National Human Rights Institutions

National Human Rights Institutions

Rules, Requirements, and Practice

DAVID LANGTRY
KIRSTEN ROBERTS LYER

OXFORD
UNIVERSITY PRESS

OXFORD
UNIVERSITY PRESS

Great Clarendon Street, Oxford, OX2 6DP,
United Kingdom

Oxford University Press is a department of the University of Oxford.
It furthers the University's objective of excellence in research, scholarship,
and education by publishing worldwide. Oxford is a registered trade mark of
Oxford University Press in the UK and in certain other countries

First Edition published in 2021

Impression: 1

Published in the United States of America by Oxford University Press
198 Madison Avenue, New York, NY 10016, United States of America

British Library Cataloguing in Publication Data

Data available

Library of Congress Control Number: 2021940517

ISBN 978–0–19–882910–2

DOI: 10.1093/oso/9780198829102.001.0001

Printed and bound by
CPI Group (UK) Ltd, Croydon, CR0 4YY

To all human rights defenders, for their tireless dedication and commitment to the promotion and protection of human rights; and to my family, for their unwavering support and encouragement throughout my career.
—David Langtry

To all those in NHRIs around the world who stand committed in the face of adversity.
For Kev, Jen, Andy, Filip, and Lucie.
—Kirsten Roberts Lyer

Preface

The purpose of this book is to provide insight into the role and functioning of National Human Rights Institutions (NHRIs) through the findings of the Sub-Committee on Accreditation (SCA) of the NHRI peer network, the Global Alliance of NHRIs (GANHRI).

NHRIs accredited to GANHRI operate in over 110 countries around the world, and as the primary state-based domestic human rights institution, they are increasingly relied upon as promoters and protectors of human rights at the national level. While NHRIs are national-level institutions, they are also promoted, and their work supported by the United Nations.

NHRIs are in the unique position of being 'graded' via a peer-review process undertaken by the SCA, for their compliance with the 1993 UN Principles relating to the Status of National Institutions (the Paris Principles).[1] This examines their independence through the NHRI's legal, structural, and procedural features. The designation and findings given to NHRIs through this peer-review process are used by governments to take such steps as may be necessary to obtain and retain the highest grade possible—'A-status'—as an indication of their compliance with national human rights and the rule of law. A-status NHRIs are also afforded enhanced recognition and access by the UN to its human rights mechanisms in their own right, giving the SCA an exceptional status within the UN framework.

Since beginning its work in 1998, and through the issuance of detailed bi-annual reports since 2008, the SCA has made considerable advances in developing the Paris Principles by applying them to the actual situations of NHRIs. Yet to date, it has not published a compilation of its 'case law'—it is this gap which the present book fills. This book sets out the assessment and findings of the SCA, based on their reasoned decisions. The findings of the SCA have been organized by thematic area, to enable readers to easily access the SCA's recommendations in a structured format for the first time.

This book will be of interest to staff and leadership of NHRIs, and the UN and other international organizations that work with NHRIs on the ground in supporting their work and strengthening their compliance with the UN Paris Principles. States that are considering the establishment of an NHRI can use this book as a reference guide in the development of their national legislation, particularly to ensure their NHRI is accredited with A-status (that is, in compliance with

[1] Principles relating to the Status of National Institutions, UNGA Res 48/134 (20 December 1993) UNGA Doc A/RES/48/134 (The Paris Principles).

the Paris Principles). Scholars working on NHRIs and those working on human rights more broadly, will also be interested in this book for its insights on NHRI practice. This book is further intended to be used as a core text for teaching in human rights courses covering national implementation of human rights and the rule of law—particularly in the context of monitoring and oversight bodies. Finally, the Paris Principles are increasingly being used as a standard for the establishment of independent national-level oversight and monitoring bodies, and the reviews by the SCA are the internationally accepted interpretation of these principles.

We have written this book to create a record of the SCA's assessments. It is the first book of its kind, and we hope that it will serve as a lasting legacy for the work of the SCA as well as a valuable tool for NHRIs and other state-based institutions working to promote and protect the rights of individuals and groups. We further hope our combined years of experience as NHRI practitioners, and as a scholar and a long-serving member of the SCA, serve to provide a unique perspective on the role and functioning of NHRIs, and that this book will contribute to the development and strengthening of NHRIs and other independent state-based institutions around the world.

David Langtry and Kirsten Roberts Lyer,
February 2021

Acknowledgements

This book would not be possible without the tireless work of those who have promoted and developed National Human Rights Institutions (NHRIs) since 1993. We particularly acknowledge Gianni Magazzeni of the UN Office of the High Commissioner for Human Rights, Professor Chris Sidoti, Kieren Fitzpatrick and Pip Dargan of the Asia-Pacific Forum Secretariat, Greg Heesom, Michel Forst, Katharina Rose of GANHRI, Gilbert Sebihogo of the African Network of NHRIs, and Debbie Kohner and Katrien Meuwissen of the European Network of NHRIs secretariat, as well as those working in the NHRI regional secretariats and NHRI representatives who have served in the leadership and Bureau and committees of the International Coordinating Committee and GANHRI over many years.

Many NHRIs would not continue to exist without the tireless work of their leadership and staff who we recognize by this book.

We particularly also wish to acknowledge those colleagues who have lost their lives because of their NHRI work, especially those from the Afghanistan Independent Human Rights Commission. This book is also dedicated to their memory.

We recognize all those scholars who work to examine and seek the improvement of NHRIs around the world, some of whom are referenced in this book.

The authors wish to sincerely thank the great research assistants who worked with us in putting together the material for this book: Isabelle Adam, Artem Galushko, Jacob McGrew, Elizaveta Potapova, Petra Skokic, Drishti Suri, Heather Tucker, and Michael Zeller. We also thank the fantastic Aron Suba.

Finally, we wish to thank our families for their support and encouragement throughout this process!

Acknowledgements

[illegible]

[illegible]

[illegible]

Contents

PART II—THE SUB-COMMITTEE ON ACCREDITATION AND THE STRUCTURE AND FUNCTIONING OF NATIONAL HUMAN RIGHTS INSTITUTIONS

Table of Cases

EUROPEAN COURT OF HUMAN RIGHTS

Table of Legislation

List of Abbreviations

ACHPR	African Commission on Human and Peoples' Rights
AHRC	Australian Human Rights Commission
AIHRC	Afghanistan Independent Human Rights Commission
ANHRIs	African Network of National Human Rights Institutions
ANNI	Asian NGO Network on National Human Rights Institutions
AOB	Austrian Ombuds Board
APF	Asia-Pacific Forum of National Human Rights Institutions
APSC	Australian Public Service Commission
APT	Association for the Prevention of Torture
CAHR	Commissioner for Administration and Human Rights (Cyprus)
CCDH	Commission Consultative des droits de l'homme (Luxembourg)
CDDH	Council of Europe Steering Committee on Human Rights
CEDAW	Convention on the Elimination of Discrimination Against Women
CEOOR	Centre for Equal Opportunities and Opposition to Racism (Belgium)
CERD	Convention on the Elimination of All forms of Racial Discrimination
CERD	Committee on the Elimination of Racial Discrimination
CESCR	Committee on Economic, Social and Cultural Rights
CFQF	Commission fédérale pour les questions féminines (Switzerland)
CFR	Commissioner for Fundamental Rights of Hungary
CHRAGG	Commission for Human Rights and Good Governance
CHRAJ	Ghana Commission on Human Rights and Administrative Justice (Ghana)
CHRC	Canadian Human Rights Commission
CHRH	Canadian Human Rights Commission (Canada)
CHRP	Commission on Human Rights of the Philippines
CNCDH	Commission Nationale Consultative des Droits de l'Homme (France)
CNCPPDH	Commission Nationale Consultative de Promotion et de Protection des Droits de l'Homme (Algeria)
CNDH	Commission Nationale des droits de l'homme (Mauritania)
CNDHCI	La Commission Nationale des Droits de l'Homme de Côte d'Ivoire
CNIDH	Commission nationale indépendante des droits de l'homme (Burundi)
CNIDH	Commission Nationale Indépendante des Droits de l'Homme (Madagascaar)
CONADEH	Comisionado Nacional de los Derechos Humanos de Honduras (Honduras)
CRC	Convention on the Rights of the Child
CRPD	Convention on the Rights of Persons with Disabilities
CSCE	Conference on Security and Co-Operation in Europe
CSDH	Comité Sénégalais des Droits de l'homme
CSW	Commission on the Status of Women
CUP	Cambridge University Press

DHCR	Defensoría de los Habitantes (Costa Rica)
DIHR	Danish Institute for Human Rights
DP	Defensoría del Pueblo (Venezuela)
DPC	Defensoria Del Pueblo of Colombia
DPE	Defensoría del Pueblo de Ecuador
DPNA	Defensor del Pueblo de la Nación Argentina
DPP	Defensoría del Pueblo de Paraguay
DPP	Defensoria del Pueblo del Peru
DPRP	Defensoría del Pueblo de la República de Panamá
DPS	Defensor del Pueblo of Spain
ECJ	European Court of Justice
ECOSOC	United Nations Economic and Social Council
ECRI	European Commission against Racism and Intolerance
ECtHR	European Court of Human Rights
EHRC	Ethiopian Human Rights Commission
EHRC	Equalities and Human Rights Commission (Great Britain)
ENNHRI	European Network of NHRIs
EOS	Equality Ombudsman of Sweden
ETC	Equal Treatment Commission (Netherlands)
EU	European Union
FCR	Federal Commission against Racism (Switzerland)
FNHRI	Finnish National Human Rights Institution
FRA	European Union Agency for Fundamental Rights
GANHRI	Global Alliance of National Human Rights Institutions (formerly ICC)
GIHR	German Institute for Human Rights
GNCHR	Greek National Commission for Human Rights
GO	General Observation
HCRC	High Commission for Human Rights (Iraq)
HRCA	Human Rights Commissioner (Ombudsman) of the Republic of Azerbaijan
HRCM	Human Rights Commission of the Maldives
HRCZ	Human Rights Commission (Zambia)
HRD	Human Rights Defender
HRDA	Human Rights Defender of the Republic of Armenia
HRORS	Human Rights Ombudsman of the Republic of Slovenia
HROT	Human Rights Ombudsman of the Republic of Tajikistan
IACmHR	Inter-American Commission on Human Rights
IACtHR	Inter-American Court of Human Rights
ICC	International Coordinating Committee of National Human Rights Institutions
ICCPR	International Covenant on Civil and Political Rights
ICESCR	International Covenant on Economic, Social and Cultural Rights
ICHRP	International Council on Human Rights Policy
IHRC	Irish Human Rights Commission
IHREC	Irish Human Rights and Equality Commission
IHROBH	Human Rights Ombudsmen of Bosnia and Herzegovina
INCHR	Independent National Commission on Human Rights (Liberia)

INDH	Instituto Nacional de Derechos Humanos (Chile)
INHRCB	Independent National Human Rights Commission of Burundi
JNCHR	National Centre for Human Rights (Jordan)
Komnas HAM	Komisi Nasional Hak Asasi Manusia (Indonesia)
LBQTIQ	lesbian, gay, bisexual, transgender/transsexual, intersex, and queer and questioning
MHRC	Malawi Human Rights Commission
MNHRC	Myanmar National Human Rights Commission
NATO	North Atlantic Treaty Organization
NCCLHR	National Council for Civil Liberties and Human Rights (Libya)
NCHR	National Commission for Human Rights of the Republic of Rwanda
NCHRF	National Commission on Human Rights and Freedom of Cameroon
NGO	non-governmental organization
NHRC	National Human Rights Commission (Nigeria)
NHRC	National Human Rights Committee (Qatar)
NHRCB	National Human Rights Commission of Bangladesh
NHRCI	National Human Rights Commission of India
NHRCK	National Human Rights Commission (South Korea)
NHRCM	National Human Rights Commission of Mongolia
NHRCT	National Human Rights Commission of Thailand
NHRI	National Human Rights Institution
NHROI	Institución Nacional de Derechos Humanos Defensoría del Pueblo (Uruguay)
NIHR	Netherlands Institute for Human Rights
NIHRB	National Institution for Human Rights (Bahrain)
NIHRC	Northern Ireland Human Rights Commission
NMM	National Monitoring Mechanism under the CRPD
NNHRI	Norwegian National Human Rights Institution
NPM	National Preventative Mechanism under the OPCAT
NRHCN	National Human Rights Commission of Nepal
NZHRC	New Zealand Human Rights Commission
OAS	Organization of American States
OAU	Organization of African Unity
OCHR	High Commissioner for Human Rights in the Russian Federation
ODIHR	OSCE Office for Democratic Institutions and Human Rights
OHCHR	Office of the United Nations High Commissioner for Human Rights
OKR	Ombudsman of the Kyrgyz Republic
ONHRC	Oman National Human Rights Commission
OORL	Ombudsman of the Republic of Latvia
OPA	Office of the People's Advocate of Moldova
OPC	Office for the Protection of Citizens (Haiti)
OPCAT	Optional Protocol to the Convention Against Torture
ORB	Ombudsman of the Republic of Bulgaria
ORC	Ombudsman of the Republic of Croatia
ORM	Ombudsman of the Republic of Macedonia

OSCE	Organization for Security and Cooperation in Europe
PA	Peoples' Advocate (Albania)
PACE	Parliamentary Assembly of the Council of Europe
PCCR	Parliamentary Commissioner for Civil Rights (Hungary)
PCRS	Protector of Citizens of the Republic of Serbia
PDDH	Procuraduría para la Defensa de los Derechos Humanos (Nicaragua)
PDH	Procurador de los Derechos Humanos (Guatemala)
PDHJ	Provedoria for Human Rights and Justice (Timor-Leste)
PDJ	Provedor de Justiça (Portugal)
PHRF	Protector of Human Rights and Freedoms (Montenegro)
PICHR	Palestine Independent Commission for Human Rights
RIHR	Romanian Institute of Human Rights
SAHRC	South African Human Rights Commission
SCA	GANHRI Sub-Committee on Accreditation
SCHRFF	Comité Supérieur des Droits de l'Homme et des Libertés Fondamentales (Tunisia)
SLHRC	Human Rights Commission of Sri Lanka
SNCHR	National Centre for Human Rights (Slovakia)
SPT	Sub-Committee on Prevention of Torture
SUHAKAM	Human Rights Commission of Malaysia
TFEU	Treaty on the Functioning of the European Union
UDHR	Universal Declaration of Human Rights
UHRC	Ugandan Human Rights Commission
UN	United Nations
UNDP	United Nations Development Program
UNESCO	United Nations Education, Scientific and Cultural Organisation
UNGA	United Nations General Assembly
UNHRC	United Nations Human Rights Council
UNIA	Interfederal Centre for Equal Opportunity and fight against racism and discrimination (Belgium)
UPCHR	Ukrainian Parliament Commissioner for Human Rights (Ukraine)
UPR	UN Human Rights Council Universal Periodic Review Process
V-dem	Varieties of Democracy Institute
WTO	World Trade Organization
ZNRC	Human Rights Commission (Zimbabwe)

Introduction

National Human Rights Institutions (NHRIs) are state-established independent national-level bodies tasked with the 'promotion and protection' of human rights under the United Nations (UN) 1993 Principles relating to the Status of National Institutions (the Paris Principles).[1] NHRIs are unique institutions in many ways. They have carved out a place for themselves within the international and national human rights architecture. For international organizations, they are an interlocutor for their goals and aims, and a domestic monitor and supporter of international human rights standards. Domestically, they function to promote and protect human rights at the national level. But while NHRIs have a potentially valuable role to play in improving human rights, their positive contribution cannot be accepted without question. NHRIs do not have value separate from their ability to foster improvements in human rights. Their existence is not a goal in and of itself. Further, as state-established institutions they run a considerable risk of being state mouthpieces, or of being restricted to the point of ineffectiveness.

With those potential risks in mind, in 1998, the peer network of NHRIs, the Global Alliance of NHRIs (GANHRI, formerly the International Coordinating Committee (ICC)), established a peer-review mechanism called the Sub-Committee on Accreditation (SCA) with the support of the United Nations Office of the High Commissioner for Human Rights (OHCHR). As will be discussed in more detail in Part I, the SCA undertakes reviews of all NHRIs who seek recognition for their compliance with the Paris Principles. From 1998 to 2019,[2] the SCA undertook reviews of 128 institutions, and provided their assessment in the form of reports to GANHRI.[3] These reports, which constitute the primary subject

[1] UN General Assembly Resolution 48/134 'Principles relating to the Status of National Institutions' (the Paris Principles) 20 December 1993.

[2] Due to the Covid-19 crisis in 2020, the SCA only undertook one session, held in December 2020. GANHRI, 'Sessions of the GANHRI Sub-Committee on Accreditation (SCA) for 2021' <https://nhri.ohchr.org/EN/AboutUs/GANHRIAccreditation/Pages/2020-Sessions.aspx> accessed 15 December 2020.

[3] The International Coordinating Committee of National Institutions for the Promotion and Protection of Human Rights (ICC), 'Report and Recommendations of the Session of the Sub-Committee on Accreditation (SCA)', subsequently the Global Alliance of National Institutions for the Promotion and Protection of Human Rights (GANHRI), 'Report and Recommendations of the Session of the Sub-Committee on Accreditation (SCA)' (hereafter SCA, Accreditation Report). GANHRI was known as the ICC until 31 March 2016 when the network changed its name. ENNHRI, 'ICC29 Highlights' (31 March 2016) <http://ennhri.org/news-and-blog/icc29-highlights/> accessed 22 February 2021.

National Human Rights Institutions. David Langtry and Kirsten Roberts Lyer, Oxford University Press. © David Langtry and Kirsten Roberts Lyer 2021. DOI: 10.1093/oso/9780198829102.003.0001

matter of this book,[4] are based on the Paris Principles, and the SCA's expansion of these principles by way of General Observations.[5] The reports provide important insight into the role and purpose of NHRIs. More broadly, they provide insight into how state-established institutions that are intended to function independently can operate effectively within national systems. For that reason, the analysis and recommendations of the SCA have relevance not just for NHRIs but for all domestic institutions that are intended to be independent from government in their operation. In addition to introducing this book as a whole, in this introduction we set out some of the discussions and approaches taken in the academic literature to NHRI independence and effectiveness. As a book focusing on the content of the SCA's assessments we do not go into detail on this literature in subsequent chapters but feel it is useful to the reader for us to introduce it here.

Ensuring and securing independence in form and function are not simple matters, as the contents of this book attest. It requires a multi-strand approach that ensures formal independence in law and structures and enables independence in practice. We have divided this book into three parts. After introducing the origins and establishment of NHRIs, as well as the process and practice of the SCA in Part I, the book's analysis of the SCA's reports is then divided into two parts, covering first NHRIs' formal structures (Part II) and then NHRI practice (Part III). Part II begins by examining SCA assessments on the enabling law of NHRIs—the formal legislation/constitutional provisions that establish the NHRI. Then it considers the critical issue of 'who runs NHRIs'. Chapter 4 considers the SCA's most extensive area of assessment—on the selection, appointment, dismissal processes, and other aspects of NHRI leadership. Chapter 5 deals with the relationship with the state. Chapter 6 considers the human rights mandate of NHRIs. Part III examines the SCA's reviews of NHRIs as human rights promoters and protectors. The chapters in this part look at NHRI practice (Chapter 7); their role as treaty-mandated bodies under specific international conventions (Chapter 8); what we term 'challenging cases' where NHRIs are operating in conflict zones, coups d'état or other difficult national situations (Chapter 9); and situations where NHRIs have 'been downgraded'; that is, where they are considered no longer to be in compliance with the Paris Principles (Chapter 10). The aim of the chapters in Parts II and III of this book is to provide a cohesive and accessible source for the content of the SCA

[4] This book utilizes the SCA reports primarily from 2008 onwards, as the reports prior to this date provided limited reasoning that do not facilitate detailed analysis. Authors' note: the citations for the SCA's accreditation reports include the name of the country, the full name of the NHRI being referred to and its acronym as used by the SCA, when the particular NHRI is mentioned for the first time in a chapter. In subsequent citations for the NHRI in the chapter, the name of the country and the acronym for the NHRI are used. Across its reports, the SCA is not consistent in its use of acronyms for particular institutions.

[5] SCA, 'General Observations of the Sub-Committee on Accreditation' (adopted on 21 February 2018) para 13 (hereafter SCA, 'General Observations' (February 2018)).

reports, however we provide a short comment at the end of each chapter with some thoughts, insights, and analysis on the area that has just been considered.

NHRIs accredited by the SCA are designated with a 'status', either A or B, depending on their assessed compliance with the Paris Principles. A-status NHRIs are those deemed to be sufficiently in compliance with the Paris Principles. Having achieved A-status, these institutions are granted a range of formal and informal advantages over those with B-status or who are unaccredited, primarily in terms of their ability to engage with the human rights bodies of the United Nations. The range of engagement is detailed further in Chapter 1, and includes access to the UN Human Rights Council, and overall provides increased prominence within the UN human rights system.

The assessments of the SCA are a means of ensuring NHRIs' independence and effectiveness. When we speak of independence in this book, what we mean is *effective functioning* for the promotion and protection of human rights. Operational independence is worth little if no positive human rights work is being done. Ensuring that NHRIs are effective in their work is important internationally and domestically. NHRIs are increasingly being given positions of prominence at the regional and international levels to speak about human rights in their country, including the compliance of their state with international human rights standards. As Pegram puts it, 'NHRIs have been granted unprecedented access to a growing set of UN venues and contexts within which they inform decision-making about human rights policy'.[6]

NHRIs—particularly those with A-status—are often taken as an authoritative voice on human rights in the country. As part of the UN Human Rights Council's Universal Periodic Review (UPR) process, for example, A-status NHRIs are given their own section (the first section) in the OHCHR compilation of stakeholders' submissions.[7] This prominence is not confined to written submissions at the international level. Expert missions to countries by international institutions to assess aspects of the national human rights situation meet with NHRIs as a matter of course. What the NHRI says often gets prominence in such assessments, as their pronouncements are given extra weight because of their status. At the domestic level, the SCA's assessments aim to assist in ensuring that the NHRI is independent in form and function. As will be seen throughout this book, the SCA's recommendations provide a means for institutions to seek support for improvement of their mandate, functioning, finances, or other essential aspects. Where the NHRI

[6] Thomas Pegram, 'Global Human Rights Governance and Orchestration: National Human Rights Institutions as Intermediaries' (September 2015) 21 European Journal of International Relations 595, 607.

[7] Human Rights Council Res 16/21, UN Doc A/HRC/RES/16/21 (12 April 2011). See for example, 'Summary prepared by the Office of the United Nations High Commissioner for Human Rights in accordance with paragraph 15(c) of the annex to Human Rights Council resolution 5/1 and paragraph 5 of the annex to Council Resolution 16/21: Rwanda' (August 2015) UN Doc A/HRC/WG.6/23RWA/317.

is not fulfilling its role as a promoter and protector of human rights, the SCA also acts as a check and means of oversight.

There is a risk in giving A-status institutions a prominent position both nationally and internationally. If NHRIs are elevated to a place where they can actually make a difference, have an impact, and change the way human rights are discussed by adding a new voice, then there is a possibility that some NHRIs who are not worthy of this position will be included. As Kumar described it in 2003, NHRIs can be a 'double-edged sword' used by regimes for political purposes.[8] The SCA's work has increasingly recognized the importance of ensuring that NHRIs merit A-status not simply because of their form and structure is compliant with the Paris Principles but also because of their practice, by considering the essential question of the substantive work undertaken by the NHRI in promoting and protecting human rights in its country, as will be seen in Part III.

The position of NHRIs is a complex one. They operate within the human rights system on multiple levels (national, regional, international), and with a variety of potentially conflicting constituencies (such as governments, non-governmental organizations (NGOs), and individual complainants). NHRIs and their multiple constituencies may also have differing views on what constitutes independence and effectiveness. As Herman and Renz concluded from their studies on non-profit effectiveness: '[it] is socially constructed ... it is not a stable construct, and that different stakeholders will judge it differently'.[9] The same can be said for NHRI effectiveness. Furthermore, NHRIs are subject to multiple, often conflicting forces. For example, they are institutions that may have a contentious relationship with the government in some aspects of their work (such as issuing critical inquiry reports), but also need to positively engage with the government in order to have their recommendations implemented. Their government-established position also opens them up to a level of pressure from the state, and the potential vulnerability of NHRIs as institutions must be borne in mind when considering their effectiveness.

Scholars assessing NHRIs have attempted to understand their effectiveness. Almost every article, chapter, or report on NHRIs mentions effectiveness, and a number of specific attempts have been made towards defining effectiveness

[8] C Raj Kumar, 'National Human Rights Institutions: Good Governance Perspectives on Institutionalization of Human Rights' (2003–2004) 19(2) American University International Law Review 259.

[9] Robert D Herman and David O Renz, 'Advancing Nonprofit Organizational Effectiveness Research and Theory: Nine Theses' (2008) 18(4) Nonprofit Management and Leadership 399, 410. See also, Herman and Renz's 2004 study on non-profit effectiveness utilizing a constituency-based approach: Robert D Herman and David O Renz, 'Doing Things Right: Effectiveness in local Nonprofit Organizations, a Panel Study' (November/December 2004) 64(6) Public Administration Review 694, 702. Harrison and Shirom similarly found 'internal and external stakeholders advocate divergent effectiveness criteria and assign different meaning and degrees of importance to any given performance measure'. Michael L Harrison and Arie Shirom, *Organizational Diagnosis and Assessment: Bridging Theory and Practice* (Sage 1999) 89.

for NHRIs.[10] Researchers in particular have assessed the usefulness of the Paris Principles as a means of establishing the effectiveness of NHRIs. Most scholars agree that the Paris Principles are at best a starting point for any assessment of NHRIs, and that in themselves they are insufficient to identify whether an NHRI is effective.[11] Scholars and practitioners have acknowledged that the Paris Principles, while useful in determining the functional requirements of NHRIs, are also not sufficient to ensure an effective institution.[12] The elaboration of General Observations by the SCA, which significantly expand the Paris Principles, is recognition of this fact, as will be seen throughout this book.

Identifying effectiveness factors is a common approach in scholarly assessments of NHRIs. Carver, for example, summarized the characteristics of effective institutions as public legitimacy, accessibility, open organizational culture, membership, diversity, relations with civil society, broad mandate, broad jurisdiction, power to monitor compliance, systematic approach to human rights issues, and adequate budget.[13] A decade later a 2013 report for Oxfam America reviewed some of the literature in the area of NHRI effectiveness to identify common factors.[14] It is interesting to note that, in just seven pieces of literature reviewed, nineteen factors of NHRI effectiveness were identified. While none of the nineteen factors enjoyed

[10] For example, International Council on Human Rights Policy (ICHRP), *Assessing the Effectiveness of National Human Rights Institutions* (International Council on Human Rights Policy 2005) ; Sanzhuan Guo, 'Effectiveness of National Human Rights Institutions in International Human Rights Law: Problems and Prospects' (2009) 14 Asian Yearbook of International Law 101; Thomas Pegram and Katerina Linos, *Interrogating Form and Function: Defining Effective National Human Rights Institutions* (The Danish Institute for Human Rights 2015).

[11] For example, C Raj Kumar, 'National Human Rights Institutions: Good Governance Perspectives on Institutionalization of Human Rights' (2003–2004) 19(2) American University International Law Review 259; Rachel Murray, 'National Human Rights Institutions: Criteria and Factors for Assessing Their Effectiveness' (2007) 25 Netherlands Quarterly of Human Rights 189.

[12] See for example, Andrew Byrnes, Catherine Renshaw and Andrea Durbach, 'A Tongue but No Teeth: The Emergence of a Regional Human Rights Mechanism in the Asia Pacific Region' (2009) 31 Sydney Law Review 211, 63; Sonia Cardenas, *Chains of Justice: The Global Rise of State Institutions for Human Rights* (University of Pennsylvania Press 2014); Richard Carver, 'National Human Rights Institutions in Central and Eastern Europe: the Ombudsman as Agent of International Law' in Ryan Goodman and Thomas Pegram (eds), *Human Rights, State Compliance and Social Change: Assessing National Human Rights Institutions* (Cambridge University Press 2012) (hereafter Goodman and Pegram, *Human Rights, State Compliance, and Social Change*); Julie Mertus, *Human Rights Matters: Local Politics and National Human Rights Institutions* (Stanford University Press 2009).

[13] Richard Carver, 'One NHRI or Many? How Many Institutions Does it Take to Protect Human Rights?—Lessons from the European Experience' (2011) 3(1) Journal of Human Rights Practice 1, referencing the criteria from his own previous work on International Council on Human Rights Policy (ICHRP) (n 11). See also, Murray (n 11); Anne Smith, 'The Unique Position of National Human Rights Institutions: A Mixed Blessing?' (November 2006) 28(4) Human Rights Quarterly 904.

[14] Ben Collins and Lesley Fleischman, 'Human Rights and Social Conflict in the Oil, Gas, and Mining Industries' (Oxfam America, 9 April 2013) <https://s3.amazonaws.com/oxfam-us/www/static/media/files/nhri-backgrounder.pdf> accessed 25 February 2021. See also, Carver (n 13); Murray (n 11); Human Rights Watch, 'Protectors or Pretenders: Government Human Rights Commissions in Africa' (1 January 2001) <https://www.hrw.org/report/2001/01/01/protectors-or-pretenders/government-human-rights-commissions-africa> accessed 25 February 2021; Smith (n 13); OHCHR, 'A Handbook on the Establishment and Strengthening of National Human Rights Institutions for the Promotion and Protection of Human Rights' (New York/Geneva 1995).

universal support across the seven UN, NGO, and academic studies, accessibility, strong mandate, selection of commissioners, civil society coordination, and adequate budget resources were identified as factors of effectiveness in four of the seven studies. In its own assessment, the Oxfam report, which focused on extractive industries, identified the following factors

- Independence: commitment to and reputation for objectivity and integrity;
- Promotion: influence on public awareness of human rights issues involved with extractive operations;
- Empowerment: support for other civil society or governmental organizations working to promote human rights norms for the extractive industries;
- Remediation: efficiency and perceived effectiveness of dispute-resolution capacity;
- Power: formal and informal influence with relevant actors.[15]

As to looking at data to determine whether NHRIs are effective in practice, there have been relatively few quantitative studies of NHRI effectiveness. However, a 2013 study in the American Sociological Review provides an interesting analysis. It looked at the question of whether the establishment or existence of an NHRI had a positive impact on certain human rights in that country.[16] The authors found that the effect of NHRIs was stronger for physical integrity abuses than for civil and political rights, and that this could be attributed to the contested nature of some civil and political rights. Furthermore, they found that this impact was positive over time. They attribute this disparity to the fact that an NHRI's establishment may bring to light more physical integrity abuses in the short term. Most interestingly, they found that NHRI effectiveness is dependent 'on the nature of the rights targeted for improvement, rather than specific organizational attributes'.[17] Cole and Ramirez's work thus suggests that less attention should be paid to organizational attributes of an institution than to its practice. It should be noted however that they conceive NHRIs broadly, not limiting their consideration those assessed for compliance with the Paris Principles,[18] but rather looking at a range of institutions that monitor the government NHRIs link the domestic public to the international human rights system and, 'foster a human rights culture'.[19]

Goodman and Pegram, and Cardenas have approached NHRI effectiveness from the perspective of norm compliance and socialization.[20] This approach considers

[15] Collins and Fleischman (n 14) 45.

[16] Francisco O Ramirez and Wade M Cole, 'Conditional Decoupling: Assessing the Impact of National Human Rights Institutions, 1981 to 2004' (2013) 78(4) American Sociological Review 702.

[17] ibid 703.

[18] They identify 180 institutions, including classical ombudsmen, human rights commissions, and human rights ombudsmen. ibid 705.

[19] ibid.

[20] Sonia Cardenas, *Chains of Justice: The Global Rise of State Institutions for Human Rights* (University of Pennsylvania Press 2014); Goodman and Pegram (n 12).

NHRIs within the complex dynamics of state adherence to international human rights standards and identifies non-mandate specific means of ascertaining NHRI effectiveness. The approach of these scholars considers the practice of NHRIs and their actual impact beyond formal adherence to the Paris Principles. Cardenas, for example, regards NHRIs as agents of accountability, and approaches their effectiveness in terms of their level of influence.[21] She identified the Ugandan NHRI as an example of effectiveness because it challenged the government and opposition and was responsive to national human rights needs.[22] Carver has also noted the importance of going beyond a 'formalistic legal analysis of the structure and competencies of NHRIs', to factors such as a systemic approach to human rights issues.[23] Scholars have criticized the use of a formalistic approach to evaluating NHRI effectiveness or impact.[24] Mertus, importantly, warns that a mandate-based approach to assessing NHRI effectiveness only requires NHRIs to advance their own agenda, regardless of whether this improves human rights.[25]

A common feature throughout the literature is that independence is viewed as a crucial factor for NHRI effectiveness.[26] However, there is a lack of empirical data to support this assertion—leaving the question open as to whether it may be possible that an NHRI can be effective while lacking independence from government. Many studies assessing independence also tend to be based upon the legal framework and Paris Principles requirements,[27] without questioning whether these criteria actually go to the issue of effectiveness.[28] There is a trend, however, in the literature suggesting that it is NHRIs' human rights work on the ground that should determine whether it is an effective institution. As will be seen throughout this book, this trend can equally be found within SCA assessments.

NHRIs have also undertaken assessments of the factors required for their own effectiveness. For example, the OHCHR undertook a survey of NHRIs in 2009. Among its findings was that for an NHRI to be accessible and effective, it needed

21 Cardenas, ibid 346.

22 ibid 347.

23 Richard Carver, 'National Human Rights Institutions in Central and Eastern Europe: the ombudsman as agent of international law' in Goodman and Pegram (n 12) 208.

24 See Julie Mertus, *Human Rights Matters: Local Politics and National Human Rights Institutions* (Stanford University Press 2009) 82.

25 ibid.

26 See for example, Kithure Kindiki, 'On the Independence of the Kenya National Commission on Human Rights: A Preliminary Comment' (2004) 2 East African Journal Human Rights & Democracy 120; Linda Reif, 'Building Democratic Institutions: The Role of National Human Rights Institutions in Good Governance and Human Rights Protection' (2000) 13 Harvard Human Rights Journal 1; Webster Zambara, 'Africa's National Human Rights Institutions and the Responsibility to Protect' (2010) 2 Global Responsibility to Protect 458, 473.

27 Kindiki, ibid. This trend is also noted by Murray (n 11).

28 A 2015 study for the Danish Institute for Human Rights by Pegram and Linos, identified twenty-two 'independence safeguards' including constitutional or legislative status, no government representation, immunity, broad human rights mandate, and investigative powers. Thomas Pegram and Katerina Linos, *Interrogating Form and Function: Defining Effective National Human Rights Institutions* (The Danish Institute for Human Rights 2015).

'diverse staff with the necessary professional skills and knowledge of human rights, as well as an organizational structure that allows for the most effective use of its resources, budget and powers'.[29] The Asia-Pacific Forum of NHRIs, (the regional secretariat for NHRIs in the Asia-Pacific), produced a capacity assessment manual that is a useful indicator of NHRIs' own perspectives on the elements that are required for an NHRI to meet its full capability. Using the United Nations Development Program (UNDP) capacity development framework as a model, the manual identifies five core areas of NHRI capacity: internal policy and procedures formulation, leadership (internal and external), knowledge, accountability, and technical and functional capacities of leadership and staff. The core areas show the overlap between NHRI internal operational functioning and the operation of the NHRI in practice. Accountability, for example, includes

> the institutional ability to ensure accountability both of individuals and of the NHRI as a whole in carrying out the mandate of the NHRI in preventing human rights violations and enforcing human rights laws. These capacities include abilities to: strengthen the national integrity of the NHRI, increase public participation and build coalitions.[30]

An important point to highlight at the outset of this book regarding the significance of the SCA's assessments is that they hold consequences outside the narrower confines of the role and functioning of NHRIs. The UN Paris Principles are increasingly used as a baseline for assessing the independence of other institutions at the domestic level that are state established, such as privacy and data protection bodies, equality bodies, ombudspersons, parliamentary human rights committees. Because they are accepted as the standard for UN-recognized NHRIs, there is a risk that the Paris Principles in themselves may be viewed as the sole basis on which independent state-based institutions can be effectively established. However, reliance solely on the text of the Paris Principles would not ensure the type of institution being sought. Both scholars and practitioners agree that the Paris Principles are an insufficient basis for such institutions and must be read with the SCA General Observations[31] and their assessments in practice, a combination which this book sets out for the first time. Furthermore, as will be seen throughout this book, the regular assessment of institutions intending to be compliant with the principles is essential. In that regard, the SCA provides a model for how peer reviews of Paris Principle-compliant institutions can be established and function over time.

[29] OHCHR, 'Survey on National Human Rights Institutions' (Geneva 2009) 18.

[30] Asia Pacific Forum of National Human Rights Institutions and UNDP, *Capacity Assessment Manual for National Human Rights Institutions* (Asia Pacific Forum of National Human Rights Institutions and UNDP 2014) 29–30.

[31] SCA, 'General Observations of the Sub-Committee on Accreditation' (adopted on 21 February 2018) General Observations 1.1, 5 (hereafter SCA, 'General Observations' (February 2018)).

The relevance of the SCA's assessments can also be viewed in the context of an increasing focus on the role of domestic structures in the implementation of international human rights standards.[32] There is logic to this focus, as international organizations are the developers and monitors of human rights standards, but their ability to ensure the implementation of these standards at the domestic level is limited by factors such as resources and political influence. Improving domestic implementation, including through the formalization of domestic structures, aims to support international organizations' work directly on the ground. Indeed, as will be seen in Chapter 1, this was one of the rationales behind the UN support for the establishment and development of NHRIs.

Practical examples of this increased focus can be seen not just in the creation of NHRIs but in the creation of dedicated national-level structures proposed in recent international human rights conventions. The Convention on the Rights of Persons with Disabilities (CRPD)[33] and the Optional Protocol to the Convention Against Torture (OPCAT)[34] explicitly reference the Paris Principles. OPCAT provides for the establishment of a National Preventative Mechanism (NPM) with the purpose of supporting the implementation of the Convention. Article 18(4) of the Optional Protocol requires States Parties to give 'due consideration' to the Paris Principles in establishing the NPM. Similarly, the CRPD provides for the establishment of a National Monitoring Mechanism (NMM), to monitor the implementation of the Convention actively. Article 33(2) requires the designation or establishment of an independent mechanism to 'promote, protect and monitor' implementation of the Convention, and the Paris Principles are to be taken into account in designating or establishing the mechanism. In both instances, states have opted in many cases to appoint the NHRI to one or both of these functions, as will be discussed in Chapter 8.

A further example of the increased attention to domestic implementation through institutionalization is the promotion by the OHCHR of the establishment of parliamentary human rights committees. A set of international principles were proposed by the UN, many of the elements of which mirror the Paris Principles. As Kirsten notes in her 2019 article on this topic:

> With explicit reference, and notable similarities to the Paris Principles, the 2018 draft principles cover the (1) mandate, (2) responsibilities and functions (both domestically and vis-à-vis the international human rights system), and

[32] See for example, Steven LB Jensen, Stéphanie Lagoutte, and Sébastien Lorion, 'The Domestic Institutionalization of Human Rights: An Introduction' (2019) 37(3) Nordic Journal of Human Rights 165–76.

[33] Convention on the Rights of Persons with Disabilities (adopted on 13 December 2006, entered into force on 3 May 2008) 2515 UNTS 3 (CRPD) Art 33.

[34] Optional Protocol to the Convention against Torture and other Cruel, Inhuman or Degrading Treatment or Punishment (adopted on 18 December 2002, entered into force on 22 June 2006) 2375 UNTS 237 (hereafter OPCAT).

(3) composition and working methods of a parliamentary human rights committee. The preamble to the draft principles specifically identifies the relevant functions of parliaments in promoting human rights implementation:

> Ratifying human rights treaties, scrutinizing legislation and overseeing the work of the executive in fulfilling its human rights obligations, are crucial in order to support and ensure the Government's own primary responsibility for the promotion and protection of human rights.[35]

Thus, the relevance of this book can be viewed on multiple levels. At the level of NHRIs undertaking reviews before the SCA, it provides a reference to the SCA's findings on a range of different aspects of NHRI role and functions. For NHRIs, it also acts as a source to aid their strengthening, providing easily accessible justification for improvements in roles and functions. More broadly, this book provides insight into important aspects of the domestic implementation of human rights. In particular, what challenges and barriers exist, and how can they be overcome to ensure effective domestic human rights institutions. Finally, and more broadly again, it can serve as a guide for the establishment and strengthening of a broad range of independent state-established bodies.

[35] Kirsten Roberts Lyer, 'Parliaments as Human Rights Actors: The Potential for International Principles on Parliamentary Human Rights Committees' (2019) 37(3) Nordic Journal of Human Rights 195. Citing OHCHR, 'Contribution of parliaments to the work of the Human Rights Council and its universal periodic review: Report of the Office of the United Nations High Commissioner for Human Rights' (17 May 2018) UN Doc A/HRC/38/25, Annex I.

PART I

THE ESTABLISHMENT AND DEVELOPMENT OF NATIONAL HUMAN RIGHTS INSTITUTIONS AND THE SUB-COMMITTEE ON ACCREDITATION

This book is divided into three parts. Part I comprises two chapters. The first chapter introduces the origins and establishment of NHRIs, providing background and context for NHRIs as a whole. The second chapter in this part sets out in detail the process and practice of the SCA. The book's analysis of the SCA's reports is then divided into two further parts, covering first NHRIs' formal structures (Part II) and then NHRI practice (Part III).

1

The Emergence of National Human Rights Institutions and their Global and Regional Networks

1.1 Introduction

National Human Rights Institutions (NHRIs)[1] are state-established independent national-level bodies tasked with the 'promotion and protection' of human rights under the United Nations (UN) Paris Principles.[2] While ideas for the establishment of this type of institution stretch back to 1945, a set of UN standards on NHRIs were not adopted until 1993. NHRIs themselves have only come to prominence since the mid-2000s, primarily due to increased focus from the international community on NHRIs as a necessary component of national human rights infrastructures. In particular, since the adoption of the Paris Principles, having an NHRI is increasingly globally accepted as a requisite part of states' international human rights commitments.

This chapter provides an overview of NHRIs and their networks, outlining the history of their establishment, introducing the Paris Principles, and looking at the role of NHRIs in engaging with regional and international organizations.

1.2 The Origins of the United Nations Paris Principles

The concept of establishing some form of national committee or body for human rights has been discussed at the international level since the founding of the UN.[3]

[1] This chapter draws in part on previous work by Kirsten Roberts Lyer, primarily Kirsten Roberts Lyer, 'National Human Rights Institutions' in Gerd Oberleitner and Steven Hoadley (eds), *Human Rights Institutions, Tribunals and Courts—Legacy and Promise* (Springer Major Reference Works handbook series 2019).

[2] Principles relating to the Status of National Institutions, UNGA Res 48/134 (20 December 1993) UNGA Doc A/RES/48/134 (The Paris Principles).

[3] For a list of recommendations relating to NHRIs, see Anna-Elina Pohjolainen, 'The Evolution of National Human Rights Institutions—The Role of the United Nations' (Danish Institute for Human Rights 2006). See also, Office of the High Commissioner for Human Rights (OHCHR), 'A Handbook on the Establishment and Strengthening of National Human Rights Institutions for the Promotion and Protection of Human Rights' (New York/Geneva 1995). The handbook outlines developments at the UN relating to NHRIs between 1946 and 1993.

National Human Rights Institutions. David Langtry and Kirsten Roberts Lyer, Oxford University Press. © David Langtry and Kirsten Roberts Lyer 2021. DOI: 10.1093/oso/9780198829102.003.0002

These early discussions focused on establishing a different type of institution from modern NHRIs called 'information groups' or 'local human rights committees'. The earliest discussions on establishing national human rights bodies took place primarily at the UN Economic and Social Council (ECOSOC) which, in its 1946 Resolution 9(II) establishing the Commission on Human Rights, invited UN Member States to 'consider the desirability of establishing information groups or local human rights committees within their respective countries to collaborate with them in furthering the work of the Commission on Human Rights'.[4] This resolution is sometimes cited as the first reference to NHRIs,[5] although what is referred to today as an NHRI is not what was envisaged in 1946. In the ECOSOC resolution, information groups or local human rights committees were regarded as national bodies for awareness raising and placed under the heading 'information groups', with no further specificity given to their role or functions. That such bodies were not seen as having an implementation or monitoring function is underscored by the presence in the resolution of a separate section on 'provisions for implementation' in which these bodies are not included. In June 1948, the Commission on Human Rights decided it could not proceed with consideration of national committees until measures on implementing the Covenant on Human Rights (the forerunner to the International Covenant on Civil and Political Rights (ICCPR)),[6] which was then being drafted alongside the Universal Declaration of Human Rights (UDHR)[7] were decided.[8] It continued to postpone its consideration of the topic for the next ten years.[9]

The initial ideas for local committees were not limited to the ECOSOC Human Rights Commission. Such bodies were also being proposed in relation to social issues,[10] and at the UN Education, Scientific and Cultural Organization (UNESCO).[11] The Sub-Commission on the Prevention of Discrimination and Protection of Minorities had also recommended national committees to 'study

[4] ECOSOC Res 9(II) (21 June 1946). See also, OHCHR NHRI Handbook (n 3).

[5] See for example, OHCHR NHRI Handbook (n 3).

[6] International Covenant on Civil and Political Rights (adopted 16 December 1966, entered into force 23 March 1976) 999 UNTS 171 (ICCPR).

[7] Universal Declaration of Human Rights (adopted 10 December 1948 UNGA Res 217 A(III) (UDHR)).

[8] Under the heading 'Functions of Information Groups and Local Human Rights Committees' the report provides: 'The Commission considered that the functions of information groups and local human rights committees, as set forth in the resolution of the Economic and Social Council of 12 June 1946, could not be defined unless the measures decided on by the Commission for implementing the Covenant on Human Rights were taken into consideration, and decided to postpone the study of this question until it had decided on these measures.' ECOSOC Commission on Human Rights 'Draft Report of the Commission on Human Rights to the Economic and Social Council' (17 June 1948) UN Doc E/CN.4/148, para 16.

[9] ECOSOC Commission on Human Rights, 'Local Human Rights Committees or Information Groups, Memorandum Submitted by the Secretary-General' (27 February 1951) UN Doc E/CN.4/519, para 5.

[10] ibid para 7.

[11] ibid para 9.

and survey' the extent of discrimination in law 'or in fact' in their jurisdiction and 'recommend to the government legal, educational and other' means of eliminating and preventing discrimination from occurring in the future.[12] However, it is clear that these committees were coordinating bodies comprising mainly or entirely government representatives, rather than being independent institutions similar to modern NHRIs.

In 1951, the UN Secretary-General again put forward proposals for local committees or information groups to take a more active role within states. His report includes a suggestion that they could 'submit recommendations to their government on ways in which existing laws and practices might be brought into conformity [with the UDHR]'.[13] He also notes they might be in a position to give useful assistance in preparing legislation,[14] replying to questionnaires, and assisting in studies on human rights.[15] This list of potential activities is interesting as it shows that elements of the functions of modern NHRIs as set out in the Paris Principles were already being considered in these earliest conceptions of national human rights bodies. It further demonstrates how the international level has shaped the development of NHRIs, rather than their having a more 'organic' emergence from national experience.

In 1959, ECOSOC again took up the question of establishing national-level bodies with responsibility for human rights. By this time, there was a shift in the approach towards national committees. In the memorandum accompanying a request by the former Chairman of the Commission to add the issue to the agenda, he proposed that 'national advisory committees on human rights, properly instituted and consisting of prominent personalities, would be of great assistance to Governments in advising regarding standards of human rights and in solving national or local human rights problems'.[16]

In its 1960 Resolution 772 on 'National Advisory Committees on Human Rights', the Commission recognized the 'importance of the contribution which can be made towards the promotion of respect for and observance of human rights by bodies representing, in each country, informed opinion on questions relating to human rights'.[17] It particularly recognized the role of such bodies 'in regard to

[12] Resolution on Future Work of the United Nations in the Field of Prevention of Discrimination and Protection of Minorities (25 October 1951) UN Doc E/CN.4/641, Res I part A III. This recommendation was submitted to the Commission in relation to the issue of local committees by the Secretary-General in ECOSOC Commission on Human Rights, 'Local Human Rights Committees or Information Groups, Note by the Secretary-General' (10 March 1952) UN Doc E/CN.4/519/Add.1.

[13] ECOSOC Commission on Human Rights, 'Local Human Rights Committees or Information Groups, Memorandum Submitted by the Secretary-General' (27 February 1951) UN Doc E/CN.4/519, para 12.

[14] ibid.

[15] ibid para 14.

[16] ECOSOC Commission on Human Rights 'National Advisory Committees on Human Rights, Note by the Secretary-General' (23 November 1959) UN Doc E/CN.4/791.

[17] ECOSOC, Res 772(XXX)B (25 July 1960).

the education of public opinion' on human rights. The resolution invited Member States, albeit in language that was rather tentative, to 'favour the formation' of local human rights committees or national advisory committees 'or to encourage them where they already exist'.[18] The resolution also called for a report on such committees by the 18th session of the Commission to be held in 1962. The 1962 report by the Secretary-General included responses from twenty governments.[19] From the responses, it is evident that there was still no consensus among the Member States as to what exactly the 1946 ECOSOC Resolution 9(II) aimed at creating. Thus, by the end of the 1960s, the idea that had emerged in 1946 of having national committees for human rights had not developed significantly beyond its earliest conceptions. In particular, there was a clear reluctance on the part of states to establish any national bodies that could detract from their sovereignty over human rights issues. Despite the slow progress between 1946 and 1960, some of the core concepts that became part of the Paris Principles had already emerged: independence from government, awareness raising, providing advice, and undertaking supervision of human rights in the country. While some of these ideas had been rejected, they were at least forming part of the debate.

The question of establishing national committees for human rights fell somewhat into abeyance after the discussions that took place in the early 1960s, and until the late 1970s, the Commission did not take up the issue again. However, it has remained firmly on the UN agenda ever since. The approach taken in the discussions in 1978 and 1979 shows clear progress from the earliest considerations of national committees in 1946 towards the 1993 Paris Principles. A key moment in the re-emergence of the debate on NHRIs in the late 1970s was a seminar that took place in Geneva in September 1978 (the Geneva Seminar). The outcome from the Geneva Seminar was General Assembly Resolution 33/46 (1978) on 'National Institutions for the Promotion and Protection of Human Rights'.[20] Most importantly in terms of the progress towards modern NHRIs, the Geneva Seminar produced a set of guidelines on the structure and functioning of national and local institutions, the issue that had stalled the development of national institutions in the 1960s.[21] Furthermore, it is clear that between 1978 and the holding of the next workshop in 1991 which produced the Paris Principles, a number of countries took steps to establish national institutions with a human rights mandate that later became NHRIs.

[18] ibid.

[19] ECOSOC Commission on Human Rights, 'National Advisory Committees on Human Rights, Report of the Secretary-General' (10 January 1962) UN Doc E/CN.4/828.

[20] National Institutions for the Promotion and Protection of Human Rights, UNGA Res 33/46 (14 December 1978) UN Doc A/RES/33/46.

[21] United Nations Division of Human Rights, 'Seminar on National and Local Institutions for the Promotion and Protection of Human Rights' (18–29 September 1978) UN Doc ST/HR/SER.A/2 'Guidelines on the Structure and Functioning of National and Local Institutions for the Promotion and Protection of Human Rights' 184–85.

The 1978 Guidelines were lengthy compared to the Paris Principles, containing fifty paragraphs, forty-one of which provided for functions, and nine of which discussed structure. It is worth listing in detail some of the relevant provisions of the 1978 Guidelines, because the similarities and differences between these guidelines and the Paris Principles can assist in understanding today's NHRIs. In truncated format, the Guidelines provided as follows regarding the functions and structures of the proposed institutions:

I. Functions

a) Act as a source of information; receive complaints; disseminate information; publish and submit periodic reports;
b) Assistance in the education of public opinion, awareness of and respect for human rights, including raising awareness and 'mobilising public opinion' against human rights violations; promote respect for rule of law; work in the national context but 'not derogate from the principles of the UDHR';[22] promote the right to self-determination and national independence;
c) 'Considering, deliberating upon and making recommendations, within their specified terms of reference, regarding any particular state of affairs that may exist nationally that the Government may wish to refer to them', they should include independent fact-finding agencies established by law, have the competence to apply concrete remedies, hold inquiries and summon witnesses;
d) 'Advising on any questions regarding human rights referred to such institutions from time to time by their national Government', periodic reviews of legislative and administrative systems, play a prominent consultative role on human rights issues, make recommendations on the administration of justice;
e) 'Studying and keeping under review the status of legislation, judicial decisions and administrative arrangements for the promotion of human rights, and preparing and, submitting, in this connexion, periodic reports at prescribed intervals to the appropriate authorities designated by the Government', including promoting incorporation, reviewing/contributing to the drafting of legislation.
f) Performing any function which the Government may wish to assign to them, assisting the government in reporting on human rights instruments, cooperating with the United Nations and channelling

[22] Para 13 provides: 'National institutions involved in promoting human rights should structure their activities in accordance with national, political, economic and social conditions and historic and cultural traditions of each nation, but in so doing the national institutions should not derogate from the principles set out in the Universal Declaration of Human Rights.' ibid 44.

information between NGOs and the UN system and facilitating research to bring national legislation into line with international standards.

II. **Structure**

1. 'National institutions should be so designed as to bring all parts of the population into the decision-making process in regard to human rights';
2. They should be statutory authorities 'created within and subject to the constitutions and laws' of the state;
3. They should be established as 'autonomous, impartial, statutory bodies';
4. Membership should reflect cross-sections of the public in its composition;
5. Appointment should be for a fixed term and persons appointed will not be arbitrarily removed;
6. They should be 'adequately staffed' to effectively discharge their statutory functions;
7. They should function regularly and 'make adequate provision for immediate access to it by any member of the public or public authority';
8. They should have local or regional 'advisory organs' where appropriate, which issue publicly available reports to the national institutions;
9. Wherever practical they should be established as local or regional organs comprising persons familiar with local problems.[23]

Although there are some clear parallels between the functions and structure proposed by the 1978 Guidelines and the Paris Principles, the Geneva Seminar in fact reported on a broad range of national institutions including judicial and legislative organs, political institutions, and educational institutions, with human rights committees or ombudsman being only a small part of the report. Indeed, the preamble to the Guidelines indicates that they relate to the 'functioning and structure of new national institutions that governments may decide to set up, *as well as for existing national institutions, comprising all governmental and public bodies concerned with promotion and protection of human rights*'.[24] This would seem to reflect both the concerns of governments regarding the establishment of new institutions and the confusion over their nature, reflected in the earlier debates from the 1950s and 1960s.

Interestingly, during these debates some states foresaw two issues of independence that, as will be seen in subsequent chapters of this book, still arise for NHRIs and are often at the heart of questions relating to how much they are truly separate from the government of their state: reporting to parliament and budgets. In that regard, the United Kingdom made this prescient statement:

[23] ibid 43–48. Direct quotations from the Guidelines are indicated by quotation marks.
[24] ibid (emphasis added).

> Whatever the financial relationship between a national body and the government, such institutions, if they are to be useful, should be truly independent and free to voice criticism and comment in accordance with the principles of free political expression and debate. They should also publish reports of their activities to the general public, not only to national authorities as suggested in paragraph 5 of the guidelines. In the United Kingdom, this objective is sometimes met by requiring bodies of the kind listed in paragraph 6(i)–(vii) to lay annual reports before Parliament.[25]

Annual General Assembly resolutions on national institutions followed the 1978 Geneva Seminar.[26] These resolutions emphasized elements of national institutions that would subsequently gain prominence in the context of modern NHRIs. General Assembly Resolution 36/134 (1982), for example, emphasized the 'importance of the integrity and independence of such national institutions'.[27] Resolution 38/123(1983) highlights a number of specific roles in its text, including the promotion and protection of the rights of individuals and groups, and the contribution of national and local institutions to the implementation of international human rights instruments.[28]

The Secretary-General's 1984 report on national institutions illustrates, however, that there remained a lack of clarity, or perhaps rather a lack of agreement, as to what 'national institutions for the protection of human rights' were, and that the term was not applied to one specific form of institution.[29] The examination of a wide variety of institutions under the heading of 'national institutions for the protection and promotion of human rights' persisted throughout the 1980s.[30] However, by the January 1991 report of the Secretary-General, which came ten

[25] ECOSOC Commission on Human Rights, 'Further Promotion and Encouragement of Human Rights and Fundamental Freedoms, Including: (b)The Importance of National Institutions in the Field of Human Rights, Addendum to Report of the Secretary-General' (7 February 1979) UN Doc E/CN.4/1321/Add.2.

[26] For example, UNGA Res 34/49 (23 November 1979) UN Doc A/RES/34/49; UNGA Res 36/134 (14 December 1981) UN Doc A/RES/36/134; UNGA Res 38/123 (16 December 1983) UN Doc A/RES/38/123; UNGA Res 39/144 (14 December 1984) UN Doc A/RES/39/144; UNGA Res 40/123 (13 December 1985) UN Doc A/RES/40/123; UNGA Res 41/129 (4 December 1986) UN Doc A/RES/41/129. The annex to UNGA Res 32/123, on the 30th Anniversary of the Universal Declaration of Human Rights suggested the 'establishment of national or local institutions for the promotion and protection of human rights' (16 December 1977) UN Doc A/RES/32/123, para (e).

[27] UNGA Res 36/134.

[28] UNGA Res 38/123.

[29] UNGA 'National Institutions for the Promotion and Protection of Human Rights, Report of the Secretary-General' (19 November 1984) 39th Session UN Doc A/39/556. The report separates institutions for promotion and those for protection. The type of institutions listed under each demonstrates the broad approach taken. Under protection, it includes judicial institutions, as well as ombudsmen, legal counselling, and legislative organs. Under 'promotion', educational bodies, healthcare systems, and social welfare systems are listed.

[30] For example, the Secretary-General's 1988 report lists the following under the heading of 'national institutions': legislative organs, judicial organs, ombudsmen (including equal opportunities and anti-corruption commissions). Under the heading of administrative organs, it lists a wide range of bodies from the Canadian Human Rights Commission to the Voluntary People's Militia of the USSR. ECOSOC Commission on Human Rights, 'National Institutions for the Promotion and Protection of

months before the workshop that drafted the Paris Principles, human rights commissions had taken greater prominence, being listed under their own heading in the report, although the report still included judicial bodies and non-governmental organizations (NGOs).[31] Indeed, a number of institutions that would be accredited as NHRIs had already been established by this time. In discussing human rights commissions, the report noted the emergence of discrete institutions, such as national commissions or committees on human rights, which 'have been established with a view to ensuring that the laws and regulations concerning the protection of human rights are effectively applied'.[32]

In October 1991, a workshop on 'National Institutions for the Promotion and Protection of Human Rights' was held in Paris.[33] This workshop adopted a series of recommendations, and a list of principles—the Paris Principles—which the 1993 Vienna World Conference on Human Rights accepted unamended (even with typographical errors).[34] From the list of participants, it is clear that, despite the broad range of institutions listed in Secretary-Generals' reports since 1978, the concept of a national institution for human rights had taken on a more specific meaning. A large number of the participants were from specialized commissions, committees, or ombudsmen. This is also in sharp contrast to the 1978 Geneva Seminar, which was primarily attended by state representatives.[35] It was this 1991 Paris workshop that refined the approach to national institutions for human rights at the UN level, and its discussions and outcomes show a definite break from the

Human Rights, Updated Report of the Secretary-General' (16 December 1988) 45th Session UN Doc E/CN.4/1989/47.

[31] ECOSOC Commission on Human Rights, 'Further promotion and encouragement of human rights and fundamental freedoms, including the question of the programme and methods of work of the Commission; Alternative approaches and ways and means within the United Nations system for improving the effective enjoyment of human rights and fundamental freedoms: National institutions for the protection and promotion of human rights' (9 January 1991) UN Doc E/CN.4/1991/23. Reif notes the following countries' commissions as being established prior to 1993: Australia (1986), Canada (1977), New Zealand (1971), Bermuda (1982), Cameroon (1992). Linda Reif, *The Ombudsman, Good Governance and the International Human Rights System* (Springer 2004) 83.

[32] ECOSOC Commission on Human Rights, 'Further promotion and encouragement of human rights and fundamental freedoms, including the question of the programme and methods of work of the Commission; Alternative approaches and ways and means within the United Nations system for improving the effective enjoyment of human rights and fundamental freedoms: National institutions for the protection and promotion of human rights' (9 January 1991) UN Doc E/CN.4/1991/23, para 50.

[33] ECOSOC Commission on Human Rights, 'Report of the International Workshop on National Institutions for the Promotion and Protection of Human Rights (Paris 7–9 October 1991)' (16 December 1991) UN Doc E/CN.4/1992/43. For a useful review of the Paris conference from the perspective of one of the key developers of the Principles, see Brian Burdekin and Jason Naum, *National Human Rights Institutions in the Asia-Pacific Region* (Martinus Nijhoff 2007).

[34] ECOSOC Commission on Human Rights, Res 1992/54 (3 March 1992) UN Doc E/CN.4/1992/L.11/Add.4, 27–30. The Commission renamed them the 'Principles relating to the status of national institutions'. The Principles were annexed to UN General Assembly, 'National institutions for the promotion and protection of human rights: Note of the Secretary-General' (19 November 1992) UN Doc A/47/701.

[35] 1978 Guidelines (n 21) 1.

previous broad approach, moving away from the idea that a range of domestic institutions could have promotion and protection functions in relation to human rights, to requiring a separate and distinct independent institution.[36]

The discussion at the Paris workshop illustrates how the Paris Principles were not created in a vacuum but were developed on the basis of a study of existing institutions that had developed over the preceding almost fifty years, and particularly since 1978. In addition, as can be seen from the details of the Paris Principles set out in the next chapter, they incorporated many of the concepts contained in the 1978 Guidelines. Thus, the process that led to the development of the Paris Principles was a long one, spanning nearly fifty years, and the text of the Paris Principles was based to a large extent on an assessment of existing institutions that had been established pursuant to previous guidelines, rather than any *de novo* consideration. Furthermore, the active involvement of NHRIs themselves in the development of the Paris Principles also set the precedent for the active engagement of NHRIs in their *further* development, as the content of this book attests.

In advance of the 1993 World Conference on Human Rights, the Office of the High Commissioner for Human Rights (OHCHR) issued a fact sheet on NHRIs, in which it explained their role and purpose vis-à-vis other types of domestic institutions:

> The concept of a national human rights institution is, however, far more specific—referring as it does to a body whose functions are specifically defined in terms of the promotion and protection of human rights. While no two institutions are exactly the same, a number of similarities can be identified which serve to separate these institutions from the various entities mentioned above. The national institutions being considered here are all administrative in nature-in the sense that they are neither judicial nor law-making. As a rule, these institutions have on-going, advisory authority in respect to human rights at the national and/or international level. These purposes are pursued either in a general way, through opinions and recommendations, or through the consideration and resolution of complaints submitted by individuals or groups. In some countries, the Constitution will provide for the establishment of a national human rights institution. More often, such institutions are created by legislation or decree. While

[36] The analysis of the rapporteur excluded from its consideration parliamentary institutions, jurisdictional institutions, NGOs, and other institutions, focusing instead on institutions whose establishment had been encouraged by the UN. A discussion on national institutions at a meeting of experts of the Conference on Security and Co-Operation in Europe (CSCE) seems to have taken a similarly broad approach to the concept of national institutions. A report noted 'it was pointed out that, in addition to the ordinary court system, including administrative courts, such institutions could comprise constitutional courts, national human rights commissions, complaints commissions, Ombudsman or mediators'. Conference on Security and Co-Operation in Europe, 'Report to the CSCE Council from the CSCE Seminar of Experts on Democratic Institutions, Oslo, November 15, 1991' (1992) 31 ILM 374, 385.

> many national institutions are attached, in some way or another, to the executive branch of government, the actual level of independence which they enjoy will depend on a number of factors including membership and the manner in which they operate.[37]

The Paris Principles were subsequently adopted at the 1993 Vienna World Conference on Human Rights. Writing in 2007, Brian Burdekin, one of the individuals who helped to establish NHRIs within the international system, wrote of the World Conference that it played a 'fundamentally important role in shifting the U.N.'s focus to concentrate more specifically on mechanisms and strategies to promote and protect human rights at the national level'. In particular, he notes that 'this shift, together with the creation of the post of U.N. High Commissioner for Human Rights and the decision by the first High Commissioner to make NHRIs a significant area of emphasis, prepared the ground for a dramatic expansion of NHRI activity throughout the 1990s'.[38]

1.3 NHRI Role and Typology

In this book, the term NHRIs is used to refer to domestic human rights institutions established by states on the basis of, or with the aim of complying with, the UN Paris Principles, and seek accreditation with the Sub-Committee on Accreditation (SCA). While it necessarily results in generalization to speak about NHRIs as a homogenous group, when there are over 120 such institutions across the world at time of writing, approaching NHRIs in this way is justifiable, given their common basis on a set of international principles, membership of a global network, review on the basis of agreed standards (by the SCA) and common modes of interaction at the international level. NHRIs accredited in line with the Paris Principles also tend to undertake broadly similar activities at the domestic level. Furthermore, as will be seen in this chapter, NHRIs operate through formally structured networks both regionally and internationally and are approached by the UN and regional human rights bodies as a homogenous group.

Nonetheless, there remains some disagreement among scholars over what constitutes an 'NHRI'. Goodman and Pegram, for example, contended in 2012 that the number of NHRIs globally ranged from 120 to 178.[39] In comparison, at this time the Global Alliance on National Human Rights Institutions (GANHRI) (then called the International Coordinating Committee of National Human Rights

[37] OHCHR, 'Fact Sheet No. 19, National Institutions for the Promotion and Protection of Human Rights' (Geneva 1993).
[38] Burdekin and Naum (n 33) 13.
[39] Ryan Goodman and Thomas Pegram (eds), *Human Rights, State Compliance and Social Change: Assessing National Human Rights Institutions* (CUP 2012).

Institutions) comprised ninety-nine A-, B-, and C-status NHRIs.[40] In her 2003 work on the UN and NHRIs, Sonia Cardenas identified 300–500 institutions.[41] This disparity between the numbers of institutions labelled as an NHRI is partly a result of a lack of agreement on whether or not to classify an institution that meets some but not all of the requirements of the Paris Principles using this nomenclature. It is also in part because GANHRI and the SCA deal with institutions that have applied for accreditation, but this is not a determination of the precise number of all NHRIs that may exist.

Perhaps adding to the challenge of clear identification is that NHRIs may be constituted in a number of different forms (see Table 1.1). Governments decide on the type of institutions that they will set up using the Paris Principles as a framework to guide the overall structure and functions. At least in principle, governments chose a model that is most closely aligned with the national legal and institutional structure. In practice, governments are likely to also choose a design that fits their political interests at the time of establishment, rather than exclusively fitting the needs of human rights promotion and protection in the country. The diversity of NHRI types is a product of the Vienna Declaration and Programme of Action,[42] as recognized by the UN General Assembly for example, in this 2008 Resolution:

> Recognizes that, in accordance with the Vienna Declaration and Programme of Action, it is the right of each State to choose the framework for national institutions that is best suited to its particular needs at the national level in order to promote human rights in accordance with international human rights standards.[43]

As noted above, the Paris Principles set out the powers and functions for NHRIs without detailing the precise form the institution should take. A broad classification of the four main NHRI types that have been established is set out in the following table:

Even within each of these categories, there are considerable differences in size, mandate, powers, structure, functions, and role in the national and international context among individual NHRIs. It may also be the case that some aspects of non-compliance with the Paris Principles will have a larger impact depending on the institution type. For example, a slow appointment process that leaves a vacancy at the head of an institution will likely have a significantly larger impact on a single-member-headed institution such as an ombudsperson, than a multi-member institution. However, irrespective of the form, the overall purpose of all

[40] International Coordinating Committee, 'Chart of the Status of National Institutions' (May 2012) <https://nhri.ohchr.org/EN/Documents/Chart%20of%20the%20Status%20of%20NIs%20(30%20May%202012).pdf> accessed 8 February 2021.

[41] Sonia Cardenas, 'Emerging Global Actors: The United Nations and National Human Rights Institutions' (2003) 9(1) Global Governance 23.

[42] UNGA, 'Vienna Declaration and Programme of Action: Note by the secretariat' (12 July 1993) UN Doc A/CONF.157/23.

[43] UNGA Res 172 (18 December 2008) UN Doc A/Res/63/172.

Table 1.1 NHRI Institution Types

Institution type	Examples of countries with A-status NHRI (2019)	Mandate and powers
Human Rights Commissions	Australia, Canada, India, Ireland, New Zealand, Nigeria, Northern Ireland, Scotland, South Africa, Uganda	Multi-member board. Broad mandate that includes protection, promotion, and monitoring, through eg reports and inquiries, legislative reviews, awareness, and education.
Ombuds Institutions/ Defensor del Pueblo	Argentina, Bolivia, Ecuador, Peru, Poland, Portugal, Spain	Usually single-member leadership (such as ombudsperson). Traditionally focusing on handling individualcomplaints
Human Rights Institutes	Denmark, Germany, Netherlands	Focusing on research, education, and advisory functions, often with a more limited protection mandate
Advisory/ Consultative Committees	France, Greece, Luxembourg, Morocco	Often have a large number of commissioners/board members with an advisory council. Greater emphasis on advisory functions

Linos and Pegram's 2015 study of the mandates of NHRIs is a particularly useful source on the different mandates and state choices on NHRI type: Thomas Pegram and Katerina Linos, Interrogating Form and Function: Defining Effective National Human Rights Institutions (The Danish Institute for Human Rights 2015).

Paris Principles-compliant NHRIs is intended to be the promotion and protection of human rights.

An important aspect of any discussion about NHRIs is recognizing their position at the national level. While NHRIs may be given prominence at the international level, their role at the national level with existing structures is not always as easily understood by domestic constituencies. This is in part because of their unusual position as 'independent' state institutions, as well as the potentially paradoxical effects of their establishment.[44] As regards their functions and mandate, NHRIs possess some features which, when combined, make them unique institutions at the national level. As neither state-representing institutions, nor NGOs, nor international organizations, they occupy a 'fourth space'[45] at the national

[44] On the paradoxical impact, see Goodman and Pegram (eds) (n 39) 16.

[45] Kirsten Roberts, 'National Human Rights Institutions as Diplomacy Actors' in Michael O'Flaherty and others (eds), *Human Rights Diplomacy: Contemporary Perspectives* (Martinus Nijhoff 2011). A number of commentators have referred to NGOs/civil society as the 'third space'; see for example, Robert Fairbanks II, 'The Political Economic Gradient' in Ram Cnaan and Carl Milofsky (eds), *Handbook of Community Movements and Local Organisations* (Springer 2007); Temma Kaplan, 'Women's Rights as Human Rights: Women as Agents of Social Change' in Marjorie Agosín (ed), *Women, Gender & Human Rights: A Global Perspective* (Rutgers University Press 2001); Gérard Fellous, *Les Institutions Nationales des Droits de l'Homme: Acteurs de Troisième Type* (Commission Nationale Consultative Des Droits de l'Homme 2006).

level.[46] This fourth space is one that NHRIs have carved out for themselves primarily from the space occupied by the three other main human rights actors: (i) governments, (ii) NGOs or civil society, and (iii) international organizations.[47]

NHRIs may be said to be an alternative to governments' traditional role when they provide a separate state-based national-level view on domestic human rights issues at the international level.[48] These reports are given considerable weight and many of the issues raised by NHRIs are subsequently raised by the international body with the state. Before the existence of NHRIs, 'official' human rights information only came from governments, with any contrary opinion presented by NGOs. Now an additional voice has the legitimacy to present authoritative human rights information and views that may challenge the government's position.

NGOs are often regarded as the primary custodians of the human rights concerns of victims and individuals at the national level. However, NHRIs have taken on some of this function through hearing individual complaints (where they have this power), engaging with individuals and interest groups, representing victims, promoting human rights, and having overall awareness of, and engagement with, the human rights situation at the national level. NHRIs have also take on some of the role of NGOs through providing an alternative independent voice from the national level. Where previously an international or regional organization may have only gone to NGOs for an independent view on the national human rights situation, now they will go to the NHRI as well, particularly where it has A-status.

Finally, the work that NHRIs can and do undertake in monitoring the application and implementation of international human rights agreements, and their national-level advisory function on the implementation of international standards, means that NHRIs have taken on some of the role that was traditionally within the remit of international organizations. A major role for NHRIs is also monitoring human rights in their state.[49] This role for NHRIs can be viewed as part of the implementation work of international human rights organizations and mechanisms.

While the fourth space created by NHRIs can be largely positive, adding a new actor to the national human rights framework, and one with legislatively mandated powers and functions at that, can be a challenging and potentially

[46] See Roberts Lyer (n 1).

[47] ibid.

[48] For example, engaging directly with the UN treaty bodies through providing shadow reports. Of thirty-four NHRI staff of European NHRIs surveyed in summer 2014, 85 per cent (29/34) reported that they had engaged with Human Rights Council's Universal Periodic Review Process, primarily through: supporting NGOs (23/34), preparing an NHRI report (18/34), commenting on the state report (18/34), and follow-up (22/34). Organization for Security and Cooperation (OSCE)—Office for Democratic Institutions and Human Rights (ODIHR) and European Network of NHRIs, 'NHRI Academy—Compilation of Pre-Academy Assignments' (June 2014) 10–11. Copy with authors. Eighty-two per cent also reported engagement with the UN Treaty Bodies, 13. Seventy-one per cent reported engagement with Special Procedures Mandate Holders, ibid 15.

[49] For example, of thirty-four staff from European NHRIs surveyed in June 2014, thirty-two indicted that their NHRI reviewed the text of laws and policies as a monitoring methodology, ibid 7.

uncomfortable position for NHRIs. They must engage with, and balance the needs of, multiple stakeholders within the realities of the national environment. They need to maintain credibility while having working relationships with all national actors including the government and NGOs. In his study of Ombudsman institutions in Latin America, Uggla illustrates how some NHRIs approach this challenge, finding that 'the institution often has to follow an essentially political logic in order to achieve its goals (for instance, by building support in society and the media, and choosing when and how to battle its opponents)'.[50] As Linnarsson and Sedletzki found in their study of national institutions for children's rights in conflict settings (which included NHRIs), such institutions were fragile even in times of peace, and the institutions' ability to engage with partners was critical because 'the trust of all actors, namely the population, civil society organizations, decision-makers, administrative and law enforcement officials, as well as international actors, is an essential element of effectiveness for independent institutions'.[51] NHRIs must be able to work with the government but also be critical of them when necessary which, due to the funding structure of NHRIs, is 'biting the hand that feeds them'. A Director of the Organization for Security and Cooperation (OSCE)-Office for Democratic Institutions and Human Rights Office for Democratic Institutions and Human Rights (ODIHR) described it thus: 'Governments never will and never should be fully comfortable with their national human rights institutions. For it is their task and their duty to be an uncomfortable partner, when and where necessary'.[52] NHRIs must also work with international and regional organizations while maintaining their own analysis and priorities and not becoming overwhelmed by the extent of cooperation or requirements placed upon them. Finally, there is a potentially negative aspect to NHRIs' occupying the fourth space: it has the risk of lessening the space for civil society, particularly in countries where civil society is already pressed. While NHRIs can be a valuable addition to the national human rights system, the fourth space is a challenging, and often fragile one. Parts II and III of this book illustrate the many challenges faced by NHRIs in ensuring that they are independent institutions with the powers and resources necessary to meet the expectations placed upon them as national promoters and protectors of human rights.

[50] Fredrik Uggla, 'The Ombudsman in Latin America' (2004) 36(3) Journal of Latin American Studies 423, 450.

[51] Ann Linnarsson and Vanessa Sedletzki, 'Independent Human Rights Institutions for Children: An Actor for the Protection of Children's Rights During Armed Conflict?' (2014) 36(2) Human Rights Quarterly 447, citing re fragility: UNICEF Office of Research, *Championing Children's Rights: A Global Study of Independent Human Rights Institutions for Children* (UNICEF 2013).

[52] Michael Georg Link, 'The Role of National Human Rights Institutions (NHRI) in Promoting and Protecting Human Rights in the OSCE Area 2015: Opening speech by Michael Georg Link Director of the Office for Democratic Institutions and Human Rights' (2015 OSCE Human Dimension Seminar, Warsaw 1–3 June 2015) <www.osce.org/files/f/documents/e/5/161271.pdf> accessed 19 January 2021.

1.4 The International and Regional NHRI Networks

Since 1993, NHRIs have taken an active role in defining their own position at the national and international levels, including the expansion of functions and the strengthening of independence.[53] The primary means through which this is done on collective basis is through GANHRI. This network was established in 1993[54] and became a legal entity under Swiss law in 2008, when it also adopted a written statute.

Pursuant to Article 5 of its founding statute, the network was established as 'an international association of NHRIs which promotes and strengthens NHRIs to be in accordance with the Paris Principles and provides leadership in the promotion and protection of human rights'.[55] The updated statute provides the following functions for GANHRI under Article 7:

b) To promote the establishment and strengthening of NHRIs in conformity with the Paris Principles, including such activities as:
   i) Accreditation of new members;
   ii) Periodic renewal of accreditation;
   iii) Special review of accreditation;
   iv) Assistance to NHRIs under threat;
   v) Encouraging the provision of technical assistance;
   vi) Fostering and promoting education and training opportunities to develop and reinforce the capacities of NHRIs.[56]

In practice, GANHRI primarily acts as a forum through which NHRIs can coordinate international engagement, as well as promote NHRI-related interests. The strength of GANHRI is largely subject to the availability and willingness of NHRI members to engage with and develop it.[57] GANHRI is headed by a Chair from one of its A-status NHRIs and its membership meets annually at the UN building in Geneva. It also holds a special meeting biennially (latterly, triennially) to discuss specific thematic issues in-depth—these have been held to date outside of Geneva

[53] Even prior to 1993, NHRIs were actively engaging in the process that led to the adoption of the Paris Principles. Burdekin and Naum (n 33).

[54] UNGA, 'National Institutions for the Promotion and Protection of Human Rights' UNGA Res 50/176 (27 February 1996) UN Doc A/RES/50/176, para 7, notes the establishment of the International Coordinating Committee in 1993.

[55] International Coordinating Committee Statute (as amended 24 March 2009) Art 7.

[56] GANHRI Statute (adopted on 5 March 2019).

[57] GANHRI is primarily funded through a membership fee elicited from its A-status members, though it has also in the past received a small annual amount from the OHCHR. See generally, Meg Brodie, 'Progressing Norm Socialisation: Why Membership Matters. The Impact of the Accreditation Process of the International Coordinating Committee of National Institutions for the Promotion and Protection of Human Rights' (2011) 80 Nordic Journal of International Law 143.

such as Bolivia (2006), Kenya (2008), Scotland (2010), Jordan (2012), Mexico (2015), and Morocco (2018).

In practice, GANHRI does not have a full-time multi-person secretariat similar to the regional networks in Africa, Asia-Pacific, and Europe, and the day-to-day operations and engagement of GANHRI are undertaken by an employee, who is provided with an office at the OHCHR in Geneva. The GANHRI Statute provides for a 'management committee', called the Bureau. Article 46 of the statute sets out the powers and functions, and it is useful to note some of them here to illustrate the type of engagement undertaken by GANHRI:

1. GANHRI Bureau is empowered to act generally in the name of GANHRI and to carry out the purpose and functions of GANHRI.
2. Without limiting the generality of the powers of management GANHRI Bureau is empowered to:
   a) decide applications for accreditation after considering a recommendation from the Sub-Committee on Accreditation;

   . . .

   d) collaborate and work with UN bodies, as well as OHCHR and UNDP, in particular work with OHCHR in connection with the GANHRI accreditation process, General Assemblies of GANHRI, meetings of the GANHRI Bureau and international conferences of NHRIs. In addition, OHCHR will facilitate and coordinate the participation of NHRIs in the Human Rights Council, its mechanisms, and the United Nations human rights treaty bodies;
   e) use and accept the services of OHCHR as the Secretariat for GANHRI, GANHRI Bureau and its SCA;

   . . .

   j) delegate any function to a nominated person, standing committee or sub-committee of persons or members;
   k) co-ordinate and arrange conferences, meetings, standing committees and sub-committees, and other activities;

   . . .

   q) adopt, amend or revoke rules of procedure in relation to the working methods of GANHRI Bureau and GANHRI sub-committees to regulate or clarify any matter contemplated by this Statute. Every decision to adopt, amend or revoke a rule shall as soon as practicable be circulated to all members of GANHRI.[58]

[58] GANHRI Statute (n 57) Art 46.

GANHRI's structure provides for four regional groups: Africa, Americas, Asia-Pacific, and Europe.[59] These regional networks, particularly in Africa, Asia-Pacific, and Europe, where there are full-time secretariats, actively and regularly engage their regional membership and undertake a considerable number of thematic initiatives at the regional level.

While it is beyond the scope of this book to detail the extent of the regional activities of the networks, it is useful to summarize each here in order to provide a fuller picture of NHRI collective engagement. While they began as an informal arrangement headed and run out of an individual NHRI, the regional networks have evolved into more formal and professional structures. In addition to the annual GANHRI meetings, the regional networks also hold their own meetings to discuss issues of regional interest and their engagement with GANHRI.

In Africa, the Network of African NHRIs (NANHRI) has been operational as a standalone secretariat based in Kenya since 2007, and it comprises forty-four institutions at the time of writing. It emerged from the Coordinating Committee of African NHRIs established in 1996, and the permanent secretariat established in 2001 within the South African NHRI.[60] ANHRI's mission is described thus: 'To support, through national, regional and international co-operation, the establishment and strengthening of NHRIs to more effectively undertake their mandate of human rights promotion, protection, monitoring and advocacy'.[61] It works on a range of thematic areas including sexual orientation and gender identity rights, torture prevention, business and human rights, and undertakes training and capacity building with NHRIs in the region. The Asia-Pacific Forum of NHRIs (APF) is also active in contributing to the strengthening of the institutions in its region. It has placed a strong focus on capacity building and protecting institutions under threat. It has also been a strong advocate for the engagement of NHRIs at the international level. Over the years, it has grown to provide individualized support to regional NHRIs. It provides assistance to governments drafting legislations for establishing NHRIs,[62] and individualized advice on accreditation and capacity-building of NHRIs,[63] as well as organizing regular conferences, workshops and

[59] In addition to the four GANHRI regional groups, NHRIs have a range of other networks at the regional or sub-regional networks. For example: The Arab Network of NHRIs, 'website' <https://annhri.org/en/2020/11/> accessed 22 February 2021; The Commonwealth Forum of National Human Rights Institutions, which was founded by David Langtry who presented the proposal to the meeting of NHRIs on the margins of the Commonwealth Heads of Government Meeting in Uganda in 2007, and served as Chair of the Forum from 2009–2011, Commonwealth Forum of National Human Rights Institutions, <https://cfnhri.org> accessed 22 February 2021; and L'Association francophone des commissions nationales des droits de l'Homme (AFCNDH), <http://afcndh.org> accessed 22 February 2021.

[60] See NANHRI, <www.NANHRI.org> accessed 19 January 2021.

[61] ibid.

[62] See for example, APF, 'APF to advise on draft legislation to establish Cambodian NHRI' (21 October 2020)<https://www.asiapacificforum.net/news/apf-advise-draft-legislation-establish-cambodian-nhri/> accessed 15 January 2021.

[63] See APF, '2019–20 Annual Report' (25 November 2020) 8–10 <https://www.asiapacificforum.net/resources/2019-2020-annual-report/> accessed 15 January 2021.

courses.[64] The European Network of NHRIs (ENNHRI), like ANHRI, was created from the previous European Group of NHRIs, when a permanent office and staff began working from Brussels in 2013. It comprises forty-five NHRIs at the time of writing. It aims to strengthen NHRIs through capacity-building and good practice, support NHRIs in accreditation and when they are under threat, and facilitate engagement with the regional mechanisms. It also coordinates reports and statements on behalf of the European NHRIs on thematic areas.[65]

The three permanent regional secretariats aim at strengthening NHRIs in their region as well as engaging on important human rights issues with a collective voice, and providing an important and active focal point for engagement with regional and international organizations.

1.5 UN-level Engagement

There are two main forms of engagement between NHRIs and the UN: formal engagement with UN mechanisms discussed in this section, and direct support from the OHCHR to the establishment and strengthening of NHRIs, which is described in the Secretary-General's 2017 Report on NHRIs:

> OHCHR provides national human rights institutions and other stakeholders with technical and legal assistance, in particular regarding constitutional and legislative frameworks relating to the establishment, nature, functions, powers and responsibilities of institutions. It also conducts and supports comparative analysis, technical cooperation projects, needs assessments and evaluation missions to establish and strengthen the capacity of national human rights institutions to discharge their mandate effectively.[66]

One of the most visible impacts at the international level of an NHRI obtaining A-status is the legitimacy and access it gains to international human rights bodies. Since the adoption of the Paris Principles,[67] the UN has not just encouraged the establishment of NHRIs at the national level but has promoted NHRIs as partners and stakeholders in a range of UN mechanisms. This inclusion of NHRIs has also

[64] ibid 14.

[65] ENNHRI, 'About ENNHRI' <http://ennhri.org/about-us/> accessed 13 January 2021.

[66] UN Secretary-General, 'National institutions for the promotion and protection of human rights: Report of the Secretary-General' (3 August 2017) UN Doc A/72/277, para 9.

[67] The third International workshop on NHRIs, held in Manila, 18–21 April 1995, recommended that the Commission on Human Rights recognize 'the unique status and independent character of national institutions and take appropriate measures to ensure that they participate in the work of the United Nations human rights bodies as individual national institutions with observer status'. ECOSOC Commission on Human Rights, 'Report of the 3rd International Workshop on National Institutions for the Promotion and Protection of Human Rights' (18–21 April 1995) UN Doc E/CN.4/1996/8, Annex V, 33.

been reflected at the regional human rights organization level to a greater or lesser extent, as will be seen further below.

The promotion of NHRIs by the UN since the adoption of the Paris Principles has fed into all of its main human rights monitoring mechanisms: the Human Rights Council,[68] including the Universal Periodic Review (UPR), the Treaty Bodies and Special Procedures, as well as specialized agencies such as the United Nations Development Program (UNDP).[69] As part of the Human Rights Council's UPR process, for example, A-status NHRIs are given their own section (the first section) in the OHCHR compilation of stakeholders' submissions.[70] The strengthening of NHRIs is also a frequent recommendation of the UPR process. As noted in the Secretary-General's 2017 report, 'During the second cycle of the universal periodic review, the establishment and strengthening of national human rights institutions in accordance with the Paris Principles were among the most frequently made recommendations to Member States'.[71] The report further notes that 'during the period under review, 19 written statements were submitted and 42 oral statements (including 11 video-recorded statements) were delivered by national human rights institutions and [GANHRI]' to the Human Rights Council.[72]

NHRIs also engage actively and directly with the UN Treaty Bodies through substantive contributions to the treaty-monitoring process. This is generally done through the submission of 'parallel' or 'shadow' reports on compliance with the treaty in their country. NHRIs also have the opportunity to meet directly with the Treaty Body members to express their concerns and emphasize their recommendations. This input, as with the UPR and at the Human Rights Council, is generally critical of their state's progress on compliance with the relevant treaty. Some treaty bodies have developed formal guidelines on their working relationship or referred to NHRIs explicitly in their jurisprudence.[73] The Committee on the Elimination

[68] UNGA Res 60/251 (3 April 2006) UN Doc A/RES/60/251, 3, establishing the Human Rights Council provides that the Council is to 'work in close cooperation in the field of human rights with Governments, regional organisations, national human rights institutions and civil society'. Human Rights Council Res 5/1 (18 June 2007) UN Doc A/HRC/RES/5/1. Rule 7 provides for the participation of NHRIs.

[69] NHRIs, particularly led by the Asia-Pacific Forum of NHRIs, have had considerable engagement and partnership with UNDP, including in the production of joint-materials (see for example, Asia Pacific Forum of National Human Rights Institutions and UNDP, *Capacity Assessment Manual for National Human Rights Institutions* (Asia Pacific Forum of National Human Rights Institutions and UNDP 2014) and in programmes for NHRI capacity building. For cooperation examples see 'APF 15: UNDP Presentation on Engagement with NHRIs in the Asia Pacific' <www.asiapacificforum.net/resources/apf-15-undp-presentation-engagement-nhris-asia-pacific/> accessed 15 February 2021.

[70] Human Rights Council Res 16/21 (12 April 2011) UN Doc A/HRC/RES/16/21. See for example, OHCHR, 'Summary prepared by the Office of the United Nations High Commissioner for Human Rights in accordance with paragraph 15(c) of the annex to Human Rights Council resolution 5/1 and paragraph 5 of the annex to Council Resolution 16/21: Rwanda' (August 2015) UN Doc A/HRC/WG.6/23/RWA/3, 17.

[71] UN Secretary-General, 'National institutions for the promotion and protection of human rights: Report of the Secretary-General' (3 August 2017) UN Doc A/72/277, para 78.

[72] ibid.

[73] For example, Committee on Economic, Social and Cultural Rights (CESCR), 'Draft General Comment No. 10: The role of national human rights institutions in the protection of economic, social

of Racial Discrimination (CERD), for example, has formalized the role of NHRIs in the hearing process, allowing NHRIs to speak during the state hearing.[74] The Committee on the Elimination of Discrimination Against Women (CEDAW) has issued a statement on its relationship with NHRIs and the roles of NHRIs in monitoring and protecting the rights of women.[75] The Committee on the Rights of the Child (CRC) has elaborated working methods specifically encouraging NHRIs to provide reports and the Committee can meet with NHRIs at their request in private. The Human Rights Council invited NHRIs to submit reports on the implementation of the ICCPR, and NHRIs may make oral statements to the Committee during the first morning meeting of every plenary session.[76] At the domestic level, NHRIs also support the involvement of NGOs and civil society organizations in the national-level treaty-body monitoring process, and raise awareness of specific treaties and the examination process at the national level.[77]

Since 2006, GANHRI has also participated in the annual inter-committee meeting of the Treaty Bodies and special procedure mandate holders. Meeting with the NHRI has also become a regular feature of the in-country visits of special procedure mandate holders. A-status NHRIs are entitled to intervene immediately after the state under consideration by a report of a mandate holder at the Human

and cultural rights' (10 December 1998) UN Doc E/C.12/1998/25; CESCR, 'General Comment No. 16, The equal right of men and women to the enjoyment of all economic, social and cultural rights' (11 August 2005) UN Doc E/C.12/2005/4; CESCR, 'General Comment No. 19, The right to social security (art. 9)' (4 February 2008) UN Doc E/C.12/GC/19; Committee on the Rights of the Child, 'General Comment No. 2 (2002), The Role of Independent National Human Rights Institutions in the Promotion and Protection of the Rights of the Child' (15 November 2002) UN Doc CRC/GC/2002/2; Human Rights Council, 'General Comment No. 31, The nature of the general legal obligation imposed on States Parties to the Covenant' (26 May 2004) UN Doc CCPR/C/21/Rev1/Add.13; CERD, 'General Recommendation No. 33, Follow-up to the Durban Review Conference' (29 September 2009) UN Doc CERD/C/GC/33; CEDAW, 'General Recommendation No. 28 on the Core Obligations of States Parties under Article 2 of the Convention on the Elimination of All Forms of Discrimination Against Women' (19 October 2010) UN Doc CEDAW/C/2010/47/GC.2. See generally, Katrien Meuwissen, 'NHRI Participation in United Nations Human Rights Procedures: International Promotion versus Institutional Consolidation' in Jan Wouters and Katrien Meuwissen (eds), *National Human Rights Institutions in Europe: Comparative, European and International Perspectives* (Intersentia Publishing 2013); Roberts Lyer (n 1).

[74] CERD, 'Rules of Procedure' (1 January 1989) UN Doc CERD/C/35/Rev3, Rule 40.

[75] CEDAW, 'Statement by the Committee on the Elimination of Discrimination against Women on its relationship with national human rights institutions' (11 February 2008) UN Doc E/CN.6/2008/CRP.1, Annex II.

[76] Human Rights Council, 'Working Methods', VIII. Participation of non-governmental organizations and national human rights institutions in the activities of the Committees <https://www.ohchr.org/EN/HRBodies/CCPR/Pages/WorkingMethods.aspx> accessed 19 January 2021.

[77] See for example, OSCE, 'Conclusions of the International Roundtable on the Role of National Human Rights Institutions and Treaty Bodies, Berlin, 23 and 24 November 2006' (16 July 2007) PC.SHDM.IO/9/07/Corr.1 presented at the Nineteenth meeting of chairpersons of the human rights treaty bodies, Geneva 21–22 June 2007; Amrei Müller and Frauke Seidensticker, *The Role of National Human Rights Institutions in the UN Human Rights Treaty Body Process* (German Institute for Human Rights 2007); OHCHR, 'Information Note on National Human Rights Institutions (NHRIs) interaction with the UN Treaty Body System' (5 April 2011).

Rights Council.[78] NHRIs are also participants in a range of other UN platforms, such as the UN Panel on Ageing.[79] The UN General Assembly issues regular resolutions on NHRIs,[80] as does the UN Human Rights Council.[81]

The efforts of NHRIs themselves have been instrumental in increasing their engagement with the UN's human rights mechanisms. There are numerous references in the UN Secretary-General's 2017 report on NHRIs, for example, on how NHRI engagement at the international level is driven forward by GANHRI.[82] Sidoti describes the emergence of a 'bottom-up' relationship between NHRIs and the UN as part of the maturation of NHRIs and their work.[83] For its part, the UN is interested in promoting NHRIs for its own institutional purposes and views NHRIs as a means of improving its human rights monitoring mechanisms, for example through NHRIs providing alternative, authoritative, national-level information, and improving the engagement between the state and the UN on human rights issues. This is in keeping with the original purpose of NHRIs seen earlier in the chapter, as institutions that support the work of the UN in the field of human rights at the national level. Further, it is worth emphasizing that the findings of the SCA are given considerable attention by the UN Treaty Bodies is a testament to both the importance of the SCA's role and the value of their reviews.

[78] Human Rights Council Res 16/21 (25 March 2011) A/HRC/RES/16/21 Annex, para 28. According to this paragraph, the A-status NHRI of the state under review shall be entitled to intervene immediately after the state during the interactive dialogue, following the presentation of a country mission report by a special procedure mandate holder.

[79] See APF, 'NHRIs to be formally included in work of UN panel on Ageing' (5 January 2017) <https://www.asiapacificforum.net/news/nhris-be-formally-included-work-un-panel-ageing/> accessed 8 January 2021.

[80] For example, National Human Rights Institutions, UNGA Res 74/156 (18 December 2019) UN Doc A/RES/74/156; Role of the Ombudsman, Mediator and Other National Human Rights Institutions in the Promotion and Protection of Human Rights, UNGA Res 72/186 (19 December 2017) UN Doc A/RES/72/186; National Institutions for the Promotion and Protection of Human Rights, UNGA Res 70/163 (17 December 2015) UN Doc A/RES/70/163; UNGA Res 63/169 (18 December 2008) UN Doc A/RES/63/169 and UNGA Res 62/207 (21 December 2010) UN Doc A/RES/65/207 on the Role of the Ombudsman, Mediator and Other National Human Rights Institutions in the Promotion and Protection of Human Rights; UNGA Res 63/172 (18 December 2008) UN Doc A/RES/63/172 and UNGA Res 64/161 (18 December 2009) UN Doc A/RES/64/161 on National Institutions for the Promotion and Protection of Human Rights.

[81] National Human Rights Institutions, Human Rights Council Res 39/17 (28 September 2018) UN Doc A/HRC/RES/39/17; Regional Arrangements for the Promotion and Protection of Human Rights, Human Rights Council Res 34/17 (11 April 2017) UN Doc A/HRC/RES/34/17; National Institutions for the Promotion and Protection of Human Rights of the UN Human Rights Council, Human Rights Council Res 27/18 (7 October 2014) UN Doc A/HRC/RES/27/18.

[82] UN Secretary-General, 'National institutions for the promotion and protection of human rights: Report of the Secretary-General' (3 August 2017) UN Doc A/72/277, Chapter IV.

[83] Chris Sidoti, 'National Human Rights Institutions and the International Human Rights System' in Goodman and Pegram (eds) (n 39) 91.

1.6 NHRIs in Regional Fora

The formalization of international organizations' engagement with NHRIs has not taken place solely at the UN. Regional organizations have also adopted NHRIs as interlocutors. The focus on NHRIs at the regional level mirrors the UN's approach of targeting NHRIs as a means of promoting institutional priorities and assisting in the implementation of international human rights standards at the domestic level. The following overview illustrates the extent of this engagement in Africa, the Americas, and Europe in order to emphasize the increasing prominence of NHRIs to international institutions interested in human rights.

The multiple organs of the Council of Europe engage with NHRIs in a range of ways. Under the heading of 'National Human Rights Structures', the Council of Europe has engaged with NHRIs as well as a range of other national bodies that may or may not be in compliance with the Paris Principles, such as national ombudsmen, thematic ombudsmen, and equality bodies established under EU legislation.[84] While the Council of Europe engages with a wide range of bodies, to date it has provided relatively little in the way of formal space for NHRIs in its monitoring activities.[85] At the Parliamentary Assembly of the Council of Europe (PACE), a resolution on 'Improving Co-operation between [NHRIs] and Parliaments in Addressing Equality and Non-discrimination Issues' was adopted in 2014.[86] The accompanying PACE Resolution called on parliaments to develop formal cooperation channels with NHRIs (with due respect for their independence) to make use of NHRI data and reports, and to debate the NHRI's annual report. It also recommended that parliaments seek the advice of the NHRI in the preparation of draft legislation and use them as sources of information and advice on human rights matters.[87]

One of the focuses of the Council of Europe's engagement with NHRIs on substantive human rights issues is in the context of the work of the European Court

[84] See for example, Council of Europe Commissioner for Human Rights, 'Co-operation with National Human Rights Structures' <www.coe.int/en/web/commissioner/co-operation-with-national-human-rights-structures> accessed 18 February 2021. See also Bruce Adamson, 'NHRI and their European Counterparts: Scope for Strengthened Cooperation and Performance towards European Human Rights Institutions' in Wouters and Meuwissen (eds) (n 73).

[85] At time of writing, the Council of Europe was in the process of drafting a new recommendation that included NHRIs, the latest meeting record stating that the Council of Europe is seeking to add 'new means and ways to strengthen the role and meaningful participation of NHRIs and ENNHRI within the Council of Europe': Council of Europe, 'Drafting Group on Civil Society and National Human Rights Institutions (CDDH-INST)' (19 March 2020) CDDH-INST(2019)R6, para 13 <https://rm.coe.int/steering-committee-for-human-rights-cddh-drafting-group-on-civil-socie/16809cf87f> accessed 7 February 2021.

[86] This arose from the following report: PACE, 'Improving co-operation between National Human Rights Institutions (NHRIs) and parliaments in addressing equality and non-discrimination issues, Committee on Equality and Non-Discrimination, Report by Katherine Zappone (Ireland)' (30 April 2014) PACE Doc 13506. The rapporteur, then-Senator Katherine Zappone, was a former member of the board of the Irish Human Rights Commission, Ireland's NHRI.

[87] ibid.

of Human Rights. The much-overloaded Court has struggled for many years with its caseload. As a result, the Court and Council have sought ways to reduce the volume of cases that reach Strasbourg. One means identified was by increasing the capacity of national-level implementation mechanisms, including NHRIs. NHRIs have the potential to take on cases (if they have a case-handling function) or to address systemic human rights issues, both of which may reduce the volume of cases submitted to the court. In terms of practical engagement by NHRIs, ENNHRI as well as individual European NHRIs have developed the practice of making third party interventions in cases before the Court.[88] In addition to this engagement, ENNHRI also held observer status on the Council of Europe Steering Committee on Human Rights (CDDH) and the Ad Hoc Committee on Preventing and Combating Violence Against Women and Domestic Violence, which resulted in the Convention on preventing and combating violence against women and domestic violence that includes specific reference to NHRIs as partners for implementation and awareness raising.[89] In its initial engagements with NHRIs, the Council of Europe secretariat appears to have largely viewed NHRIs as institutions in need of capacity building support (particularly in eastern Europe, the Balkan region, and the Caucasus).[90] However, this is shifting as their role at the UN correspondingly grows, and with the increasing focus on domestic implementation mechanisms. Since 2018, the Council of Europe has recognized the important role played by NHRIs in the promotion of human rights and implementation of human rights obligations and commitments of Member States.[91] It is also notable that the

[88] ENNHRI, 'Third Party Interventions Before the European Court of Human Rights: Guide for National Human Rights Institutions' (October 2020) Annex 1 <http://ennhri.org/wp-content/uploads/2020/10/Third-Party-Interventions-Before-the-European-Court-of-Human-Rights-Guide-for-NHRIs.pdf> accessed 25 February 2021, provides a list of selected NHRI third party interventions by ENNHRI members. The then-named European Group of NHRIs also participated in the Interlaken process on the reform of the Court, including making statements on the reform process at the Interlaken Ministerial Meeting and at the High-Level Conference on the Future of the European Court of Human Rights held in Izmir, Turkey in 2011. European Group of National Human Rights Institutions, 'Intervention of the European Group of National Human Rights Institutions at the Interlaken Ministerial Conference on the Future of the European Court of Human Rights', Interlaken 18–19 February 2010. Copy on file with authors. European Group of National Human Rights Institutions, 'Oral Statement of the European Group of National Human Rights Institutions at the Izmir High-Level Ministerial Conference on the Future of the European Court of Human Rights, 26–27 April 2011'. Copy on file with authors. The Group was also an active participant in the High-Level Conference on the Future of the European Court of Human Rights held in Brighton in April 2012. See for example, ENNHRI, 'Submission to Council of Europe's Committee of experts on the reform of the European Court of Human Rights (DH-GDR) on the longer-term future of the system of the European Convention on Human Rights, and the European Court of Human Rights' (27 January 2014) <www.ihmisoikeuskeskus.fi/@Bin/256832/ENNHRI%20sub%20obn%20Conv%20system%20270114%20Final.pdf> accessed 19 January 2021.

[89] Council of Europe, Convention on Preventing and Combating Violence against Women and Domestic Violence (Istanbul Convention) CETS No. 210, Art 7(3) (comprehensive and coordinated policies) and Art 13 (awareness raising).

[90] See for example, the peer-to-peer project set out in Adamson (n 84).

[91] Council of Europe, Recommendation CM/Rec(2018)11 of the Committee of Ministers to Member States on the need to strengthen the protection and promotion of civil society space in Europe (adopted

European Commission for Democracy Through Law (Venice Commission) regularly provides its opinions on NHRI laws.[92]

Since its establishment in 2008, the EU Agency for Fundamental Rights recognized and engaged with EU NHRIs. NHRIs are formally recognized within the Regulation founding the Agency, Council Regulation (EC) No 168/2007, which provides that the Agency shall cooperate with NHRIs among others.[93] The first and second directors of the Agency were a former head of the A-status Danish NHRI and the International Coordinating Committee (forerunner to GANHRI) and the former head of another A-status institution. The Agency holds annual meetings with NHRIs and has published two major reports on NHRIs in EU Member States.[94] EU NHRIs are also invited to input into the Annual Work Programme of the Agency and are invited for discussions on thematic issues such as disability, data protection, migration, and human rights education.

Engagement by the EU with NHRIs has been increasing since the adoption of the EU Action Plan on Human Rights and Democracy in 2015.[95] ENNHRI has been making efforts to engage with the EU's other bodies for a number of years and this has seen results in the increased references to NHRIs in EU official publications. The European Council in its ten-year review of the EU Charter of fundamental rights underlined 'the necessity of safeguarding an enabling environment for independent [NHRIs], equality bodies and other mechanisms', emphasizing that they 'play a crucial role in the protection and promotion of fundamental rights and in ensuring compliance with the Charter'.[96] The European Parliament issued a resolution in support of NHRIs in 2009, urging Member States to set up NHRIs and ensure their independence, in light of the important preventative function that their work entails.[97] In 2020, it recalled the 'indispensable role' to be played by NHRIs, among others, in the annual monitoring cycle,[98] and listed NHRIs among

on 28 November 2020). At the time of writing, the Council of Europe is in the process of drafting a new recommendation on the development and strengthening of NHRIs. See Council of Europe, 'Civil society and national human rights institutions' <https://www.coe.int/en/web/human-rights-intergovernmental-cooperation/human-rights-development-cddh/civil-society-and-human-rights-institutions> accessed 23 February 2021.

[92] For example, Venice Commission, 'Opinion on the Draft Amendments to the Law on the Protector of Human Rights and Freedoms of Montenegro' (13 October 2009) Opinion No 540/2009.

[93] Council Regulation (EC) No 168/2007 of 15 February 2007 establishing a European Union Agency for Fundamental Rights [2007] OJ L 53/1.

[94] EU Agency for Fundamental Rights, *National Human Rights Institutions in the EU Member States—Strengthening the fundamental rights architecture in the EU* (European Union Agency for Fundamental Rights 2010); European Union Agency for Fundamental Rights, *Strong and Effective National Human Rights Institutions—Challenges, Promising Practices and Opportunities* (European Union Agency for Fundamental Rights 2020).

[95] Council of the EU, 'Council Conclusions on the Action Plan on Human Rights and Democracy 2015–2019' (20 July 2015) 10897/15RC/oza. 4. DGC 2B.

[96] Council of the European Union, 'Council Conclusions on the Charter of Fundamental Rights after 10 Years: State of Play and Future Work' (20 September 2019) 12357/19, para 22.

[97] Adamson (n 84) 148–49; Jan Wouters, Katrien Meuwissen, and Ana Sofia de Barros, 'The European Union and National Human Rights Institutions' in Wouters and Meuwissen (eds) (n 73) 187–220.

[98] European Parliament, 'The establishment of an EU Mechanism on Democracy, the Rule of Law and Fundamental Rights' (7 October 2020) P9-TA(2020)0251, para 10.

the stakeholders that must be closely involved with the mechanism.[99] Notably, it specifically 'points out that the accreditation status of [NHRIs] and the space for civil society may themselves serve as indicators for assessment purposes'.[100] A 2020 EU Strategy released on the implementation of the EU Charter of Fundamental Rights includes a section on 'strong and effective' NHRIs and invites Member States to establish or strengthen their NHRI.[101]

The OSCE formally recognized NHRIs prior to the elaboration of the Paris Principles. The 1990 Copenhagen Document provided participating states should 'facilitate the establishment and strengthening of independent national institutions in the area of human rights and the rule of law'.[102] The OSCE, through ODIHR, and its regional offices, also engages in capacity building for NHRIs on the ground. For example, in 2012, the OSCE published a handbook on NHRIs and Gender Equality.[103] ODIHR also supports an annual capacity-building Academy for NHRIs in cooperation with ENNHRI.[104]

In terms of formalized engagement between the organization and NHRIs, in 2007, ODIHR established a Focal Point for Human Rights Defenders and National Human Rights Institutions. From 14–15 April 2011, the OSCE held a Supplementary Human Dimensions Meeting on NHRIs.[105] At the meeting, NHRIs proposed a set of recommendations as to how NHRIs could be supported by participating states and the OSCE. The aim of these recommendations was to provide impetus towards the adoption of a new set of OSCE Commitments relating to NHRIs.[106] NHRIs are increasingly viewed as having an important role in the implementation of ODIHR priorities.[107] ODIHR also regularly issues opinions on draft NHRI laws with the aim of promoting compliance with the Paris Principles.[108]

[99] ibid para L.

[100] ibid.

[101] European Commission, 'Strategy to strengthen the application of the Charter of Fundamental Rights in the EU' (2 December 2020) COM(2020) 711 final.

[102] OSCE, 'Document of the Copenhagen Meeting of the Conference on the Human Dimension of the CSCE' (29 June 1990) <www.osce.org/files/f/documents/9/c/14304.pdf> accessed 19 January 2021.

[103] OSCE, *Handbook for National Human Rights Institutions on Women's Rights and Gender Equality* (ODIHR 2012).

[104] ENNHRI, 'NHRI Academy' <http://ennhri.org/our-work/nhri-academy/> accessed 17 February 2021.

[105] OSCE, 'Supplementary Human Dimension Meeting on National Human Rights Institutions (ombudsinstitutions, commissions, institutes and other mechanisms)' 14–15 April 2011, Vienna, <www.osce.org/event/shdm2011_1> accessed 15 February 2021.

[106] Adamson (n 84) 152–53.

[107] For example, in 2015, the OSCE held a Human Dimension Seminar on 'National Human Rights Institutions Promoting and Protecting Human Rights in the OSCE Area', where the head of ODIHR stated that 'any support for our claims is even more credible when it is voiced by a National Human Rights Institution'. Michael Georg Link, 'The Role of National Human Rights Institutions (NHRI) in Promoting and Protecting Human Rights in the OSCE Area 2015: Opening speech by Michael Georg Link Director of the Office for Democratic Institutions and Human Rights' (2015 OSCE Human Dimension Seminar, Warsaw 1–3 June 2015) <https://www.osce.org/files/f/documents/e/5/161271.pdf> accessed 19 January 2021.

[108] See for example, ODIHR, 'Opinion on the Draft Federal Law on the Support to the National Human Rights Institution of Switzerland' (31 October 2017) Opinion-Nr.: NHRI-CHE/312/2017 [AlC]; ODIHR, 'Opinion on the Draft Act on the Independent National Human Rights Institution of Iceland' (6 February 2017) Opinion-Nr.: NHRI-ISL/301/2017 [AlC]; ODIHR, 'Opinion on the on the Law of the Republic of Lithuania on the Seimas Ombudsmen' (21 September 2011) Opinion-Nr.: NHRI–LTU/187/2011 (AT).

The Commonwealth,[109] through the Commonwealth Secretariat, has taken an active role in the development of NHRIs in the countries that belong to this association. For example, in 2000, a conference was held in Cambridge aimed at developing a consensus on progress based on the Paris Principles and 'encourage the move towards a new era of human rights thinking'.[110] The Commonwealth has produced guidelines on the strengthening of NHRIs, and on the engagement between NHRIs and parliaments. There is also a specific Commonwealth Forum of NHRIs, which acts as a networking and information sharing forum, as well as hosting working groups and initiatives on a range of human rights issues.[111] The Forum also provides input to the Commonwealth on NHRIs and human rights matters.[112]

The Organization of American States (OAS)[113] has actively promoted the concept of NHRIs through a series of resolutions. The OAS places strong emphasis on the accreditation status of the NHRI. For example, a 2009 resolution on 'Strengthening the Role of National Institutions for the Promotion and Protection of Human Rights in the Organization of American States' decided to grant participation and speaking rights to A-status NHRIs that are members of the Americas regional network.[114] The OAS has, moreover, established a close relationship between the Inter-American Commission on Human Rights (IACmHR) and NHRIs in recent years. The IACmHR signed a Declaration of Commitment for Technical Cooperation with NHRIs from a number of OAS Member States to establish information exchange processes and broaden the participation of NHRIs within the

[109] The Commonwealth comprises fifty-four states, primarily current and former UK colonies and dependencies. It became an international organization in 1949 <www.thecommonwealth.org/about-us> accessed 15 February 2021.

[110] Commonwealth Secretariat, *National Human Rights Institutions: Best Practice* (Commonwealth Secretariat 2001) 5.

[111] Commonwealth Forum of NHRIs, <https://cfnhri.org/> accessed 20 January 2021. See for example, Commonwealth Forum of NHRIs, 'Strategic Plan 2019–2021' <https://cfnhri.org/wp-content/uploads/2020/01/CFNHRIStrategicPlanFinalDraft.pdf> accessed 23 February 2021.

[112] See for example, Commonwealth Forum of NHRIs, 'CFNHRI Communiqué to Commonwealth Heads of Government CHOGM 2013' (Colombo, Sri Lanka 2013) <https://thecommonwealth.org/sites/default/files/events/documents/CHOGM%202013%20Communique_0.pdf> accessed 20 January 2021.

[113] For a detailed discussion on NHRIs in Latin America, see Thomas Pegram, 'National Human Rights Institutions in Latin America: Politics and Institutionalization' in Goodman and Pegram (eds) (n 39) ch 9.

[114] OAS, 'Strengthening the Role of National Institutions for the Promotion and Protection of Human Rights in the Organization of American States' General Assembly Res AG/RES. 2448 (XXXIX-O/09) (4 June 2009). See also, OAS, 'Strengthening of the National Human Rights Systems of the Member States and Support for the Work of Defenders of the People, Defenders of the Population, and Human Rights Attorneys or Commissioners (Ombudsmen)' General Assembly Res AG/RES. 2221 (XXXVI-O/06) (6 June 2006); OAS, 'Strengthening the Role of National Institutions for the Promotion and Protection of Human Rights in the Organization of American States' General Assembly Res AG/RES. 2421 (XXXVIII-O/08) (3 June 2008); OAS, 'Strengthening of the National Human Rights Systems of the Member States and Support for the Work of Defenders of the People, Defenders of the Population, and Human Rights Attorneys or Commissioners (Ombudsmen)' General Assembly Res AG/RES. 2411 (XXXVIII-O/08) (3 June 2008); OAS, 'Permanent Council Report on Strengthening the Role of National Institutions for the Promotion and Protection of Human Rights in the Organization of American States' (29 April 2009) OEA/Ser.G CP/CG-1770/09 rev 2.

IACmHR's mechanisms.[115] This is complemented by regular meetings organized by the IACmHR on best practice for NHRIs.[116]

NHRIs have also been given formal recognition by a number of African regional mechanisms.[117] Article 26 of the African Charter on Human and Peoples' Rights explicitly provides that States Parties have a duty to 'allow the establishment and improvement of appropriate national institutions entrusted with the promotion and protection of the rights and freedoms guaranteed by the present Charter'.[118] In furtherance of this provision, NHRIs have had observer status at the African Commission on Human and Peoples' Rights (ACHPR) since 1998,[119] and affiliate status since 2010.[120] The resolution granting observer status calls NHRIs 'an essential partner in the implementation of the Charter at National Level'.[121] NHRIs are required to submit an activities report to the Commission every two years.[122] Those with an affiliate status are further required to assist the Commission with promotion of human rights at the national level. NHRIs are thus given a position of some prominence by the Commission and actively engage with it. For example, the Director of secretariat of the Africa Group of NHRIs made an opening statement at the 56th Ordinary Session of the African Commission on Human and Peoples' Rights held in 2015 and spoke about human rights issues on the continent, as well as the Africa Group's plans for greater engagement with regional mechanisms.[123] In addition, NHRIs may also engage with the Court pursuant to Article 30 of the 2008 Protocol on the Statute of the African Court of Justice and Human Rights, which provides that NHRIs are entitled to submit cases to the Court.[124]

[115] OAS, 'IACHR and National Human Rights Institutions (NHRIs) sign Declaration of Commitment for Technical Cooperation' (19 November 2018) Press release no 246/18 <http://www.oas.org/en/iachr/media_center/PReleases/2018/246.asp> accessed 15 January 2021.

[116] OAS, 'IACHR Holds Successful Third Meeting on Best Practice for National Human Rights Institutions' (27 January 2008) Press release no 016/20 <https://www.oas.org/en/iachr/media_center/PReleases/2020/016.asp> accessed 15 January 2021.

[117] For example, Rachel Murray, *The Role of National Human Rights Institutions at the International and Regional Levels: The Experience of Africa* (Hart Publishing 2007).

[118] African Charter on Human and Peoples' Rights (adopted 27 June 1981, entered into force 21 October 1986) (1982) 21 ILM 58 (African Charter).

[119] ACHPR, 'Resolution on the Granting of Observer Status to National Human Rights Institutions in Africa' ACHPR/Res 31(XXIV)98 (Banjul 31 October 1998).

[120] Rules and Procedure of the African Commission on Human and People's Rights (adopted in May 2010) Rule 67. The criteria for affiliate status were amended in ACHPR, 'Resolution on the Granting of Affiliate Status to National Human Rights Institutions in Africa' ACHPR/Res 370(LX)2017 (Niamey 22 May 2017).

[121] ibid.

[122] These reports can be found on the Commission's website: African Commission on Human and Peoples' Rights, 'National Human Rights Institutions' <www.achpr.org/network> accessed 3 February 2021.

[123] Gilbert Sebihogo, 'Opening Statement by the Network of National Human Rights Institutions' (56th Ordinary Session of the African Commission on Human and Peoples' Rights, Banjul, Gambia, 21 April–7 May 2015) <www.achpr.org/sessions/statements?id=80> accessed 20 January 2021.

[124] Protocol to the African Charter on Human and Peoples' Rights on the Establishment of an African Court (adopted on 10 June 1998, entered into force 25 January 2004) OAU Doc.OAU/LEG/EXP/AFCHPR/PROT(III).

1.7 Conclusion

The 1993 UN Paris Principles, the foundational standards for all modern NHRIs, by no means arrived 'out of the blue' and reflect concepts that were considered by the international community for almost fifty years. The development of Paris Principles-compliant NHRIs can be divided into three phases: 1946–1960, 1978–1991, and from 1991 on. In the earliest phase, there was clearly a great reluctance on the part of states to establish national bodies for human rights that would detract in any way from states' autonomy over human rights. And although promoted by the UN, by the 1960s the idea had stalled. The late 1970s saw a re-emergence of interest in national-level institutions for human rights, and the development of guidelines in 1978, which are the predecessor to the Paris Principles. The second phase, between the elaboration of the 1978 Guidelines and the adoption of the Paris Principles, was characterized by a lack of clarity as to what was intended, with a wide range of domestic institutions being listed as potential national human rights bodies that would meet the requirements of the 1978 Guidelines. What these bodies would look like in practice was left to individual states. However, by 1993, it was clear that what was envisaged were autonomous national-level bodies that would support the international community's human rights efforts. Since 1993, shaping NHRIs has gradually shifted from states to NHRIs themselves, who have taken on an active and progressive role in promoting NHRIs and in seeking to remedy defects in, and expand on, the provisions of the Paris Principles.

Far from the hesitant beginnings of NHRIs from 1946 to 1991, the period following the adoption of the Paris Principles has produced widespread acceptance of the concept of establishing an autonomous national human rights body. By November 2019, 124 NHRIs were accredited to GANHRI, 80 of which had A-status.[125] Although this is more than double the number of A-status NHRIs that existed in 2002, when there were thirty-seven, growth has been relatively slow, with forty-three A-status institutions added to GANHRI within this period (2002–2019).[126] Outstripping the growth in the *number* of NHRIs has been the increase in the *attention* given to NHRIs and their status at the international level. To a significant extent, this has been because of the efforts and organization of NHRIs themselves through both GANHRI and the regional networks.

The 'why' of NHRI establishment is less clear than the 'how'; why, in 1993, were the Paris Principles adopted? Why was the concept of independence finally accepted? While the official documentation may not be clear on this point, one

[125] GANHRI, 'Accreditation Status as of 27 November 2019' <www.ohchr.org/Documents/Countries/Cooperation/StatusAccreditationChart.pdf> accessed 15 January 2021. There were thirty-four B-status and ten C-status accredited NHRIs.

[126] In 2002, there were thirty-seven A-status NHRIs and twelve B-status. In 2005, there were fifty-one NHRIs with A-status, and eight with A(R) status ('A-reserve' status, which is no longer applied—see further, Chapter 2), meaning fifty-nine in total.

purpose for NHRIs flows through the entire discussion; that they were envisaged as a link between the international and national levels, with the aim of furthering the work of the UN in the area of human rights. This may be why the UN not only kept the idea on the agenda since 1946 but actively pushed for the establishment of NHRIs. One consequence of this process is that the UN has conferred legitimacy on NHRIs. This legitimacy is closely tied to the accreditation process, which enables NHRIs to demonstrate that they are not merely 'window dressing' but active promoters and protectors of human rights. That it is A-status NHRIs which are given the highest level of access particularly at the UN mechanisms, shows that the SCA's pronouncements are given weight and have created confidence over the course of their development.

The next chapter will examine the SCA and the requirements of the accreditation process in more detail.

2

The Operation of the Sub-Committee on Accreditation in Practice

2.1 Introduction

As seen in the previous chapter, scholars and practitioners alike acknowledge that the United Nations (UN) Paris Principles,[1] while useful in determining the functional requirements of National Human Rights Institutions (NHRIs), are not sufficient to ensure an effective institution. The Paris Principles thus required elaboration to facilitate their application to the realities of these institutions as well as a peer-review mechanism that would monitor the compliance of NHRIs with the Principles. This was recognized and acted upon by the Global Alliance of NHRIs' (GANHRI) Sub-Committee on Accreditation (SCA). This chapter examines the functioning of the SCA, as well as the process of development of its General Observations, and the formalities of the accreditation process.

Outside of representation of NHRIs at the international level, GANHRI's main role is the accreditation of the compliance of NHRIs with the Paris Principles. According to GANHRI:

> [r]eviewing NHRIs' compliance with the Paris Principles, through its accreditation and reaccreditation process (i.e. through the work of its Sub-committee on Accreditation), is one of the main functions of the GANHRI. In accordance with the Statute of the GANHRI, the Sub-Committee on Accreditation (the Sub-committee) has the mandate to consider and review applications for accreditation, re-accreditation and accreditation reviews of NHRIs on the basis of written evidence submitted. The GANHRI Bureau is vested with the power to decide applications for accreditation after considering the recommendation from the Sub-Committee on Accreditation.[2]

In 1998, the then-named International Coordinating Committee (the ICC, now GANHRI) began accrediting NHRIs through the SCA, comprising four

[1] Principles relating to the Status of National Institutions, UNGA Res 48/134 (20 December 1993) UNGA Doc A/RES/48/134 (The Paris Principles).

[2] International Coordinating Committee (ICC), 'Guidelines for Accreditation & Re-Accreditation of National Human Rights Institutions to the International Coordinating Committee of National Human Rights Institutions' (June 2009) 1.

National Human Rights Institutions. David Langtry and Kirsten Roberts Lyer, Oxford University Press. © David Langtry and Kirsten Roberts Lyer 2021. DOI: 10.1093/oso/9780198829102.003.0003

members: representing one A-status NHRIs from each of the four GANHRI regions.[3] The SCA was established in order to assess NHRIs against the Paris Principles and provide an accreditation 'grade' of A,[4] B, or C. NHRIs that are assessed as fully compliant with the Principles are given A-status,[5] those partly compliant are given B-status.

The allocating of a non-compliant status (C-status) was discontinued in 2011. The last two C-status accreditations were for Switzerland (2010) and Romania (2011). The SCA had discussions about the merit of dealing with C-status institutions. First, examining these institutions required the same time commitment both by Office of the High Commissioner for Human Rights (OHCHR) and the SCA members to receive, review, consider, and discuss these institutions, and to identify and explain the shortcomings the institution had when preparing the report. Secondly, there was a point raised that if C-status means 'not compliant' with the Paris Principles, then arguably the institution was not an NHRI at all, and ought not to be considered by an organization that accredits NHRIs. Thirdly, and related to the second point, there was the risk of a perception that a C-status institution might still have had some credibility as being an NHRI and that those institutions could rightfully say that they had 'been accredited by the ICC/GANHRI'. For these reasons, when the SCA Rules of Procedure were amended in 2018, section 10 referred to A- and B-statuses only. Section 6.4 was also inserted, which provided that if there was a question as to whether an institution was an NHRI, the matter would be put to the SCA for determination at the beginning of its next session. This allowed for the following process: the OHCHR, as the secretariat to the SCA, would determine if it believed an applicant institution was not an NHRI (ie would be accredited as C-status). It would advise the institution of this and provide its reasons to the SCA. The institution could then submit its response and information to the SCA to justify it being able to apply for A- or B-status (ie that it was in fact an NHRI). This process ensures that it remains the SCA that makes the determination

[3] The 2001 SCA Report refers to the first report of the sub-committee being 1998, and the accreditation status report reflects one 1998 entry for Switzerland: Federal Commission Against Racism. ICC, 'Report of the Accreditation Sub-Committee' (April 2001).

[4] When the accreditation process began, through to the April 2006 session of the SCA, in addition to 'A' status the SCA also accredited certain NHRIs with 'A(R)' status, which was defined as 'Accreditation with reserve—granted where insufficient documentation is submitted to confer A status'. See for example, SCA, 'Report and Recommendations of the Sub-Committee on Accreditation' (April 2006), para 4 (hereafter SCA, 'Accreditation Report'). The final time the SCA applied the A(R) accreditation was in the case of the NHRI of Armenia: SCA, 'Accreditation Report—Armenia (Human Rights Defender (HRD))' (April 2006) 2, with the SCA stating: 'The Sub-Committee recommends accreditation status A(R) at this time and recommends that the Human Rights Defender provide additional information regarding how the requirement of pluralism is ensured through the expert council and provide additional information describing the scope and nature of its role in promoting human rights.'

[5] The process of accreditation was set out in the ICC Rules of Procedure (as amended on 14 April 2008) annexed to the ICC Statute (adopted on 23 March 2012). See also, UNGA 'Report of the Secretary-General on the Process Currently Utilized by the International Coordinating Committee of National Institutions for the Promotion and Protection of Human Rights to Accredit National Institutions in Compliance with the Paris Principles' (18 January 2010) UN Doc A/HRC/13/45.

of eligibility to apply for accreditation, based on consideration of input from both OHCHR and the NHRI. It also avoids the SCA undertaking a lengthy review of all aspects of the institution that may not be an NHRI at all. Should the SCA nonetheless decide that the applicant institution is an NHRI then the full application process would be undertaken.

The SCA's published reports for the first few years simply listed the accreditation decision made, with no explanations or rationale. In 2002, limited explanations appeared together with a table setting out short comments for each application. The SCA continued to develop and expand the reports to provide more information on what issues were considered by it for each application. The SCA met once a year until 2006, when it began to meet twice a year. At its second session in 2006, the SCA developed the first General Observations (discussed further in Section 2.3) and established a Working Group to consider the accreditation process and make recommendations for improvement. The Working Group developed a Decision Paper which was adopted by the ICC (GANHRI) in 2008.[6]

This Decision Paper acknowledged the purpose of GANHRI (the ICC) to be the creation and strengthening of NHRIs, and the evolving and growing importance by international and national actors to members of GANHRI. The paper stated:

> In light of the changing role of National Institutions, and in order to remain true to its original purpose, it is paramount that the ICC reviews its accreditation process, with a view to strengthening the credibility and efficiency of the process, as well as that of its inherent fairness. With this in mind, the Working Group recommends that a new accreditation process be developed. To ensure that the process is fair and impartial, and that it satisfies the principles of natural justice, the Working Group recommends that it be based on the following three guiding principles: 1. Transparency 2. Rigour 3. Independence.[7]

Among other things, the result was that the SCA Rules of Procedure were amended to provide for decisions to be based on written documentation, dialogue/consultation with applicants, one-year notice of intention to downgrade, regional bodies were also welcomed to attend sessions as observers, and it was clarified that the SCA 'decisions' were rather recommendations to the GANHRI (ICC) Bureau, which could be challenged by the applicant within one month of the recommendation and the Bureau would have twenty days to approve or reject the recommendation. The Working Group continued to develop and refine the process, as well as reviewing and revising General Observations over the years.

[6] SCA, 'Report and Recommendations of the Sub-Committee on Accreditation' (April 2008) Annex 5 (hereafter Decision Paper (April 2008)).

[7] ibid 5–6.

With the development of the SCA procedures, the SCA has been recognized by the UN and accepted by states as the authoritative interpreter of the Paris Principles. For example, the UN General Assembly Resolution 63/172, adopted in December 2008, explicitly encouraged engagement:

> *Encourages* national institutions to seek accreditation status through the International Coordinating Committee of National Institutions, and notes with satisfaction the strengthening of the accreditation procedure and the continued assistance of the Office of the High Commissioner in this regard, as well as the assistance of the Office to the conferences of the International Coordinating Committee.[8]

In the Report of the Secretary-General to the Human Rights Council of 18 January 2010, on the SCA process, the Secretary-General stated:

> The Secretary-General acknowledges that the accreditation process carried out by the Subcommittee on Accreditation of the International Coordinating Committee, with the support of the Office of the High Commissioner for Human Rights, is a dynamic process, and expresses appreciation for its increasing rigorousness, fairness and transparency. The Secretary-General also stresses the importance of this process in strengthening the independence and effectiveness of national human rights institutions which, ultimately, will result in strengthening the national human rights protection system.[9]

The recommendations of the SCA, although addressed to NHRIs, are often issues that governments must act to rectify. The SCA recognizes that NHRIs are reliant on their government for the implementation of many of the elements of the Paris Principles.[10] The accreditation process is thus somewhat unusual, given that the NHRI has not been responsible for its own establishment, nor for many of the issues that the SCA highlights as concerns, such as its basis in national legislation, the procedure for the appointment of members and staff, and designation and size of budgets. However, although it may not be in a position to make all the recommended changes itself, the NHRI should not be passive in response to the SCA's recommendations. The SCA intends that its recommendations be used by the NHRI to lobby the government or parliament for improvements.[11] As will be seen

[8] UNGA Res 172 (18 December 2008) UN Doc A/Res/63/172, para 19 (emphasis in original).

[9] Human Rights Council, 'Process currently utilized by the International Coordinating Committee of National Institutions for the Promotion and Protection of Human Rights to accredit national institutions in compliance with the Paris Principles: Report of the Secretary-General' (18 January 2010) UN Doc A/HRC/13/45, para 16.

[10] SCA, 'General Observations of the Sub-Committee on Accreditation' (adopted on 21 February 2018) para 13 (hereafter SCA 'General Observations' (February 2018)).

[11] ibid.

in subsequent chapters, the SCA uses the level of effort put in by the NHRI to improve its own situation as a benchmark for the institution's legitimacy as an NHRI. The SCA's recommendations have also been used by international bodies such as UN Treaty Bodies and the HRC as a basis on which to call on Member States to strengthen their NHRIs.

2.2 The Functioning of the SCA

SCA members serve for a renewable term of at least three years.[12] Alternate members are also appointed by the regional networks in case of conflict of interest or if the SCA member NHRI is under notice of intention to downgrade.[13] Although nominated by their respective regional networks, members are intended to 'participate as impartial, objective and independent experts'.[14] Further, they should not represent any interests: 'They must make decisions based on an objective assessment of an applicant's compliance with the Paris Principles and the General Observations, and without consideration of national or regional interests'.[15]

One of the four members of the SCA is selected as chairperson for a one-year term, renewable twice. The functions of the chairperson are:

- authorize the agenda for sessions;
- preside over meetings;
- consult with members on issues arising between sessions;
- report to the GANHRI Bureau and General Meetings; and
- authorize all communications from the SCA, whether issued by the Secretariat or the Chair. The Secretariat shall assume responsibility for regular communications.[16]

The chairperson position is expected to rotate between the regional networks.[17]

The SCA meets twice a year in Geneva.[18] Each member has one vote, though the Rules of Procedure dictate that decisions should be by consensus where possible. Decisions may be made by a vote in favour by three members. Where there is a tie, the chairperson has a casting vote.[19] Meetings are confidential, and members are expected to remove themselves where they have 'a real or perceived conflict of

[12] Rules of Procedure for the GANHRI Sub-Committee on Accreditation (adopted on 4 March 2019) 3.1 (hereafter SCA Rules of Procedure).
[13] ibid.
[14] ibid.
[15] ibid.
[16] ibid 3.2.
[17] ibid 3.2.
[18] ibid 4.
[19] ibid 4.5.

interest'.[20] NHRIs under review may also request an SCA member be removed for a real or perceived conflict of interest, and the final decision rests with the GANHRI bureau.[21]

The SCA is a voluntary body in that the work is carried out by its members without remuneration and on top of their regular work within their own NHRIs. In practice, the SCA is supported by the OHCHR, which has played a critical and significant role since the inception of the SCA in 1998, serving as Secretariat of the ICC at that time. Rule 2.4 of the Rules of Procedure of the SCA prior to 2018 provided that the OHCHR 'shall be a permanent observer to the Committee and in its capacity as Secretariat of the GANHRI, support the Sub-Committee's work'; amendments to the Rules in 2018 provided that the OHCHR 'shall be a permanent observer to the SCA and shall serve as its Secretariat'.[22] The OHCHR is usually the first point of contact for NHRIs seeking accreditation, and it is responsible for receiving and reviewing all materials required for accreditation, preparing and presenting a summary of all applications, arranging, attending, and participating in all sessions of the SCA (without voting rights and without advocating for a particular accreditation classification).[23]

The OHCHR's role was set out in the Secretary-General's 2017 Report on NHRIs:

> OHCHR provides substantive support, technical advice and secretariat services to the Subcommittee on Accreditation of the Global Alliance of National Human Rights Institutions. During the period under review, the Subcommittee met twice, in November 2016 and March 2017, and reviewed 28 institutions leading to 23 re-accreditations, four new accreditations and one special review.
>
> The Secretary-General has stated in his biannual reports to the Human Rights Council on the activities of the Global Alliance in accrediting national institutions in compliance with the Paris Principles (A/HRC/33/34, para. 31, and A/HRC/27/40, para. 26) that the presence of OHCHR at all the meetings of the Subcommittee was instrumental to attesting to the compliance of the accreditation process with the established rules of procedure and contributed to its transparency, fairness and rigour.[24]

Given, as noted above, that the SCA is a voluntary body, the support of OHCHR is essential for the efficient and effective operation of the SCA.

Representatives from regional secretariats may also attend as permanent observers. Their role is to 'assist SCA members in understanding any relevant regional

[20] ibid 4.7.
[21] ibid.
[22] ibid 5.1.
[23] ibid 5.1.
[24] UN Secretary-General, 'National institutions for the promotion and protection of human rights: Report of the Secretary-General' (3 August 2017) UN Doc A/72/277, 11.

context; and improve their understanding of the accreditation process to assist them in helping their members to participate in that process'.[25] Similarly, a representative from the GANHRI head office may attend the SCA sessions as a permanent observer.[26]

2.3 The General Observations

Since 2006, the SCA has published General Observations to elaborate on the contents of the Paris Principles. As will be seen throughout the book, in practice, it is the General Observations that are utilized for the SCA's reviews of NHRIs. Since their first iteration, these have been enhanced and developed into substantive explanations of the Paris Principles, and they serve as important guides in practice.

The General Observations are applied to assess NHRIs during the accreditation process. The SCA considers that the General Observations are relevant to all NHRIs, 'being independent of a specific set of facts pertaining to a single domestic context, are universal in their application and provide guidance in both individual cases and more generally'.[27]

In Parts II and III of this book, specific General Observations are discussed in more detail. Here we discuss their general purpose as explained by the SCA. According to the Rules of Procedure of the SCA:

> The SCA may develop General Observations to explain the meaning and practical application of the Paris Principles.
>
> General Observations should:
> - promote a clear understanding of the Paris Principles and their application to decisions on accreditation, re-accreditation, or special review;
> - assist NHRIs in developing their own practices and procedures in compliance with the Paris Principles; and
> - facilitate NHRI advocacy with their domestic governments to address issues relating to Paris Principles compliance.
>
> Where an NHRI falls substantially short of the standards articulated in the General Observations, the SCA may determine that the NHRI is not or is no longer compliant with the Paris Principles.
>
> General Observations must be approved by the GANHRI Bureau.[28]

[25] SCA Rules of Procedure (n 12) 5.2.
[26] ibid 5.3.
[27] SCA, 'General Observations' (February 2018) (n 10) para 8; see also, para 12.
[28] SCA Rules of Procedure (n 12) 2.

The first General Observations were adopted in 2006 and focused on four areas, providing a relatively short elaboration of each: limitation of powers of NHRIs due to national security reasons; ensuring pluralism in and selection and appointment of the governing body; encouraging ratification or accession to international human rights instruments; and government representatives on NHRIs.[29] The SCA has made a concerted effort to develop its General Observations and to clarify the requirements for NHRIs. In May 2011, it created a Working Group tasked with reviewing the General Observations with a view to improving their 'relevance and clarity'.[30] Revised General Observations were approved by the ICC (GANHRI)'s Bureau meeting in Geneva in May 2013. The revision saw the division of the General Observations into two categories: 'Essential requirements of the Paris Principles' and 'Practices that directly promote Paris Principles compliance'.[31] Per the 2018 General Observations, the essential requirements are:

1.1 The establishment of NHRIs
1.2 Human rights mandate
1.3 Encouraging ratification or accession to international human rights instruments
1.4 Interaction with the international human rights system
1.5 Cooperation with other human rights bodies
1.6 Recommendations by NHRIs
1.7 Ensuring pluralism of the NHRI
1.8 Selection and appointment of the decision-making body of NHRIs
1.9 Political representatives on NHRIs
1.10 Adequate funding of NHRIs
1.11 Annual reports of NHRIs

Practices considered as promoting compliance with the Paris Principles, but not essential, are:

[29] SCA, 'ICC Sub-Committee on Accreditation Report' (October 2006) 7–8. The General Observations were numbered 6.2 to 6.6 as they were under heading 6 of the SCA report.

[30] SCA, 'ICC Sub-Committee on Accreditation General Observations' (adopted in May 2013) para 11 (hereafter SCA 'General Observation' (May 2013)) explains that the decision of ICC/GANHRI in 2011 was to develop new General Observations through a multi-stage process, that being '[t]he first stage consists of a discussion amongst SCA members, representatives of GANHRI Regional Networks, and OHCHR on the topic of the General Observation. Secondly, a Working Group is established. It canvasses GANHRI members, through the Regional Networks, for their views on the topic to be addressed. Thirdly, the Working Group, taking into account any comments received from the GANHRI membership, develops a draft and presents it to the SCA for review and comment. Lastly, once approved, the SCA will recommend the revised draft be formally adopted through its sessional reports to the GANHRI Bureau.'

[31] SCA, 'General Observations' (February 2018) (n 10) 4–5.

2.1 Guarantee of tenure for members of the NHRI decision-making body
2.2 Full-time members of an NHRI
2.3 Protection from criminal and civil liability for official actions and decisions undertaken in good faith
2.4 Recruitment and retention of NHRI staff
2.5 NHRIs during the situation of a coup d'état or a state of emergency
2.6 Limitation of power of NHRIs due to national security
2.7 Administrative regulation of NHRIs
2.8 Assessing NHRIs as National Preventive and National Monitoring Mechanisms
2.9 The quasi-judicial competency of NHRIs (complaints-handling)[32]

In practice, the SCA has been careful to avoid describing the categorization of General Observations other than as set out in the observations themselves, that 'the categorization of the General Observations into the … two sections clarifies for all stakeholders which of the General Observations are direct interpretations of the Paris Principles, and which are drawn from the SCA's extensive experience in identifying proven practices to ensure independent and effective NHRIs in line with the Paris Principles'. Thus, those issues viewed as direct interpretations of the Paris Principles went into part one, while 'best practices' went into part two.

As noted above, the General Observations have been enhanced and developed over time and serve as important guides in practice. To further assist NHRIs, the SCA developed Practice Notes beginning in 2017, which provided explanation on issues which, in the experience of the SCA, appeared to be misunderstood or unclear to NHRIs.[33] Four Practice Notes were issued in 2017: (1) Deferrals; (2) Special Reviews; (3) Assessing the Performance of National Human Rights Institutions; and (4) National Human Rights Institutions in Transition. In 2018 the SCA issued Practice Note 5: Sources of information to assess the performance of NHRIs. Practice Notes are explanatory only and are developed and issued by the SCA; they do not require approval by the GANHRI Bureau or membership.

2.4 The Process of Accreditation

There are a number of different forms of accreditation envisaged by the GANHRI Statute:

- first-time accreditation for new or reformed institutions

[32] ibid.
[33] GANHRI, Practice Notes, <https://nhri.ohchr.org/EN/AboutUs/GANHRIAccreditation/General%20Observations%202/Forms/Default%20View.aspx> accessed 18 February 2021.

- regular or periodic re-accreditation
- special review[34]

First-time accreditation and periodic re-accreditation apply essentially the same process, with some minor differences in requirements—for example, newly established institutions must wait one year until they can apply.[35] Special reviews are dealt with separately below in Section 2.5. Applications and supporting documents are sent to and processed by the National Institutions and Regional Mechanisms Section of the OHCHR as the GANHRI Secretariat.[36]

2.4.1 Periodic Re-accreditation

Once NHRIs have obtained A-status,[37] they are subject to periodic re-accreditation to verify their continued compliance with the Paris Principles. According to Article 15 of the GANHRI Statute:

> All NHRIs that hold 'A' status are subject to re-accreditation on a five year cyclical basis. Articles 10, 11 and 12 apply to NHRIs undergoing re-accreditation. In particular, reference to an application for accreditation means both the initial application and the application for re-accreditation.[38]

The process of re-accreditation of A-status NHRIs began in 2006 and was done to ensure that those existing NHRIs merited retention of A-status. The initial accreditations by the SCA prior to that date were done in the absence of detailed criteria and essentially sole reliance on the Paris Principles, which were broad principles only and lacked specificity to allow for a clearer guide to determine A-, B-, or C-status. This came about through experience over the years following the establishment of the SCA, and that experience led to the development of General Observations beginning in 2006. Given the growing stature and importance afforded to A-status institutions, it was believed a review process was required to

[34] GANHRI Statute (adopted on 5 March 2019) (hereafter GANHRI Statute).

[35] SCA Rules of Procedure (n 12).

[36] GANHRI, Guidelines for Accreditation Applications, Compilation of the Rules and Working Methods of the SCA, (February 2014). <https://nhri.ohchr.org/EN/ICC/GeneralMeeting/27/Theme%202%20ICC%20accreditation%20process/Compilation%20of%20the%20Rules%20and%20Working%20Methods%20of%20the%20SCA_Eng_February_2014.pdf> accessed 5 February 2021.

[37] B-status institutions are not subject to periodic re-accreditation. While this was envisaged in the 2008 Decision Paper (n 6) and would have been welcomed by the SCA, it was not included in the ICC Statute. Further, in practice it was not feasible to have B-status institutions be periodically re-accredited given the workload that existed at the time, which required two full weeks in Geneva. However, it remains fully open to these institutions to apply to be 'upgraded' to A-status should they consider they have achieved Paris Principles compliance.

[38] GANHRI Statute (n 34) Art 15.

ensure those institutions that had originally been given A-status still merited that status, or had the institution become less Paris Principles-compliant and thus ought to be downgraded.

As this was a new procedure by the SCA, and given that the process was still not as rigorous, transparent, and detailed as it became later, there was a reluctance to downgrade an NHRI without giving it notice of the deficiencies which it needed to address over the following five years. Indeed, it would be reasonable for an NHRI to question why it was being challenged for something that it was doing when initially granted A-status, which had not, at that time, been flagged as a problem. The SCA was also of the view that it could be very difficult for a state to agree to amend legislation for its NHRI when it had been A-status for many years and the legislation had remained the same for all those years. The SCA thus made the decision that for the first re-accreditation it would identify any issues of non-compliance with the Paris Principles and recommend that the NHRI attend to remedying the issue. On the next round of periodic re-accreditations (which began in 2011), the SCA was firmer in looking at whether the NHRI had addressed the issue previously raised, and what steps, if any, the NHRI had taken to do so. The recommendations thus became stronger, and the SCA informed NHRIs that it would be increasingly strict in requiring issues be dealt with if an NHRI was to retain its a-status.

An example of this progression is the NHRI of Germany, the German Institute for Human Rights (GIHR), which had a problematic enabling law. The SCA first considered it in 2001 and granted it A(R)-status with the reservation that the GIHR did not have an annual report. In 2003 the SCA lifted the reservation because a report on activities had been submitted by the GIHR. No other issues of concern were noted. The first re-accreditation was done in 2008, at which time the GIHR was re-accredited with A-status. The SCA stated in its report, however, that:

> The Sub-Committee expresses its concern that the GIHR is founded by a Motion of the Bundestag (Motion 14/4801). Notwithstanding the fact that the Motion was unanimously adopted and that the GIHR is functioning independently and effectively under this arrangement, the Sub-Committee reiterates the need for an NHRI to be established in a constitutional or legal text and therefore recommends the adoption of a stronger legal basis for the Institute.[39]

The GIHR came before the SCA for its next accreditation in 2013, at which time consideration was deferred by the SCA, stating:

> The SCA commends the work undertaken by the GIHR to address recommendations made by the SCA in 2008. In particular, it notes that the GIHR successfully

39 SCA, 'Accreditation Report—Germany (GIHR)' (November 2008) 7.

advocated for the introduction of legislation, but that parliament completed its term before the legislation had been passed.

The SCA notes that the GIHR is established by a Motion of the Parliament (Motion 14/4801). Notwithstanding the fact that the Motion was adopted unanimously and that the GIHR is functioning effectively under this arrangement, the SCA reiterates the need for an NHRI to be established by constitutional or legislative text.

It encourages the GIHR to continue to advocate for the adoption of legislation to formalise its existing mandate, and for such legislation to include the responsibilities referenced in the Paris Principles.[40]

The SCA next considered the GIHR at its first session of 2015, and deferred the re-accreditation to its second session, noting that draft legislation had been approved by the Federal Cabinet and would be submitted to parliament. At its second session, the SCA recommended the GIHR be re-accredited with A-status, stating:

> The SCA welcomes the adoption of a new law that establishes the GIHR in primary legislation. It commends the GIHR for its sustained efforts to advocate for the passage of this legislation.[41]

All accredited NHRIs are expected to go through periodic re-accreditation. Failure to apply for re-accreditation may result in suspension of accreditation classification. The following provisions of the GANHRI statute apply:

> Art. 19 An accreditation classification held by a NHRI may be suspended if the NHRI fails to submit its application for re-accreditation or fails to do so within the prescribed time without justification.
>
> Art. 20 An accreditation classification may lapse if a NHRI fails to submit an application for re-accreditation within one (1) year of being suspended for failure to reapply.
>
> ...
>
> Art. 22 NHRIs whose accreditation status has lapsed or been revoked may regain accreditation only by re-applying for accreditation as provided for in Article 10 of this Statute.
>
> Art. 23 In the event that accreditation lapses or is revoked or suspended, all rights and privileges conferred on that NHRI through accreditation immediately cease. In the event that a NHRI is under review, it shall retain the accreditation status it has been granted until such time as the body determining membership

[40] SCA, 'Accreditation Report—Germany (GIHR)' (November 2013) 21.
[41] SCA, 'Accreditation Report—Germany (GIHR)' (November 2015) 14.

comes to a decision as to its compliance with the Paris Principles or its membership lapses.[42]

2.4.2 Submission of Information for Accreditation

Under the GANHRI Statute, the accreditation process requires a copy of the NHRI's establishing instrument, an outline of its organizational structure including staff and annual budget, its most recent annual report, and 'a detailed statement showing how it complies with the Paris Principles as well as any respects in which it does not so comply and any proposals to ensure compliance'.[43]

The Rules of Procedure of the SCA provide that any NHRI applying for either its first accreditation or re-accreditation must complete a 'statement of compliance with the Paris Principles' plus additional supporting material.[44] The statement of compliance is the core component of the application and should be supported by accompanying materials.[45] In addition to the statement, the NHRI must submit the following:

- a copy of the legislation or other instrument by which it is established and empowered in its official or published format;
- an outline of its organizational structure, including staff complement;
- its annual budget; and
- a copy of its most recent annual report or equivalent document in its official or published format.[46]

Applicants for re-accreditation should also provide information on how they have addressed any previous recommendations made by the SCA.[47] Where an NHRI fails to submit the relevant documentation, the application will be rejected.[48] In addition to information from the NHRI, information may also be received from third parties, such as non-governmental organizations (NGOs), relevant to the accreditation status of the NHRI.[49] The information is provided to the NHRI for their comment and response.[50]

Special consideration is given to NHRIs working in volatile situations, per the Rules of Procedure:

[42] GANHRI Statute (n 34) Arts 19, 20, 22, 23.
[43] ibid Art 10.
[44] SCA Rules of Procedure (n 12) 6.
[45] ibid 6.1.
[46] ibid 6.1.
[47] ibid 6.1.
[48] ibid 6.2.
[49] ibid 6.7.
[50] ibid 6.2.

> 8.4. Applications from NHRIs in volatile contexts
> The context in which an NHRI operates may be so volatile that the NHRI cannot be reasonably expected to be in full conformity with all the provisions of the Paris Principles. When formulating its recommendation on the accreditation status in such cases, the Sub-Committee will give due consideration to factors such as:
> - political instability;
> - conflict or unrest;
> - lack of state infrastructure, including excessive dependency on donor funding; and
> - the NHRI's execution of its mandate in practice.[51]

The template for the statement of compliance is provided to all NHRIs and is generally available online at the GANHRI website.[52] The template is twelve-pages long and thus cannot be replicated here at length. However, it is useful to set out the overall areas covered. The template is divided into three main sections. The first section, called 'Character of the NHRI', provides details of the information NHRIs must provide in relation to their establishment, independence, composition, selection and appointment, tenure, infrastructure, staffing, premises, and their accessibility. They are further required to discuss the regularity of their meetings and the establishment, mandate, composition, and working methods of any working groups established by the NHRI. Under the second section, 'General Mandate', NHRIs are asked to describe their general competence and responsibilities, including their mandate to promote and protect human rights, the various other functions they perform, as well as their relationship with relevant human rights stakeholders and other bodies. The final section is optional and covers the specific mandate of NHRIs as National Preventative Mechanisms (NPMs) under the Optional Protocol to the Convention Against Torture (OPCAT).[53]

2.4.3 NHRIs in Transition: Mergers and Structural Changes

Periodically, NHRIs undergo structural changes or mergers with other national institutions imposed by the state. The SCA has provided guidance as to whether the institution should be regarded as a new institution, or a continuing one for the purposes of accreditation, as set out in Practice Note 4 (2017):

[51] ibid 8.4.

[52] GANHRI, 'Compilation of the SCA Rules, Working Methods and Template for the Statement of Compliance' <https://nhri.ohchr.org/EN/AboutUs/GANHRIAccreditation/Documents/Forms/DispForm.aspx?ID=172> accessed 5 February 2021.

[53] Optional Protocol to the Convention against Torture and other Cruel, Inhuman or Degrading Treatment or Punishment (adopted on 18 December 2002, entered into force on 22 June 2006) 2375 UNTS 237 (hereafter OPCAT). The SCA's reviews of these NHRIs are examined in Chapter 8.

NHRIs in transition are advised to seek assistance and advice from OHCHR and their Regional Networks throughout the process.

The SCA will consider as soon as practicable whether the institution will be considered new or continuing for the purposes of accreditation. It will advise the NHRI accordingly.

In making this determination, the SCA will first and foremost consider the wording of the new enabling legislation, including whether it:

- changes the name of the existing institution;
- dissolves the previously-existing institution;
- provides that the newly-created institution is a continuation of the previously-existing institution; and
- contains appropriate continuation provisions.

The SCA will further consider whether the newly-created institution:

- maintains or expands its previous mandate; and
- maintains equivalent or strengthened protections in relation to its structure and functioning.[54]

The decision that a merged or substantially changed institution is to be considered as a new institution for the purposes of accreditation has significant implications for the NHRI, as outlined by the SCA in the Practice Note:

> Where the SCA determines that a newly-created institution will be considered a new institution for the purposes of accreditation, it immediately ceases to hold status and cannot rely on the status of its predecessor institution.
>
> General Observation 1.11 on 'Annual reports of NHRIs' requires that new institutions must be in operation for one (1) year prior to submitting their application for accreditation. It further requires that they submit a published annual report to the SCA. In relevant and exceptional circumstances, the SCA may consider accepting an alternate unpublished report from a new institution for the purposes of accreditation.[55]

2.5 Special Reviews and Status Suspensions

Outside the regular accreditation process just outlined, the SCA can initiate a special review in accordance with Article 16.2 of the GANHRI Statute, 'where it is of

[54] SCA, 'Practice Note 4: NHRIs in Transition' (adopted on 6 March 2017).
[55] ibid.

the view that the circumstances of the NHRI have changed in such a way as to affect its ongoing compliance with the Paris Principles'.[56] The SCA has elaborated on what this looks like in practice:

> In practice, this may include, but is not limited to, situations where:
>
> - the enabling law of the NHRI has been amended significantly;
> - there has been a significant political change that impacts adversely on the ability of the NHRI to fulfil its mandate;
> - the conduct of the NHRI—such as a failure to respond adequately or in a timely manner to serious rights violations—calls into question the institution's independence; or
> - the SCA has received credible information from a third party that the circumstances of the NHRI have changed.[57]

The SCA also further explains what type of credible third party information it will consider:

> Credible third party information may emanate from a variety of sources including:
>
> - observations and recommendations of the international human rights system, including from the UPR, the Treaty Bodies, and from Special Procedures mandate holders;
> - observations and recommendations of a regional human rights mechanism;
> - media reports; and
> - submissions or public reports made by civil society or other organizations.

It also explains how this third-party information is handled:

> The weight given to third-party information is determined on a case-by-case basis by the members of the SCA, taking into account that an effective NHRI can expect to face criticism from a variety of actors. When considering whether to initiate a Special Review, the NHRI will be provided with reasons, including any information that has been received from third-party sources, and will be provided with an opportunity to respond.[58]

The SCA makes it clear that a decision of the SCA to initiate a special review is not subject to challenge.[59] The review of the accreditation classification of an NHRI must be finalized within eighteen months.[60]

[56] SCA Rules of Procedure (n 12) 11.
[57] SCA, 'Practice Note 2: Special Reviews' (adopted on 6 March 2017).
[58] ibid.
[59] GANHRI Statute (n 34) Art 16.3; SCA Rules of Procedure (n 12) 6.2.
[60] ibid Art 16.4.

There is also provision in the GANHRI Statute for the urgent suspension of accreditation status, prompting a special review. According to Article 18.2 of the Statute:

> Art 18.2 Authority to immediately suspend accreditation in exceptional circumstances
> Where, in the opinion of the GANHRI Chairperson, an exceptional circumstance exists necessitating the urgent suspension of the accreditation status of an 'A' status NHRI, the GANHRI Bureau may decide to immediately suspend the accreditation classification of that NHRI and request the SCA to initiate a special review, pursuant to Article 16.2.

Article 18.4 defines 'exceptional circumstances' as 'a sudden and drastic change in internal political order of a State'. The following examples are given:

- breakdown in the constitutional or democratic order; or
- a declared state of emergency; or
- gross violations of human rights;

<u>and</u> this is accompanied by any of the following:

- there is a change in the NHRI enabling legislation or other applicable law that is contrary to the Paris Principles; or
- there is a change in the composition of the NHRI that is not undertaken in accordance with the established selection and/or appointment process; or
- the NHRI acts in a way that seriously compromises its compliance with Paris Principles.[61]

The Statute also sets out the process involved:

Art 18.3 Process for immediate suspension of accreditation in exceptional circumstances

The decision of the GANHRI Bureau in such exceptional circumstance is final and is subject to the following process:

(i) The GANHRI Chairperson, through the GANHRI Secretariat, will immediately notify the GANHRI Bureau and the NHRI in question of the alleged existence of an exceptional circumstance pursuant to Article 18.2 and the recommendation to suspend the accreditation classification of that NHRI;

[61] ibid Art 18.4 (emphasis in original).

(ii) The NHRI can challenge the recommendation by submitting a letter addressed to the GANHRI Chairperson and copied to the GANHRI Secretariat, within twenty-eight (28) days of the date of communication of the recommendation;

(iii) Any member of the GANHRI Bureau that supports the challenge of the NHRI shall, within twenty (20) days, notify the GANHRI Chairperson and the GANHRI Secretariat. If the challenge does not receive the support of at least one (1) GANHRI Bureau member within twenty (20) days, the recommendation to suspend will be deemed accepted by the GANHRI Bureau;

(iv) If at least one (1) member of the GANHRI Bureau supports the challenge of the NHRI within these twenty (20) days, the GANHRI Secretariat will notify all GANHRI Bureau members as soon as practicable of this support and will provide any additional relevant material;

(v) Once provided with this notification and any additional relevant material, any other member of the GANHRI Bureau that supports the challenge of the NHRI shall, within twenty (20) days, notify the GANHRI Chairperson and the GANHRI Secretariat of this support.

(vi) If at least two (2) GANHRI Bureau members in total coming from not less than two (2) regions support the challenge pursuant to Article 18.3 (iv) and (v) of the NHRI, the recommendation shall be referred to the following GANHRI Bureau meeting for decision. Otherwise, the recommendation to suspend the accreditation classification is deemed approved by the GANHRI Bureau.

Where an accreditation status is suspended, Article 21 of the GANHRI Statute sets out the following provision:

> NHRIs whose accreditation has been suspended remain suspended until the body determining their compliance with the Paris Principles under this Statute comes to a determination of their accreditation status or until their accreditation lapses.[62]

2.6 How the SCA Makes its Decisions

The SCA conducts its sessions in accordance with its published working methods.[63] The SCA primarily uses a summary of accreditation information provided by the OHCHR, but may obtain additional information as follows:

[62] GANHRI Statute (n 34) Art 21.

[63] SCA, Working Methods, Compilation of the SCA Rules and Working Methods of the SCA (2019) <https://nhri.ohchr.org/EN/AboutUs/GANHRIAccreditation/Documents/Forms/DispForm.aspx?ID=172> accessed 6 February 2021 (hereafter SCA, Working Methods).

1.4 If further clarification is requested during its deliberations, the SCA will make conference calls with relevant NHRIs. Prior to the meeting all concerned NHRIs will be informed about this new way of seeking clarifications and are requested to provide a name and phone number in each NHRI in case the Sub-Committee needs to contact the Institution.

1.5 OHCHR Desk Officers and, as appropriate, field offices are made available to the Sub-Committee members to introduce individual NHRIs considered by the Sub-Committee and provide further information, as needed.[64]

In terms of the substance of the review itself, this is set according to the SCA Rules of Procedure, as follows:

The SCA assesses an applicant's compliance with the Paris Principles in both law and practice. In doing so, it considers whether:

- the applicant's legal base is compliant with the Paris Principles; and
- an applicant's actions demonstrate that it is effectively fulfilling its mandate to promote and protect human rights.

To undertake this assessment, the SCA shall review:

- the NHRI's enabling legislation and any other relevant laws, rules or regulations;
- any relevant policies and procedures;
- the NHRI's organizational structure, including staff complement and annual budget;
- a current annual report and other reports;
- the concluding recommendations / observations of international human rights mechanisms, including the Universal Periodic Review, UN Treaty Bodies and Special Procedures;
- credible third party reports, including from civil society; and
- other relevant documentation, as required.[65]

In addition, where there is a re-accreditation, section 8.3 of the Rules of Procedure provides for consideration of issues raised in previous reviews:

- In considering an application for re-accreditation, the SCA will also assess what action an NHRI has taken to address concerns raised at the NHRI's previous accreditation review.
- If there is insufficient evidence to show that an NHRI has taken reasonable steps to address past concerns, or has failed to offer a reasonable explanation why previous concerns have not been addressed, the SCA may, depending on

64 ibid 1.4.
65 SCA Rules of Procedure (n 12) 8.1.

> the seriousness of the issues previously raised, interpret such lack of progress as an indication of non-compliance with the Paris Principles.[66]

Following its review, the SCA makes its recommendations. These recommendations are contained in reports published after each session. It is these reports that are the primary material for Parts II and III of this book. In its report, the SCA makes its accreditation recommendation to the GANHRI Bureau.

Pursuant to Article 18.1, where there is a recommendation to remove A-status, this is not implemented for a year:

> Any decision that would serve to remove accredited 'A' status from an applicant can only be taken after the applicant is informed of this intention and is given the opportunity to provide in writing, within one (1) year of receipt of such notice, the written evidence deemed necessary to establish its continued conformity to the Paris Principles.

The process followed by the SCA leading up to and at each session is set out in GANHRI's 'A Practical Guide to the Work of the Sub-Committee on Accreditation'.[67] The guide was prepared on behalf of GANHRI by the Canadian Human Rights Commission in December 2017 and updated in November 2018. It is useful to set it out in some length here, as it provides details on how the process works in practice:

> BEFORE THE SESSION
> All information provided by an NHRI under review, including its Statement of Compliance and supporting documentation, is made available to SCA members soon after they are received by the Secretariat via a private web portal to which only members and permanent observers have access.
>
> All members attending the session are to provide to the Secretariat,[[68]] in writing, the names and titles of those participating on its behalf at least thirty (30) days before the session. This information is posted by the Secretariat on the website of the SCA at least twenty-eight (28) days before the beginning of the session. Where an NHRI under review feels that a member of the SCA attending the session has a real or perceived conflict of interest, they are to inform the Secretariat of this in

[66] ibid 8.3.

[67] GANHRI, 'A Practical Guide to the Work of the Sub-Committee on Accreditation' (2018) <https://nhri.ohchr.org/EN/AboutUs/GANHRIAccreditation/Documents/GANHRI%20Manual_online(1).pdf> accessed 6 February 2021 (hereafter GANHRI Guide).

[68] The term 'Secretariat' in the GANHRI Guide refers to the OHCHR, per the SCA Rules of Procedure (2018) which states that the OHCHR is 'permanent observer to the SCA and shall serve as its Secretariat'.

writing at least twenty-one (21) days before the SCA session. The Secretariat will then forward the correspondence to the GANHRI Chairperson. The final decision on whether a real or perceived conflict of interest exists is to be decided by the GANHRI Bureau at least seven (7) days before the SCA session.

The SCA may receive information from multiple sources related to an application for accreditation or re-accreditation. This includes information submitted by the NHRI, and can also include publicly-information and information provided by third-party sources such as civil society organizations. This information assists the SCA in assessing the performance of NHRIs and their compliance with the Paris Principles.

There may be publicly-available information about an NHRI that is relevant to the review of their application. This can include:

- Observations and recommendations of the international human rights system, including the Universal Periodic Review, Treaty Bodies and Special Procedures mandate holders;
- Observations and recommendations of regional human rights mechanisms; and
- Press releases and other documents issued by the NHRI itself.

Because this information is publicly available, an NHRI under review is expected to be aware of its existence. As such, it will not generally be forwarded to the NHRI for a response prior to the relevant SCA session. However, such information may be the subject of questions during the telephone interview with the NHRI at the session.

Other sources of information may also be publicly available, but may not reasonably be known to an NHRI under review. This can include:

- Media reports; and
- Public reports from civil society or other published sources.

Where information contained in these documents gives rise to concerns, the SCA will ensure that the information is provided to the NHRI under review as soon as practicable, and in any event prior to the telephone interview conducted by the SCA at the relevant session. The NHRI under review is not required to formally respond to this information in writing, as it will be given a chance to do so during the interview.

The Secretariat, from time to time, receives other submissions in relation to the review of a particular NHRI. This can include:

- Third-party submissions addressed to the SCA or GANHRI bodies by civil society organizations or individuals; and
- Official, non-public notes from Special Procedures mandate holders.

All third-party submissions are subject to the same fixed dates for submission to the Secretariat:

- For information related to an NHRI being reviewed at the SCA's first session of a calendar year, third-party information must be received by the Secretariat on December 1st of the preceding calendar year.
- For information related to an NHRI being reviewed at the SCA's second session of a calendar year, third-party information must be received by the Secretariat no later than August 1st.

Submissions from Special Procedures mandate holders are not subject to these fixed dates and may be received any time prior to the relevant SCA session. This is because these individuals are part of the international human rights system and, as such, their contributions are not considered third-party submissions.

Such information is generally not in the public domain and, in order to ensure procedural fairness, must be sent to the NHRI concerned prior to the SCA session in order to provide an opportunity to respond to the issues identified. The NHRI may wish to respond in writing to the issues identified, however this is not mandatory as the NHRI will be provided with an opportunity to respond during the interview.

The Secretariat prepares a summary of all information that is relevant to the accreditation of the NHRI under review. This summary also includes information contained in the reports, recommendations or observations of international human rights mechanisms. The summary is provided to the NHRI under review prior to it being distributed to members. The applicant NHRI is provided with one (1) week to review the summary and correct any factual errors by providing their comments to the Secretariat in writing. The Secretariat will then post the summary, along with the NHRI's unedited response, on the SCA members' web portal.

The Secretariat also prepares a programme of work for each session based on the arrangements it has made with each NHRI under review as to the date and time when they will be considered. This programme is distributed to SCA members and observers in advance of the session.

AT THE SESSION

The process undertaken by the SCA is the same for each NHRI under review:

1. The staff member of the Secretariat who prepared the summary provides an overview of the NHRI's application, including any potential issues of concern the Secretariat has identified. Members and observers are provided an opportunity to ask questions.
2. Additional information may be provided, as needed. This may include an overview of the domestic context in which the NHRI is operating and information about any activities that OHCHR has undertaken with the NHRI. SCA members and observers are provided with an opportunity to ask questions.
3. The SCA Chair will then ask the Regional Network representative and the representative of the GANHRI Head Office to provide information about their knowledge of and work with the NHRI under review, as well as any relevant national, regional or international context.
4. Following these verbal reports, the members will develop a list of questions to pose to the NHRI during an interview. These questions most often pertain to issues raised in the NHRI's application that require further clarification or those that have not been addressed fully by the NHRI in its Statement of Compliance. It is the practice of the SCA to also ask the NHRI under review whether there are any recommendations that the SCA could make that would assist the NHRI in strengthening their institution. In all cases where the SCA wishes to rely on information that is adverse to the NHRI under review, and to which the NHRI has not yet been provided an opportunity to respond, the SCA will raise this information in the interview and provide the NHRI with an opportunity to respond. This includes in respect of publicly-available information and other additional information that has been provided during the session.
5. Interviews are conducted by telephone only. Some NHRIs have, in the past, requested that they be able to do the interview via videoconference or in person. However, in order to ensure that the process is fair for all NHRIs and does not favour those who have greater resources, or are geographically closer to Geneva, the SCA permits interviews only by telephone. The working language of the SCA is English. However, NHRIs can be interviewed in another of the GANHRI languages—French, Spanish or Arabic—should they choose, and their answers will be translated to English following the interview, for the benefit of those SCA members who do not speak the chosen language. NHRIs under review may wish to consider using a local interpreter fluent in English and the local/national language so that they can both speak in the language in which they are most comfortable during the interview and best ensure that members of the SCA are able to fully understand their responses to questions.

The interview conducted by the SCA provides the NHRI under review with an opportunity to respond to any questions or concerns related to the review of its application, including any that have been arisen as a result of publicly-available information or other submissions received in relation to the NHRI.[69]

Based on the totality of information available to them, including the responses provided by the NHRI during the interview, the members will deliberate until a decision is reached.

Though SCA members are provided with the summary from the Secretariat, this is not the only information they consider when reviewing an NHRI. They are also provided with, and consider, all information provided by the NHRI under review. This includes, for example:

- the Statement of Compliance prepared by the NHRI;
- the provisions of the NHRI's enabling law;
- any other relevant laws, rules or regulations;
- the practices and procedures of the NHRI;
- the NHRI's organizational structure, including staff complement and budget;
- annual and other reports of the NHRI; and
- statements and media releases issued by the NHRI.

As noted above, the SCA may also consider information about the NHRI that is provided by other sources. This information enables the SCA to better assess the performance of the applicant NHRI and strengthens the credibility of the accreditation process itself by ensuring that all relevant information is taken into consideration.

The weight that is given to third-party information is determined on a case-by-case basis by the members of the SCA. In practice, where the information received is congruent with other available information, detailed, and makes reference to relevant facts, the SCA is more likely to attach importance to it.89 The SCA acknowledges that even an effective NHRI may be criticized by a variety of stakeholders for the way it undertakes its mandate, and that the SCA must, therefore, ensure that it independently assesses whether those criticisms are, or are not, well-founded. Where the NHRI has responded to allegations made by a third party, the SCA will carefully consider this response.

Each member of the SCA has one (1) vote. The ultimate results of deliberations are the sole responsibility of SCA members. Permanent observers do not have voting rights and, therefore, do not participate in the deliberations.

[69] NHRIs may also address concerns to the SCA as part of the telephone interview done with every NHRI under review. At the end of the call the SCA asks if there are any recommendations it might make that they would find helpful in their efforts to improve their structure, resources, mandate, or other aspects.

In all instances, the SCA must make every effort to reach its decisions by consensus. Where this is not possible, decisions may be made by a vote of three (3) members. In the rare circumstance where a vote is tied and further deliberation is unlikely to result in a decision, the SCA Chairperson has a casting or deciding vote.

During deliberations, SCA members will decide not only what accreditation classification they will recommend, but also what recommendations should be made to the NHRI under review. The Secretariat prepares a draft report following each meeting based on the decisions made by members and circulates it for the review of the members. On the final day of the SCA session, all members together review the draft SCA report and make final decisions in respect of the issues of concern that are to be highlighted and the recommendations to be made. All members and observers participate in the drafting of the report.[70]

The GANHRI Guide explains its status recommendations in detail, as follows:

The SCA may recommend that an NHRI be accredited or re-accredited with A-status, which is described as denoting 'full compliance' with the Paris Principles. In reality, however, it has been the experience of the SCA that no NHRI operates in perfect compliance with the Paris Principles, and, therefore, recommendations for improvement are always made by the SCA. What A-status does signal, therefore, is that the issues of concern noted by the SCA are not of sufficient severity to impact the NHRI's ability to act in an effective and independent manner. The SCA may also recommend that an NHRI be accredited or re-accredited with B-status, which denotes 'partial compliance' with the Paris Principles. The SCA understands that most NHRIs applying for accreditation do so in the hopes of being awarded A-status and having the rights and privileges associated with that status. However, it should be emphasized that a determination by the SCA to recommend B-status is not necessarily an indicator that an NHRI is not an effective body.

Most often, a decision to recommend B-status will be based on a determination that there are multiple issues of concern relating to structure, effectiveness, independence, or a combination of those factors. The SCA recognizes that, in these cases, the NHRI may not fully understand which issues were of significant concern and need to be addressed in order to improve their compliance with the Paris Principles to the point that they would be eligible for accreditation as A-status. Accordingly, the SCA has developed a practice of outlining the recommendations made in its report into those that it 'notes with concern' which the NHRI should address as a priority and those that it merely 'notes' which the NHRI should address in due course.

70 GANHRI Guide (n 67) 32–34.

In some cases, there may be a single issue of concern that is structural in nature and, in the view of the SCA, is sufficiently serious that the NHRI cannot be considered to be operating in 'full compliance' with the Paris Principles. Such situations are varied and dependent on the particular facts related to a given application. Past examples include the following:

— In one instance, the founding legislation of an NHRI required that all members of the decision-making body be adherents to a particular religion. The SCA viewed that this clause was not in compliance with the Paris Principles requirement for pluralism.[71]
— In another case, an NHRI was operating with a dual role as a department at a university and as an NHRI, but was not established either by legislation or by the constitution with a broad mandate to both promote and protect human rights.[72]

Finally, the SCA may recommend that an A-status NHRI be downgraded to B-status. Where this recommendation is made, the NHRI is given one (1) year to address the issue or issues of concern noted and demonstrate continued compliance with the Paris Principles. The NHRI maintains its status during this time.

- In some cases, the SCA may recommend a downgrade where an NHRI applying for re-accreditation has not taken steps to address the issues of concern previously noted by the SCA, and these are, in the view of the SCA, sufficiently serious to impact the NHRI's ability to act in an effective and independent manner. The accreditation process has become more rigorous over time. As such, even an NHRI that has been accredited with A-status for a number of years is expected to take steps to improve its compliance with the Paris Principles, in line with the recommendations previously made by the SCA. An NHRI may be downgraded if it has not done so. Generally, it is the practice of the SCA to defer the application for re-accreditation prior to recommending a downgrade in order to allow the NHRI to take the necessary steps to address the issues of concern or to provide sufficient justification as to why it is not able to do so.
- In other cases, the concerns of the SCA may be related to the conduct of an NHRI, either as a result of a single incident of sufficient severity or a pattern of conduct. Examples of such situations are varied and depend on the facts of a particular case, but they often relate to the conduct of an NHRI in situations of political unrest or in the face of credible allegations of grave human rights violations having been committed by government authorities:

[71] See SCA, 'Accreditation Report—Maldives (Human Rights Commission of The Maldives (HRCM))' (March/April 2010) 6.
[72] See SCA, 'Accreditation Report—Norway (Norwegian Centre for Human Rights (NCHR))' (October 2011) 16.

- o In one instance, an NHRI failed to respond to credible allegations of human rights violations having taken place following a coup d'état.[73]
- o In two similar such instances, the SCA was of the view that the NHRIs had failed to demonstrate—through their actions and/or inactions—a willingness to address all human rights issues in response to credible allegations that gross violations of human rights had been committed.[74]75

Additionally, a new paragraph has been added to the preamble of the reports, beginning in May 2018:

> 1.9 In the interests of clarity and as a good practice, where the SCA has recommended that an NHRI be accredited with other than A status, it has divided its recommendations between those that it 'notes with concern' and those that it 'notes'. The issues that have been noted 'with concern' constitute the primary reasons for which the NHRI has not been accredited with A status.[76]

The process after a decision is outlined by the SCA in its Guidelines on Accreditation:

> a) After the Sub-Committee meeting
> The process for approving the Sub-Committee's recommendations is set out in Art 12.1 of the GANHRI Statute. After the evaluation of an NHRI application, OHCHR sends the recommendation of the Sub-Committee first to relevant applicant NHRIs. These NHRIs have 28 days to react to the recommendation, if they so wish. Immediately after that 28-day period, OHCHR sends the Report and Recommendations of the Sub-Committee (and any response from the applicant NHRI) to the 16 members of the GANHRI Bureau. The Bureau members have twenty (20) days to approve or object to the recommendations.
>
> Any member of the GANHRI Bureau who disagrees with the recommendation must notify the Chair of the Sub-Committee and the GANHRI Secretariat within these 20 days. The GANHRI Secretariat then notifies all other Bureau members and provides all information to clarify that objection. If at least four members of the GANHRI Bureau (coming from not less than two regional groups) notify the GANHRI Secretariat that they hold a similar

[73] Honduras' NHRI was first given one-year notice of intention to downgrade SCA, 'Accreditation Report—Honduras (Comisionado Nacional de los Derechos Humanos de Honduras (CONADEH))' (October 2010) 9, confirmed by SCA, 'Accreditation Report—Honduras (CONADEH))' (October 2011) 20.

[74] See SCA, 'Accreditation Report—Venezuela (Defensoria del Pueblo (DPV))' (March 2015) 25–26; and SCA, 'Accreditation Report—Thailand (National Human Rights Commission of Thailand (NHRCT))' (November 2015) 40–41.

[75] GANHRI Guide (n 67) 36–37 (bullet points in original).

[76] SCA, 'Accreditation Report' (May 2018) 5–6.

objection within twenty (20) days of receipt of this information, the recommendation shall be referred to the next GANHRI Bureau meeting for decision. If the required number of members does not raise any objection to the recommendation within the 20 day period, it will be deemed to be approved by the GANHRI Bureau.

b) Approval of Recommendations
The decision of the GANHRI Bureau on accreditation, based on the Sub-Committee's review, is final. Unapproved decisions are referred for consideration at the next GANHRI meeting.[77]

2.7 Deferrals

Article 14 of the GANHRI Statute deals with situations where an application for accreditation is deferred:

> Art. 14.1 The SCA may decide to defer an application rather than make a decision on status. The deferral decision(s) shall be limited to a period of two (2) years, except in exceptional circumstances that may justify a longer period. In any event, the total duration of the deferral shall not exceed the periodic cycle set out in Article 15.

> Art. 14.2 A decision of the SCA to defer an application for accreditation or re-accreditation is not a recommendation to the GANHRI Bureau and cannot be challenged under the provisions of Article 12.[78]

Once the SCA began the five-yearly re-accreditation process in 2006, resulting in all A-status NHRIs needing to be scheduled for consideration by the SCA, and with growing interest in accreditation resulting in increased first-time applications for accreditation, the SCA found it difficult to be able to deal with all applicants in a one-week annual session. This difficulty was compounded by deferring applications to subsequent sessions, creating a backlog of re-accreditations, first-time applications, and deferred applications. The SCA recognized that it ought not to defer an application 'easily' or as a matter of course, but also recognized that there were situations where deferral was necessary or desirable for various reasons, and at times it found there were issues that in its view should be dealt with prior to the next five-year re-accreditation review of the NHRI. Given the desire to avoid

[77] SCA, Guidelines for Accreditation Applications, Compilation of the Rules and Working Methods of the SCA (2019) <https://nhri.ohchr.org/EN/AboutUs/GANHRIAccreditation/Documents/Forms/DispForm.aspx?ID=172> accessed 8 February 2021 (emphasis in original).
[78] GANHRI Statute (n 34).

deferrals, the SCA developed a practice of re-accrediting the NHRI with A-status, and setting out those issues of concern, with a decision to reconsider those issues in less than five years, while the balance of issues was to be dealt with at the next five-year re-accreditation.[79]

An example of this is the NHRI of Nepal, the National Human Rights Commission (NHRC). At the time of its re-accreditation in 2007, the SCA recommended A-status:

> The Sub-Committee notes the following:
>
> 1) It refers to the General Observation on 'Adequate funding', in particular sub-paragraphs b) and c) and that financial systems should be such that the NHRI has complete financial autonomy.
> 2) It refers to the General Observation on 'Selection and appointment of the governing body', in particular sub-paragraphs a), b) and d).
> 3) It encourages the NHRI to strengthen its interaction with civil society organisations.
> 4) It refers to the General Observation on 'Interaction with the International Human Rights System', in particular with regard to engagement with the United Nations Human Rights Treaty Bodies, the Human Rights Council and the ICC.
> 5) It has reviewed the draft bill and compared its provisions with the Interim Constitution, and will continue to monitor the developments and progress of the bill as to its consistency with the Interim Constitution and the Paris Principles.
>
> The Sub-Committee will again consider issue number 1 at its October 2008 session.[80]

When the SCA considered NHRC again in 2008, it decided as follows:

> Recommendation: The Sub-Committee confirms the status A accreditation of the NHRC.

[79] As regards scheduling, during David's time on the SCA, the SCA developed a practice that on the final day of each session, the calendar for future session(s) was reviewed, and there was discussion and debate on how to balance workload limitations on the number of applications that could be processed per session, with new applications, re-applications, special reviews, and deferrals, while ensuring regional balance. It was considered important to ensure that new applicants did not have to wait too long to have their application heard, but that deferrals and special reviews needed to be dealt with when they were scheduled. The SCA did not want to put off re-accreditations much beyond the five-year review timeline, while at the same time wanting to make sure each of the four GANHRI regions was treated equally. At times the decision on how long to defer was determined by the calendar—that is, at times the SCA would defer to the next session, other times for a year, or year and a half away.

[80] SCA, 'Accreditation Report—Nepal (NHRC)' (October 2007) 9–10.

> The Sub-Committee acknowledges NHRC's response to the concerns it raised in October 2007, particularly with regard to the issue of financial autonomy. Having completed its review, it also reiterates the comments it made in its October 2007 report regarding adequate funding and selection and appointment of the governing body.
>
> In the course of the review, the Sub-Committee noted that the NHRC legislation has not yet been adopted by the Parliament and therefore it encourages the NHRC to promote the development of legislation in full compliance with the Paris Principles.
>
> The Sub-Committee encourages the NHRC to increase its cooperation with statutory institutions for the promotion and protection of human rights as well as civil society organizations. It refers to General Observation 1.5 'Cooperation with other human rights institutions'.
>
> The Sub-Committee will again consider these issues at its October/November 2009 session.[81]

At its 2009 session the SCA deferred consideration of the NHRC to 2010, and at that time the SCA made the following recommendation:

> The SCA informs the NHRC of its intention to recommend the ICC Bureau that the NHRC be accredited with B status, and gives the Institution the opportunity to provide, in writing, within one year of such notice, the documentary evidence deemed necessary to establish its continued conformity with the Paris Principles. The NHRC retains its A status during this period.
>
> The SCA notes that, pursuant to article 16.3 of the ICC Statute, which provides that 'any review of the accreditation classification of a NHRI must be finalized within 18 months', the SCA is required to make a decision on the accreditation classification of the NHRC at this session, as the review of the NHRC began in March 2008. The recommendations of the SCA made at that time have not been met.[82]

At its 2011 session the SCA recommended the NHRC maintain its A-status, noting 'with satisfaction the actions undertaken by the NHRCN to address the concerns and recommendations made by the SCA in its first session in 2010'.[83]

[81] SCA, 'Accreditation Report—Nepal (NHRC)' (November 2008) 11.
[82] SCA, 'Accreditation Report—Nepal (NHRC)' (March/April 2010) 13.
[83] SCA, 'Accreditation Report—Nepal (NHRCN)' (May 2011) 23–24. The acronym used in the SCA report changed from the previous NHRC to NHRCN in this report.

In 2012, questions were raised by NHRIs as to whether the SCA could or should be 're-considering' NHRIs in less than the five-year period of re-accreditation set out in the GANHRI statute. The SCA reviewed the practice it began in 2007 and decided that it would cease accrediting A-status with a review of certain issues in less than five years and decided that it would instead rely solely on deferrals to deal with issues of concern that the SCA determined should be dealt with prior to accrediting/re-accrediting NHRIs with A-status. As will be seen throughout Parts II and III, deferrals are frequently used by the SCA.

Given that there were varying reasons for the SCA to decide to defer an application, and as there appeared to be misunderstanding of and opposition to deferral by some NHRIs from time to time, in its 6 March 2017 Practice Note 1, the SCA elaborated as to the reasons behind a deferral:

> The SCA may decide to defer an application rather than making a recommendation as to the accreditation status of an NHRI. It may do this where, for example:
>
> - the SCA has identified significant concerns that may impact adversely on the NHRI's accreditation status and would like to provide the NHRI with an opportunity to provide additional information or to take action to address its concerns;
> - SCA recommendations made at a previous review remain unaddressed, and the NHRI has not explained why no action has been taken or why the issues have not been addressed in the intervening five-year period;
> - significant legislative reforms are pending that may impact on the accreditation status of an NHRI;[84] or
> - the political or security situation in the state in which the NHRI is operating is so volatile as to make a proper review of the NHRI impossible.[85][86]

2.8 Challenges to Accreditation Decisions

Beginning with the Decision Paper in 2008,[87] amendments were made to the provisions dealing with challenges to the SCA recommendations. These changes clarified the process to make it clear how challenges could be made.

These changes came about as follows. Because of the time spent by the SCA reviewing all materials, interviewing the NHRI, hearing from regional representatives

[84] For example, in the case of Malawi, repeated deferrals were utilized pending the adoption of new legislation. See further, Chapter 4.3.2.

[85] For example, in the case of Egypt where the SCA deferred the re-accreditation of the National Council for Human Rights of Egypt for an extended period from 2011 to 2018, including because of delays in the reform of its enabling law as a result of the situation in the country during that time. See further, Chapter 7.3.1.

[86] SCA, 'Practice Note 1: Deferrals' (adopted on 6 March 2017).

[87] Decision Paper (April 2008) (n 6).

and GANHRI, and deliberating/discussing the application in reaching a decision on the accreditation, there was considerable deference given to the SCA recommendations by the Bureau. Further, Bureau members did not have the benefit of all that the SCA members had read, seen, and heard during the week-long SCA session, and thus the Bureau relied on the expertise and independence of the SCA and accepted the recommendations made by the SCA. At the same time, however, NHRIs considered that if they had a legitimate concern with the recommendation made, they ought to be 'heard' by the Bureau to present their case. In an effort to balance the desire of NHRIs to have a challenge recourse with the deference given to the SCA's work, the decision was made to require one-quarter (four members) of the Bureau to support an NHRI's challenge. As the Bureau has four members from each region, it was decided that the four members required to support the challenge must come from at least two regions in order to avoid a challenge going forward with only the four Bureau members from the challenging NHRI's region supporting the challenge.

Timelines were developed to balance the desire to finalize recommendations and the ability to challenge, and a twenty-eight-day period was established for the NHRI to file a challenge the SCA recommendation. If an NHRI filed a challenge within the twenty-eight days, the Bureau would be advised of that challenge and the documentation before the SCA is provided to the Bureau members so they can consider the challenge submitted and review the documents available, to decide whether or not to support the challenge. Bureau members have twenty days to consider the challenge. If no Bureau member supports the challenge within the twenty days, then the SCA recommendation becomes a final decision. If a Bureau member does support the challenge, the Secretariat informs the other Bureau members accordingly and a further twenty-day period then begins for the remaining Bureau members to consider whether or not to support the challenge. If four members in total do not support the challenge within this subsequent twenty-day period, the SCA recommendation becomes a final decision. If four Bureau members support the challenge, the recommendation is referred to the next Bureau meeting for decision.

The Bureau developed a procedure for deliberation on a challenge brought before it. This is explained in the GANHRI Guide as follows:

> This procedure provides that the issues to be considered by the Bureau are limited to those put forward by the applicant NHRI in its challenge letter. However, the Bureau will not consider any information—whether contained in the challenge letter or brought to the attention of the Bureau in another way—that was not before the SCA at the time of its recommendation. For example, if an NHRI has taken steps in the intervening period to address the issues of concern identified by the SCA at the time of its recommendation, this information will not be considered by the Bureau in determining whether or not to accept the recommendation of the SCA.

The standard for review by the Bureau is whether the SCA recommendation sufficiently demonstrates that the applicant NHRI falls substantially short of the standards set out in the Paris Principles and the General Observations. The Bureau may find that an SCA recommendation does not meet this standard where:

- it is based on a consideration not contained in the Paris Principles as interpreted through the General Observations;
- it is based on a manifest disregard of the Paris Principles as interpreted through the General Observations;
- it is manifestly erroneous or arbitrary; or
- it is not sufficiently comprehensive as to permit a finding that the applicant NHRI falls substantially short of the standards articulated in the Paris Principles as interpreted through the General Observations.

If, after deliberations, Bureau members are satisfied that the SCA recommendation sufficiently demonstrates non-compliance with the Paris Principles, it will accept the recommendation. If Bureau members find that the SCA recommendation does not meet this standard, it will direct the SCA to re-consider the application at its next session and submit its revised recommendation to the Bureau.

It should be noted that, in order to ensure all challenges are handled fairly and consistently, an NHRI whose challenge is being heard by the Bureau, and who is also a Bureau member, is excluded from participating in the meeting at which the challenge will be heard and decided.[88]

The first instances of a challenge to a recommendation being supported by four Bureau members was in 2016. Greece was supported in its challenge of the recommendation to downgrade to B-status after one year, and Venezuela was supported in its challenge of the recommendation to downgrade to B-status immediately, following the one-year notice to downgrade made in 2015.[89] This required the development of a cover page to the SCA reports to specify which recommendations became final decisions and those which were referred to the Bureau for final decision. Ultimately, the October 2016 Bureau upheld the recommendations made for both Greece and Venezuela that were made in the May 2016 SCA report.[90] While there have been subsequent challenges that have received the requisite support, none have resulted in reversal of the SCA recommendation to date.

[88] GANHRI Guide (n 67) 42, 45.

[89] SCA, 'Accreditation Report—Greece (Greek National Commission for Human Rights (GNCHR))' (May 2016) 37; SCA, 'Accreditation Report—Venezuela (Defensoria del Pueblo (DPV))' (May 2016) 55. Greece was able to establish its Paris Principles compliance when reviewed by the SCA again in 2017. See Chapter 7.3.1.1 (Venezuela) and Chapter 10.3.1 (Greece).

[90] SCA, 'Accreditation Report' (May 2016).

2.9 Developing Practice: David Langtry—Reflections on Ten Years in the SCA

From the time of the first accreditations of NHRIs in 1998, the SCA has endeavoured to improve, enhance, and strengthen its processes through the ongoing review and revision of its Rules of Procedure, development of General Observations, issuance of practice notes and manuals, and conducting information sessions and providing guidance and advice to NHRIs interested in pursuing accreditation.

As the accreditation process evolved, A-status-accredited NHRIs were given increasing significant participation rights and independent access to UN human rights mechanisms. This increasing stature meant that there was ever-increasing scrutiny of the accreditation process by the UN, states, human rights players, and NHRIs themselves.

The development of the accreditation process by GANHRI illustrates the seriousness with which it is taken by NHRIs. The process has been gradually imposing stricter requirements for NHRI effectiveness based on practice. Indeed, writing in 2011, Okafor argued that 'the NHRI evaluation model is so significantly limited and incomplete that it requires extension and enlargement' in order, he suggested, to increase the 'transformative potential' of NHRIs.[91] This process has been underway apace since the early 2010s. The legitimacy given to the SCA decisions, by NHRIs, states and the UN and other international and regional organizations, means that the SCA has considerable importance, and responsibility.

GANHRI/the SCA must therefore be vigilant in ensuring that the accreditation process is, and is seen to be, fair, impartial, transparent, rigorous, and independent. Accreditation decisions must be able to be justified by the facts presented to the SCA and withstand comparison to decisions made in cases of similar situations of other NHRIs from different regions, structures, and political and legal systems. It is critically important that those accredited with A-status are objectively seen to be 'A-status' in both law and in practice.

GANHRI must also continue to ensure that the SCA itself is functioning effectively, fairly, and impartially. The amendments to the Rules of Procedure in 2018 to require the posting in advance the names of individuals attending the upcoming session, clarifying quorum requirements, providing for resolution of tied votes, and dealing with situations of real or perceived conflict of interest, in part serve to promote the transparency of the process. Just as the SCA assesses the effectiveness of NHRIs in practice, so, too, should the SCA remain aware that it will be 'assessed' by the way it functions in practice.

[91] Obiora C Okafor, 'National Human Rights Institutions in Anglophone Africa' in Ryan Goodman and Thomas Pegram (eds), *Human Rights, State Compliance and Social Change: Assessing National Human Rights Institutions* (CUP 2012) 126.

Given that GANHRI's accreditation process is unique, in that it is a peer review of NHRIs, and given the stature accorded to A-status institutions by the UN mechanisms, there will be continued scrutiny of the accreditation from many fronts, including, among others: states that may be denied A-status accreditation for their human rights body; NHRIs which believe they are wrongly denied A-status; human rights players that argue they ought to have the same opportunity to have peer-review accreditation; human rights scholars, academics, and activists; and A-status NHRIs themselves which recognize that an unwarranted accreditation of A-status to an NHRI can bring the entire accreditation process into disrepute.

The recommendations of the Decision Paper remain as true today as they did in 2008:

> In light of the changing role of National Institutions, and in order to remain true to its original purpose, it is paramount that the (GANHRI) reviews its accreditation process, with a view to strengthening the credibility and efficiency of the process, as well as that of its inherent fairness ... To ensure that the process is fair and impartial, and that it satisfies the principles of natural justice, it [must] be based on the following three guiding principles: 1. Transparency 2. Rigour 3. Independence.[92]

[92] Decision Paper (April 2008) (n 6), 5–6.

PART II

THE SUB-COMMITTEE ON ACCREDITATION AND THE STRUCTURE AND FUNCTIONING OF NATIONAL HUMAN RIGHTS INSTITUTIONS

This book is divided into three parts. Part I comprised two chapters introducing the origins and establishment of NHRIs, and setting out in detail the process and practice of the SCA. This part begins the book's analysis of the SCA's reports. Covering NHRIs' formal structures, Part II begins with an examination of NHRIs' legal basis, before moving onto the critical question of who runs NHRIs. It then considers NHRIs relationship with the state and their human rights mandate. NHRI practice is examined in Part III.

3
National Human Rights Institutions' Legal Basis: The Enabling Law

3.1 Introduction

The status of a National Human Rights Institution's enabling legislative instrument is fundamental to ensuring that the institution is formally part of the state structure. This aspect of National Human Rights Institution (NHRI) establishment is regarded by the Sub-Committee on Accreditation (SCA) to be of central importance in guaranteeing both the permanency and independence of the NHRI. Significant amendments to the enabling law may result in the initiation of a special review by the SCA (see Chapter 2.5).

The requirement of the NHRI's enabling law being set in the law of the state derives from the Paris Principles, which requires NHRIs to be properly established as a state body in law:

> [A].2. A national institution shall be given as broad a mandate as possible, which shall be clearly set forth in a constitutional or legislative text, specifying its composition and its sphere of competence.[1]

While relatively few NHRIs have received recommendations solely on the formal status of their enabling law (just twelve such recommendations were made between 2008 and 2017), reflecting the fact that most states have established their NHRI as part of the formal domestic structure, the *content* of that enabling law is the subject of a significant number of recommendations, as will be seen throughout Part II of this book. This is because the content of the enabling law is crucial for a wide range of other issues that may impact the NHRI's functioning, including the institution's appointment mechanisms, terms and conditions of office, mandate and powers, funding, and lines of accountability. The content and status of the enabling legislation is also closely connected to the operation of administrative regulations (Chapter 5.5) as these may allow the government to make changes to the mandate, powers, or functions of the NHRI, or its methods of operation, without going through a formal legislative process. The SCA thus makes reference to the enabling

[1] Principles relating to the Status of National Institutions, UNGA Res 48/134 (20 December 1993) UNGA Doc A/RES/48/134 (The Paris Principles).

National Human Rights Institutions. David Langtry and Kirsten Roberts Lyer, Oxford University Press. © David Langtry and Kirsten Roberts Lyer 2021. DOI: 10.1093/oso/9780198829102.003.0004

law in many of its recommendations, further, as can be seen in the sections on the appointment process (Chapter 4.4) is closely connected to any discussion on the content of the enabling law. This chapter focuses on the status of the enabling law at the national level and the requirements for that law in relation to the NHRI's annual report.

The SCA has elaborated on Paris Principles A.2 in its General Observation 1.1 (2018):

> An NHRI must be established in a constitutional or legislative text with sufficient detail to ensure the NHRI has a clear mandate and independence. In particular, it should specify the NHRI's role, functions, powers, funding and lines of accountability, as well as the appointment mechanism for, and terms of office of, its members. The establishment of an NHRI by other means, such as an instrument of the Executive, does not provide sufficient protection to ensure permanency and independence.[2]

The SCA further explained this with the following rationale:

> The SCA recognizes that NHRIs are created in different socio-economic circumstances and political systems, which may in turn impact on the manner in which they are formally established. Nonetheless, the Paris Principles are clear on the requirement that NHRIs, regardless of the constitutional and legal system in which they operate, be formally entrenched in law and in this way be distinguished from an agency of state, a nongovernment organization, or an ad hoc body. Further, it is necessary that the constitutional or legislative text set out the NHRI's mandate as well as the composition of its leadership body. This necessarily requires the inclusion of complete provisions on the NHRI's appointment mechanisms, terms and conditions of office, mandate, powers, funding and lines of accountability.
>
> The SCA considers this provision to be of central importance in guaranteeing both the permanency and independence of the Institution.[3]

It particularly emphasizes the insufficiency of executive instruments as a legal basis:

> The creation of an NHRI in other ways, such as by a decision of the Executive (through a decree, regulation, motion, or administrative action) and not by the legislature raises concerns regarding permanency, independence from government and the ability to exercise its mandate in an unfettered manner. This is because instruments of the Executive may be modified or cancelled at the whim of

[2] SCA, 'General Observations of the Sub-Committee on Accreditation' (adopted on 21 February 2018) GO 1.1, 5 (hereafter SCA 'General Observations' (February 2018)).

[3] ibid.

> the Executive, and such decisions do not require legislative scrutiny. Changes to the mandate and functions of an independent agency of state charged with the promotion and protection of human rights should be scrutinised by the legislature and not be at the fiat of the Executive. Any amendment or repeal of the constitutional or legislative text establishing the NHRI must require the consent of the legislature to ensure its guarantees of independence and powers do not risk being undermined in the future.[4]

The requirements for the formal basis of NHRIs in national law as discussed in this chapter, thus includes three interconnected elements:

- Foundation in law, which should be either in a constitutional provision or a legislative text adopted by the parliament;
- Procedure for making changes to the law, which should be via parliament; and
- Content of the law, which should include sufficient detail on the mandate and functions of the NHRI.

Issues relating to the content of the law feature throughout Chapters 4–6 and substantive powers of NHRIs are specifically discussed in Chapter 6.

3.1.1 NHRI Based in the Constitution or Legislation

NHRIs should be established under the constitution or in national legislation. The SCA has determined that instruments outside these, such as establishment by an executive decree or decision, are insufficient to provide for the stability of the NHRI and protect it from untoward interference. The SCA has therefore called for improved legislative basis for NHRIs that are founded by presidential decree, as such decrees are not sufficient to ensure the 'permanency and independence' of the institution.[5] In the case of Mauritania, for example, the SCA recommended at the NHRI's first accreditation that it be given B-status as it was founded by presidential decree.[6] This decree was replaced by an Act of Parliament in 2010, and the NHRI was subsequently upgraded to A-status in May 2011.[7] For Switzerland's Federal Commission against Racism (FCR), which applied for accreditation in March 2010, the lack of a founding legislative text was one of several issues that prevented

[4] ibid.

[5] SCA, 'Report and Recommendations of the Session of the Sub-Committee on Accreditation (SCA)—Kazakhstan' (March 2012) 7 (hereafter, 'SCA, 'Accreditation Report'). See also, SCA, 'Accreditation Report—Algeria (Commission Nationale Consultative de Promotion et de Protection des Droits de l'Homme (CNCPPDH))' (March 2009) 8.

[6] SCA, 'Accreditation Report—Mauritania (Commission National des Droits de l'Homme (NHRC))' (November 2009) 4.

[7] SCA, 'Accreditation Report—Mauritania (CNDH)' (May 2011) 15.

it from obtaining a Paris Principles-compliant status. In that case, the FCR had been established by an executive decision of the Federal Council and was in fact an extra-parliamentary commission.[8]

As discussed in Chapter 2.4, the situation of the German Institute for Human Rights (GIHR) illustrates the importance placed on the status of the enabling law by the SCA.[9] Long a leading institution in the NHRI network, from the time of its establishment, the GIHR operated on the basis of a parliamentary motion rather than legislation.[10] The non-Paris Principles-compliant nature of this was raised during the institution's periodic re-accreditation in 2008, however, the institution retained A-status. The unanimous adoption of the relevant Motion of the Bundestag (Motion 14/4801), and the 'independent and effective functioning' of the NHRI were factors taken into account by the SCA in its assessment.[11] Nonetheless, the recommendation was made for the adoption of a stronger legal basis. When the institution came up for periodic re-accreditation again in 2013, consideration was deferred, with one of the reasons cited being the need for the NHRI 'to be established by constitutional or legislative text'.[12] The next review did not in fact take place until March 2015, when re-accreditation was again deferred, with the SCA noting that draft legislation had been approved by the Federal Cabinet and was due for submission to Parliament.[13] In November 2015, the NHRI was recommended for re-accreditation with A-status, on the basis that the new law had been adopted.[14] Thus, in terms of the formality of its enabling law, the German NHRI was given a significant 'grace period' by the SCA to allow it to get its legislation in place. Coupled with the proper *de facto* functioning of the institution and the efforts it had made to have its legislative basis formalized, this was sufficient to allow the SCA to defer re-accreditation for a period of two years. However, the NHRI was clearly placed on notice that its A-status was in jeopardy should the issue not have been resolved. The SCA has taken a similar approach in the case of Malawi, where the accreditation was deferred due to proposed substantive amendments to the enabling law (see further, Chapter 4.3.2).[15]

[8] SCA, 'Accreditation Report—Switzerland (Federal Commission against Racism (FCR))' (March/April 2010) 12. The Federal Commission was one of the few institutions to be accredited with the now-discontinued C-status. See Chapter 2.1.

[9] The early accreditations of the GIHR were also noted in the previous chapter in relation to the developing practice of the SCA.

[10] SCA, 'Accreditation Report—Germany (German Institute for Human Rights (GIHR))' (November 2008) 7.

[11] ibid.

[12] SCA, 'Accreditation Report—Germany (GIHR)' (November 2013) 20.

[13] SCA, 'Accreditation Report—Germany (GIHR)' (March 2015) 39.

[14] SCA, 'Accreditation Report—Germany (GIHR)' (November 2015) 14.

[15] See also, Nepal: In confirming the National Human Rights Commission of Nepal's A-status in 2008, the SCA also noted that it would review the question of pending legislation in the following year. SCA, 'Accreditation Report—Nepal (National Human Rights Commission (NHRC))' (November 2008) 11.

The SCA has been willing to overlook the requirement of an enabling law being set in legislative or constitutional basis where there are extenuating circumstances making a better alternative impossible. For many years, the A-status NHRI of Palestine had operated without a formal legislative basis. First highlighted during its accreditation in March 2009,[16] at the time of its 2015 re-accreditation, the NHRI of Palestine was still not based in founding legislation because of the disruption to the operation of the adopting authority, the Palestinian Legislative Council.[17] The draft legislation had been prepared in 2005 but the activities of the Council had been disrupted from 2006, prior to the adoption of the law. Further, the NHRI itself had adopted bylaws 'in the spirit of an enabling law'.[18]

The SCA has also given leeway to NHRIs in states where the particular legislative or governance structure is such that a 'regular' type of enabling law is not possible. The NHRI of Belgium (UNIA) was established pursuant to an inter-federal agreement rather than an explicit law. The SCA considered that since this inter-federal agreement had the status of law and had been adopted 'on the basis of legislative enactments by the eight(8) parliamentary assemblies that make up Belgium'.[19] Further, the SCA appeared to take into account that there was a positive purpose behind the chosen legal basis, namely, 'that this structure was chosen in order to promote the accessibility of the institution for all people in Belgium and guarantees its independence and full geographic coverage'.[20] The SCA therefore arrived at the finding that the inter-federal agreement was not an instrument of the executive but was equivalent to a legislative act.[21] However, it did express some concern for the stability of this enabling law because the agreement provided for a three-year renewal and that any of the constituent parliamentary assemblies could withdraw unilaterally, with potential impact for the functioning and jurisdiction of the NHRI.[22] Despite the SCA's acceptance of this enabling law, it still encouraged the NHRI to advocate for a fully Paris Principles-compliant enabling law.[23]

16 SCA, 'Accreditation Report—Palestine (Palestine Independent Commission for Human Rights (PICHR))' (March 2009) 7.

17 SCA, 'Accreditation Report—Palestine (PICHR)' (November 2015) 34.

18 ibid.

19 SCA, 'Accreditation Report—Belgium (The Interfederal Centre for Equal Opportunity and fight against racism and discrimination (UNIA))' (May 2018) 9.

20 ibid.

21 ibid.

22 ibid.

23 ibid.

3.1.2 NHRI Seeking Improvements to its Enabling Law

While NHRIs are not responsible for the adoption of their own enabling law, the SCA does expect the NHRI to advocate for changes to its legislation when needed.[24] The requirement for the NHRI to advocate for changes to its enabling law can be found across the range of issues covered in Part II of this book.

The SCA recognizes that neither it nor GANHRI have any power over the state to cause laws to be passed but that the NHRI should advocate for the changes set out in the SCA reports, arguing that those changes are needed to avoid downgrading to B (or to achieve A-status if currently B-status). The SCA tries to balance the necessity for Paris Principles compliance with the reality that the NHRI cannot pass laws. That is, the SCA must consider and determine whether or not an NHRI should be 'punished' for the actions/inactions of the state. By requiring an NHRI to advocate for changes, the SCA can then consider whether the NHRI has done so, what the response of the state has been, and what likelihood there will be that the law/amendments will be passed.

The emphasis placed on the requirement for the NHRI to be active in advocating for change to its enabling law can be seen clearly in the case of Thailand. While the *status* of the NHRI's enabling law was not specifically at issue, but rather the adoption of an amended law in line with the 2007 Constitution, the emphasis by the SCA on the actions of the NHRI is illustrative of the importance for the NHRI to be proactive. The revision of the Thailand NHRI's new enabling law had been awaiting parliamentary approval for six years when the SCA considered the re-accreditation of the institution in November 2013.[25] While it was not raised by the SCA as problematic per se that the new law had not come into effect, the SCA was concerned by the lack of activity of the NHRI in seeking amendments to the law to strengthen its compliance with the Paris Principles. Re-accreditation was deferred to the following year, and the same issue was raised in SCA reviews in March 2014,[26] and October 2014,[27] when the NHRI was recommended to be downgraded to B-status (see Chapter 9.2 for more on the downgrading of Thailand). The level of engagement of the NHRI with the reforms going on in the country, without it having at the time of the re-accreditation process advocated for improvements in its own laws, was an important point of consideration for the SCA.[28] The SCA

[24] See for example, the NHRI of Nigeria; in its October 2010 review, the SCA commended the efforts of the institution, but deferred its decision as it was awaiting presidential signature. SCA, 'Accreditation Report—Nigeria (National Human Rights Commission (NHRC))' (October 2010) 6. See also SCA, 'Accreditation Report—Rwanda (The National Commission for Human Rights of the Republic of Rwanda (NCHR))' (May 2013) 16.

[25] SCA, 'Accreditation Report—Thailand (National Human Rights Commission of Thailand (NHRCT))' (November 2013) 27.

[26] SCA, 'Accreditation Report—Thailand (NHRCT)' (March 2014) 17.

[27] SCA, 'Accreditation Report—Thailand (NHRCT)' (October 2014) 32–35.

[28] The SCA noted 'that the NHRCT [Thailand NHRI] is actively involved in the current constitutional reforms and that it intends to re-submit a proposal to amend its enabling law'. ibid 34.

recognizes where efforts are made by the NHRI,[29] as will be seen elsewhere in this book. In accrediting the NHRI of Croatia in 2013, it 'noted with appreciation' the institution's efforts to improve its legislative basis, and 'applauded' its efforts.[30] Similarly in 2015, it commended efforts made by the NHRI of Morocco, including the placement of the CNDH in the Constitution and efforts to amend the legislation regarding it selection and appointment process.[31]

3.2 The Annual Report in the Enabling Law

3.2.1 Introduction

As noted in the introduction to this chapter, the enabling law is important to a wide range of issues relevant to the Paris Principles-compliant functioning of an NHRI. This section considers one of the elements not examined elsewhere in this book: the provisions for the formal publication and deliberation on the NHRI's annual report in the enabling law. Other considerations relating to the annual report are provided in separate parts of this book, including problematic content of an annual report (see eg in the cases of Mauritania and Honduras, Chapter 10.2.2 and Chapter 9.2 respectively), and the ability of the state to determine the form and content of the annual report (see Chapter 5.5 on administrative regulation).

For many years, the SCA has emphasized the importance of the annual report, both that the NHRI publish one, and that it be substantive, addressing 'opinions, recommendations and proposals' on human rights issues. It was the subject of forty recommendations from 2008 to 2017. SCA General Observation 1.11 provides that:

> Annual, special and thematic reports serve to highlight key developments in the human rights situation in a country and provide a public account, and therefore public scrutiny, of the effectiveness of an NHRI. The reports also provide a means by which an NHRI can make recommendations to government and monitor respect for human rights by government.
>
> The importance for an NHRI to prepare, publicize and widely distribute an annual report on its national situation with regard to human rights in general, and on more specific matters, is stressed. This report should include an account of the activities undertaken by the NHRI to further its mandate during that year and

[29] SCA, 'Accreditation Report—Algeria (The National Human Rights Council of Algeria (CNDH))' (May 2018) 15.

[30] SCA, 'Accreditation Report—Croatia (Ombudsman of the Republic of Croatia (ORC))' (May 2013) 8.

[31] SCA, 'Accreditation Report—Morocco (Conseil National des Droits de l'Homme (CNDH))' (November 2015) 32.

> should state its opinions, recommendations and proposals to address any human rights issues of concern.
>
> The SCA considers it important that the enabling laws of an NHRI establish a process whereby its reports are required to be widely circulated, discussed and considered by the legislature. It is preferable for the NHRI to have an explicit power to table reports directly in the legislature rather than through the Executive and, in so doing, to promote action on them.
>
> Where an NHRI has made an application for accreditation or re-accreditation, it will be required to submit a current annual report, that is, one from the preceding year's reporting period ... The SCA finds it difficult to assess the effectiveness of an NHRI and its compliance with the Paris Principles in the absence of a current annual report.[32]

In its justification, the SCA cites Paris Principle A.3 in support of this requirement:

> Section A.3(a) of the Paris Principles requires National Institutions to be responsible for, '*submit[ting] to the Government, Parliament and any other competent body, ... reports on any matters concerning the promotion and protection of human rights.*' It states that institutions '*may decide to publicize them*', and enumerates the four areas that these reports shall relate to:
>
> (i) Recommendations on the creation or amendment of any legislative or administrative provisions, including bills and proposals;
> (ii) Any situation of violation of human rights;
> (iii) Human rights in general and on more specific matters; and
> (iv) Proposals to put an end to human rights violations, and its opinion on the proposals and reaction of government to these situations.[33]

The SCA clarified what this means in practice in relation to the content of the report, publication and the enabling law:

> *Content of reports*—The annual report of an NHRI is a vital public document that not only provides a regular audit of the government's performance on human rights but also an account of what the NHRI has done. As such, this report should include an account of the activities undertaken by the NHRI to further its mandate during that year and should state its opinions, recommendations and proposals to address any human rights issues of concern, and the government's action on its recommendations;
>
> *Publication of reports*—It is important for an NHRI to publicize and widely distribute an annual report on its national situation with regard to human rights in

[32] SCA 'General Observations' (February 2018) (n 2) GO 1.11, 30.
[33] ibid (emphasis in original).

general, and on more specific matters. It is vitally important that all the findings and recommendations of the NHRI be publicly available as this increases the transparency and public accountability of the NHRI. In publishing and widely disseminating its annual report, the NHRI will play an extremely important role in educating the public on the situation of human rights violations in the country;

Submission of reports—The NHRI should be given the legislative authority to table its reports directly to the legislature rather than through the Executive. The legislature should be required to discuss and consider the reports of the NHRI, so as to ensure that its recommendations are properly considered by relevant public authorities.[34]

The General Observation on annual reports thus combines several requirements: the technical or procedural requirements for the adoption and consideration of the report, and the substantive content of the report. This section will consider further the SCA's review of the provisions relating to the annual report in the enabling law. In this regard, it may be noted that the SCA has accepted where there is a different format that results in the same outcome. The Sri Lankan NHRI submitted quarterly activity reports to parliament that, combined, made up its annual report.[35]

3.2.2 Annual Report Adoption Procedure and Consideration by Parliament

In applying General Observation 1.11, the SCA has emphasized the requirement that the enabling law should include specific provision for the annual report, even where such a report is, in practice, issued by the NHRI.[36] The enabling law should also explicitly require that the annual report will be made public.[37]

The SCA is also concerned with the procedure by which the annual report is adopted and considered formally within the state. The SCA requires that the NHRI's annual report be considered by the parliament, and this requirement should

[34] ibid 31.

[35] SCA, 'Accreditation Report—Sri Lanka (The Human Rights Commission of Sri Lanka (SLHRC))' (May 2018) 38.

[36] For example, in its March 2017 review of the Philippines NHRI (CHRP), the SCA found that '[t]he Constitution and [Executive Order] 163 are silent on the requirement for the CHRP to produce annual and other reports, and on the method of tabling and publicizing such reports. The SCA acknowledges that the CHRP, in practice, prepares annual reports on the situation of human rights and distributes these reports to regional offices for public dissemination, and to government offices such as Congress, the Senate and the department of budget and management. The SCA notes that section 38 of the proposed CHR Act provides that the CHRP shall prepare and make public an annual report on its activities.' SCA, 'Accreditation Report—Philippines (Commission on Human Rights of the Philippines (CHRP))' (March 2017) 32.

[37] SCA, 'Accreditation Report—Congo (Commission Nationale des Droits de l'Homme (CNDH))' (October 2010) 4–5.

explicitly be provided for in the enabling law. The SCA 'considers it preferable that the enabling laws of an NHRI establish a process whereby the Institution's reports are required to be widely circulated, discussed and considered by Parliament'.[38] In its assessment of the NHRI of Finland in October 2014, for example, the SCA recommended a change in procedure in the enabling law to ensure that the parliament had the opportunity to discuss the NHRI's report and, further, called on the NHRI to provide a consolidated annual report text to the whole parliament and not just a parliamentary committee.[39] This underscores that the provision of the annual report should be to the whole parliament; a requirement in the enabling law for submitting the annual report to the head of parliament is not sufficient.[40] State bodies should not have the authority to edit the NHRI's annual report.[41]

Closely related to this is the requirement that the procedure for the adoption of the annual report in the enabling law should allow for the NHRI to submit its own report directly to the parliament rather than have to go through any ministerial or governmental body first. In the case of Tanzania, the SCA called on the NHRI 'to advocate for changes to its enabling law to provide the explicit power to table all reports directly in the legislature, rather than through the Executive, and in doing so to promote action on them'.[42] Similarly, when reviewing the B-status NHRI of Libya, the SCA stated that it 'considers it preferable that an NHRI has the explicit power to submit reports directly to parliament rather than through the

[38] SCA, 'Accreditation Report—Finland (Finnish National Human Rights Institution (FNHRI))' (October 2014) 9. In reviewing Bosnia and Herzegovina in November 2016, the SCA also recommended that the enabling law include specific reference to the consideration of the report by the Parliament as there was 'no requirement in the enabling Law that the annual report is considered by or discussed in the relevant Parliaments'. SCA, 'Accreditation Report—Bosnia and Herzegovina (Human Rights Ombudsmen of Bosnia and Herzegovina (IHROBH))' (November 2016) 16. See also the subsequent review in November 2017: SCA, 'Accreditation Report—Bosnia and Herzegovina (IHROBH)' (November 2017) 8–12. The SCA also made this recommendation to Namibia (A-status) and Nigeria (A-status) in November 2016. SCA, 'Accreditation Report—Namibia (Office of the Ombudsman (Ombudsman))' (November 2016) 43; SCA, 'Accreditation Report—Nigeria (National Human Rights Commission (NHRC))' (November 2016) 49.

[39] The SCA found that '[i]n accordance with Section 12 of the Parliamentary Ombudsman Act, the annual report of the Ombudsman is tabled in Parliament and is discussed in the presence of the Ombudsman. The report of the HRC is presented to the Constitutional Law Committee, to other Committees depending upon the content of the report, and to members of Parliament. However, it is neither tabled nor discussed in Parliament. The SCA is of the view that, as a result of this difference in procedure, Parliament is not provided with a complete account of the work of the FNHRI.' SCA, 'Accreditation Report—Finland (FNHRI)' (October 2014) 9. This recommendation was repeated in October 2019: SCA, 'Accreditation Report—Finland (FNHRI)' (October 2019) 10.

[40] SCA, 'Accreditation Report—Cameroon (The National Commission on Human Rights and Freedom of Cameroon (NCHRF))' (November 2017) 17.

[41] SCA, 'Accreditation Report—Oman (Oman National Human Rights Commission (ONHRC))' (November 2013) 15.

[42] SCA, 'Accreditation Report—Tanzania (Commission for Human Rights and Good Governance (CHRAGG))' (November 2016) 51. Per the SCA 'in accordance with section 33(1) of the [NHRI] Act and article 131(3) of the Constitution, the annual report of the CHRAGG is submitted to the National Assembly through the responsible Minister'. ibid. See also, SCA, 'Accreditation Report—Armenia (Human Rights Defender of the Republic of Armenia (HRDA))' (May 2013) 7–8.

government'.[43] The SCA specifically noted that 'the [Enabling] Law is silent on the procedure by which the reports of the NCCLHR are to be provided to the appropriate authorities'.[44] In the case of Zambia, the SCA was concerned that the enabling law required the NHRI's annual report to be first submitted to the President, despite a constitutional provision that 'commissions shall submit annual reports to the National Assembly', and called on the NHRI to advocate for changes to its enabling law to clarify its 'explicit power' to table reports to the Assembly.[45]

Any restriction on the ability of the NHRI to submit its report directly to the parliament will cause concern for the SCA. Even where the provision is closer to a formality than any impediment, the SCA has still called for these requirements to be removed from the enabling law. In the case of Northern Ireland, the NHRI submitted its report to the Secretary of State, who then tabled the report before parliament. Despite noting the NHRI's clarification that 'the Minister's role is limited to tabling the document before Parliament, and that he or she is not permitted to modify the report or require that modifications be made', the SCA still called on the NHRI to 'advocate for changes to its enabling law to provide the explicit power to table reports directly in the legislature, rather than through the Executive'.[46] In addition to the NHRI being able to table its annual report before parliament, specific provision should be made for parliament to debate the report.[47] The SCA has

[43] SCA, 'Accreditation Report—Libya (National Council for Civil Liberties and Human Rights (NCCLHR))' (October 2014) 15. See also, SCA, 'Accreditation Report—Greece (Greek National Commission for Human Rights (GNCHR))' (March 2015) 33: 'In accordance with article 5 of the Law, the annual report of the GNCHR is submitted to the Prime Minister, the President of Parliament, and the leaders of political parties that are represented in the national and European Parliament. However, there is no requirement to either table or discuss the report in Parliament.'

[44] SCA, 'Accreditation Report—Libya (NCCLHR)' (October 2014) 15. In relation to Cameroon, the SCA recommended a change in the enabling law as the NHRI's reports were to be submitted to the President rather than the Parliament: SCA, 'Accreditation Report—Cameroon (NCHRF)' (March 2015) 38. See also, SCA, 'Accreditation Report—Greece (GNCHR)' (May 2016) 37, and a similar recommendation in relation to Myanmar: SCA, 'Accreditation Report—Myanmar (Myanmar National Human Rights Commission (MNHRC))' (November 2015) 14) which used a similar process. Concerns were also raised in relation to Zimbabwe: SCA, 'Accreditation Report—Zimbabwe (Human Rights Commission (ZHRC))' (May 2016) 24.

[45] SCA, 'Accreditation Report—Zambia (Human Rights Commission (HRCZ))' (November 2016) 59–60. This was raised again in October 2018, where the SCA noted that an amendment bill would address this issue: SCA, 'Accreditation Report—Zambia (HRCZ)' (October 2018) 20. See also a similar recommendation to Nepal: SCA, 'Accreditation Report—Nepal (National Human Rights Commission of Nepal (NHRCN))' (March 2019) 29.

[46] SCA, 'Accreditation Report—Northern Ireland (Northern Ireland Human Rights Commission (NIHRC))' (May 2016) 45–46. See also recommendations to New Zealand: SCA, 'Accreditation Report—New Zealand (New Zealand Human Rights Commission (NZHRC))' (May 2016) 43–44, and Tanzania: SCA, 'Accreditation Report—Tanzania (Commission for Human Rights and Good Governance of (CHRAGG))' (November 2016) 51 and SCA, 'Accreditation Report—Tanzania (CHRAGG)' (November 2017) 35.

[47] See for example, SCA, 'Accreditation Report—Malaysia (Human Rights Commission of Malaysia (SUHAKAM))' (November 2015) 31: 'In accordance with section 21 of the Act, SUHAKAM may present annual and thematic reports to Parliament. However, there is no requirement for the Government to table and debate the report in Parliament. The SCA acknowledges with appreciation SUHAKAM efforts since its establishment in calling on the Parliament to discuss its annual reports. However, the SCA is of the view this practice should be enshrined in the Act.' See also, SCA, 'Accreditation Report—Samoa (Office of the Ombudsman (Ombudsman))' (May 2016) 21; SCA, 'Accreditation Report—Canada

recommended that the enabling law, or bylaws, provide for the 'relevant government ministries and the competent parliamentary committees to hold discussion on [NHRI] reports and their recommendations'.[48] There should be an explicit process in the enabling law whereby the NHRI's reports are required to be discussed by the legislature 'to ensure that relevant public authorities properly consider its recommendations'.[49]

The SCA has raised concerns where the formal procedure relating to the annual report is excessively slow, such as in the case of India, where the publication of annual reports faced a multi-year delay as a result of a government procedure not to table the report in parliament before it had prepared a response to the NHRI's recommendations, effectively preventing publication.[50] This is closely connected to the question of the power of the NHRI to publish its own report, as in this instance the ability of the NHRI to publish its report was circumscribed by the government. Where the NHRI itself is slow in producing its annual report, it will also face criticism from the SCA, for example in relation to Ghana where at the time of its review in March 2019, the 2016 annual report had still not been published or tabled before parliament.[51]

Finally, it may be noted that an annual report is a critical part of the accreditation process, and NHRIs are required to provide a recent report, translated into one of the official GANHRI languages.[52] Similarly, where NHRIs are given a significantly

(Canadian Human Rights Commission (CHRC))' (May 2016) 28, and SCA, 'Accreditation Report—Malaysia (SUHAKAM)' (November 2015) 31.

[48] SCA, 'Accreditation Report—Palestine (PICHR)' (November 2015) 36.

[49] SCA, 'Accreditation Report—Togo (La Commission Nationale Des Droits De L'homme Du Togo (CNDH))' (October 2019) 19.

[50] SCA, 'Accreditation Report—India (National Human Rights Commission of India (NHRCI))' (May 2011) 15. In November 2016, the SCA acknowledged the Indian NHRI's efforts to mitigate this limitation by publishing other reports on thematic issues or the state of human rights. The SCA encouraged the NHRI to 'seek a solution to this issue, and to continue to advocate for its annual reports to be tabled in Parliament and made public as soon as possible', SCA, 'Accreditation Report—India' (November 2016) 28. In its deferred review in November 2017, the SCA noted that the NHRI had proposed an amendment to the enabling law so that annual reports could be presented to parliament without the Government's memorandum of action, SCA, 'Accreditation Report—India (NHRCI)' (November 2017) 21. See also, SCA, 'Accreditation Report—Luxembourg (Commission Consultative des droits de l'homme (CCDH))' (November 2015) 27; SCA, 'Accreditation Report—Tanzania (CHRAGG)' (November 2017) 35–36.

[51] SCA, 'Accreditation Report—Ghana' (March 2019), 24. This was a problem previously for the NHRI of Ghana. In 2014 the SCA noted that the annual report from 2011 was just then before the parliament and the annual reports for 2012 and 2013 had not yet been published, SCA, 'Accreditation Report—Ghana Commission on Human Rights and Administrative Justice (CHRAJ))' (March 2014) 14. See also, SCA, 'Accreditation Report—Tanzania (CHRAGG)' (November 2016) 51.

[52] See for example, SCA, 'Accreditation Report—Algeria (CNCPPDH)' (April 2008) 4; SCA, 'Accreditation Report—Ukraine (Ukrainian Parliament Commissioner for Human Rights (UPCHR))' (April 2008) 9; CA, 'Accreditation Report—Ghana (CHRAJ)' (November 2008) 7; SCA, 'Accreditation Report—Mongolia (National Human Rights Commission (NHRC))' (November 2008) 9; SCA, 'Accreditation Report—Sri Lanka (SLHRC)' (March 2009) 5; SCA, 'Accreditation Report—Honduras (CONADEH)' (October 2010) 9–10; SCA, 'Accreditation Report—Ethiopia (EHRC))' (November 2013) 7.

broadened mandate they should provide a report on at least one year's activities when applying for accreditation.[53]

3.3 Comment

The question of the status of the NHRI's enabling law within the national legal system could be regarded as merely a technical issue, and in and of itself, this issue has not seen a huge number of comments by the SCA compared to other areas discussed in subsequent chapters. However, the status of the founding law is crucial to the stability and independence of the institution. Where an enabling law is properly constituted, changes will require legislative scrutiny, which acts as a means of protecting the NHRI's independence. For this reason, foundation by executive decision is deemed insufficient, given the risk of arbitrary changes. Another important point noted by the SCA in its General Observations is that the establishment of the NHRI in the law of the state is a clear signal of the nature of the institution; it is not an agency of state, NGO, or ad hoc body. Further, the status of the legal basis underpinning the NHRI confers it with legitimacy in the exercise of its mandate.[54]

The lack of founding legislation is one of a number of factors that may impact Paris Principles compliance. The importance placed by the SCA on this issue reflects the legitimacy and stability that such a status affords the NHRI. However, the SCA has also understood and accepted that there are different legal and governance systems that may require a nuanced approach. For the NHRI in Oman, the SCA noted that it understood that 'in Oman a Royal Decree is equivalent to legislation',[55] meaning that the Paris Principles requirement was met. This illustrates how the SCA approaches this requirement with recognition of the system of governance in the country. These examples contrast somewhat with the NHRI of Palestine, whose legal status has not been made regular, but this issue is mentioned repeatedly as one that should be rectified where possible. As seen above, in reviewing the NHRI of Belgium (UNIA) in 2018, the SCA also illustrated how it accepts difference national governance systems.[56]

The literature in the field supports the importance of the status of the enabling law. In their 2015 survey of NHRI experts, Linos and Pegram found that constitutional or legal status was ranked as 4.8 out of a score of 5 in terms of its importance,

[53] SCA, 'Accreditation Report—Haiti (Office for the Protection of Citizens (OPC))' (May 2013) 7.

[54] Katerina Linos and Tom Pegram, 'Interrogating Form and Function: Designing Effective National Human Rights Institutions' (Danish Institute for Human Rights, 2015) Matters of Concern Human Rights Research Paper Series No 2015/8, 22.

[55] SCA, 'Accreditation Report—Oman (Oman National Human Rights Commission (ONHRC))' (November 2013) 12. See also, SCA, 'Accreditation Report–Qatar (National Human Rights Committee (NHRC))' (October 2010) 13.

[56] SCA, 'Accreditation Report—Belgium (The Interfederal Centre for Equal Opportunity and fight against racism and discrimination (UNIA))' (May 2018) 9.

on the rationale that 'establishment by constitution or legislation makes [an] NHRI charter harder to amend, and [the] NHRI more stable',[57] with a 'general consensus' of its importance and that this was generalizable across settings.[58] Linos and Pegram argue that it is not merely a '*de jure* guarantee' but 'a safeguard of *de facto* autonomy in the performance of an NHRIs' functions', and is 'among the most significant structural guarantees of NHRI independence'.[59] Part of the rationale for this is the 'higher threshold and scrutiny required to secure reversal of legislation or constitutional amendments imposes significant costs', compared to an executive instrument.[60]

The requirement for an establishing law based in the constitution or national legislation has been reflected in recommendations relating to ombudspersons from the Parliamentary Assembly of the Council of Europe (PACE).[61] The Organization for Security and Cooperation in Europe (OSCE) has similarly found that the establishment in the constitution or legislation 'to establish permanence' is an essential characteristic for the independence of national institutions (broadly defined to include ombudsmen).[62] The UN Committee Against Torture has made a similar determination in its Guidelines on national preventative mechanisms.[63] The European Commission for Democracy Through Law (Venice Commission)'s advice on ombudspersons supports constitutional-level provision for the ombudsperson 'to promote and preserve the independence and neutrality ... as well as the respect in the national and the place of importance among other institutions'.[64] The Venice Commission, PACE, and the OSCE's approach emphasizes that there is a clear preference for constitutional provision for ombudspersons. However, the Venice Commission has commented that despite the 'general recognition' of the desirability of a constitutional guarantee, 'the principle involved is not universally regarded as indispensable' with some institutions operating under legislation.[65] It

[57] Linos and Pegram (n 54) 14, Table 1.

[58] ibid 15, 17.

[59] ibid 20.

[60] ibid 20–23. Linos and Pegram cite several examples where an NHRI was not shut down despite national pressure, in support of this hypothesis. ibid 21.

[61] For example, Parliamentary Assembly of the Council of Europe (PACE), 'Strengthening the Institution of Ombudsman in Europe', Res 1959 (2013), para 4.1; PACE, Recommendation 1615 (2003).

[62] OSCE, 'Ombudsman and Human Rights Protection Institutions in OSCE Participating States, OSCE Human Dimension Implementation Meeting October 1998 Background Paper 1' (21 September 1998) 9; OSCE, 'Report of the Second Meeting in the ODIHR Human Rights Discussion Series for Representatives of the Forum for Security Co-operation: The Role of Ombuds Institutions in Protecting Human Rights of Armed Forces Personnel' (Vienna, 14 October 2013) 18, noting that constitutionally based Ombuds institutions have 'added legitimacy in relation to governmental institutions, a more secure and permanent basis for its mandate, and greater security of tenure' compared to those established by executive decree.

[63] Committee Against Torture, 'Guidelines on national preventative mechanisms' (9 December 2010) UN Doc CAT/OP/12/5, para 7.

[64] Venice Commission, 'Compilation on the Ombudsman Institution' (1 December 2011) CDL(2011)079, 4. See also the International Ombudsman Institute (IOI), 'Bylaws' (adopted on 13 November 2012), 2(a).

[65] ibid.

proposes that this may be for historical reasons because the 'significance of the role of the Ombudsman in relation to human rights and freedoms was not as strongly recognized as it is today' or because the procedure for amending the constitution is cumbersome and 'provision for an institution such as the Ombudsman is difficult to make except in the course of a wider constitutional revision process'.[66] The SCA's approach emphasizes the importance of a stable legislative provision but does not over emphasize the constitutional aspect and cannot be said to be absolutist in the requirement for a constitutional provision or legislation but rather as taking a pragmatic approach.

The SCA also requires that the enabling law contains provision for the publication of an annual report, including specific provision for the NHRI to lay the report before parliament absent any intermediary. This is important in order to underscore the NHRI's independence and to avoid the possibility of interference with the integrity of the NHRI in its ability to disseminate its findings and information on its activities publicly. This includes cases of delay, as seen above in relation to India and Tanzania. Even where the process of an executive intermediary is merely '*pro forma*' as in the case of Northern Ireland, the symbolism of the transmission of the report through the executive branch was problematic. The requirement is not only that the enabling law provide a clear ability for the NHRI to place the report before parliament, but also that parliament must consider it. It is thus an active requirement and not one that a passive placing of the report before parliament can fulfil. Similarly, placing the annual report before a committee of parliament, or before its president but not the plenary, is insufficient to meet this requirement. The approach of the SCA here is in keeping with the general approach taken by other bodies. The Venice Commission has found that parliaments should be obliged to consider the recommendations of the ombudsperson.[67] PACE similarly considers that it is an essential characteristic of an ombudsperson that they are able to present their annual report, and other reports, to parliament.[68] While this chapter has examined the status of the enabling law, the next chapter will focus on the largest area of SCA recommendations, many of which also relate to the content of those enabling laws: namely, the selection and appointment, and terms and conditions of NHRI leadership.

[66] ibid 4.
[67] ibid 19.
[68] PACE, Recommendation 1615(2003), 7.14.

4
Who Runs National Human Rights Institutions? Membership, Leadership, and Staffing

4.1 Introduction

This chapter examines a range of crucial issues for National Human Rights Institutions (NHRIs), central to which is the question of who runs the NHRI? Issues of leadership, both executive and appointed, as well as board members (in multi-member institutions) and staffing are critical to the independence and functioning of NHRIs.

This chapter begins by considering the question of pluralism. The Sub-Committee on Accreditation (SCA) has emphasized that pluralism in leadership and staffing is a requirement for NHRIs and should reflect the nature of the society in which the NHRI operates, including representation of women and diverse societal groups. The chapter then moves to the area that has received the most focus in SCA accreditations: the selection and appointments process. Issues covered under this heading include the formalization of the selection and appointment process in the enabling law, the composition of the selection panel, and the process for nomination and appointment. Finally, this chapter considers the related issues of security of tenure, functional immunity, and staffing. Together, the issues dealt with in this chapter go to the heart of the functional and structural requirements for the compliance of NHRIs with the Paris Principles.[1]

4.2 Ensuring Pluralism

The SCA's concerns regarding pluralism arise from the need for the NHRI to be representative and accessible for the entirety of the population of the country. The issue is one of the more frequently raised concerns by the SCA.

In its 2018 General Observation 1.7 on ensuring pluralism, the SCA set out a number of ways in which pluralism should be achieved:

[1] Principles relating to the Status of National Institutions, UNGA Res 48/134 (20 December 1993) UNGA Doc A/RES/48/134 (The Paris Principles).

National Human Rights Institutions. David Langtry and Kirsten Roberts Lyer, Oxford University Press. © David Langtry and Kirsten Roberts Lyer 2021. DOI: 10.1093/oso/9780198829102.003.0005

A diverse decision-making and staff body facilitates the NHRI's appreciation of, and capacity to engage on, all human rights issues affecting the society in which it operates, and promotes the accessibility of the NHRI for all citizens.

Pluralism refers to broader representation of national society. Consideration must be given to ensuring pluralism in the context of gender, ethnicity or minority status. This includes, for example, ensuring the equitable participation of women in the NHRI.

The SCA notes there are diverse models for ensuring the requirement of pluralism in the composition of the NHRIs as set out in the Paris Principles. For example:

a) Members of the decision-making body represent different segments of society as referred to in the Paris Principles. Criteria for membership of the decision-making body should be legislatively established, be made publicly available and subject to consultation with all stakeholders, including civil society. Criteria that may unduly narrow and restrict the diversity and plurality of the composition of the NHRI's membership should be avoided;
b) Pluralism through the appointment procedures of the governing body of the NHRIs for example, where diverse societal groups suggest or recommend candidates;
c) Pluralism through procedures enabling effective cooperation with diverse societal groups, for example advisory committees, networks, consultations or public forums; or
d) Pluralism through staff that are representative of the diverse segments of society. This is particularly relevant for single member NHRIs, such as an Ombudsperson.[2]

Pluralism thus needs to be realized through the provisions in the enabling law on the appointment process for the leadership, the implementation of the appointment process itself, and thorough the operation of the NHRI in practice. As noted by the SCA in its justification to General Observation 1.7, the Paris Principles explicitly refer to pluralism and diversity as requirements for the NHRI, connected to the composition of the members:

Ensuring the pluralistic composition of the NHRI is a central requirement of the Paris Principles as a guarantee of institutional independence. Section B.1 states: 'The composition of the national institution and the appointment of its members . . . shall be established in accordance with a procedure which affords all

[2] SCA, 'General Observations of the Sub-Committee on Accreditation' (adopted on 21 February 2018) GO 1.7, 20 (hereafter, SCA, 'General Observations').

necessary guarantees to ensure the pluralist representation of the social forces (of civilian society) involved in the promotion and protection of human rights.'

The same provision highlights that pluralism is intended to promote effective cooperation with an indicative list of stakeholders representing:

a) Non-governmental organizations responsible for human rights and efforts to combat racial discrimination, trade unions, concerned social and professional organizations, for example, associations of lawyers, doctors, journalists and eminent scientists;
b) Trends in philosophical or religious thought;
c) Universities and qualified experts;
d) Parliament;
e) Government departments.

The SCA considers the pluralistic composition of the NHRI to be fundamentally linked to the requirement of independence, credibility, effectiveness and accessibility.[3]

The requirement for pluralism is often mentioned by the SCA in conjunction with the selection and appointments process for the leadership and/or board of the NHRI.[4] However, the SCA has also expanded the pluralism requirement to include pluralism in staffing, *inter alia*, to cover single-member institutions such as ombudspersons:

Where the members and staff of NHRIs are representative of a society's social, ethnic, religious and geographic diversity, the public are more likely to have confidence that the NHRI will understand and be more responsive to its specific needs. Additionally, the meaningful participation of women at all levels is important to ensure an understanding of, and access for, a significant proportion of the population. Likewise, in multilingual societies, the NHRI's capacity to communicate in all languages is key to its accessibility.

The diversity of the membership and staff of an NHRI, when understood in this way, is an important element in ensuring the effectiveness of an NHRI and its real and perceived independence and accessibility.[5]

[3] ibid 20–21 (ellipsis in original).

[4] For example, SCA, 'Report and Recommendations of the Session of the Sub-Committee on Accreditation (SCA)'—Algeria (Commission Nationale Consultative de Promotion et de Protection des Droits de l'Homme (CNCPPDH))' (October 2010) 10 (hereafter, SCA, 'Accreditation Report'); SCA, 'Accreditation Report—Austria (Austrian Ombudsman Board (AOB))' (May 2011) 11; SCA, 'Accreditation Report—Indonesia (Indonesian National Commission on Human Rights (Komnas HAM))' (March 2012) 19.

[5] SCA, 'General Observations' (February 2018) (n 2) GO 1.7, 21.

On the issue of selection and appointments, the SCA elaborates on its importance in creating a pluralistic NHRI:

> Ensuring the integrity and quality of members is a key factor in the effectiveness of the NHRI. For this reason, selection criteria that ensure the appointment of qualified and independent decision-making members should be legislatively established and made publicly available prior to appointment.
>
> The SCA recommends that the adoption of such criteria be subject to consultation with all stakeholders, including civil society, to ensure the criteria chosen is appropriate and does not exclude specific individuals or groups.
>
> The SCA cautions that criteria that may be unduly narrow and restrict the diversity and plurality of the composition of the NHRI's membership and staff body, such as the requirement to belong to a specific profession, may limit the capacity of the NHRI to fulfil effectively all its mandated activities. If staff and members have a diverse range of professional backgrounds, this will help to ensure that issues are not narrowly framed.[6]

In applying the pluralism requirement in practice, the SCA has focused on two issues:

- The requirement for pluralism in membership should be reflected in the law; and
- Ensuring the equitable participation of women in the NHRI.

This section will begin with consideration of the SCA's findings in relation to the requirements for the enabling law, before looking at pluralism in practice and in NHRI staffing.

4.2.1 Pluralism in the Enabling Law

The requirement for pluralism to be reflected in the enabling law of the NHRI has long been an issue of concern to the SCA, which has called for the enabling law specifically to include provisions to ensure pluralism.[7] This is even where the NHRI is pluralistic in practice.[8] As noted above, the requirement for pluralism is broadly

[6] ibid.

[7] SCA, 'Accreditation Report—Luxembourg (Commission Consultative des Droits de l'Homme of Luxembourg (CCDH))' (March 2009) 9; SCA, 'Accreditation Report—Qatar (National Human Rights Committee (NHRC))' (March/April 2010) 15. See also SCA, 'Accreditation Report—Costa Rica (Defensoría de los Habitantes (DHCR))' (November 2016) 20–21; SCA, 'Accreditation Report—Mexico (Comisión Nacional de los Derechos Humanos (CNDH))' (November 2016) 38–39; SCA, 'Accreditation Report—Namibia (Office of the Ombudsman (Ombudsman))' (November 2016) 43–44; SCA, 'Accreditation Report—Philippines (The Commission on Human Rights of the Philippines (CHRP))' (March 2017) 30; SCA, 'Accreditation Report—Nicaragua (Procuraduría para la Defensa de los Derechos Humanos of Nicaragua (PDDH))' (November 2017) 47–48.

[8] For example, the NHRI of Panama the SCA noted that, 'the law does not explicitly require pluralistic composition of the DPRP. However, the SCA recognizes the efforts undertaken by DPRP to address

interpreted by the SCA. In examining the NHRI of Mali in 2012, the SCA specified that the pluralism requirement is not just about particular actors in the country but also about gender, ethnicity, and representation of minorities:

> The founding law specifies that members are to come from a variety of designated groups including civil society, professional associations, trade unions, the judiciary, parliament and government. In determining representation from these groups, consideration must be given to ensuring pluralism in the context of gender, ethnicity or minority status.[9]

The SCA has emphasized that pluralism must be ensured 'particularly with regard to ethnic minorities'.[10] It has gone so far as to recommend the inclusion of specific minority groups within a country.[11] However, pluralism should also not be limited just to specific ethnicities. For the NHRI of Bosnia and Herzegovina, the SCA criticized the provision in the law that required the appointment of ombudspersons from '"the three constituent peoples" that is, Bosniaks, Croats and Serbs' as being insufficient to support 'a broad interpretation of pluralism beyond ethnicity'.[12]

Where there are explicit provisions limiting the participation of one or more ethnic or other groups, this is likely to be fatal to the NHRI obtaining A-status. In its review of the NHRI of the Maldives in 2010, the SCA noted that the enabling law 'continues to provide that all members of the Commission must be Muslim' and called for the clause to be removed due to its discriminatory nature.[13] The NHRI was accredited with B-status, with this issue being central to that decision.[14]

pluralism including that it reports that out of the twelve (12) current directors, seven (7) are women, and that out of the eleven (11) regional branches chiefs, eight (8) are women'. Nonetheless, it encouraged the NHRI to propose amendments to its enabling law. SCA, 'Accreditation Report—Panama (The Defensoría del Pueblo de la República de Panamá (DPRP))' (November 2017) 24. See also SCA, 'Accreditation Report—Guatemala (Procurador de los Derechos Humanos (PDH))' (May 2018) 24; SCA, 'Accreditation Report—Moldova (The Office of the People's Advocate of Moldova (OPA))' (May 2018) 26; SCA, 'Accreditation Report—Nicaragua (PDDH)' (May 2018) 32; SCA, 'Accreditation Report—Spain (The Defensor del Pueblo of Spain (DPS))' (May 2018) 34; SCA, 'Accreditation Report—Sri Lanka (The Human Rights Commission of Sri Lanka (SLHRC))' (May 2018) 37.

[9] SCA, 'Accreditation Report—Mali (Commission Nationale des Droits de l'Homme (CNDH))' (March 2012) 12.

[10] SCA, 'Accreditation Report—Croatia (Ombudsman of the Republic of Croatia (ORC))' (April 2008) 7–8.

[11] In reviewing Burundi, November 2012, the SCA noted that the Batwa minority group was not represented in the staff of the NHRI. SCA, 'Accreditation Report—Burundi (Independent National Human Rights Commission of Burundi))' (November 2012) 7–8. See also, SCA, 'Accreditation Report—India (The National Human Rights Commission of India (NHRCI))' (November 2017) 18: 'It encourages the NHRCI to continue these efforts, in particular by ensuring that diversity of Indian society is represented including, but not limited to, Dalits and other religious or ethnic minorities.'

[12] SCA, 'Accreditation Report—Bosnia and Herzegovina (Institution of Human Rights Ombudsmen of Bosnia and Herzegovina (IHROBH))' (November 2012) 11.

[13] SCA, 'Accreditation Report—Maldives (Human Rights Commission of the Maldives (HRCM))' (March/April 2010) 6.

[14] The NHRI was invited to apply for re-accreditation once these issues had been addressed. At time of writing, this had not taken place.

The concept of pluralism should not however be limited solely to ethnicity. For the NHRI of Macedonia, the Ombudsman's Act required 'an adequate and equitable representation of citizens belonging to all the communities in the Republic of Macedonia' and where Deputy Ombudspersons 'currently include ethnic Macedonians and Albanians'. The SCA emphasized that pluralism, 'in the context of Paris Principles, refers to broader representation of Macedonian society, not just ethnicity'.[15] The SCA has also specified that pluralism includes persons with disabilities as a distinct category of persons who should be represented in the NHRI.[16]

However, the SCA has come up against the issue of NHRIs not being permitted, by reason of national equality laws, particularly in the European Union (EU), to undertake diversity hiring. It has recommended amendments to NHRI laws in these circumstances.[17] The issue for the SCA is that, while there are many situations where the law does not permit inquiry as to a person's 'background', the law could nonetheless provide for self-identification and encourage the hiring of persons from diverse backgrounds. Thus, the SCA is not taking issue with the laws per se but rather that the law should still find appropriate ways to provide that an NHRI be required to have a pluralistic composition in its membership and staff.

4.2.2 Pluralism in Practice

The enabling law should require pluralism, but pluralism should also be implemented in practice.[18] Even where the enabling law is Paris Principles-compliant in requiring gender parity, for example, as in the case of Myanmar, the SCA will also consider whether the NHRI's practice is compliant.[19]

Efforts by the NHRI in this regard should be clear. The SCA has paid particular attention to issues of gender equality in leadership and staff since it began

[15] SCA, 'Accreditation Report—Macedonia (Ombudsman of the Republic of Macedonia (ORM))' (October 2011) 9.

[16] SCA, 'Accreditation Report—Poland (Human Rights Defender (HRD))' (November 2012) 22, and SCA, 'Accreditation Report—Poland (HRD)' (November 2017) 27.

[17] For example, the NHRI of Poland reported to the SCA that it was 'prohibited by law from inquiring about citizens' ethnic, religious or other background, but reports that its staff is inclusive of members of these groups'. SCA, 'Accreditation Report—Poland (HRD)' (November 2017) 28.

[18] SCA, 'Accreditation Report—Qatar (NHRC)' (November 2015) 37: 'The decree law does not require pluralism in the membership of the NHRC. The SCA notes that, at present, only three (3) of the thirteen (13) NHRC members are women.' This contrasts with SCA, 'Accreditation Report—Serbia (Protector of Citizens (PCRS))' (March 2015) 23: 'The Law does not require pluralism in the membership of the PCRS. However, the SCA notes that, at present, two of the four current Deputies of the Protector of Citizens are women and one is from a national minority . . . While the SCA notes that the PCRS indicated that its membership reflects the diversity of Serbian society, the SCA encourages the PCRS to advocate for the inclusion of provisions in its enabling law to ensure diversity in its membership and staff.'

[19] SCA, 'Accreditation Report—Myanmar (Myanmar National Human Rights Commission (MNHRC))' (November 2015) 12: 'while section 7(c) of the enabling law requires equitable representation of men and women, at present only two (2) of the eleven (11) NHRC members are women'.

its reviews. In recent years, it has been increasingly critical of disparities in representation on the board and in the leadership and executive structure.[20] For the NHRI of Afghanistan, the SCA welcomed specific provisions in the enabling law requiring the representation of women in its membership, as well as the adoption of a specific gender policy:

> The SCA notes with appreciation the AIHRC's efforts to improve gender balance, in particular by:
> - the inclusion of a provision in the presidential decree requiring that 4 of its 9 members must be women;
> - the adoption of a Gender Policy to promote greater gender equity and opportunities for advancement.
>
> [The SCA] encourages the AIHRC to continue to accord priority to its gender initiatives and to take the necessary practical steps to implement its new Gender Policy.[21]

Conversely, in its 2012 review of the Indonesia NHRI (Komnas HAM), the SCA criticized the NHRI for having only one woman on the governing body, an issue it had previously raised with the institution:

> During the 2007 review of Komnas HAM, the SCA expressed concern about lack of pluralism in the governing body, in particular, the low representation of women. The representation of women remains low with only one in the current governing body. The SCA is therefore not satisfied that Komnas HAM has taken sufficient action to address the concerns raised in 2007.[22]

By the institution's 2017 review, this issue had been somewhat rectified, with four out of thirteen members being women, and representation of eight ethnic groups, earning praise from the SCA.[23] Similarly, the SCA welcomed an initiative by the NHRI of Liberia which reported it would aim to hire 60 per cent women in its future recruitment efforts.[24]

[20] SCA, 'Accreditation Report—Côte d'Ivoire (La Commission Nationale des Droits de l'Homme de Côte d'Ivoire (CNDHCI))' (May 2016) 14: 'The SCA notes that women are not sufficiently represented in the CNDHCI's different bodies. For example, in the Executive Bureau 7 of 22 members and 13 of 43 staff are women.'

[21] SCA, 'Accreditation Report—Afghanistan (Afghanistan Independent Human Rights Commission (AIHRC))' (October 2014) 1617. The SCA also referred to Paris Principles B.2 and General Observations 2.4 on 'Recruitment and retention of NHRI staff'.

[22] SCA, 'Accreditation Report—Indonesia (Komnas HAM)' (March 2012) 19. See also, SCA, 'Accreditation Report—Burundi (INHRCB)' (November 2012) 7–8.

[23] SCA, 'Accreditation Report—Indonesia (Komnas HAM)' (March 2017) 25.

[24] SCA, 'Accreditation Report—Liberia (Independent National Commission on Human Rights (INCHR))' (March 2017) 8.

Tokenistic gestures, however, are not sufficient to meet the gender equality requirement. The NHRI of Niger reported to the SCA that representation of women on its governing body was guaranteed because one of the members was from a women's rights organization.[25] This was regarded as insufficient and compounded by the low level of female representation among the NHRI's staff (27 per cent).[26]

The NHRI of India's (National Human Rights Commission—NHRCI) efforts in practice to promote pluralism were similarly considered by the SCA to be insufficient:

> The SCA further acknowledges the NHRCI's position that the presence of 'deemed members' from the National Commissions addressing caste, women's rights, minorities, scheduled tribes, and children's rights—two (2) of whom are women—on the statutory full commission contributes to the pluralism of the NHRCI. However, the SCA notes that the NHRCI reported that the member from the National Commission on scheduled castes rarely attends full statutory commission meetings and that the SCA has received information from civil society organizations indicating that the other deemed members similarly rarely attend meetings where decisions on the focus, priorities and core business of the NHRCI's non-judicial functions are made. Accordingly, the SCA remains of the view that this method of ensuring pluralism is insufficient.
>
> Finally, the SCA notes that the NHRCI reports that, of its 468 staff, 92 (20%) are women. The SCA is accordingly of the view that the NHRC has not taken the necessary steps to ensure pluralism of its institution through its staff complement.[27]

Re-accreditation of the NHRCI at the time was deferred a year until November 2017, when the SCA noted that the institution had taken some limited steps to improve the gender balance in its membership and staff:

> With respect to its membership, the SCA notes that a woman was appointed in April 2017, and that the NHRCI has advocated for changes to its Act to increase the number of members and provide that one (1) be a woman. The SCA notes, however, that the proposed amendment has not been adopted, and that having only one (1) member who is a woman does not represent appropriate gender balance. It encourages the NHRCI to continue to advocate for changes to its enabling law to provide for appropriate gender balance in the composition of its membership.

[25] SCA, 'Accreditation Report—Niger (Commission Nationale des Droits Humains (CNDH))' (March 2017) 12.
[26] ibid.
[27] SCA, 'Accreditation Report—India (NHRCI)' (November 2016) 24.

> With respect to its staff, the SCA notes the efforts made by the NHRCI in recent appointments to increase the representation of women, as well as the gender sensitization programme it organized for its staff in July 2017 in collaboration with APF. It encourages the NHRCI to continue these efforts, in particular by ensuring that diversity of Indian society is represented including, but not limited to, Dalits and other religious or ethnic minorities.[28]

Despite the limited nature of the improvements, the SCA considered that the NHRI's actions were sufficient to prevent it being at risk from downgrading to B-status on this basis.

4.2.3 Pluralism in Staffing

As noted above, the SCA has expanded on the Paris Principles' requirement regarding pluralism to include staff, finding that '[a] diverse staff facilitates the NHRI's appreciation of, and capacity to engage on all human rights issues affecting the society in which it operates, and promotes the accessibility of the NHRI for all citizens'.[29] Pluralism in staffing as a distinct issue featured in thirty-four SCA reviews from 2007 to 2019.

In its November 2008 examination of the German NHRI (German Institute for Human Rights (GIHR)), the SCA stressed 'the importance of ensuring pluralism at all levels in the GIHR on a more permanent and formal basis and in a manner distinct from the length of the contracts of the staff in particular with regard to gender balance and ethnic diversity'.[30] The SCA also called for the staff of the NHRI of the Kyrgyz Republic to be representative of the society and for this to be reflected in the law, as well as for the NHRI to 'develop policies and procedures to ensure that staff representation is broad and pluralistic'.[31]

The requirement for pluralism in staffing is emphasized by the SCA as particularly important for single-member institutions such as ombudspersons.[32]

[28] SCA, 'Accreditation Report—India (NHRCI)' (November 2017) 17–18.

[29] SCA, 'Accreditation Report—Peru (The Defensoria del Pueblo del Peru (DPP))' (March 2012) 23. See also, SCA, 'Accreditation Report—Hungary (Commissioner for Fundamental Rights (CFR))' (November 2013) 12.

[30] SCA, 'Accreditation Report—Germany (GIHR)' (November 2008) 7. See also, SCA, 'Accreditation Report—Luxembourg (CCDH)' (November 2008) 8.

[31] SCA, 'Accreditation Report—Kyrgyz Republic (The Ombudsman of the Kyrgyz Republic (OKR))' (March 2012) 10–11.

[32] See for example the following SCA Accreditation Reports: SCA, 'Accreditation Report—Tajikistan (The Human Rights Ombudsman of the Republic of Tajikistan (HROT))' (March 2012) 15; SCA, 'Accreditation Report—Colombia (The Defensoria Del Pueblo of Colombia (DPC))' (March 2012) 18; SCA, 'Accreditation Report—Peru (DPP)' (March 2012) 24; SCA, 'Accreditation Report—Azerbaijan (The Human Rights Commissioner (Ombudsman) of the Republic of Azerbaijan (HRCA))' (March 2012) 30; SCA, 'Accreditation Report—Panama (DPP)' (November 2012) 21. See also re: diversity in staffing in the enabling law: SCA, 'Accreditation Report—Cyprus (Commissioner for Administration

As also noted above, the SCA has gone so far as to recommend the inclusion of specific societal groups in the staff of the NHRI,[33] and requires gender parity in staffing.[34] Where efforts are made by the NHRI to promote gender equality in staffing, such as in the case of Panama's NHRI, where seven out of twelve directors and eight out of eleven regional branch chiefs were women, the SCA has expressed particular appreciation.[35]

4.3 Criteria for NHRI Members and Leadership

In keeping with the concept of pluralism discussed in the previous section, the SCA also requires that the criteria for membership of the board or other leadership are not unduly restrictive or onerous. For example, the SCA has found that a requirement of a doctorate for the leadership of an NHRI may 'unduly limit the pool of candidates from which he or she can be chosen'.[36] Similarly, it has expressed concern where the eligibility requirement in the enabling law is limited to lawyers.[37] However, the SCA did not express its concern regarding the requirement for ten years' experience 'as a lawyer, a judge or a university professor of legal sciences', only expressing concern for the doctorate requirement.[38]

One of the more challenging cases as regards the leadership of the NHRI has been in relation to the NHRI of India (NHRCI), whose leadership pool was extremely narrowly drawn. The enabling law required that the Commission consist of:

and Human Rights (CAHR))' (November 2015) 9–10; SCA, 'Accreditation Report——Honduras (National Commissioner for Human Rights (CONADEH))' (May 2016) 20–21; SCA, 'Accreditation Report—Mexico (CNDH)' (November 2016) 39; SCA, 'Accreditation Report—Namibia (Office of the Ombudsman (Ombudsman))' (November 2016)' (November 2016) 43–44; SCA, 'Accreditation Report—Nicaragua (PDDH)' (November 2016) 47; SCA, 'Accreditation Report—Georgia (The Office of the Public Defender (OPD))' (October 2018) 10; SCA, 'Accreditation Report—Timor-Leste (Provedoria dos Direitos Humanos e Justica (PDHJ))' (October 2018) 16; SCA, 'Accreditation Report—Haiti (Office de la Protection du Citoyen (OPC))' (March 2019) 26.

[33] In reviewing Burundi, November 2012, the SCA noted that the Batwa minority group was not represented in the staff of the NHRI. SCA, 'Accreditation Report—Burundi (INHRCB)' (November 2012) 7.

[34] See SCA, 'Accreditation Report— Côte d'Ivoire (CNDHCI)' (May 2016) 14; SCA, 'Accreditation Report—Niger (CNDH)' (March 2017) 12; SCA, 'Accreditation Report—Liberia (INCHR)' (March 2017) 8–9.

[35] SCA, 'Accreditation Report—Panama (DPRP)' (November 2017) 24.

[36] SCA, 'Accreditation Report—Ecuador (Defensoría del Pueblo de Ecuador (DPE))' (March 2015) 16: 'In accordance with Article 216 of the Constitution, the Defensor must 1) hold a Doctorate of Law from a recognized university and 2) have at least 10 years' experience as a lawyer, a judge or a university professor of legal sciences.'

[37] SCA, 'Accreditation Report—Ghana (The Commission on Human Rights and Administrative Justice (CHRAJ))' (March 2019) 21. This issue was also raised with Ghana in its 2014 periodic review. In the 2018 review, the SCA noted that a proposed amendment would remove this provision.

[38] SCA, 'Accreditation Report—Ecuador (DPE)' (March 2015) 16.

a) a Chairperson who has been a Chief Justice of the Supreme Court;
b) one member who has been a Judge of the Supreme Court;
c) one member who has been Chief Justice of the High Court;
d) two members amongst persons having knowledge of, or practical experience in, matters relating to human rights.[39]

The SCA reiterated its previously expressed concerns from 2006 and 2011, that 'the requirement that the Chair be a former Chief Justice of the Supreme Court and the majority of members be recruited from the senior judiciary severely restricts the potential pool of candidates, particularly as it relates to the representation of women in the governing body of the NHRCI'.[40] The SCA did not accept the stated justification for the requirement—that the NHRI had a quasi-judicial function—as this was just one of the ten functions for the NHRI set out in the enabling law, and that legislation provided the possibility for the appointment of 'two members amongst persons having knowledge of, or practical experience in, matters relating to human rights, who are not required to be chosen from the judiciary'. Furthermore, the SCA noted that no women had been appointed to any of the positions on the governing body of the NHRI since 2004.[41]

A similarly restrictive requirement was introduced into the enabling law of the NHRI of Rwanda:

> According to Article 11.5 of the law, 'for a person to be a commissioner, he or she shall fulfil the following: "be experienced in administration or was once an administrator"'. It understands that such a requirement is interpreted to mean that only a person who is or was in the Government administration becomes eligible to be a commissioner.[42]

This requirement was part of the reason for the SCA to recommend downgrading the NHRI to B-status, a fate avoided by the NHRI when changes were made to the selections and appointments process by May 2013.[43]

Thus, limiting provisions in enabling laws on who can be chosen to lead the NHRI have been a cause of concern for the SCA, including requirements that the ombudsperson 'be graduated lawyers who have passed the bar exam and have had a distinguished career of at least 10 years in the legal profession',[44] or that they

[39] SCA, 'Accreditation Report—India (NHRCI)' (November 2016) 24. See also, discussion on India's NHRI in Section 4.4.
[40] SCA, 'Accreditation Report—India (NHRCI)' (November 2016) 24.
[41] ibid.
[42] SCA, 'Accreditation Report—Rwanda (The National Commission for Human Rights of the Republic of Rwanda (NCHR))' (March 2012) 27.
[43] SCA, 'Accreditation Report—Rwanda (NCHR)' (May 2013) 16.
[44] SCA, 'Accreditation Report—Bosnia and Herzegovina (IHROBH)' (November 2012) 11–12.

must be lawyers.[45] The SCA noted that the only provision for leadership of the NHRI of Zambia provided in the enabling law was that 'the Chairperson and Vice-Chairperson shall be persons who have held, or are qualified to hold, high judicial office', absent further detail.[46] Similarly, requirements in the Philippines that 'the Chairman and members must be Philippine citizens at least 35 years of age who were not candidates for any elective positions immediately preceding their appointment, and a majority must be members of the Philippine Bar' were also considered by the SCA as insufficiently broad (in addition to lacking other necessary features to ensure a broad selection and appointment process).[47] However, a proposal expanding the merit criteria 'to include a requirement to have a deep and comprehensive knowledge of, and practical experience for at least ten (10) years on human rights protection, promotion and policy advocacy' was considered as acceptable.[48] A draft amendment to the law of the NHRI of Egypt, providing that 'members should be selected from among public figures well-known for their experience, the independence of their opinion, and distinguished performance in the field of human rights' and provisions requiring the advertising of vacancies 'to allow concerned authorities relating to human rights to propose candidates and to ensure pluralism' were also considered sufficient by the SCA.[49]

The enabling law must be clear as to the requirements for membership of the board. The NHRI of Qatar was to comprise seven members from civil society representatives and four from government ministries. The law indicated that the civil society representatives should have interest and experience in human rights but was 'otherwise silent on the process and criteria used to determine the suitability of applicants'.[50] This same concern had been raised in 2009, however the NHRI was re-accredited with A-status in 2015, despite no change in the enabling law (the NHRI had, however, formed its own nomination committee).[51] The enabling law must contain details on the criteria to be used for the identification and evaluation of candidates.[52]

[45] SCA, 'Accreditation Report—Macedonia (ORM)' (October 2011) 9–10. See also, SCA, 'Accreditation Report—Liberia (INCHR)' (March 2017) 9: 'In accordance with article 9(4) of the Act, the Chairperson shall be a senior lawyer who has demonstrated excellence and a commitment to human rights and the rule of law. The Act is silent on the merit criteria for Commissioners.' This point was examined under General Observation 1.8 on selections and appointment.

[46] SCA, 'Accreditation Report—Zambia (Human Rights Commission (HRCZ))' (November 2016) 56; SCA, 'Accreditation Report—Zambia (HRCZ)' (October 2018) 19. This point was examined under General Observation 1.8 on selections and appointment.

[47] SCA, 'Accreditation Report—Philippines (CHRP)' (March 2017) 30–31. This point was examined under General Observation 1.8 on selections and appointment.

[48] ibid 30.

[49] SCA, 'Accreditation Report—Egypt (NCHR)' (March 2017) 35.

[50] SCA, 'Accreditation Report—Qatar (NHRC)' (November 2015) 37.

[51] ibid.

[52] SCA, 'Accreditation Report—Georgia (OPD)' (October 2018) 10–11.

Criteria for leadership should be clear and uniform. The SCA criticized the appointment procedure for the Great Britain NHRI, the Equalities and Human Rights Commission (EHRC), which had the following process:

> In accordance with paragraph 1(1) of Schedule 1 of the Act, the Secretary of State shall appoint members of the EHRC. Paragraph 2(1) provides that an individual may be appointed if he or she (i) has experience or knowledge relating to a relevant matter (discrimination or human rights) or (ii) is suitable for appointment for some other special reason, having regard to the desirability of the Commissioners together having experience and knowledge relating to relevant matter (discrimination or human rights).[53]

The SCA commented that this was not sufficiently broad and transparent, including a lack of clear and uniform criteria to assess the merit of candidates, particularly regarding the criterion of 'some other special reason', which the SCA considered as 'not sufficiently defined ... and ... open to abuse'.[54]

As regards the criteria for membership, as was noted above, the SCA requires a merit-based appointments process. Merit in this case relates to human rights-relevant experience or qualifications.[55] The SCA has stated that membership of parliament or a political party are not in themselves relevant criteria for selection of the governing body.[56] In reviewing selection and appointment processes the SCA has also emphasized the need for merit-based selection,[57] and that there should be some educational or human rights experience prescribed in the law, an issue closely aligned with questions of pluralism.[58]

The SCA has also been critical where the requirements for the head of the executive restrict pluralism, such as where the head must be a civil servant.[59]

[53] SCA, 'Accreditation Report—Great Britain (EHRC)' (November 2015) 18–19.

[54] ibid 19.

[55] SCA, 'Accreditation Report—Afghanistan (AIHRC))' (November 2013) 17, noting, '[t]he AIHRC law provides that the President should consider a limited set of qualifications for potential members of the Commission (Article 11) but it does not otherwise provide any details on the process for seeking candidates, or their subsequent assessment, selection and appointment. Members, including the Chairperson, are therefore appointed largely at the discretion of the President of the Republic. Information before the SCA indicated that recent appointments have been the subject of national and international criticism regarding the suitability of some appointees and their compliance with the criteria in Article 11 of the AIHRC law, particularly the requirement for practical experience in human rights'.

[56] SCA, 'Accreditation Report—Egypt (National Council for Human Rights (NHCR))' (May 2013) 10. This issue closely connects to concerns regarding the actual perceived independence of the NHRI, as noted by the SCA in that instance. ibid.

[57] SCA, 'Accreditation Report—Kazakhstan (The Commissioner for Human Rights (CHR))' (March 2012) 8; SCA, 'Accreditation Report—Philippines (CHRP)' (March 2012) 25.

[58] SCA, 'Accreditation Report—Kyrgyz Republic (OKR)' (March 2012) 10. See also, SCA, 'Accreditation Report—Denmark (DIHR)' (November 2012) 13, where the SCA remarked that 'the enabling law does not specify the eligibility criteria to become a member of the Board'.

[59] SCA, 'Accreditation Report—Macedonia (ORM)' (October 2011) 10.

Finally, it may be noted that the in the context of the requirement of pluralism also extends to 'ensuring representation of different segments of society and their involvement in suggesting or recommending candidates to the governing body'.[60] This is discussed further below in Section 4.4 on the selection and appointment process.

4.3.1 Political Representatives on the NHRI Decision-making Body

The issue of political representatives on boards or leadership of NHRIs is one that the SCA has been concerned with since its creation. Political representation goes to the heart of the requirement of independence of the NHRI from the government. The progress of the SCA's general observations on this issue illustrate that it is an area where the SCA has been strengthening its position. In 2009, the SCA's General Observation provided:

> Government representatives on National Institutions: The Sub-Committee understands that the Paris Principles require that Government representatives on governing or advisory bodies of National Institutions do not have decision making or voting capacity.[61]

The SCA's 2013 General Observations elaborated on these requirements, and there was a further additional paragraph (below, italics) added in its 2017 and 2018 revisions:

> General Observation 1.9 Political representatives on NHRIs
>
> The SCA notes that the Paris Principles require an NHRI to be independent from government in its structure, composition, decision-making and method of operation. It must be constituted and empowered to consider and determine the strategic priorities and activities of the NHRI based solely on its determination of the human rights priorities in the country, free from political interference.
>
> For these reasons, government representatives and members of parliament should not be members of, nor participate in, the decision-making of organs of an NHRI. Their membership of, and participation in, the decision-making body of the NHRI has the potential to impact on both the real and perceived independence of the NHRI.

[60] SCA, 'Accreditation Report—Malaysia (National Human Rights Commission of Malaysia (SUHAKAM))' (April 2008) 5.

[61] SCA, 'ICC Sub-Committee on Accreditation General Observations' (adopted in June 2009) GO 2.3.

The SCA recognizes that it is important to maintain effective working relationships, and where relevant, to consult with government. However, this should not be achieved through the participation of government representatives in the decision-making body of the NHRI.

Where government representatives or members of parliament, or representatives of government agencies, are included in the decision-making body, the NHRI's legislation should clearly indicate that such persons participate only in an advisory capacity. In order to further promote independence in decision making, and avoid conflicts of interest, an NHRI's rules of procedure should establish practices to ensure that such persons are unable to inappropriately influence decision-making by, for example, excluding them from attending parts of meetings where final deliberations and strategic decisions are made.

The participation of government representatives or members of parliament, or representatives of government agencies, should be restricted to those whose roles and functions are of direct relevance to the mandate and functions of the NHRI, and whose advice and cooperation may assist the NHRI in fulfilling its mandate. In addition, the number of such representatives should be limited and should not exceed the number of other members of the NHRI's governing body.[62]

The added paragraph particularly aims to address the argument that having such representatives on the NHRI would be beneficial to the institution. While the Paris Principles do not directly reference this issue, the SCA notes the importance to several elements of an NHRI's operation in its justification for this General Observation:

Paris Principle C(a) states that an NHRI must be able to 'freely consider any question falling within its competence'.

Paris Principle B.2 states that the requirement of an appropriate infrastructure is intended to ensure the NHRI is 'independent of the government'.

Paris Principle B.3 requires that members of an NHRI are appointed officially, thereby promoting a stable mandate 'without which there can be no real independence'.

Paris Principle B.1 specifically provides that representatives of government departments can participate 'only in an advisory capacity'.[63]

[62] SCA, 'General Observations' (February 2018) (n 2) GO 1.9, 24. The paragraph beginning 'Where government representatives . . .' was added in 2017: SCA, 'General Observations of the Sub-Committee on Accreditation' (adopted in March 2017) GO 1.9, 29 (hereafter SCA, 'General Observations' (March 2017)).

[63] SCA, 'General Observations' (February 2018) (n 2) GO 1.9, 24–25.

The SCA further elaborated on why this issue is so critical to independence:

> By clearly promoting independence in the composition, structure and method of operation of an NHRI, these provisions seek to avoid any possible interference in the NHRI's assessment of the human rights situation in the State and the subsequent determination of its strategic priorities. It follows therefore that members of parliament, and especially those who are members of the ruling political party or coalition, or representatives of government agencies, should not in general be represented on, nor should they participate in decision making, since they hold positions that may at times conflict with an independent NHRI.
>
> The SCA acknowledges the value in developing and maintaining effective links with relevant ministers and government agencies, particularly where cooperation will assist in promoting the NHRI's mandate. However, it stresses that this must be done in a way that ensures both real and perceived independence of decision making and operation, and avoids a conflict of interest. The creation of Advisory Committees is an example of a mechanism where such relationships can be maintained without impacting on the NHRI's independence.
>
> The SCA notes that Paris Principle B.1 specifically states that representatives of government agencies have only an advisory role, while no such restriction is explicitly stated in relation to representatives of parliament. It notes, however, that in providing an indicative list of relevant stakeholders, Paris Principle B.1 envisages either the "presence" or the ability to establish "effective cooperation" with such representatives. Given the explicit requirements for independence stated throughout the Paris Principles, examples of which are referenced above, the SCA is of the view that a similar restriction must apply to members of parliament, and particularly those who are members of the ruling political party or coalition.
>
> Excerpt from the Paris Principles
>
> B) Composition and guarantees of independence and pluralism—
>
> 1. The composition of the national institution and the appointment of its members, whether by means of an election or otherwise, shall be established in accordance with a procedure which affords all necessary guarantees to ensure the pluralist representation of the social forces (of civilian society) involved in the promotion and protection of human rights, particularly by powers which will enable *effective cooperation to be established with, or through the presence of*, representatives of:
>
> ...
>
> (d) Parliament
>
> (e) Government departments (if these are included, their representatives *should participate in the deliberations only in an advisory capacity*).
>
> 2. The national institution shall have an infrastructure which is suited to the smooth conduct of its activities, in particular adequate funding. The purpose

> of this funding should be to enable it to have its own staff and premises, in order to be independent of the Government and not be subject to financial control which might affect its independence.
> 3. In order to ensure a stable mandate for the members of the national institution, without which there can be no real independence, their appointment shall be effected by an official act which shall establish the specific duration of the mandate. This mandate may be renewable, provided that the pluralism of the institution's membership is ensured.[64]

A number of NHRIs received recommendations from the SCA because of political representation on the board. The SCA's views on this as expressed in its reports have evolved over time, as was seen in the evolution of the general observations above. For the SCA, 'political representatives' refers to both government representatives and parliamentarians.[65] The SCA has raised concerns repeatedly with Germany's NHRI, where there were both government and parliamentary representatives on the governing body. This concern was raised in 2008, and again in November 2013, by which time the SCA's recommendations had developed closer to a 'ban' on political representatives on the governing body. In the SCA's 2015 review the issue had not only not resolved itself but had deteriorated with the retention of voting rights for the members of the German parliament and an increase in the number of government representatives.[66]

The SCA expects that the NHRI will seek changes to remove voting rights of political representatives.[67] Reviewing the NHRI of Qatar in 2009, the SCA noted that legislative amendments had increased the number of civil society representatives and removed voting rights for government representatives.[68] This seems to have been sufficient for the SCA at the time as despite the continuation of this situation,

[64] SCA, 'General Observations' (February 2018) (n 2) GO 1.9, 25–26 (emphasis in original).

[65] SCA, 'Accreditation Report—Germany (GIHR)' (November 2008) 7: 'While article 24(2) of the GIHR's Statute provide that the German Government's representatives on the Board of the Trustees have no voting rights, article 24(1) indicates that two of the GIHR's Trustees must be members of the German's Bundestag's Committee on Human Rights and Humanitarian Aid. The Statute does not exclude these representatives from voting on decisions made by the Board of Trustees.' See also, SCA, 'Accreditation Report—Chad (Commission National des Droits de l'Homme (CNDH))' (November 2009) 7.

[66] SCA, 'Accreditation Report—Germany (GIHR)' (November 2015) 15–16.

[67] SCA, 'Accreditation Report—Slovakia (National Centre for Human Rights (SNCHR))' (March 2014) 9. The NHRI had one member of Parliament on its administrative board, who also had voting rights, and the SCA called for the NHRI to advocate for changes to its governance structure to remove voting rights. See also, SCA, 'Accreditation Report—Jordan (National Centre for Human Rights (JNCHR))' (November 2015) 23 and SCA, 'Accreditation Report—Jordan (JNCHR)' (November 2016) 30. For Bahrain, four members of the Council of Commissioners were sitting parliamentarians and two, including the Chair, were members of the Shura Council whose members are directly appointed by the King. SCA, 'Accreditation Report—Bahrain (National Institution for Human Rights (NIHRB))' (May 2016) 9; SCA, 'Accreditation Report—Mauritania (Commission Nationale des droits de l'homme (CNDH))' (November 2016) 34.

[68] SCA, 'Accreditation Report—Qatar (NHRC)' (March 2009) 4.

with four members from government ministries on the Commission, the SCA in its November 2015 review of the NHRI, did not raise the issue directly.[69]

Where a majority of members of a governing body are from the government, an NHRI is unlikely to receive A-status.[70] The NHRI of Greece had not addressed the SCA's concerns regarding voting rights for members of parliament on the governing body in the year between two reviews of the NHRI, with proposed amendments being insufficient as the parliamentary representatives retained their voting rights.[71] The SCA therefore recommended the NHRI be downgraded to B-status, with the required one-year notice. The NHRI avoided being downgraded and was re-accredited with A-status. After the one-year review, as the SCA noted the actions taken by the NHRI included amendments to its laws and that 'the proposed amendments and other actions taken fully address the SCA's concerns with respect to political representatives on NHRIs, full-time members, and annual reports'.[72]

The Cameroon NHRI was also recommended to make changes to its governance structure to remove voting rights from parliamentary representatives.[73] The NHRI of Côte d'Ivoire had two members of the NHRI who were parliamentarians, and six were representatives of government departments. While the latter participated in an advisory capacity, the parliamentarians had voting rights. In that instance, the

[69] SCA, 'Accreditation Report—Qatar (NHRC)' (November 2015) 36–38.

[70] See SCA, 'Accreditation Report—Oman (Oman National Human Rights Commission (ONHRC))' (November 2013) 12: 'The Royal Decree provides for the appointment of 14 commissioners out of which 2 are members of parliament and 6 are government officials. All have voting rights, and together are in the majority on the governing body.'

[71] SCA, 'Accreditation Report—Greece (Greek National Commission for Human Rights (GNCHR))' (March 2015) 30: 'The membership of the GNCHR includes the President of the Special Parliamentary Committee on Institutions, representatives of the political parties recognized in accordance with the Regulations of Parliament, and representatives of various Ministries. While Article 2(5) of the Law specifies that the representatives of the Ministries do not have voting rights, the President of the Special Parliamentary Committee and representatives of political parties do have voting rights. In addition, in accordance with Article 2(4) of the Law, the President of the Special Parliamentary Committee is eligible to be elected as President or Vice President of the GNCHR.' SCA, 'Accreditation Report—Greece (GNCHR)' (May 2016) 35: 'The SCA notes that the legislative amendment would make the President of the Special Parliamentary Committee on Institutions and Transparency ineligible for election as President or Vice President of the GNCHR. However, the SCA is of the view that this amendment does not sufficiently address its stated concerns as, during the review, the GNCHR confirmed to have one representative from Parliament with voting rights ... The SCA encourages the GNCHR to advocate for the necessary changes in its Law to ensure that representatives of political parties, including the President of the Special Parliamentary Committee, have no voting rights.'

[72] SCA, 'Accreditation Report—Greece (GNCHR)' (March 2017) 23.

[73] SCA, 'Accreditation Report—Cameroon (National Commission on Human Rights and Freedoms (NCHRF))' (March 2015) 35: 'In accordance with section 6 of the Law, four members of the NCHRF are Members of Parliament, two are representatives of the Senate, and four are representatives of government departments in charge of social affairs, justice, penitentiary affairs and women's affairs, respectively. The SCA notes that, while the representatives of government departments participate only in an advisory capacity, the Members of Parliament and representatives of the Senate have full rights, including voting rights ... The SCA encourages the NCHRF to advocate for the necessary changes in its governance structure to ensure that Members of Parliament and representatives of the Senate do not have voting rights.' See also, India's NHRI, where the Chairperson of the National Commission for Scheduled Castes was a Member of Parliament and had voting rights in the full statutory commission. SCA, 'Accreditation Report—India (NHRCI)' (November 2016) 27.

NHRI was accredited with B-status, although it may be noted that there were nine other issues of concern with the Côte d'Ivoire institution.[74]

The enabling law must also be sufficiently clear on this point. For Niger, the enabling law stated that membership of the NHRI included two members appointed by the National Assembly with voting rights.[75] The NHRI assured the SCA that these were not political representatives but rather experts appointed by parliament, though it had nonetheless proposed that these members not have voting rights. The SCA considered that the law was insufficiently clear.[76]

Overall, the SCA seems to be uncomfortable with any political representatives on NHRIs but recognizes that this is a reality for some countries. Thus, the presence of political representatives on boards will not in and of itself be fatal, however they should not have voting rights. With regards to political representation on the NHRI, the SCA views it in the context of the NHRI overall. Recognizing the potential for political representation on the governing body to impact the independence and perceived independence of the NHRI, the SCA has developed its recommendations in this area over time, strengthening them to the point where it strongly recommends that no political representatives are on a board. In terms of its impact on an NHRI's status, it seems that where there is a majority of political or governmental representation, such as in the cases of Oman and Bahrain, the SCA will take a particularly strong line.

4.3.2 State Body Representation on the NHRI Decision-making Body

In some instances, other national bodies may have a representative on the NHRI decision-making body. In the case of the Malawi NHRI, the Malawi Human Rights Commission (MHRC), it was not political representatives but other national bodies on the board that raised concerns for the SCA. In March 2012, the SCA stated:

> The Law Commissioner and the Ombudsman are ex officio members of the MHRC, however the Constitution is silent on whether they have voting rights. In addition, the SCA notes that the Law Commissioner and the Ombudsman

[74] SCA, 'Accreditation Report— Côte d'Ivoire (CNDHCI)' (May 2016) 13. See also, SCA, 'Accreditation Report—Algeria (CNDH)' (May 2018) 16, where two members of the NHRI were parliamentarians with voting rights. Further, the law of the NHRI did not specify that holding of elected office was only incompatible with membership of the NHRI (it specified this only for the President of the institution and not for the other members). See also, SCA, 'Accreditation Report—Madagascar (Commission Nationale Indépendante des Droits de l'Homme (CNIDH))' (March 2019) 8.

[75] SCA, 'Accreditation Report—Niger (CNDH)' (March 2017) 13.

[76] ibid.

> constitute the selection committee for membership of the MHRC. Together, these two elements may impact on the independence, or perceived independence of the MHRC.[77]

In its November 2012 review, the SCA elaborated on its concerns:

> The MHRC reports that the Law Commissioner and Ombudsman are, like the MHRC Commissioners, independent statutory office holders and that there [*sic*] involvement has not compromised the objectivity and transparency of its operations. However, the SCA emphasizes that the Paris Principles require that the institution function independently, and both the Ombudsman and the Law Commissioner have statutory functions that must take precedence over the functions of the MHRC. Should the Law Commissioner and the Ombudsman remain members of the governing board, they should do so in an advisory capacity only.[78]

The re-accreditation of the NHRI was deferred to November 2013 due to the ongoing process of adopting the NHRI legislation, however the SCA acknowledged the 'extensive efforts' made by the NHRI to address its recommendations.[79] The accreditation was deferred again in 2014 and 2015, due to the ongoing legislative process. The issue of voting rights of the law commissioner and ombudsperson was one of the issues that was tabled for amendment by the Malawi government.[80] When the NHRI was re-accredited with A-status in November 2016, the voting rights had been removed for both the ombudsperson and law commissioner.[81]

4.4 Selection and Appointment of the Decision-making Body

One of the most significant areas of criticism and frequent areas for recommendation by the SCA is in relation to the selection and appointment process of the decision-making body of the NHRI. This issue received the largest number of interventions from 2008 to 2019, with 174 reviews mentioning this issue. The very first set of General Observations, adopted in 2006, contained an observation on selection and appointment process:

> The Sub-Committee notes the critical importance of the selection and appointment process of the governing body in ensuring the pluralism and independence

[77] SCA, 'Accreditation Report—Malawi (Malawi Human Rights Commission (MHRC))' (March 2012) 22 (re-accreditation deferred).

[78] SCA, 'Accreditation Report—Malawi (MHRC)' (November 2012) 19.

[79] SCA, 'Accreditation Report—Malawi (MHRC)' (November 2013) 23.

[80] SCA, 'Accreditation Report—Malawi (MHRC)' (May 2016) 42.

[81] SCA, 'Accreditation Report—Malawi (MHRC)' (November 2016) 31.

of the National Institution. In particular, the Sub-Committee emphasizes the following factors:

a) A transparent process
b) Broad consultation throughout the selection and appointment process
c) Advertising vacancies broadly
d) Maximizing the number of potential candidates from a wide range of societal groups
e) Selecting members to serve in their own individual capacity rather than on behalf of the organization they represent.[82]

While these five basic criteria have remained, reflecting the increasingly rigorous requirements the SCA places on the accreditation process, since the 2013 General Observations the SCA has formulated a detailed justification for the selection and appointment of the decision-making body of NHRIs. The 2018 General Observations provide as follows:

G.O. 1.8 Selection and appointment of the decision-making body of NHRIs
It is critically important to ensure the formalisation of a clear, transparent and participatory selection and appointment process of the NHRI's decision-making body in relevant legislation, regulations or binding administrative guidelines, as appropriate. A process that promotes merit-based selection and ensures pluralism is necessary to ensure the independence of, and public confidence in, the senior leadership of an NHRI. Such a process should include requirements to:

a) Publicize vacancies broadly;
b) Maximize the number of potential candidates from a wide range of societal groups;
c) Promote broad consultation and/or participation in the application, screening, selection and appointment process;
d) Assess applicants on the basis of pre-determined, objective and publicly available criteria; and
e) Select members to serve in their own individual capacity rather than on behalf of the organization they represent.[83]

In its justification for this General Observation, the SCA refers to Paris Principle B.1 in support of its approach, and provides considerable detail on the rationale for these requirements:

[82] SCA, 'Accreditation Report' (October 2006) para 6.4. See also, SCA, 'General Observations' (June 2009) (n 61) GO 2.3, contained in SCA, 'Accreditation Report' (March 2009) Annex II, 26–31.
[83] SCA, 'General Observations' (February 2018) (n 2) 22.

Section B.1 of the Paris Principles specifies that: 'The composition of the national institution and the appointment of its members, whether by means of *an election or otherwise*, shall be established in accordance with *a procedure which affords all necessary guarantees to ensure the pluralist representation* of the social forces (of civilian society) involved in the promotion and protection of human rights.'

Section B.1 further enumerates which groups may be included in this process. These are 'representatives of:

(a) Non-governmental organizations responsible for human rights and efforts to combat racial discrimination, trade unions, concerned social and professional organizations, for example, associations of lawyers, doctors, journalists and eminent scientists;
(b) Trends in philosophical or religious thought;
(c) Universities and qualified experts;
(d) Parliament;
(e) Government departments (if these are included, their representatives should participate in the deliberations only in an advisory capacity).'

The SCA interprets the reference to an election or other like process, together with the reference to broad participation, as requiring a clear, transparent, merit-based and participatory selection and appointment process.

Such a process is fundamental in ensuring the independence and effectiveness of, and public confidence in, the NHRI.

For this reason, it is important that the selection process be characterized by openness and transparency. That is, it should be under the control of an independent and credible body and involve open and fair consultation with NGOs [non-governmental organizations] and civil society. Not only is this a means of developing a good relationship with these bodies, but consideration of the expertise and experience of NGOs and civil society is likely to result in an NHRI with greater public legitimacy.

Advertising vacancies broadly maximises the potential number of candidates, thereby promoting pluralism.

Promoting broad consultation and participation in the application, screening, selection and appointment process promotes transparency, pluralism and public confidence in the process, the successful candidates and the NHRI.

The assessment of applicants on the basis of pre-determined, objective and publicly available criteria promotes the merit-based appointment of candidates, limits the capacity for undue interference in the selection process, and serves to ensure the appropriate management and effectiveness of the NHRI.

Selecting members to serve in their own individual capacity rather than on behalf of the organization they represent is likely to result in an independent and professional membership body.

It is recommended that the selection and appointment process, bearing the hallmarks described above, be formalized in relevant legislation, regulations or binding administrative guidelines, as appropriate.

Excerpt from the Paris Principles

B) Composition and guarantees of independence and pluralism—

1. The composition of the national institution and the appointment of its members, whether by means of an election or otherwise, shall be established in accordance with a procedure which affords all necessary guarantees to ensure the pluralist representation of the social forces (of civilian society) involved in the promotion and protection of human rights, particularly by powers which will enable effective cooperation to be established with, or through the presence of, representatives of:

(a) Non-governmental organizations responsible for human rights and efforts to combat racial discrimination, trade unions, concerned social and professional organizations, for example, associations of lawyers, doctors, journalists and eminent scientists;
(b) Trends in philosophical or religious thought;
(c) Universities and qualified experts;
(d) Parliament;
(e) Government departments (if these are included, their representatives should participate in the deliberations only in an advisory capacity).[84]

There is necessarily some overlap as regards the selection and appointment process with other areas, such as pluralism, previously described, the terms and conditions of the head of the NHRI, and security of tenure. This section focuses primarily on the SCA's recommendations on the technical and practical requirements of the selection and appointment process. This can be broken down further into the following areas, each of which has its own sub-section in this chapter:

1. Formalization of the appointment process in the enabling law (Section 4.4.1);
2. Content of the selection and appointment process (Section 4.4.2);
3. Composition of the selection panel (Section 4.4.3);
4. Nominations (Section 4.4.4);
5. Appointment by government (Section 4.4.5);
6. Extension of term outside of normal limits (Section 4.4.6).

[84] SCA, 'General Observations' (February 2018) (n 2) 22–24.

4.4.1 Formalization of Selection and Appointment Process in the Enabling Law

A frequent recommendation by the SCA is that detailed provisions on the selection and appointment process be reflected in the enabling law,[85] with particular emphasis on transparency, broad consultation, and 'participation of diverse societal forces'.[86] Where this does not exist, the NHRI should advocate for changes to its legislation.[87] The selection and appointment process should not be simply by way of 'internal regulatory document'[88] but must be set out in the enabling law or some other formal instrument.[89] As stated in the General Observation, where the process is formalized in 'regulations or binding administrative guidelines', this is sufficient.[90]

Provisions on the selection and appointment process should also be permanent, rather than temporary measures,[91] and not be subject to a requirement that they be re-issued for each appointment process.[92]

[85] See for example, SCA, 'Accreditation Report—El Salvador (Procuraduría para la Defensa de los Derechos Humanos (PDDH))' (November 2016) 22; SCA, 'Accreditation Report—Liberia (Independent National Commission on Human Rights (INCHR))' (March 2017) 9–10; SCA, 'Accreditation Report—Egypt (NCHR)' (May 2018) 21; SCA, 'Accreditation Report—Nicaragua (PDDH)' (May 2018) 31; SCA, 'Accreditation Report—Argentina (The Defensor del Pueblo de la Nación Argentina (DPNA))' (October 2018) 23; SCA, 'Accreditation Report—Paraguay (Defensoría del Pueblo de Paraguay (DPP))' (March 2019) 10–11; SCA, 'Accreditation Report—Finland (Finnish National Human Rights Institution (FNHRI))' (October 2019)' (October 2019) 9–10; SCA, 'Accreditation Report—Honduras (CONADEH)' (October 2019) 12–13; SCA, 'Accreditation Report—Togo (La Commission Nationale Des Droits De L'homme Du Togo (CNDH))' (October 2019) 18; SCA, 'Accreditation Report—Hungary (CFR)' (October 2019) 24–25; SCA, 'Accreditation Report—Russia (High Commissioner for Human Rights in the Russian Federation (OCHR))' (October 2019) 28–29.

[86] SCA, 'Accreditation Report—Guatemala (PDH)' (May 2013) 14.

[87] See for example, SCA, 'Accreditation Report—Georgia (OPD)' (May 2013)12–13; SCA, 'Accreditation Report—Haiti (OPC)' (May 2013) 8.

[88] SCA, 'Accreditation Report—Luxembourg (CCDH)' (March 2009) 9.

[89] SCA, 'Accreditation Report—Mauritania (CNDH)' (November 2009) 4; SCA, 'Accreditation Report—Belgium (Centre for Equal Opportunities and Opposition to Racism (CEOOR))' (March/April 2010) 11; SCA, 'Accreditation Report—Switzerland (Federal Commission against Racism (FCR))' (March/April 2010) 12; SCA, 'Accreditation Report—Congo (Commission Nationale des Droits de l'Homme (CNDH))' (October 2010) 4.

[90] SCA, 'Accreditation Report—El Salvador (PDDH)' (May 2011) 13; SCA, 'Accreditation Report—New Zealand (New Zealand Human Rights Commission (NZHRC))' (May 2011) 17; SCA, 'Accreditation Report—Netherlands (Netherlands Institute for Human Rights (NIHR))' (March 2014) 7.

[91] See SCA, 'Accreditation Report—Indonesia (Komnas HAM)' (March 2017) 25–26: 'In accordance with article 83(1) of the Law, the members of Komnas HAM are selected by the House of Representatives based on the recommendation of Komnas HAM and validated by the President. The SCA notes that, in accordance with article 86 of the Law, Komnas HAM has issued Regulation 3/2016 on the Establishment of a Selection Committee for Komnas HAM Members. However, the SCA notes that this process is applicable only to the 2017–2022 selection process and is not a permanent addition to Komnas HAM's regulatory framework.'

[92] SCA, 'Accreditation Report—Panama (DPRP)' (November 2017) 24–25: 'In accordance with article 6(2) of the Law, the Ombudsperson is appointed by an absolute majority vote of the National Assembly, based on the recommendation of the Human Rights Commission. The DPRP reports that, in 2016, the Human Rights Commission issued a Selection Regulation to make the process more transparent and consultative, including by requiring that vacancies be advertised in the media and on

The formalization of the selection and appointment process should be provided in law even where practice indicates a process is more closely aligned to the requirements of the Paris Principles.[93] This includes where a process is in practice conducted openly and transparently.[94] For the NHRI of Spain, the Defensor del Pueblo of Spain (DPS), for example, it was insufficient that vacancies were not formally advertised even though the DPS reported that 'the public is aware that the selection process will take place as a result of media attention surrounding the expiration of the term of the Defensor'.[95] Similarly for Sri Lanka's NHRI (SLHRC), even though vacancies were made 'online and in national newspapers' the SCA recommended that there be a specific requirement in the law regarding advertising.[96]

In reviewing the NHRI of South Africa in 2017, the SCA noted that the process was not based on any formal instrument:

a) Section 193 (5) of the Constitution stipulates that the National Assembly must recommend persons (a) nominated by a committee of the Assembly proportionally composed of members of all parties represented in the Assembly. However, the process of attaining the names of appointees does not appear to

the National Assembly website. It further reports that, in practice, candidates are interviewed by the Human Rights Commission in a publicly-broadcast interview on the National Assembly's television channel, and that citizens and civil society are free to participate. The SCA notes, however, that the regulation has not been provided to the SCA and that the DPRP reports that a new regulation is issued each time there is a selection and appointment process.'

[93] SCA, 'Accreditation Report—New Zealand (NZHRC)' (May 2016) 42–43: 'In accordance with section 28(1)(b) of the Crown Entity Act (CEA) Commissioners are appointed by the Governor General on the recommendation of the Minister. The SCA acknowledges that the NZHRC reports that, in practice, positions are advertised, applications from interested parties and nominations from members of Parliament are sought, an independent panel interviews short-listed candidates, and advice is provided to the Minister of Justice. However, the SCA is of the view that the process currently enshrined in the Law is not sufficiently broad and transparent. In particular, it does not:—require the advertisement of vacancies; or—promote broad consultation and / or participation in the application, screening, selection and appointment process'. See also, SCA, 'Accreditation Report—Zimbabwe (Human Rights Commission (ZHRC))' (May 2016) 22; SCA, 'Accreditation Report—Canada (Canadian Human Rights Commission (CHRC))' (May 2011) 12; SCA, 'Accreditation Report—Egypt (NCHR)' (May 2018) 21; SCA, 'Accreditation Report—Nicaragua (PDDH)' (May 2018) 31; SCA, 'Accreditation Report—Argentina (DPNA)' (October 2018) 23; SCA, 'Accreditation Report—Paraguay (DPP)' (March 2019) 10–11; SCA, 'Accreditation Report—Armenia (The Human Rights Defender of the Republic of Armenia (HRDA))' (March 2019) 14–15.

[94] SCA, 'Accreditation Report—Scotland (Scottish Human Rights Commission (SHRC))' (March 2015) 17–18. In that instance, the process was via 'a selection panel consisting of the convener of the most relevant Committee of the Scottish Parliament and between four and seven other Members of Parliament makes a recommendation on the appointment. Further, in accordance with paragraph 1(3) of Schedule 1 of the Act, the other members of the SHRC are appointed by the Scottish Parliamentary Corporate Body, which is chaired by the Presiding Officer of the Scottish Parliament and consist of four other Members of Parliament drawn from government and the opposition parties.' ibid 17. See also, SCA, 'Accreditation Report—Norway (Norwegian National Human Rights Institution (NNHRI))' (March 2017) 15. See also on recommendations on the content of the enabling law: SCA, 'Accreditation Report—Uganda (The Uganda Human Rights Commission (UHRC))' (May 2018) 39.

[95] SCA, 'Accreditation Report—Spain (DPS)' (May 2018) 33.

[96] SCA, 'Accreditation Report—Sri Lanka (SLHRC)' (May 2018) 36. See also, SCA, 'Accreditation Report—Bulgaria (Ombudsman of the Republic of Bulgaria (ORB))' (March 2019) 16–17.

be stipulated in any legal document, although the information indicates that a consultative process including a nation-wide announcement of the vacancies is undertaken and that an ad hoc committee to consider nominations received from the public and interviews of candidates is established, which are then submitted in a shortlist to the National Assembly.

b) Section 193 of the Constitution stipulates that civil society may be involved in the recommendation process of members of the Commission but the exact role of civil society is not defined in any legislation.

c) The SAHRC Act S. 5(1)(a)(i) states the minimum criteria for the appointment of SAHRC Commissioners.

While acknowledging that the process reportedly used in recent appointments was clear, transparent and participatory, the SCA notes that the process is not formalized in legislation, regulation, or in a binding administrative guideline.[97]

The law containing the selection and appointment process should be sufficiently detailed to ensure that qualified candidates are selected, and to remove the possibility of the process being overly discretionary,[98] although the criteria for selecting candidates should also not be overly restrictive, as noted in Chapter 4.3. The SCA has also made it clear that NHRIs are expected to pursue legislative amendments to ensure a Paris Principles-compliant process.[99]

The method of public consultation should be explicitly provided for in the enabling law 'or another binding regulation', and include NGOs and civil society.[100] It should not just be a matter of practice.[101] Vacancies must be advertised and the law

[97] SCA, 'Accreditation Report—South Africa (South African Human Rights Commission (SAHRC))' (November 2017) 31. See also, SCA, 'Accreditation Report—Denmark (Danish Institute for Human Rights (DIHR))' (November 2017) 39: 'In accordance to Section 3 (2) of the Act, the Board is comprised of thirteen (13) members who are appointed in their personal capacity by various authorities. Six are appointed by the Council of Human Rights, four by the Rectors of various universities, two by the Conference of Rectors under Universities Denmark and one elected by the employees of the DIHR. Further, Section 5 of the Act provides that the Council of Human Rights is composed to reflect the prevailing views among civil society organizations working in the field of human rights, following a public announcement. The law is otherwise silent on the selection and appointment process. The SCA took note that the Council of Human Rights of the DIHR has decided to change its appointment procedure and now publishes vacancies, calls for candidates amongst its membership, and that its chairmanship recommends six board members for the Council's approval. However, the SCA notes that this process is not formalized in the DIHR's legislation, in regulation, or in another binding administrative guideline.'

[98] SCA, 'Accreditation Report—Afghanistan (AIHRC)' (November 2013) 17: 'Members, including the Chairperson, are therefore appointed largely at the discretion of the President of the Republic.'

[99] SCA, 'Accreditation Report—Morocco (Conseil Consultatif des Droits de l'Homme (CCDH))' (October 2010) 13.

[100] SCA, 'Accreditation Report—Mexico (CNDH)' (November 2016) 38. See also, SCA, 'Accreditation Report—Peru (DPP)' (March 2017) 27–28; SCA, 'Accreditation Report—Bulgaria (ORB)' (March 2019) 16–17.

[101] SCA, 'Accreditation Report—Bahrain (NIHRB)' (May 2016) 7: 'In accordance with article 5 of the Law, members of the Council of Commissioners are appointed by Royal Decree in consultation with relevant civil society organizations and various other groups. While the NIHRB reports that it calls for an open meeting with civil society organizations in addition to conducting private consultations,

must specify the process for ensuring consultation.[102] Consultation should not be indirect, so, for example, with regard to the process for the NHRI of Guatemala, the SCA made the following recommendations in 2018:

> With respect to the involvement of civil society in the parliamentary process for selecting the Procurador, the SCA is of the view that this involvement should be direct rather than through members of parliament. This could be achieved, for example by:
> - directly soliciting proposals from civil society; or
> - allowing civil society to directly participate in the evaluation process.[103]

It is insufficient for public consultation to be limited to a public presentation in front of the legislature where members of parliament can ask questions.[104]

Transparency in the process is also critical. For the NHRI of B-status Oman, appointments were made by the Sultan and not advertised publicly, nor was the process transparent.[105] The NHRI of Malaysia was praised for positive steps to promote transparency:

> Vacancies were published in various Malay and English newspapers in Peninsular Malaysia and the States of Sabah and Sarawak, as well as on official websites. In addition, letters were sent to over 70 organisations from a wide variety of civil society organisations inviting them to nominate qualified candidates for the positions.[106]

the Law is otherwise silent on the process for selection and appointment of members of the Council of Commissioners. The SCA is of the view that the process currently enshrined in the Law is not sufficiently broad and transparent. In particular, it does not: require the advertisement of vacancies; establish clear and uniform criteria upon which all parties assess the merit of eligible applicants; and specify the process for achieving broad consultation and/or participation in the application, screening, selection and appointment process.' See also, SCA, 'Accreditation Report—Ghana (CHRAJ)' (March 2019) 22–23; SCA, 'Accreditation Report—Haiti (OPC)' (March 2019) 26; SCA, 'Accreditation Report—Nepal (National Human Rights Commission of Nepal (NHRCN))' (March 2019) 28; SCA, 'Accreditation Report—Ukraine (Ukrainian Parliament Commissioner for Human Rights (UPCHR))' (October 2019) 21–22.

[102] SCA, 'Accreditation Report—Nigeria (National Human Rights Commission (NHRC))' (November 2016) 48. See also on advertising: SCA, 'Accreditation Report—Democratic Republic of Congo (CNDH)' (May 2018) 13–14.

[103] SCA, 'Accreditation Report—Algeria (CNDH)' (May 2018) 15. Similar recommendations were made to Croatia: SCA, 'Accreditation Report—Croatia (ORC)' (March 2019) 18; SCA, 'Accreditation Report—Ukraine (UPCHR)' (October 2019) 21–22.

[104] SCA, 'Accreditation Report—Russia (OCHR)' (October 2019) 28–29.

[105] SCA, 'Accreditation Report—Oman (ONHRC)' (November 2013) 13. See also, SCA, 'Accreditation Report—Nepal (NHRCN)' (October 2014) 37–38; Hungry, SCA, 'Accreditation Report—Hungary (CFR)' (October 2014) 9–10.

[106] SCA, 'Accreditation Report—Malaysia (SUHAKAM)' (November 2015) 29. However, the SCA remained concerned about the process. See also on transparency; SCA, 'Accreditation Report—Moldova (OPA)' (May 2018) 26.

The SCA clearly expects that its recommendations will be followed by the NHRI. For example, a recommendation was made in 2008 to the Russian NHRI to ensure a transparent appointment process. However, by its 2013 re-accreditation review, no progress had been made, and the SCA deferred consideration for twelve months.[107] In October 2014, the SCA noted that the NHRI had initiated an open and transparent process that involved civil society consultations. Due to its efforts, the NHRI was re-accredited with A-status, despite the fact that the process in the enabling law failed to:

- require the advertisement of vacancies for Commissioners;
- establish clear and uniform criteria upon which all nominating parties assess the merit of eligible applicants; and
- promote broad consultation and/or participation in the application, screening, selection and appointment process.[108]

Related to this, the SCA takes a particularly positive view of the NHRI's commitment to the Paris Principles where there are concerted efforts to make improvements to the existing selection and appointment provisions. For the NHRI of Afghanistan (Afghanistan Independent Human Rights Commission (AIHRC)), the SCA commended its 'response to SCA recommendations made in November 2013, including its successful advocacy for a Presidential Decree establishing a merit-based selection and appointment process for Commissioners, and increased funding from the government'.[109] In that instance, a Presidential Decree in September 2014 formalized a process that established a pluralistic selection committee to 'undertake a competency-based review of all applicants' and nominate twenty-seven qualified candidates 'taking into consideration diversity in terms of ethnicity, language, gender and origin of living', at least half of whom were to be women, from which the President would select nine, at least four of whom were to be women.[110]

Paris Principles-compliant provisions should also be made for the appointment of deputy ombudspersons.[111] Under the law of the NHRI of Timor-Leste (PDJH), the head of the institution (*Provedor*) had the power to appoint two or more deputies for renewable periods of four years 'on the basis of transparent and objective criteria, giving consideration, notably, to their integrity, independence, impartiality and qualifications'. This in itself was insufficient, but the PDHJ developed a

[107] SCA, 'Accreditation Report—Russia (OCHR)' (November 2013) 25.
[108] SCA, 'Accreditation Report—Russia (OCHR)' (October 2014) 31.
[109] SCA, 'Accreditation Report—Afghanistan (AIHRC)' (October 2014) 16.
[110] ibid 16–17.
[111] SCA, 'Accreditation Report—Bolivia (Defensoría del Pueblo (DPB))' (March 2017) 19, where the law provided that deputy ombudspersons were selected by the Ombudsperson and ratified by the senate, without further detail. See also SCA, 'Accreditation Report—El Salvador (PDDH)' (November 2016) 22.

binding administrative guideline 'establishing the procedures regarding appointment criteria for the Deputies' and this was considered sufficient for the purposes of Paris Principles compliance. Nonetheless, the SCA recommended that the provisions be put into the enabling law.[112]

4.4.2 Content of the Selection and Appointment Process

Since its early reviews (2006–2009), the SCA had recommended a 'clear and transparent' appointment and dismissal process,[113] which should be in the 'founding legal documents'.[114] The consultation process should be 'broad and formal',[115] include the public,[116] civil society,[117] and 'vulnerable groups'.[118] The selection process should also be consultative.[119] The appointment process should be transparent,[120] and 'based on a broad advertisement of the vacancy'.[121] Part of the requirement for transparency was that the appointment process be formalized in the enabling legislation.[122] The government should not have the exclusive authority to nominate members without consultation,[123] nor should the ultimate selection and appointment of members be with the state.[124] The SCA was particularly concerned about any efforts to reform the appointment process that were not aimed at enhancing independence, transparency, and effectiveness.[125]

The SCA has been consistent in its recommendations on the selection and appointment process, and after the adoption of revised General Observations in March 2009, the five requirements set out in General Observation 1.8 in the introduction to this Section became standard in the recommendations on selection and

[112] SCA, 'Accreditation Report—Timor-Leste (PDHJ)' (October 2018) 17.
[113] SCA, 'Accreditation Report—Algeria (CNCPPDH)' (April 2008) 4.
[114] SCA, 'Accreditation Report—Malaysia (SUHAKAM)' (April 2008) 5.
[115] SCA, 'Accreditation Report—Mauritius (National Human Rights Commission (NHRC))' (April 2008) 6. See also, SCA, 'Accreditation Report—Korea (National Human Rights Commission (NHRCK))' (November 2008) 10.
[116] SCA, 'Accreditation Report—Korea (NHRCK)' (November 2008) 10.
[117] SCA, 'Accreditation Report—Mongolia (National Human Rights Commission (NHRC))' (November 2008) 9. See also, SCA, 'Accreditation Report—Korea (NHRCK)' (November 2008) 10; SCA, 'Accreditation Report—Malaysia (SUHAKAM)' (March 2009) 10.
[118] SCA, 'Accreditation Report—Thailand (National Human Rights Commission (NHRC))' (November 2008) 10–11.
[119] SCA, 'Accreditation Report—Sri Lanka (SLHRC)' (March 2009) 5.
[120] SCA, 'Accreditation Report—Russia (OCHR)' (November 2008) 5. See also, SCA, 'Accreditation Report—Albania (People's Advocate (PA))' (November 2008) 6; SCA, 'Accreditation Report—Mongolia (NHRC)' (November 2008) 9; SCA, 'Accreditation Report—Sri Lanka (SLHRC)' (March 2009) 5.
[121] SCA, 'Accreditation Report—Albania (PA)' (November 2008) 6. See also, SCA, 'Accreditation Report—Korea (NHRCK)' (November 2008) 10, requiring 'public advertisement'.
[122] SCA, 'Accreditation Report—Ireland (Irish Human Rights Commission (IHRC))' (November 2008) 7–8.
[123] SCA, 'Accreditation Report—Luxembourg (CCDH)' (November 2008) 8.
[124] SCA, 'Accreditation Report—Algeria (CNCPPDH)' (March/April 2010) 6–7.
[125] SCA, 'Accreditation Report—Afghanistan (AIHRC)' (November 2008) 11.

appointment process.[126] As noted in Section 4.4.1, the SCA frequently makes the recommendation for their inclusion in the enabling law. The SCA has also made it clear that the appointing authority should utilize the Paris Principles in the selection process.[127] The requirements for transparent, participatory, and pluralistic processes set out in legislation or other instrument have remained a key point of emphasis for the SCA,[128] including in particular the need for consultation with civil society,[129] that is clearly set out[130] and in a sufficient level of detail.[131] The process should also be public.[132]

An interesting and rare example where the SCA did not recommend any changes to NHRI legislation—suggesting that it found it Paris Principles compliant—was for the NHRI of Samoa, where the draft legislation specified the following:

> Section 7 and 8 of the Act provide that the Head of State may appoint a person recommended by the Legislative Assembly as the Ombudsman.
>
> The process is set out in Schedule 3 of the Act is as follows:
>
> - the Government is responsible to advertise the position in a newspaper having wide circulation in Samoa when the position of Ombudsman becomes vacant;
> - an independent Screening Committee, comprising the Chairperson of the Public Service Commission, a retired judge/lawyer and a representative of civil society groups is established to review applicants;
> - the Screening Committee considers applications based on a detailed set of specific and general criteria set out in the law and prepares a short list;
> - the Committee sends a report to the Legislative Assembly including the Committee's opinion on suitable candidates;
> - the Legislative Assembly considers the report and makes a recommendation to the Head of State.

[126] See for example, SCA, 'Accreditation Report—Switzerland (Commission fédérale pour les questions féminines (CFQF))' (March 2009) 6; SCA, 'Accreditation Report—Ukraine (UPCHR)' (March 2009) 7.

[127] SCA, 'Accreditation Report—Ecuador (DPE)' (March 2009) 9.

[128] See for example, SCA, 'Accreditation Report—Senegal (Comité Sénégalais des Droits de l'homme (CSDH))' (May 2011) 23; SCA, 'Accreditation Report—Bulgaria (ORB)' (October 2011) 7; SCA, 'Accreditation Report—Bulgaria (Commission for Protection against Discrimination of the Republic of Bulgaria (CPD))' (October 2011) 9; SCA, 'Accreditation Report—Egypt (NCHR)' (October 2011) 13–14; SCA, 'Accreditation Report—Zambia (HRCZ)' (October 2011) 19; SCA, 'Accreditation Report—Senegal (CSDH)' (October 2011) 21; SCA, 'Accreditation Report—Malawi (MHRC)' (November 2012) 18; SCA, 'Accreditation Report—Spain (DPS)' (November 2012) 27; SCA, 'Accreditation Report—South Africa (SAHRC)' (November 2012) 29; SCA, 'Accreditation Report—Germany (GIHR)' (November 2015) 14–15.

[129] SCA, 'Accreditation Report—Costa Rica (DHCR)' (October 2011) 13; SCA, 'Accreditation Report—Poland (HRD)' (November 2012) 22–23.

[130] SCA, 'Accreditation Report—Spain (DPS)' (November 2012) 27.

[131] SCA, 'Accreditation Report—Mali (CNDH)' (March 2012) 12: 'The founding law does not specify a process by which nominating organisations are to seek or assess applicants.'

[132] SCA, 'Accreditation Report—Myanmar (MNHRC)' (November 2015) 11.

The SCA notes that the process provided by the Act has not yet been implemented in practice as the current Ombudsman was appointed before the enactment of the Act. It encourages the full application of these provisions when future vacancies arise.[133]

4.4.3 Composition of the Selection Panel

As noted in Section 4.4.2, the requirement for representation from a diverse section of society extends to the composition of the selection panel.[134] Even prior to its detailed formalization in revised General Observations in 2013, the SCA raised concerns about the composition of selection panels, for example in the case of Bangladesh where the committee was 'primarily comprised of government appointees and the quorum requirements would appear to allow nominations solely by those members'.[135] The process for Thailand's NHRI, the National Human Rights Commission of Thailand (NHRCT), was criticized by the SCA for having a selection panel composed 'exclusively . . . of officials from a small number of public institutions'.[136] Proposed reforms to create a seven-member panel composed of judges, parliamentarians, and two other persons selected by the Supreme Court and Administrative Court were also considered insufficient as they failed to provide for a sufficiently broad and diverse panel.[137] The SCA deferred consideration of A-status re-accreditation for six months. At the subsequent review in March 2014, re-accreditation was again deferred as the new draft law had not yet been approved by parliament, with the SCA noting its concern regarding the lack of a transparent and participatory process.[138] In October 2014, the NHRI was downgraded to B-status, in part because of serious concerns by the SCA regarding the appointment process, but primarily because of insufficient efforts by the NHRI (in particular, though the NHRIs failure to act on serious human rights violations and open display of political affiliation by some of its staff appears to have been the determining factor).[139] The NHRI had proposed that the Supreme Court and Administrative Court select two members from civil society. This proposal, however, did not establish a transparent and participatory, merit-based selection in the view of the SCA.[140] At the next review of the NHRI in November 2015, these issues

[133] SCA, 'Accreditation Report—Samoa (Office of the Ombudsman (Ombudsman))' (May 2016) 19–20.

[134] The SCA also highlights the need for the selection process to be pluralistic. SCA, 'Accreditation Report—Great Britain (EHRC)' (November 2008) 4–5.

[135] SCA, 'Accreditation Report—Bangladesh (National Human Rights Commission of Bangladesh (NHRCB))' (May 2011) 7.

[136] SCA, 'Accreditation Report—Thailand (National Human Rights Commission of Thailand (NHRCT))' (November 2013) 27.

[137] SCA, 'Accreditation Report—Thailand (NHRCT)' (November 2013) 28.

[138] SCA, 'Accreditation Report—Thailand (NHRCT)' (March 2014) 17.

[139] SCA, 'Accreditation Report—Thailand (NHRCT)' (October 2014) 32–33.

[140] ibid.

had still not been addressed and the downgrading to B-status was confirmed. The SCA expressed the following concerns regarding the selection process:

- There is no requirement to advertise vacancies on the NHRCT;
- The selection committee established by Section 8(1) of the enabling law is composed of officials from a very small number of public institutions, with no clear representation, or a requirement for consultation with key stakeholder groups or civil society;
- There is no provision for broad consultation and/or participation, in the application, screening and selection process;
- There does not appear to be clear and detailed criteria upon which to assess the merit of eligible applicants.[141]

In May 2013, the SCA recommended a special review of the NHRI of Nepal. One of the issues for discussion was that a constitutional provision required that members of independent constitutional bodies were to be selected by the Constitutional Council of the Prime Minister, Chief Justice, speaker of the legislature and three ministers designated by the Prime Minister.[142] Despite the candidates receiving a public hearing in the parliament, the SCA was still concerned that the process was not clear, transparent, participatory, and promoting merit-based selection.[143] In that examination, the SCA took into account the political situation, noting that 'the current political environment "presented challenges that would likely hamper the selection and appointment of new members ... to replace the existing members whose term[s] were set to expire in 2013"'.[144] The SCA deferred the review to its October 2014 session, by which time five commissioners had been appointed.[145]

A proposed revision to the NHRI law in Cameroon, which provided that 'vacancies be advertised, and for the use of an ad hoc committee in screening candidates' was sufficient to substantially address the previous concerns of the SCA.[146] However, the SCA noted that the ad hoc committee was 'comprised primarily of political representatives, and that the draft law does not specify the process for achieving participation of civil society in the application, screening, selection and appointment process'.[147] For the NHRI of Malawi (MHRC), the SCA expressed

[141] SCA, 'Accreditation Report—Thailand (NHRCT)' (November 2015) 39. This was one of a number of concerns raised about the Thailand NHRI. For more on the NHRI's downgrading, see Chapter 9.2 on challenging cases.
[142] SCA, 'Accreditation Report—Nepal (NHRC)' (May 2013) 23.
[143] ibid.
[144] SCA, 'Accreditation Report—Nepal (NHRC)' (November 2013) 32.
[145] SCA, 'Accreditation Report—Nepal (NHRC)' (October 2014) 37. The commissioners had not been appointed by the deferred review in March 2014, thus the matter was deferred to the October session.
[146] SCA, 'Accreditation Report—Cameroon (NCHRF)' (November 2017) 12.
[147] ibid 13.

concern that 'the role of the Law Commissioner and the Ombudsman as the Selection Committee for members is incompatible with their role as ex officio members of the MHRC'.[148]

Overly political panels have been criticized by the SCA as not meeting the requirements of the Paris Principles. The SCA critiqued the provisions for selection and appointment for the NHRI of India, where recommendations were made by a committee 'consisting of the Prime Minister, the Speaker of the House of the People, the Minister in-charge of the Ministry of Human Affairs in the government of India, the Leader of the Opposition in the House of the People, the Leader of the Opposition in the Council of States, and the Deputy Chairperson of the Council of States'.[149] Despite the NHRI's initiative in changing the law to include advertising of vacancies and 'clear and uniform' assessment criteria, the SCA in November 2017 still found that:

> 1) these proposed changes would not address the previously-stated concerns of the SCA with respect to the requirement that there be broad consultation and/or participation in the application, screening, selection and appointment process, and 2) it is unclear whether the process would be formalized in legislation, regulation, or in another binding administrative guideline.[150]

Similar concerns were raised regarding the NHRI of South Korea. As noted above the SCA had previously expressed concern regarding the process set out in the enabling law, which provided for appointment by the President from '4 persons selected by the National Assembly, 4 persons nominated by the President, and 3 persons nominated by the Chief Justice of the Supreme Court'.[151] The SCA called on the NHRI to advocate for a clear, transparent and merit-based appointment process.[152] In March 2015, the criteria had not been amended, with the SCA noting that the enabling law specified 'very limited eligibility criteria'.[153] However, it commended the NHRI for taking steps to remedy the situation including making recommendations on qualification standards for Commissioners and a broad consultation in the selection process.[154] Despite the SCA's concerns at this point, again the activity and engagement of the NHRI itself was crucial to its retaining A-status, and this is evident in the May 2016 re-accreditation where the SCA commended the NHRI for advocating for improvements to the rules on selections and

[148] SCA, 'Accreditation Report—Malawi (Malawi Human Rights Commission (MHRC))' (March 2012) 21.
[149] SCA, 'Accreditation Report—India (NHRCI)' (November 2016) 25.
[150] SCA, 'Accreditation Report—India (NHRCI)' (November 2017) 18.
[151] SCA, 'Accreditation Report—Korea (NHRCK)' (March 2014) 14.
[152] ibid 14–15.
[153] SCA, 'Accreditation Report—Korea (NHRCK)' (March 2015) 40.
[154] ibid 39.

appointments process and promoting broad participation and consultation during the process.[155]

In the case of the B-status NHRI of Algeria, a selection committee comprising the First President of the Supreme Court, the President of the Council of State, the President of the Court of Auditors, and the President of the National Economic and Social Council, with the role of ensuring that the composition was 'based on criteria of competency, probity, societal and institutional pluralism, as well as representation of women' was not considered sufficiently broad and transparent due to the lack of advertisement of vacancies, lack of clear and uniform criteria for candidates, and lack of broad consultation.[156] In the case of Sri Lanka's NHRI (SLHRC), the SCA noted that recommendations were made to the President from the Constitutional Council, a ten-member body that included the Prime Minister, Speaker of Parliament, Leader of the Opposition, and at least three other members of parliament.[157] The SCA specifically recommended that the SLHRC follow the 2017 recommendations of the UN Special Rapporteur on the independence of judges and lawyers that 'the composition of the Constitutional Council should balance the number of active politicians with representation from civil society, the Bar Association and academia so as to avoid the politicization of the appointment processes', and that the NHRI should publish the criteria used to evaluate candidates.[158]

The creation of selection panels should not be overly complex. The NHRI of Slovakia, the National Centre for Human Rights, which applied for its first accreditation in March 2014, had a particularly complicated appointment process for its administrative board, which comprised members 'selected by nine separate appointing authorities, each of which can define its own selection criteria', and failed to meet the required standard for a clear, transparent, merit-based appointment process, with the institution only receiving B-status.[159] However, the SCA will accept complex processes in certain instances where they result from a complex national system and meet the Paris Principles requirements in practice. So, for example, in the case of the Belgian NHRI there was an arrangement whereby the six constituent parliamentary assemblies designated members, but the process was sufficiently broad and transparent.[160]

The composition of the selection committee must be precise enough to ensure that the panel is Paris Principles compliant in practice. The NHRI of Iraq was appointed by a panel of 'not more than 15 experts representing the Council

155 SCA, 'Accreditation Report—Korea (NHRCK)' (May 2016) 41.
156 SCA, 'Accreditation Report—Algeria (CNDH)' (May 2018) 15.
157 SCA, 'Accreditation Report—Sri Lanka (SLHRC)' (May 2018) 36.
158 ibid.
159 SCA, 'Accreditation Report—Slovakia (SNCHR)' (March 2014) 8–9.
160 SCA, 'Accreditation Report—Belgium (The Interfederal Centre for Equal Opportunity and fight against racism and discrimination (UNIA))' (May 2018) 10–11.

of Representatives, the Council of Ministers, the High Judicial Council, civil society, and the UN Office for Human Rights in Iraq select individuals to be recommended to the Council of Representatives for appointment'.[161] It did not specify how many members from each segment of society should be included in the committee; the possibility was left open for the committee to comprise 'predominantly of government representatives'.[162] Furthermore, the previous selection committee had contained only two representatives of civil society.[163] Similarly for Myanmar, the law required the selection board for the NHRI to comprise 'the Chief Justice of the Union; Minister of Home Affairs; Minister of Social Welfare, Relief and Resettlement; Attorney General; one representative from the Bar Council; two representatives from the Parliament; one representative from the Myanmar Women's Affairs Federation; and two representatives from registered NGOs'.[164] This board then adopted the procedures for nomination and submitted a list of thirty nominees to the President, who 'selects and appoints suitable members, in coordination with the Speakers of both Houses of the Parliament'.[165] The SCA expressed its concern that there were a significant number of members of the government, and no quorum requirement. There were also concerns regarding the practice, where 'the designation of, and process for selection of civil society representatives (in particular from 'registered' civil society organisations) is not sufficient to ensure a transparent and participatory selection process'.[166]

The SCA must also be convinced that any selection panel is independent. For example, in its 2017 review of the NHRI of Mauritania (Commission Nationale des droits de l'homme (CNDH)), the SCA stated:

> The SCA notes that the legislative amendments establish a selection committee comprising CNDH President, one representative of the Mauritanian Bar Association, one law professor of Nouakchott Al Aasriya University and two civil society representatives.
>
> The SCA notes that it has received information from civil society and from the Special Rapporteur on extreme poverty and human rights that the composition of the CNDH, and the absence of an explanation as to why particular organizations have been chosen to nominate members, has resulted in a lack of independence in the decision-making body.
>
> The SCA notes that the CNDH disputes the characterization of its decision-making body as lacking independence and indicates that its selection and appointment process is clear, transparent and participatory.

[161] SCA, 'Accreditation Report—Iraq (High Commission for Human Rights (HCHR))' (March 2015) 7.
[162] SCA, 'Accreditation Report—Iraq (HCHR)' (March 2015) 7.
[163] ibid.
[164] SCA, 'Accreditation Report—Myanmar (MNHRC)' (November 2015) 11.
[165] ibid.
[166] ibid.

> The SCA is of the view that, while the new provisions in the law have addressed some of the concerns raised in November 2016, they are not sufficient to address the substance of its previously-stated concerns, which related to the independence of the selection and appointment process.[167]

The NHRI was recommended by the SCA to be downgraded to B-status in part because of this issue, though as noted previously in the case of Thailand, the main reason for the downgrading was failure to speak out on human rights violations (see Chapter 7.3 and Chapter 9.2). In its October 2018 review of Mauritania, the SCA noted that the CNDH still considered that the existing process was broad and transparent. However, the SCA found that the CNDH 'has not adequately responded to the substance of the SCA's concerns regarding the actual or perceived independence of the members who are selected by the various appointing entities'.[168]

Even where there is provision in the enabling law for a diverse selection committee, the SCA may require specificity in the numbers of each body represented on that committee. For example, in its 2013 review of Rwanda, the SCA noted that the relevant law and presidential decree provided for 'a Selection Committee composed of five members originating from four different entities, i.e. NGOs for the promotion and protection of human rights, the Public Service Commission, Civil Society, and experts with expertise and skills in human rights'.[169] However, the law failed to specify the exact number of representatives from each of these bodies.[170] In this instance, the SCA was clearly concerned about the integrity and independence of the process, recommending to the NHRI to advocate for amendments and noting that:

> There should not be any interference in the NGO consultations and proceedings towards the appointment of their representatives in the Selection Committee and in the NCHR membership.[171]

Further, while having NGOs as part of the selection process is welcomed, there should be broader representation, in line with the identification of specific groups in Paris Principles B1.[172]

167 SCA, 'Accreditation Report—Mauritania (CNDH)' (November 2017) 21–22.
168 SCA, 'Accreditation Report—Mauritania (CNDH)' (October 2018) 26–27.
169 SCA, 'Accreditation Report—Rwanda (NCHR)' (May 2013) 16.
170 ibid.
171 ibid.
172 For example, the members of the NHRI of Luxembourg were to be selected by 'the proposal of an internal selection committee comprised of [*sic*] members of CCDH, and the opinion of an external selection committee comprised of [*sic*] the heads of five (5) non-governmental organizations. The SCA considered 'that it would be preferable for the process also to include greater representation from diverse segments of society, such as those listed in the Paris Principles at B1'. SCA, 'Accreditation Report—Luxembourg (CCDH)' (November 2015) 26.

4.4.4 Nominations

Nominations for leadership and board members by political entities appear to be a relatively common cause for concern for the SCA, as it may go against the broad consultation process. For the NHRI of Georgia, the enabling law provided for candidates to be 'nominated by the President, by parliamentary factions, or by a group of at least 6 parliamentarians who do not belong to any faction', and positions were not advertised broadly, nor was there a consultation process.[173] However, the process in fact included public consultations with civil society and media, and the Public Defender advocated for amendments to address the SCA's recommendations. For Guatemala, the SCA called for a more transparent and consultative process where the head of the NHRI (*Procurador*) was nominated by the congressional Human Rights Commission.[174] For the NHRI of Qatar, where the NHRI considered and proposed new members and this was then referred to the Emir, the legislation did not establish a clear, transparent, and pluralistic nomination process.[175] Thus, particularly at issue, is the *process* that is used, not the fact of nomination by this means per se.

The enabling law must provide for a participatory selection process that promotes merit-based selection. In Haiti, the process was for both chambers of parliament to submit a list of eligible applicants and 'the successful candidate is determined by consensus of the President of the Republic, the President of the Senate and the President of the National Assembly'.[176] However, the SCA expressed concern that the process did not clearly promote participation and merit-based selection.[177] Similarly, where the head of the institution is selected by the legislature from a list of candidates proposed by the President that was not as a result of a broad consultation process, this is not considered sufficient.[178] For the NHRI of Azerbaijan, which was downgraded to B-status in 2017 for its failure to address the human rights situation in the country (see Chapter 10.2.1), the election of an Ombudsperson by parliamentary majority from three candidates proposed by the President was not sufficient to meet Paris Principles requirements.[179] In Mongolia,

173 SCA, 'Accreditation Report—Georgia (OPD)' (November 2012) 16–17.

174 SCA, 'Accreditation Report—Guatemala (PDH)' (May 2013) 14; SCA, 'Accreditation Report—Guatemala (PDH)' (May 2019) 24.

175 SCA, 'Accreditation Report—Qatar (NHRC)' (March 2009) 4–5.

176 SCA, 'Accreditation Report—Haiti (OPC)' (November 2013) 8.

177 ibid.

178 SCA, 'Accreditation Report—Colombia (DPC)' (March 2012) 17–18. The issue arose again at Colombia's re-accreditation in March 2017, 'In accordance with article 281 of the Constitution and article 2 of the Law, the Ombudsperson is elected by the Chamber of Representatives based on a list of three (3) candidates presented by the President. Once the list is received, the Chamber of Representatives holds a public audience before the plenary of the Congress introducing presented candidates.' The SCA recognized the efforts made by the NHRI, and the institution was re-accredited with A-status. SCA, 'Accreditation Report—Colombia (DPC)' (March 2017) 21.

179 SCA, 'Accreditation Report—Azerbaijan (HRCA)' (March 2017) 18–19.

candidates for Commissioners were nominated by the Speaker of the parliament on the basis of proposals from the President, the Parliamentary Standing Committee on Legal Affairs, and the Supreme Court, with parliament taking the decision. However, the SCA's primary concern was the absence of broad consultation and the advertisement of vacancies.[180]

For the NHRI of Australia, the Australian Human Rights Commission (AHRC), the SCA was concerned that despite a detailed appointments process, ultimately the decision rested with a political appointee, who was not required to follow the recommendations set out in guidelines:

> The Guidelines include requirements to advertise vacancies; provide detailed selection criteria; and assess candidates by a panel that includes the independent representative of the [Australian Public Service Commission (APSC)] whose role is to ensure the process is in accordance with the Guidelines. On the completion of the assessment process, the panel determines a pool of suitable candidates and provides a report to the Commissioner of the APSC for endorsement and transmission to the Attorney General. The Attorney-General then writes to the Prime Minister seeking approval for the candidate to be appointed as an AHRC Commissioner by the Governor-General. However, the SCA notes that: if the Attorney-General is not satisfied with the proposed candidates, he or she may unilaterally propose an alternate appointee; and that, in one instance in 2013, the Attorney-General proposed the appointment of a Commissioner without following the merit-based selection process outlined above. Such appointment has the potential to bring into question the legitimacy of the appointees and the independence of the NHRI.[181]

The overall process must be transparent and consultative, whatever the ultimate appointing authority. For the NHRI of Panama, the enabling law provided 'that the Defensor(a) is appointed by the legislature, on the basis of a nomination by its Human Rights Commission and a majority vote of a plenary session of the National Assembly', however the SCA called for a more open, transparent, and inclusive process.[182] A similar provision for the NHRI of Nicaragua was also criticized.[183] In that instance, a provision that 'when a position becomes vacant, the Board of Directors

[180] SCA, 'Accreditation Report—Mongolia (NHRCM)' (November 2013) 23–24. A decision on accreditation was deferred to the following year, where changes advocated by the NHRI were still considered as insufficient to ensure a transparent process as they lacked provision for broad consultation with civil society. SCA, 'Accreditation Report—Mongolia (NHRCM)' (October 2014) 25.

[181] SCA, 'Accreditation Report—Australia (AHRC)' (November 2016) 10–11.

[182] SCA, 'Accreditation Report—Panama (DPP)' (November 2012) 20.

[183] 'Pursuant to Articles 138(9)(d) of the Constitution and 1(2) and 8 of the Law, the Ombudsperson and Deputy Ombudsperson are appointed by 60% majority vote of the Parliament. The enabling laws are otherwise silent on the selection process. The SCA is of the view that the selection process currently enshrined in the existing legislation is not sufficiently broad and transparent.' SCA, 'Accreditation Report—Nicaragua (PDDH)' (November 2016) 46.

requests that the plenary approve a resolution to call for an election, and that this call is published in a media publication with national circulation' was not sufficiently broad or transparent.[184] For the NHRI of Portugal (The Provedor de Justiça (PDJ)), Article 5(1) of the enabling law provided that the *Provedor* is elected by the Parliament with a two-thirds majority of the members present, but the procedure was not sufficiently broad or transparent:

> The SCA acknowledges that the PDJ reports that the selection and appointment process is governed by Parliament's Rules of Procedure, which provide for the ability of groups of between ten (10) and twenty (20) members of parliament to nominate candidates, and for public hearings with the candidates. However, the SCA is of the view that the selection process currently enshrined in the enabling law is not sufficiently broad and transparent. In particular, it does not:
> - require the advertisement of vacancies;
> - establish clear and uniform criteria upon which all parties assess the merit of eligible applicants; and
> - specify the process for achieving broad consultation and/or participation in the application, screening, selection and appointment process.[185]

The nomination process should also not be overly political. For example, for the NHRI of Albania, only candidates supported by at least twenty-eight members of the Parliament were able to be considered,[186] which the SCA was concerned may 'unreasonably exclude otherwise meritorious candidates'.[187] The SCA criticized the process for the appointment of the Commissioner of the Ukraine NHRI which provided that candidates were to be proposed by the Chairman of the Parliament or 'no less than one-fourth of People's Deputies'. Such an appointment was considered as unreasonably excluding otherwise meritorious candidates.[188]

Where nominations are put forward by a number of different bodies, challenges can arise in ensuring the necessary Paris Principles-compliant process is undertaken. There should also be uniformity in the nomination process where there are a number of nominating bodies.[189] The process must still be clear, participatory,

[184] SCA, 'Accreditation Report—Nicaragua (PDDH)' (November 2017) 46.

[185] SCA, 'Accreditation Report—Portugal (The Provedor de Justiça (PDJ))' (November 2017) 29–30.

[186] SCA, 'Accreditation Report—Albania (PA)' (November 2013) 20; SCA, 'Accreditation Report—Albania (PA)' (October 2014) 19.

[187] SCA, 'Accreditation Report—Albania (PA)' (October 2014) 18–19.

[188] SCA, 'Accreditation Report—Ukraine (UPCHR)' (October 2014) 35–36.

[189] SCA, 'Accreditation Report—Greece Rights (GNCHR)' (March 2015) 29: 'In accordance with article 2 of the Law, the members of the GNHRC are appointed by a decision of the President based on the nominations of various entities. The SCA notes that each body makes nominations and this may result in different processes being employed by each entity.' SCA, 'Accreditation Report—Greece (GNCHR)' (May 2016) 33: 'The SCA notes that the legislative amendment specifies that members are "designated by" the various entities rather than being "representatives of" these entities. However, this does not address the concern of the SCA that having each body make nominations may result in different processes being employed by each entity.' Concern about the process was reiterated by the SCA in SCA,

broad, and transparent.[190] An argument by the NHRI of Denmark (Danish Institute for Human Rights (DIHR)) that it could not set the selection criteria for candidates was rejected by the SCA:

> the SCA notes that 4 members are appointed by 4 universities and 2 by the Conference of Rectors according to different criteria. The SCA acknowledges the DIHR's view that to further circumscribe the process would interfere with the independence of the universities. However, the SCA is of the view that providing for different stakeholders to select members according to their rules of operation may result in different entities using different processes for selection, and that a consistent, transparent, merit-based and broadly consultative selection process should be used across all appointing entities.[191]

The SCA recommended that the Danish NHRI seek amendments to its law, and 'in the interim, the SCA encourage the DIHR to consider policy and/or administrative options that would allow it to provide general guidance to nominating entities about their selection processes in a manner that both respects the principle of academic freedom and the requirements of the Paris Principles'.[192] The DIHR responded to these recommendations by amending its bylaws and the appointing entities adopting guidelines.[193] For the NHRI of Zambia (the Human Rights Commission (Zambia) (HRCZ), the SCA called for harmonization of the process across nominating bodies:

> in accordance with Section 6 (1) of the Amendment Bill, Commissioners are appointed by the President, subject to ratification by the National Assembly. It further provides that the Commission is to consist of a Chairperson, a Vice chairperson, and a representative of each of nine different entities. Section 6 (5) of the Amendment Bill provides that the entities referred to nominate their member.
>
> The SCA is of the view that the proposed selection process is not sufficiently broad and transparent, in particular it does not:
>
> - require the advertisement of vacancies;

'Accreditation Report—Greece (GNCHR)' (March 2017) 23–24. See also, SCA, 'Accreditation Report—Cameroon (NCHRF)' (March 2015) 34: 'in accordance with section 6 of the Law, the Commissioners are appointed by decree of the President upon the proposal of the services, socio-professional associations or bodies to which they belong. The SCA notes that these proposals are made according to the internal procedures of the concerned bodies and, consequently, this may result in different processes being employed between institutions', and SCA, 'Accreditation Report—Cameroon (NCHRF)' (May 2016) 28–29; SCA, 'Accreditation Report—Morocco (Conseil National des Droits de l'Homme (CNDH))' (November 2015) 32–33; SCA, 'Accreditation Report—Korea (NHRCK)' (May 2016) 41.

190 SCA, 'Accreditation Report—Greece (GNCHR)' (March 2017) 23–24.

191 SCA, 'Accreditation Report—Denmark (DIHR)' (November 2017) 39.

192 ibid.

193 SCA, 'Accreditation Report—Denmark (DIHR)' (October 2018) 8.

- establish clear and uniform criteria upon which the nominating entities assess the merit of eligible applicants;
- provide that the members selected by nominating entities serve in their individual capacity rather than on behalf of the organisation they represent; and
- promote broad consultation and/or participation in the application, screening, selection and appointment process for the Chairperson and the Vice chairperson.

The SCA further notes that providing for different nominating entities to select members may result in different entities using different processes for selection. The SCA is of the view that these processes should be harmonized across all nominating entities.[194]

4.4.5 Appointment by Government

The SCA is not primarily concerned about the issue of who ultimately appoints the members of the NHRI. Recognizing that in most countries the appointment has to be made by the Prime Minister or President. The focus of the SCA's concerns is on the nature of the *process* by which selection and appointments are made. For example, under the relevant law, the Chairperson, Deputy Chairperson, and members of every division of the Mauritius NHRI were to be appointed 'by the President, acting on the advice of the Prime Minister ... [who] will consult with the Leader of the Opposition prior to tendering his or her advice to the President'.[195] This was considered by the SCA as insufficiently transparent and inclusive, and the NHRI was encouraged to advocate for a revised process.[196] Similarly, the Jordanian NHRI was to be 'supervised by a Board of Trustees of no more than twenty-one (21) members, whose Chairman and members are appointed by Royal Decree at the recommendation of the Prime Minister'.[197] Parliamentary appointments are insufficient where there is a lack of a proper process.[198] Thus, rather than focusing on the appointment authority, the SCA reiterated the need for a broad and

194 SCA, 'Accreditation Report—Zambia (HRCZ)' (October 2018) 19. A similar recommendation was made to Madagascar: 'providing for the different entities to select members according to their rules of procedure may result in them using different processes for selection, and that a consistent, transparent, merit-based and broadly consultative selection process should be used across all of the entities'. SCA, 'Accreditation Report—Madagascar (CNIDH))' (March 2019) 7.

195 SCA, 'Accreditation Report—Mauritius (NHRC)' (October 2014) 22.

196 ibid.

197 SCA, 'Accreditation Report—Jordan (JNCHR)' (November 2015) 22–23. This was reiterated in the SCA recommendations in November 2016. SCA, 'Accreditation Report—Jordan (NCHR)' (November 2016) 29. Despite its concern, the NHRI was re-accredited with A-status. The SCA commended the work of the NHRI in seeking to strengthen its mandate.

198 SCA, 'Accreditation Report—Nicaragua (PDDH)' (May 2018) 31, where the law provided that the ombudsperson and deputy ombudsperson are appointed by 60 per cent majority in parliament.

transparent process with advertising of vacancies, clear and uniform criteria, and public consultation.

The SCA does not have a stated preference for which national body makes the appointments formally. What is critical is that the requirements from the General Observations are met. The process must be clear, transparent, and participatory.[199] It must ensure by way of enabling law or regulation a consultative element in the application, screening, and appointment process, including with civil society and NGOs, even where this happens in practice.[200] Involvement of the legislature may have some preferential features that would allow the process to be undertaken in the manner required by the General Observations, but care must be taken that it does not result in an overly onerous process or be allowed to interfere with the effective operation of the NHRI. For Peru's NHRI, for example, 'the process of election of a candidate took more than five years due to the requirement for the candidate to receive the vote by two thirds (2/3) of the members of Parliament'.[201]

Formal appointment by the executive or another branch of government is thus not fatal to A-status in and of itself. For example, the enabling law of the NHRI of Mauritania stipulated 'the appointment of 4 members by the President of the Republic, on the basis of their competence and experience in the field of human rights'.[202] However, it was the lack of any formal selection and appointment procedure in the enabling law that was problematic.[203]

The SCA may find that where the government has sole authority to appoint and dismiss the head of the NHRI, in the absence of any appointment process, it is a factor indicating that the NHRI is not an independent institution in accordance with the Paris Principles.[204] This will be seen in Section 4.5. The SCA has also raised concerns where candidates are selected and appointed solely by political bodies.[205]

[199] SCA, 'Accreditation Report—Bosnia and Herzegovina (IHROBH)' (November 2016) 14. See also, SCA, 'Accreditation Report—Egypt (NHRC)' (March 2017) 35, where the SCA noted that 'in accordance with article 2(3) of the draft law, the Bureau of the House of Representatives examines the candidates and submits a list to Plenary of the House of Representatives for election … However, beyond the ability to propose candidates, it is unclear that a process would be in place to achieve broad consultation and/or participation in the application, screening, selection and appointment process.' See also, SCA, 'Accreditation Report—Argentina (DPNA)' (November 2017) 38: 'In accordance with Article 2 of the Law, the selection process to nominate the Head of the Defensoría del Pueblo should be carried out by a bicameral commission formed by 7 Congress members and 7 Senate members. The bicameral commission revises the candidatures and must propose 1 to 3 candidates to the Senate and to the Congress. Within the next 30 days both the Senate and the Congress shall select and appoint the Defensor by 2/3 of votes. The SCA notes that the process for selection and appointment currently enshrined in the enabling Law is not sufficiently broad and transparent. In particular, it does not: require the advertisement of vacancies; establish clear and uniform criteria upon which all parties assess the merit of eligible applicants; and promote broad consultation and / or participation in the application, screening, selection and appointment process.'

[200] SCA, 'Accreditation Report—Bosnia and Herzegovina (IHROBH)' (November 2017) 8–9.

[201] SCA, 'Accreditation Report—Peru (DPP)' (March 2017) 28.

[202] SCA, 'Accreditation Report—Mauritania (CNDH)' (May 2011) 15.

[203] ibid.

[204] SCA, 'Accreditation Report—Sweden (Equality Ombudsman of Sweden (EOS))' (May 2011) 9.

[205] SCA, 'Accreditation Report—Bulgaria (CPD)' (October 2011) 9: 'The CPD consists of 9 Commissioners, of which 5 are elected by the National Assembly and 4 are appointed by the President of the Republic of Bulgaria'.

Where there is an appointment process with considerable executive discretion, the SCA may find that the Paris Principles' requirements are not met. For example, in considering the NHRI of Malaysia in 2015, the SCA stated:

> In accordance with section 5(2) of the Act, the King, on recommendation of the Prime Minister, appoints SUHAKAM Commissioners. Before making a recommendation, the Chairperson must consult a Selection Committee comprised of the Chief Secretary to the Government, the Chairperson of the Commission, and three (3) members of civil society, appointed by the Prime Minister, who have knowledge of or practical experience in human rights matters. The law therefore provides the Prime Minister with discretion to nominate the three civil society candidates on the Selection Panel.
>
> In addition, the SCA is concerned that, while the Prime Minister must consult the Selection Committee, there is no legal requirement that he or she make recommendations from the list of candidates that were been determined by the independent Selection Committee to be suitable for appointment.
>
> The SCA noted these concerns in 2009 and highlighted that the combination of these two factors leaves open the potential for political interference.[206]

A Constitutional provision on the appointment of the Ombudsperson and Deputy Ombudsperson by the President on the recommendation of the Judicial Service Commission was not considered sufficiently broad and transparent in the case of Namibia because it lacked the requisite detail for a broad and transparent process.[207] Similarly, where an appointment process is not set out in the enabling law and is operated by a governmental (sponsoring) department, this may be problematic.[208]

4.4.6 Delays or Extension of Appointment outside Regular Procedures

In a number of instances, the term of the head of an NHRI has expired and been extended outside a formal appointment and selection process, raising concerns

[206] SCA, 'Accreditation Report—Malaysia (SUHAKAM)' (November 2015) 29.

[207] SCA, 'Accreditation Report—Namibia (Ombudsman)' (November 2016) 41. The SCA repeated this recommendation in October 2018: SCA, 'Accreditation Report—Namibia (Ombudsman)' (October 2018) 12–13.

[208] SCA, 'Accreditation Report—Northern Ireland (Northern Ireland Human Rights Commission (NIHRC))' (May 2016) 45: 'The NIHRC reports that, in practice, the appointment process is subject to detailed guidance from the Office of the Commissioner for Public Appointments. and includes the advertising of vacancies, the use of a selection panel who make recommendations to the Secretary of State, and the ability to appeal the process for selection of the Chief Commissioner through the Employment Tribunal. However, this process is undertaken by the NIHRC's sponsor department, and is not set out in the legislation, in regulations, or in binding administrative guidelines.'

for the SCA. Where the appointment of the head of the NHRI is done outside of the required selection and appointment procedure, the SCA takes a particularly strong line. In the case of Rwanda, the 'the former Chairperson of the NCHR was appointed Deputy Chief Justice of Rwanda on December 9, 2011. The new Chairperson was appointed by the government very recently without any apparent process being followed.'[209] The lack of process demonstrated that 'neither the NCHR nor the government of Rwanda made any efforts to address the concerns of the SCA as expressed in 2007'.[210] The SCA recommended that the NHRI be downgraded to B-status.[211] The following year, the NHRI had made sufficient changes to receive re-accreditation to A-status, including in particular changes to the selection and appointment procedure, which by law included pluralistic representation of NGOs and human rights experts.[212]

In the case of Nicaragua, the extension of the head of the institution was done by presidential decree, resulting (at time of re-accreditation) in the head of the NHRI (*Procurador*) being in place for an additional one year and five months, with the SCA expressing its concerns as follows:

> The SCA notes that this situation may be due to factors that are beyond the control of the NHRI and that a political stalemate has caused the extension of the terms of office for over 50 officials. However, the SCA notes that the existing legislation provides that an appointment or a re-appointment of the *Procurador* can be made upon a vote of 60% in Parliament. The SCA would welcome a timely resolution of this situation through use of the existing legislative provisions to appoint a new, or to re-appoint the existing *Procurador*.[213]

In the case of the Azerbaijan NHRI (the Human Rights Commissioner (Ombudsman) of the Republic of Azerbaijan (HRCA)), the SCA expressed 'concern over the delays and transparency of the appointment procedure, which call into question the independence of the HRCA'.[214] The Ombudsperson's term had expired in 2017, but as of May 2018 there had been no developments.[215]

The First Deputy Ombudsperson of Argentina (DPNA) was left in an acting position from 2009 to October 2011, which seemed to have been as a result of elections in the country and a corresponding delay in the appointment process. The SCA, while raising concern, seemed satisfied that there would be a new

[209] SCA, 'Accreditation Report—Rwanda (NCHR)' (March 2012) 27.
[210] SCA, 'Accreditation Report—Rwanda (NCHR)' (March 2012) 27. See SCA, 'Accreditation Report—Rwanda (NCHR)' (October 2007) 3. However, no elaboration is provided on this point in the 2007 report.
[211] SCA, 'Accreditation Report—Rwanda (NCHR)' (March 2012) 26.
[212] SCA, 'Accreditation Report—Rwanda (NCHR)' (May 2013) 16.
[213] SCA, 'Accreditation Report—Nicaragua (PDDHN)' (May 2011) 18.
[214] SCA, 'Accreditation Report—Azerbaijan (HRCA)' (May 2011) 22.
[215] SCA, 'Accreditation Report—Azerbaijan (HRCA)' (May 2018) 45.

ombudsperson appointed in March 2012 and the NHRI was re-accredited with A-status.[216] However, at its re-accreditation in November 2016, it was clear that an ombudsperson had still not been appointed some seven years later, with an 'under-secretary' acting in the role despite legislative provision for one of the deputy ombudspersons to undertake this role. The SCA expressed its concern that:

> [t]he delay in the appointment of the Ombudsperson and Deputy Ombudspersons could restrict DPNA's ability to speak out on significant and controversial human rights concerns. The SCA acknowledges the recent establishment of the Permanent Bicameral Commission, which is expected to lead to the appointment of an Ombudsperson and two Deputy Ombudspersons.
>
> The SCA encourages a prompt resolution of the process of appointing the Ombudsperson and Deputy Ombudspersons of the DPNA.[217]

The NHRI of Paraguay's re-accreditation with A-status was deferred in 2013, in part because no new ombudsperson had been appointed since 2008.[218] In that instance, the UN Human Rights Committee had also expressed its concern about both the lack of appointment and the lack of clarity.[219] This was coupled with serious concerns about the effective performance of the Defensor. Consideration was deferred because recent elections were expected to result in a new appointment.[220]

The NHRI of Nepal came under special review in 2013, as it was without a chairperson or commissioners. In March 2014, a decision on accreditation was again deferred with the SCA noting that 'while the NHRCN remains without a Chairperson and Commissioners, it continues to operate effectively as a NHRI under powers formally delegated to the Acting Secretary'.[221] However, in the absence of a chairperson or commissioners, the SCA stated that it could not make a decision. The institution was re-accredited with A-status in October 2014 following the appointment of commissioners.[222]

[216] SCA, 'Accreditation Report—Argentina (DPNA)' (October 2011) 11.

[217] SCA, 'Accreditation Report—Argentina (DPNA)' (November 2016) 8. The accreditation of the DPNA was deferred repeatedly. In October 2019—the latest SCA report available at time of writing—the SCA commented as follows: 'The SCA is of the view that, in the absence of policy advice from the GANHRI Bureau, the application by the DPNA cannot be determined reasonably at this time, based on the facts that are available. Pursuant to Section 8.5 of the SCA Rules of Procedure, the SCA shall seek policy guidance from the GANHRI Bureau.' SCA, 'Accreditation Report—Argentina (DPNA)' (October 2019) 23.

[218] SCA, 'Accreditation Report—Paraguay (DP)' (November 2013) 24.

[219] ibid.

[220] ibid.

[221] SCA, 'Accreditation Report—Nepal (National Human Rights Commission (NHRC))' (March 2014) 22.

[222] SCA, 'Accreditation Report—Nepal (NHRCN))' (October 2014) 37. Note: The SCA utilizes a different acronym for the same institution.

4.5 Security of Tenure for Board Members and Leadership

The requirement for security of tenure for NHRI leadership derives from the Paris Principles stipulation that NHRIs have a 'stable mandate'. The Paris Principles provide:

> In order to ensure a stable mandate for the members of the national institution, without which there can be no real independence, their appointment shall be effected by an official act which shall establish the specific duration of the mandate. This mandate may be renewable, provided that the pluralism of the institution's membership is ensured.[223]

In its General Observation 2.1 (2018), the SCA elaborated that:

> [t]he SCA is of the view that in order to address the Paris Principles requirements for a stable mandate, which is important in reinforcing independence, the enabling legislation of an NHRI must contain an independent and objective dismissal process, similar to that accorded to members of other independent State agencies.
>
> The dismissal must be made in strict conformity with all the substantive and procedural requirements as prescribed by law.
>
> The grounds for dismissal must be clearly defined and appropriately confined to only those actions which impact adversely on the capacity of the member to fulfil their mandate.
>
> Where appropriate, the legislation should specify that the application of a particular ground must be supported by a decision of an independent body with appropriate jurisdiction.
>
> Dismissal should not be allowed based solely on the discretion of appointing authorities.
>
> Such requirements ensure the security of tenure of the members of the governing body and are essential to ensure the independence of, and public confidence in, the senior leadership of a National Institution.[224]

As seen in some of the instances above, NHRIs can suffer from lack of stability, such as where there is a vacancy with no appointment made, or an appointment is not reconfirmed. Thus, the SCA has interpreted a stable mandate as containing five essential interconnected requirements: an independent and objective dismissal process set out in the enabling law, that conforms to due process requirements, based on limited and clearly defined grounds, not based of the discretion of the appointing authority, and preferably are subject to the decision on an independent body.

[223] Paris Principles (n 1).
[224] SCA, 'General Observations' (February 2018) (n 2) GO 2.1, 34.

In its justification for its approach, the SCA provided the following explanation:

> In prescribing the conditions to ensure a stable mandate for members of the NHRI decision-making body, section B.3 of the Paris Principles is silent on the scenario of their dismissal. Nonetheless, it is the view of the Sub-Committee that ensuring the security of tenure of NHRI members is consistent with the Paris Principles requirements regarding the composition of the National Institution and its guarantees of in dependence and pluralism.
>
> Appropriate procedural protections and due process are essential aspects of all human rights but are especially pertinent in relation to a matter such as ensuring the independence of the NHRI and its membership. That is, NHRI members must be able to undertake their responsibilities without fear and without inappropriate interference from the State or other actors. In this light, the Sub-Committee highlights the following:
>
> - Members may be dismissed only on serious grounds of misconduct or incompetence, in accordance with fair procedures ensuring objectivity and impartiality set out in the national law.
> - The dismissal of members by the Executive, such as before the expiry of the term for which they have been appointed, without any specific reasons given to them and without effective functional immunity being available to contest the dismissal, is incompatible with the independence of the NHRI.[225]

While the majority of its focus is on dismissal, the question of institutional stability also relates to the length of the term of office for NHRI leadership.

4.5.1 Length of Term of Office

The issue of security of tenure is closely connected to issues around the length of term of office for NHRI office holders. In this regard, prior to the formalization of the SCA's views in the revisions to the General Observations in 2013, the SCA had criticized terms of office of just two years,[226] and also where there was no provision specifying length of term.[227] It suggested a length of office of between three and

[225] ibid 34–35.

[226] SCA, 'Accreditation Report—Malaysia (SUHAKAM)' (April 2008) 5; SCA, 'Accreditation Report—Togo (CNDH)' (October 2019) 19–20, where the law provided for a two-year appointment for members, renewable twice.

[227] SCA, 'Accreditation Report—Namibia (Ombudsman)' (May 2011) 16, where the enabling law did not limit the term, and while retirement age for the Ombudsman was 65, it could be extended by the President to 70 under the Constitution. See also, SCA, 'Accreditation Report—Romania (Romanian Institute of Human Rights (RIHR))' (May 2011) 21.

seven years, renewable once.[228] These recommendations were formalized in the updated and expanded 2013 General Observations. The enabling law should also provide for minimum terms of appointment.[229] Security of tenure requires that the language in the enabling law on the NHRI is sufficiently precise on this point. In the case of New Zealand's NHRI, the SCA recommended a change from 'not longer than 5 years' to a minimum term.[230] Terms of office of three years for the head of an institution have, however, been considered as too short by the SCA in some circumstances, even where that term is renewable.[231] For members, renewable terms in the enabling law should clearly state how many times they can be reappointed in order to remove the possibility of an unlimited term.[232] Appointments should be for a fixed term and clearly defined in law.[233] Thus, for Ghana's NHRI, the SCA considered that a proposed change to the Constitution from provisions whereby the Commissioner and Deputy Commissioners ceased to hold office upon reaching seventy years and sixty-five years respectively, to provision for a non-renewable ten-year term, would meet the requirements for a fixed term of office.[234] Where the term is at or above the maximum length recommended by the SCA, it should be limited to one reappointment.[235]

4.5.2 Dismissal of Leadership

A critical aspect for NHRIs as regards security of tenure is the process for dismissal of leadership. The SCA requires that there be clear criteria in the enabling law for the removal of office holders.[236] Prior to their formalization in the 2013 General

[228] SCA, 'Accreditation Report—Colombia (DPC)' (March 2012) 18. See also, SCA, 'Accreditation Report—South Africa (SAHRC)' (November 2012) 30 noting the need for a clear fixed term.

[229] SCA, 'Accreditation Report—New Zealand (NZHRC)' (May 2016) 43–44.

[230] SCA, 'Accreditation Report—New Zealand (NZHRC)' (May 2011) 17.

[231] SCA, 'Accreditation Report—El Salvador (PDDH)' (November 2016) 23, where the SCA 'remains concerned that the duration of the term is too short to promote the independence of members and ensure the continuity of programs and services'. The enabling law contained no limitation on the number of times the Procurador could be renewed. This issue was considered under General Observation 2.2. See also, SCA, 'Accreditation Report—Tanzania (Commission for Human Rights and Good Governance of (CHRAGG))' (November 2016) 54. For Zambia, a three-year renewable term was considered too short: SCA, 'Accreditation Report—Zambia (HRCZ)' (October 2018) 22.

[232] SCA, 'Accreditation Report—Algeria (CNDH)' (May 2018) 19; SCA, 'Accreditation Report—Afghanistan (AIHRC)' (October 2019) 8; SCA, 'Accreditation Report—Honduras (CONADEH)' (October 2019) 14; SCA, 'Accreditation Report—Ukraine (UPCHR)' (October 2019) 22.

[233] SCA, 'Accreditation Report—Northern Ireland (NIHRC)' (May 2016) 46 where Commissioners had a term 'not more than 3 years', and the Chief Commissioner a 'maximum of five years'.

[234] SCA, 'Accreditation Report—Ghana (CHRAJ)' (March 2019) 23.

[235] SCA, 'Accreditation Report—Croatia (ORC)' (March 2019) 19. See also SCA, 'Accreditation Report—Armenia (HRDA)' (March 2019) 15, where the SCA recommended a six-year term be limited to one re-election.

[236] See for example, SCA, 'Accreditation Report—Rwanda (NCHR)' (October 2018) 15–16; SCA, 'Accreditation Report—Honduras (CONADEH)' (October 2019) 14; SCA, 'Accreditation Report—Norway (NNHRI)' (March 2017) 15–16; SCA, 'Accreditation Report—Colombia (The Defensoria Del Pueblo of Colombia (DPC))' (March 2017) 22–23.

Observations, in its reports the SCA had set out requirements for objective and transparent criteria,[237] that were 'substantiated and transparent'[238] and well defined in the enabling law,[239] with objective grounds,[240] and should not be in the sole hands of the government, including a government department.[241] Dismissal criteria should also not be overly broad, with terms for dismissal for reasons such as 'incompetence' or 'misbehaviour'.[242]

More unusual reasons for dismissal have been challenged by the SCA, such as the provision for the B-status Kyrgyz Republic Ombudsperson that they may be dismissed in the event of 'non-approval of a report they have submitted to the parliament'.[243] A member of Malawi's NHRI could be removed for 'lack of "impartiality"' and, despite jurisprudence on the issue of dismissal including on the basis of impartiality, this provision was overly broad and had the potential for misuse.[244] The SCA similarly questioned provisions allowing removal for 'physical or psychological incapacity (with determination by a medical practitioner and with a vote of 2/3 of the members of the National Assembly)' noting that an 'independent and objective' dismissal process was required with grounds clearly defined in the legislation.[245] The SCA's concern here was that the decision to dismiss should not be based solely on the discretion of the appointing body but rather by an independent body with appropriate jurisdiction. This would remove the possibility of political influence/decisions where there may be a majority-controlled legislature.

The SCA has gradually become more specific in its requirements for what constitutes insufficiently defined criteria for removal. The grounds must be clearly

[237] SCA, 'Accreditation Report—Mauritius (NHRC)' (April 2008) 6; SCA, 'Accreditation Report—Algeria (CNCPPDH)' (October 2010) 10.

[238] SCA, 'Accreditation Report—Maldives (HRC)' (April 2008) 8.

[239] SCA, 'Accreditation Report—Great Britain (ECHR)' (April 2008) 9; SCA, 'Accreditation Report—Ireland (IHRC)' (November 2008) 7–8; SCA, 'Accreditation Report—Luxembourg (CCDH)' (November 2008) 8; SCA, 'Accreditation Report—Thailand (NHRC)' (November 2008) 10–11; SCA, 'Accreditation Report—Qatar (NHRC)' (March 2009) 4 (where there were no provisions in the enabling law for dismissal); SCA, 'Accreditation Report—Switzerland (CFQF)' (March 2009) 6; SCA, 'Accreditation Report—Palestine (Palestine Independent Commission for Human Rights (PICHR))' (March 2009) 7; SCA, 'Accreditation Report—Switzerland (FCR)' (March/April 2010) 12; SCA, 'Accreditation Report—Morocco (CCDH)' (October 2010) 13; SCA, 'Accreditation Report—Hungary (PCCR)' (May 2011) 8–9; SCA, 'Accreditation Report—Egypt (NCHR)' (October 2011) 13–14; SCA, 'Accreditation Report—Philippines (CHRP)' (March 2012) 25; SCA, 'Accreditation Report—Denmark (DIHR)' (November 2012) 14.

[240] SCA, 'Accreditation Report—Algeria (CNCPPDH)' (March/April 2010) 7.

[241] SCA, 'Accreditation Report—Netherlands (Equal Treatment Commission (ETC))' (March/April 2010) 10.

[242] SCA, 'Accreditation Report—Zambia (HRCZ)' (October 2011) 19–20, and SCA, 'Accreditation Report—Zambia (HRCZ)' (October 2018) 21. In respect of Zambia, the SCA noted 'that the HRCZ membership may be terminated by the President on several grounds, including a finding of gross misconduct following an investigation. The SCA is of the view that these amendments, if passed in their present form, would address the previously stated concerns.' Similarly challenged by the SCA was a provision that the NHRI of Rwanda could be 'removed from office by the organ that appointed him/her': SCA, 'Accreditation Report—Rwanda (NCHR)' (March 2012) 28.

[243] SCA, 'Accreditation Report—Kyrgyz Republic (OKR)' (March 2012) 11.

[244] SCA, 'Accreditation Report—Malawi (MHRC)' (November 2012) 18–19.

[245] SCA, 'Accreditation Report—Panama (DPP)' (November 2012) 21.

stated,[246] as well as specific. For the NHRI of Haiti, for example, dismissal could be carried out by the High Judicial Court for 'grave offences' committed in the performance of his/her duty where requested by two-thirds of the Parliament's Lower Chamber. The Deputy could be removed by the President at the request of the Citizen's Protector (head of the institution).[247] However, there were no further details on the grounds for dismissal or the meaning of grave offences.[248] A provision allowing removal for 'extremely weighty reasons' was also rejected as unclear.[249] Dismissal for a 'shameful act that is incompatible with his or her status' was regarded as 'vague and open to misuse'.[250] Dismissal where a person is, in the opinion of a member of the government, 'unable, unfit or unwilling to perform his functions' has also been criticized.[251] Loss of position for 'physical incapacity' or 'as a result of acts or practices that are inconsistent with the obligations associated with membership in the Council' were also considered overly vague and open to misuse.[252] Grounds providing that a member of the NHRI could be dismissed for 'misusing one's prerogatives for other than discharging the [NHRI's] mandate, breach of confidentiality of deliberations, or inability to carry out one's function' were also insufficiently clear.[253] General terms such as 'misbehaviour' or 'misconduct' will also not meet the requirement if they are not clearly defined.[254]

Where terms for dismissal are clear in the overall context of national law, this will likely be sufficient to meet the Paris Principles' requirements. For example, in the Canadian NHRI, members hold office while maintaining 'good behaviour' but may be removed by the Governor in Council on address of the Senate and House of Commons, while 'good behaviour' was not defined in the Act, but 'its meaning is circumscribed by other statutes, guidelines and judicial decisions'.[255] Thus, terms in NHRIs' enabling laws such as 'inability to carry out their functions' require clarity to 'avoid misinterpretation' and reduce the possibility of political influence of manipulation being used to remove a member who is critical of the government

[246] For example, SCA, 'Accreditation Report—Portugal (PDJ)' (November 2017) 30.

[247] SCA, 'Accreditation Report—Haiti (OPC)' (November 2013) 9.

[248] ibid.

[249] SCA, 'Accreditation Report—Finland (Finnish National Human Rights Institution (FNHRI))' (October 2014) 8.

[250] SCA, 'Accreditation Report—Latvia (Ombudsman of the Republic of Latvia (OORL))' (March 2015) 10.

[251] SCA, 'Accreditation Report—Great Britain (ECHR)' (November 2015) 20.

[252] SCA, 'Accreditation Report—Morocco (CNDH)' (November 2015) 33–34.

[253] SCA, 'Accreditation Report— Côte d'Ivoire (CNDHCI)' (May 2016) 10–11.

[254] SCA, 'Accreditation Report—Tanzania (CHRAGG)' (November 2016) 53–54. See also, SCA, 'Accreditation Report—Zambia (HRCZ)' (November 2016) 56–57 'Section 7(2) of the enabling Law provides that a Commissioner may be removed from office for "inability to perform the functions of their office, whether arising from infirmity of body or mind, incompetence or for misbehaviour". The enabling Law does not define these terms, and is silent on the process for dismissal.' See also, South Africa, where the terms 'misconduct' and 'incompetence' were not defined. However, the SCA requested supporting evidence from the NHRI to its claim that these terms were well defined in jurisprudence. SCA, 'Accreditation Report—South Africa (SAHRC)' (November 2017) 32–33.

[255] SCA, 'Accreditation Report—Canada (CHRC)' (May 2016) 26.

of the day.[256] Even where terms are accompanied by relevant jurisprudence, such as in the case of Denmark's NHRI, where members could be removed for lack of 'personal and professional integrity', the SCA recommended that 'in the interests of clarity and consistency' greater precision should be provided.[257] A constitutional provision in Uganda for the Ugandan Human Rights Commission (UHRC) that 'a member of the UHRC can be dismissed in the same manner as a judge of the High Court "with the necessary modifications"' was considered insufficient to meet the requirements of an independent and objective dismissal process, as the term was not defined in law.[258]

Where provisions include removal for 'incapacity', the SCA considers that any such determination should be made by an independent medical professional or tribunal.[259]

Where criteria are particularly far-reaching, the SCA has expressed considerable concern, such as for the NHRI of the Philippines (Commission on Human Rights of the Philippines (CHRP)):

> The SCA notes that EO 163 [the enabling law] is silent on the dismissal process for the Chairman and members of the CHRP. The SCA further notes that the CHRP has indicated that grounds and procedures for dismissal for the Chairman and members are currently governed by Republic Act number 6713, Code of Conduct and Ethical standards for public officials.
>
> The SCA notes that section 9 of the proposed CHR Act provides that the Chairman and members may be removed for office for a) disloyalty to the Republic of the Philippines; b) culpable violation of the Constitution; c) bribery and graft and corruption, other high crimes or betrayal of trust; d) dishonesty, misconduct in office, gross negligence, or dereliction of duty; e) commission of any offence involving moral turpitude or an offence punishable by imprisonment for more than six (6) years; and f) abuse of authority. The SCA is of the view that the grounds for dismissal outlined in the proposed CHR Act are far-reaching and may be open to misuse.
>
> Further, the SCA notes that section 9 of the proposed CHR Act provides that the dismissal process is commenced by the filing of a verified complaint with the Office of the Ombudsman. The SCA notes that the enabling law does not appear to place limitations placed on who may initiate such a complaint.[260]

[256] SCA, 'Accreditation Report—Bosnia and Herzegovina (IHROBH)' (November 2016) 14–15; SCA, 'Accreditation Report—Bosnia and Herzegovina (IHROBH)' (November 2017) 9.
[257] SCA, 'Accreditation Report—Denmark (DIHR)' (October 2018) 9.
[258] SCA, 'Accreditation Report—Uganda (UHRC)' (May 2018) 39–40.
[259] See for example, SCA, 'Accreditation Report—Malaysia (SUHAKAM)' (November 2015) 31–32; SCA, 'Accreditation Report—Qatar (NHCR)' (November 2015) 38. There must at least be appropriate medical evidence. See SCA, 'Accreditation Report—South Africa (SAHRC)' (November 2017) 32–33.
[260] SCA, 'Accreditation Report—Philippines (CHRP)' (March 2017) 32–33.

In practice, the requirements for objective criteria and a dismissal process that is not discretionary are closely intertwined. There must be clear grounds for the dismissal procedure in the enabling law,[261] and it should be clear how these provisions operate in practice. In the enabling law of the NHRI of Timor-Leste, conflicting provisions raised concerns as to how they applied in practice:

> [the] Provedor can be terminated by article 19 of the Statute Law 7/2004. In this regard:
>
> - Article 19(e) stipulates 'final conviction for a criminal offence that carries a prison sentence exceeding one (1) year';
> - Article 19(f) stipulates 'final conviction for a criminal offence punished by actual imprisonment'.
> - Article 21(1)(d) provides that the Parliament can remove the Provedor from office if he is convicted for a criminal offence that carries a prison sentence of less than one year.[262]

The following detailed provisions in the law of the NHRI of Algeria were considered insufficient:

> In accordance with Article 16 of the Law, membership in the CNDH can be terminated by: a) the expiry of the term of the member; b) resignation; c) unjustified absence at three consecutive plenary assembly meetings; d) loss of membership under which he/she was elected; e) conviction for crime or voluntary offence; f) death; and g) serious and repeated act or behaviour inconsistent with his/her obligations. For cases covered by c), e) and g), the dismissal is decided by the absolute majority of the CNDH plenary assembly.[263]

In that instance, the SCA highlighted the lack of independence because dismissal was at the sole discretion of the plenary assembly and not an independent authority.

A provision for 'recall' by the appointing authority is insufficient to meet the requirements of an independent and objective process.[264] In October 2007, the SCA referred to the 'sudden dismissal' of the Executive Secretary and ex-officio

[261] For example, SCA, 'Accreditation Report—Oman (ONHRC)' (November 2013) 14; SCA, 'Accreditation Report—Libya (National Council for Civil Liberties and Human Rights (NCCLHR))' (October 2014) 13; SCA, 'Accreditation Report—Jordan (JNCHR)' (November 2015) 24: 'The SCA acknowledges that the JNCHR has advocated for changes to its enabling law to provide for dismissal under the following conditions: a) resignation; b) conviction by a regular court for a felony or misdemeanor of a moral and ethical nature; c) loss of any of the eligibility requirements; or d) the expiration of the Board term. The SCA notes that the proposed amendment continues to be silent on the process for dismissal.'; SCA, 'Accreditation Report—Mexico (CNDH)' (November 2016) 30.

[262] SCA, 'Accreditation Report—Timor-Leste (PDHJ)' (November 2013) 31.

[263] SCA, 'Accreditation Report—Algeria (CNDH)' (May 2018) 19.

[264] SCA, 'Accreditation Report—Slovakia (SNCHR)' (March 2014) 10; SCA, 'Accreditation Report—Cameroon (NCHRF)' (March 2015) 36; SCA, 'Accreditation Report—Cameroon (NCHRF)' (May 2016) 30; SCA, 'Accreditation Report—Cameroon (NCHRF)' (November 2017) 14–15.

Commissioner of the NHRI of Nigeria (the National Human Rights Commission of Nigeria) who was also at the time the head of the coordinating mechanism of African NHRIs. The NHRI was downgraded to B-status.[265] The NHRI did not regain A-status until May 2011, following legislative amendments.[266] Where a recall is because of 'loss of status that justified their appointment' such a recall may allow for the removal of a commissioner for 'inappropriate reasons'.[267]

An example of a process that seems to meet the requirements of the SCA was identified for Egypt. While not enacted at the time of the review, the SCA noted:

> article 4 of the draft law provides that membership in the NCHR is terminated in the case of resignation, death, or the issuance of a final tribunal verdict against a member for a dishonorable office or one of the crimes that constitutes a violation of human rights. Also in accordance with article 4, termination of membership is effected by a two-thirds (2/3) majority vote of the NCHR. It appears that these amendments would address the above-noted concern [that the enabling law is silent on the grounds and process for dismissal].[268]

Where dismissal is by the parliament, it must be by a majority in practice.[269] The inclusion of a provision for a parliamentary investigation prior to any decision by the parliament has been cautiously welcomed, but it must ensure that there cannot be dismissal for political reasons.[270] The process for removal by the parliament should be clearly set out in law.[271] Provisions for Scotland's NHRI, the Scottish Human Rights Commission, that 'the Chair or Members may be dismissed if Parliament decides by a 2/3 vote that 1) the Chair or relevant Member has breached the terms of appointment, or 2) that the Parliament has lost confidence in the member's

[265] SCA, 'Accreditation Report—Nigeria (NHRC)' (October 2007) 10.

[266] SCA, 'Accreditation Report—Nigeria (NHRC)' (May 2011) 18.

[267] SCA, 'Accreditation Report—Cameroon (NCHRF)' (March 2015) 36; SCA, 'Accreditation Report—Cameroon (NCHRF)' (November 2017) 14–15.

[268] SCA, 'Accreditation Report—Egypt (NHRC)' (March 2017) 36.

[269] SCA, 'Accreditation Report—Latvia (OORL)' (March 2015) 10, 'Further, in accordance with section 10(2), such a dismissal may be proposed by not less than one-third of the Saeima and approved by an absolute majority vote of the Saeima. The SCA understands that a decision to dismiss the Ombudsman could be undertaken with the support of only 26 members of the Saeima.'

[270] SCA, 'Accreditation Report—Latvia (OORL)' (March 2015) 10, 'The SCA welcomes the introduction of a requirement that an investigation be undertaken by the Parliamentary Investigation Commission, and be submitted to the Parliament, in advance of a decision being taken. However, the SCA is of the view that the process, even as amended, does not provide sufficient procedural safeguards to ensure that dismissal of the Ombudsman will not be undertaken for political reasons.'

[271] SCA, 'Accreditation Report—Bosnia and Herzegovina (IHROBH)' (November 2016) 11. See also, SCA, 'Accreditation Report—El Salvador (PDDH)' (November 2016) 22–23: 'In accordance with article 9 of the Law, the Ombudsperson may be dismissed by a two-thirds (2/3) majority vote of the Legislative Assembly for various reasons, including manifest breach of their constitutional and legal obligations and gross negligence in the performance of their duties. It is not clear what the precise procedure for dismissal is, however, including, for example, who proposes a vote and whether a hearing is held.'; SCA, 'Accreditation Report—Norway (NNHRI)' (March 2017) 15–16.

willingness, suitability or ability to perform the member's functions', were criticized as being potentially open to misuse.[272]

In addition to the process for dismissal, the authority to dismiss itself must be clearly set out in the enabling law.[273] It should be clear who can initiate a process for dismissal.[274] The SCA has been particularly critical of provisions that leave room for considerable degrees of discretion to members of the government. For Malaysia's NHRI, the provisions were 'ill defined' and insufficient to protect against political interference:

> In accordance with section 10(d) of the Act, the King may remove a member, on the advice of the Prime Minister, if he is of the opinion that the members: (i) has engaged in any paid office or employment which conflicts with his duties as a members of the Commission; (ii) has misbehaved or conducted himself in such a manner as to bring disrepute to the Commission; or (iii) has acted in contravention of the Act and in conflict with his duties as a members of the Commission. This provision provides significant discretion to the Prime Minister in recommending the removal of a member, and, as the grounds are ill defined, may not provide sufficient protection against political interference.[275]

For New Zealand's NHRI, the provisions established that:

> the Governor General may, at any time for just cause, on the advice of the responsible Minister given after consultation with the Attorney-General, remove a member from office. In accordance with section 41, the responsible Minister may advise the removal of a member with as little formality and technicality, and as much expedition, as is permitted by the principles of natural justice, a proper consideration of the matter, and the different requirements of the Act in relation to the different types of statutory entity.[276]

The SCA found this to be insufficient as a clearly defined, independent, and objective dismissal process.[277]

[272] SCA, 'Accreditation Report—Scotland (SHRC)' (March 2015) 18.

[273] SCA, 'Accreditation Report—Jordan (NCHR)' (November 2016) 30–31: 'In accordance with article 13 (3) of the law, membership of the Board shall expire for various grounds. However, the SCA notes the authority to dismiss and the process for determining the existence of the ground in the event of loss of civil qualification, health incapacitation or absence without acceptable excuse is not specified.'

[274] SCA, 'Accreditation Report—Mexico (CNDH)' (November 2016) 37–38.

[275] SCA, 'Accreditation Report—Malaysia (SUHAKAM)' (November 2015) 31–32.

[276] SCA, 'Accreditation Report—New Zealand (NZHRC)' (May 2016) 43.

[277] ibid. See also, SCA, 'Accreditation Report—Australia (AHRC)' (November 2016) 11: 'the Governor-General may remove the Commissioner on the advice of the Executive Council, for the following reasons: (i) physical or mental incapacity; (ii) misbehaviour; (iii) absence from duty; and (iv) bankruptcy under their respective applicable above cited laws. The precise process for dismissal is not further described in the Act.'

The head of an institution should also not be able to remove a deputy without an independent and objective dismissal procedure,[278] backed by transparent and objective criteria.[279] These provisions may be contained in legislation, regulation, or another binding administrative guideline, but ideally should be in the enabling law.[280]

There must be a right to appeal within dismissal procedures.[281] Even where the provisions for dismissal include the possibility of review by a supposedly independent tribunal, the SCA will take into account the reality of the situation in which the NHRI is operating. Reviewing Zimbabwe's NHRI in 2016, the President had the power to remove a commissioner for 'inability to discharge the functions of the office whether arising from infirmity of body or mind or any other cause, or for misbehavior' and this was subject to review by a tribunal composed of 'a Chairperson who is or has been a judge of the Supreme Court or the High Court, and two (2) other members, one of whom shall be a person who is and has been qualified to practice as a legal practitioner in Zimbabwe for not less than seven (7) years'.[282] Because the members of the tribunal were appointed by the President, the SCA considered the process to be insufficient and open to misuse.[283] A similar situation arose for Tanzania, where 'pursuant to Article 10(2) of the Act, where the question of the removal of a Commissioner arises, the President appoints a special tribunal comprised of a chairman and at least two (2) other members to investigate the matter and report back' as the members of the special tribunal were appointed at the discretion of the President.[284] Imprecise provisions such as requiring that there be 'a hearing' will also not meet the requirements.[285]

Where NHRIs have board members appointed by different bodies, there must still be clear dismissal procedures in place. So, in the case of Germany, the enabling law provided that 'if a voting member of the Board of Trustees leaves the organisation or institution which has appointed him or her, or resigns from his or her position on the Board, then his or her replacement is elected or appointed for the remaining duration of the term of the Board'. The SCA was concerned that the statute and law were 'otherwise silent on the dismissal procedure for members of the Board'.[286]

278 SCA, 'Accreditation Report—Timor-Leste (PDHJ)' (November 2013) 31–32.
279 SCA, 'Accreditation Report—Mauritius (NHRC)' (October 2014) 22.
280 SCA, 'Accreditation Report—Timor-Leste (PDHJ)' (October 2018) 17.
281 SCA, 'Accreditation Report—Paraguay (DPP)' (March 2019) 11; SCA, 'Accreditation Report—Namibia (Ombudsman)' (October 2018) 13–14.
282 SCA, 'Accreditation Report—Zimbabwe (ZHRC)' (May 2016) 24.
283 ibid.
284 SCA, 'Accreditation Report—Tanzania (CHRAGG)' (November 2016) 52–53.
285 SCA, 'Accreditation Report—Mauritania (CNDH)' (November 2016) 36: 'According to Article 17 of the Law, a member can only be removed after a hearing for serious misconduct, default, repeated and non-justified absences, impediment or loss of membership qualities under which he was elected. Also in accordance with article 17 of the Law, dismissal occurs after being heard in accordance with the conditions set forth in the law. The Law is otherwise silent on the dismissal process.'
286 SCA, 'Accreditation Report—Germany (GIHR)' (November 2015) 17. See also, SCA, 'Accreditation Report—Greece (Greek National Commission for Human Rights (GNCHR))' (March 2017) 24–25.

4.5.3 Changes to Employment Conditions

Related to security of tenure are changes to the employment conditions of leadership. Changes to terms and conditions such as reductions in salary,[287] re-assignment mid-tenure,[288] or re-appointment in the absence of clear provisions in the enabling law,[289] have been considered by the SCA as problematic. The SCA has emphasized:

> In this regard, clearly establishing the terms and conditions of service of members at the commencement of their appointment is fundamental, as is the requirement that their terms and conditions must not be modified to the detriment of a member during their period of appointment. Furthermore, the terms and conditions of members should be equivalent to those with similar responsibilities in other independent State agencies, as pursuant to the Paris Principles B.2.[290]

NHRI leadership should be appropriately compensated. In reviewing the Ombudsman of Slovenia in 2010, the SCA expressed its concern regarding a change in salary provisions:

> [The SCA] received advice from the Ombudsman that recent domestic legislative changes in Slovenia have annulled the provision in the Law of the Human Rights Ombudsman that entitled the Ombudsman to a salary equal to that of the President of the Constitutional Court, and entitled the Deputies to a salary equivalent to Constitutional Court judges. This change may impact the independence and efficiency of the institution and affect the security of tenure of the current Ombudsman and Deputies.[291]

4.6 Full-time Board Members

In its 2009 General Observations, the SCA emphasized the need for members to be full-time:

> 2.8 Full-time Members: Members of the NHRIs should include full-time remunerated members to:

[287] SCA, 'Accreditation Report—Slovenia (Human Rights Ombudsman of the Republic of Slovenia (HRORS))' (March/April 2010) 9.
[288] SCA, 'Accreditation Report—Sweden (EOS)' (May 2011) 10, where the Ombudsperson was reassigned despite having four years left of her term.
[289] SCA, 'Accreditation Report—Guatemala (PDH)' (May 2013) 14.
[290] SCA, 'Accreditation Report—Slovenia (HRORS)' (March/April 2010) 8.
[291] SCA, 'Accreditation Report—Slovenia (HRORS)' (March/April 2010) 9.

a) Ensure the independence of the NHRI free from actual or perceived conflict of interests;
b) Ensure a stable mandate for the members;
c) Ensure the ongoing and effective fulfilment of the mandate of the NHRI.[292]

In its early reviews of NHRIs, the SCA recommended that members should be full-time,[293] even where they opt for part-time status, as it 'assists in promoting the independence of the NHRI by ensuring a more stable mandate for members, provides more effective leadership for staff; and promotes the ongoing and effective fulfilment of the NHRI's functions'.[294] This requirement was elaborated in the 2013 General Observations, and restated in 2018 General Observation 2.2 on Full-time members of an NHRI as follows:

> The enabling law of the NHRI should provide that members of its decision-making body include full-time remunerated members. This assists in ensuring:
> a) the independence of the NHRI free from actual or perceived conflict of interests;
> b) a stable tenure for the members;
> c) regular and appropriate direction for staff; and
> d) the ongoing and effective fulfilment of the NHRI's functions.[295]

The SCA explained the rationale behind this requirement:

> An appropriate minimum term of appointment is crucial in promoting the independence of the membership of the NHRI, and to ensure the continuity of its programs and services. An appointment period of three (3) years is considered to be the minimum that would be sufficient to achieve these aims. As a proven practice, the SCA encourages that a term of between three (3) and seven (7) years with the option to renew once be provided for in the NHRI's enabling law.
>
> A further requirement in ensuring the stability of a member's mandate, and the independence of a NHRI and its members, is the requirement that the terms and conditions of a member's service cannot be modified to their detriment during their period of appointment. Additionally, such terms and conditions should

[292] SCA, 'General Observations' (June 2009) (n 61) GO 2.8, 3.
[293] SCA, 'Accreditation Report—Luxembourg (CCDH)' (November 2008) 8; SCA, 'Accreditation Report—Luxembourg (CCDH)' (March 2009) 9; SCA, 'Accreditation Report—Switzerland (CFQF)' (March 2009) 6; SCA, 'Accreditation Report—Chad (CNDH)' (November 2009) 7; SCA, 'Accreditation Report—Algeria (CNCPPDH)' (March/April 2010) 7; SCA, 'Accreditation Report—Algeria (CNCPPDH)' (October 2010) 11; SCA, 'Accreditation Report—Zambia (HRCZ)' (October 2011) 19–20; SCA, 'Accreditation Report—Senegal (CSDH)' (October 2011) 21.
[294] SCA, 'Accreditation Report—Malawi (MHRC)' (March 2012) 22. See also, SCA, 'Accreditation Report—Senegal (CSDH)' (November 2012) 26.
[295] SCA, 'General Observations' (February 2018) (n 2) GO 2.2, 36.

> be equivalent to those with similar responsibilities in other independent State agencies.[296]

In its justification, the SCA outlined the importance of a stable mandate:

> Section B.3 of the Paris Principles sets out the requirements to ensure a stable mandate for the members of the NHRI. It specifies that, 'their appointment shall be effected by an official act which shall establish the specific duration of the mandate'. It further clarifies that, 'this mandate may be renewable . . .'.
>
> Although the provision is silent on the duration of the appointment, the SCA is of the view that specifying an appropriate minimum term in the NHRI's enabling law is crucial in both promoting the independence of the membership and of the NHRI, and to ensure the continuity of its programs and services. Consistent with international good practices, it therefore recommends an appointment period that extends between three and seven years with the option to renew once.
>
> In prescribing the conditions to ensure a stable mandate for members of the NHRI's decision-making body, section B.3 of the Paris Principles does not address the issue of whether members are required to be full-time or whether they are to be remunerated. The SCA is of the view that the appointment of members on a full-time basis promotes stability, an appropriate degree of management and direction, and limits the risk of members being exposed to conflicts of interest upon taking office. Furthermore, it clearly establishes the terms and conditions of service, including proper remuneration of members, and serves to reinforce their independence and integrity.
>
> Excerpt from the Paris Principles
>
> B) Composition and guarantees of independence and pluralism—
>
> 3. In order to ensure a stable mandate for the members of the national institution, without which there can be no real independence, their appointment shall be effected by an official act which shall establish the specific duration of the mandate. This mandate may be renewable, provided that the pluralism of the institution's membership is ensured.[297]

The requirement for all members to be full-time is not absolute. Where the membership of the board is large, such as for the NHRI of France with sixty-four members (in 2013), the SCA has recommended that the decision making body *include* full-time remunerated members:

> The Sub-Committee is of the view that the appointment of members on a full-time basis promotes stability, an appropriate degree of management and

[296] ibid (ellipsis in original).
[297] ibid 36–37 (ellipsis in original).

> direction, and limits the risk of members being exposed to conflicts of interest upon taking office. Furthermore, it clearly establishes the terms and conditions of service, including proper remuneration of members, and serves to reinforce their independence and integrity.[298]

Board members should not serve on a voluntary basis.[299] Ideally, they should be full-time and remunerated.[300] This requirement should be clearly stated in the enabling law.[301] The head of the institution should also not be part-time.[302] Even where there may be a sound logic for the use of part-time members, such as for Greece where members were intended to be part time 'in order that they remain professionally active and up-to-date with current affairs and the everyday practices of those entities they represent', the SCA still recommends the inclusion of full-time remunerated members.[303] This is still the case even where the institution is run by a full-time director, where there should still be full-time remunerated members of the decision-making body.[304] Whether commissioners are part-time or full-time (and which ones) should be set out in the enabling law.[305] There should not be the potential for arbitrary or vague terms regarding the duration of appointment.

The issue of full-time membership is closely connected to the length of tenure and fixed term in office, under General Observation 2.1 (see Chapter 4.5.1). Where a term of office ceases at a specified age (such as sixty-five years) rather than at the end of the term of office, the SCA has recommended amendments be made.[306] Discussion by the SCA under General Observation 2.2 has also included consideration of the terms and conditions of appointment. Where the leadership and staff of the Mauritius NHRI were to be appointed by the President 'on such terms and conditions as [he/she] thinks fit', the SCA commented:

> in order to ensure the stability of the mandate and the independence of members of its decision-making body, the terms and conditions of service should be

[298] SCA, 'Accreditation Report—France (Commission Nationale Consultative des Droits de l'Homme (CNCDH))' (May 2013) 12. See also, SCA, 'Accreditation Report—Greece (GNCHR)' (March 2015) 31, which had no full-time members and there was a voluntary agreement by the members not to accept the honorarium.

[299] SCA, 'Accreditation Report—Jordan (JNCHR)' (November 2015) 23; SCA, 'Accreditation Report—Luxembourg (CCDH)' (November 2015) 26.

[300] SCA, 'Accreditation Report—Malaysia (SUHAKAM)' (November 2015) 30. See also, SCA, 'Accreditation Report—Bahrain (NIHRB)' (May 2016) 9–10; SCA, 'Accreditation Report—Zambia (HRCZ)' (November 2016) 57; SCA, 'Accreditation Report—Denmark (DIHR)' (November 2017) 42–43.

[301] SCA, 'Accreditation Report—Zambia (HRCZ)' (October 2018) 21.

[302] SCA, 'Accreditation Report—Palestine (PICHR)' (November 2015) 35.

[303] SCA, 'Accreditation Report—Greece (GNCHR)' (May 2016) 36.

[304] SCA, 'Accreditation Report—Belgium (UNIA)' (May 2018) 11.

[305] SCA, 'Accreditation Report—Northern Ireland (NIHRC)' (May 2016) 44.

[306] SCA, 'Accreditation Report—Ghana (CHRAJ)' (March 2014) 13, where 'the Commissioner and Deputy Commissioners cease to hold office upon attaining the ages of seventy and sixty-five, respectively'.

> equivalent to office holders with similar responsibilities in other independent State agencies. Further, these terms and conditions should not be modified to their detriment during the period of appointment.[307]

Issues of stability arise where the terms and conditions of members are vague or subject to determination by government. For example, for the Great Britain NHRI (EHRC):

> All members of the EHRC work on a part-time basis. The number of days members are expected to work each year is determined by the Secretary of State in consultation with the EHRC, and is set out in members' terms and conditions of appointment. According to paragraph 1(3) of Schedule 1 of the Act, EHRC members hold office for a fixed term ranging from two (2) to five (5) years, and a member whose period of membership has expired may be re-appointed.[308]

Similarly, for the NHRI of Namibia, the SCA was concerned that a fixed, renewable term was not set out in the enabling law.[309] Terms of office should also not be indefinitely renewable.[310]

4.7 Functional Immunity for Board Members, Leadership, and Staff

Functional immunity for board members has been an increasing focus of the SCA's reviews in recent years. While there were only sixteen mentions in the five years between 2008 and 2013, there were thirty-one between November 2013 and October 2019.

In the General Observations in 2009, immunity was addressed in the following terms: 'It is strongly recommended that provisions be included in national law to protect legal liability for actions undertaken in the official capacity of the NHRI'.[311] The earliest recommendations by the SCA in relation to the need for improvements to functional immunity for the members of the NHRI included those to

[307] SCA, 'Accreditation Report—Mauritius (NHRC)' (October 2014) 23.

[308] SCA, 'Accreditation Report—Great Britain (ECHR)' (November 2015) 19. See also, SCA, 'Accreditation Report—South Africa (SAHRC)' (November 2017) 32, where the SCA expressed concern regarding provisions in the enabling law that 'the commissioners may, on the recommendation of the National Assembly, be appointed as full-time or part-time commissioners and hold office for such fixed term as the National Assembly may determine at the time of such appointment, but not exceeding seven (7) years'.

[309] SCA, 'Accreditation Report—Namibia (Ombudsman)' (November 2016) 42–43. See also, SCA, 'Accreditation Report—Tanzania (CHRAGG)' (November 2017) 37.

[310] SCA, 'Accreditation Report—Nicaragua (PDDH)' (November 2016) 46.

[311] SCA, 'General Observations' (June 2009) (n 61) GO 2.5.

Luxembourg,[312] Qatar,[313] Switzerland (Commission fédérale pour les questions féminines (CFQF)),[314] Tunisia,[315] Morocco,[316] Romania,[317] and Bulgaria.[318] From 2012 onwards, the issue began to gain even more attention from the SCA.[319] The General Observations relating to functional immunity were elaborated in 2013, and further strengthened with the addition of a new paragraph in 2017,[320] which provided additional rationale as to why functional immunity is so important and reflected SCA practice.[321] A further update in 2018 changed the title of the General Observation from 'guarantees of functional immunity' to '[p]rotection from criminal and civil liability for official actions and decisions undertaken in good faith', considered to be a clearer provision particularly for those NHRIs without a national tradition of immunity for office holders. The updated General Observation 2.3 (2018) provides:

> Protection from criminal and civil liability for official actions and decisions undertaken in good faith
>
> External parties may seek to influence the independent operation of an NHRI by initiating, or by threatening to initiate, legal proceedings against a member of the decision-making body or a staff member of the NHRI. For this reason, members and staff of an NHRI should be protected from both criminal and civil liability for acts undertaken in good faith in their official capacity. Such protections serve to enhance the NHRI's ability to engage in critical analysis and commentary on human rights issues, safeguard the independence of senior leadership, and promote public confidence in the NHRI.
>
> While the SCA considers it preferable for these protections to be explicitly entrenched in NHRI legislation or another applicable law of general application, it acknowledges that such protection may also exist by virtue of the specific legal context in which the NHRI operates.

312 SCA, 'Accreditation Report—Luxembourg (CCDH)' (November 2008) 9; SCA, 'Accreditation Report—Luxembourg (CCDH)' (March 2009) 10; SCA, 'Accreditation Report—Luxembourg (CCDH)' (October 2010) 12, under previous General Observation 2.5 'immunity'.

313 SCA, 'Accreditation Report—Qatar (NHRC)' (March 2009) 4.

314 SCA, 'Accreditation Report—Switzerland Commission fédérale pour les questions féminines (CFQF)' (March 2009) 6.

315 SCA, 'Accreditation Report—Tunisia (Comité Supérieur des Droits de l'Homme et des Libertés Fondamentales (SCHRFF))' (November 2009) 6.

316 SCA, 'Accreditation Report—Morocco (CCDH)' (October 2010) 13.

317 SCA, 'Accreditation Report—Romania (RIHR)' (May 2011) 21.

318 SCA, 'Accreditation Report—Bulgaria (CPD)' (October 2011) 8–9.

319 See for example, SCA, 'Accreditation Report—Kazakhstan (CHR)' (March 2012) 9; SCA, 'Accreditation Report—Mali (CNDH)' (March 2012) 13; SCA, 'Accreditation Report—Indonesia (Komnas HAM)' (March 2012) 20 (the SCA had also raised this concern in 2007). See also, SCA, 'Accreditation Report—Malawi (MHRC)' (March 2012) 20–21, where the SCA noted it had raised this concern in 2007 and that despite the NHRI's efforts, provision for immunity had not been included in the NHRI's enabling law.

320 The first paragraph of General Observation 2.3 (2018) was added in 2017.

321 While this provision was added in the 2017 General Observations, the formulation was used by the SCA since March 2014. SCA, 'Accreditation Report—Netherlands (NIHR) (March 2014) 7–8.

> It is acknowledged that no office holder should be beyond the reach of the law and thus, in certain exceptional circumstances it may be necessary to lift these protections. However, the decision to do so should not be exercised by an individual, but rather by an appropriately-constituted body such as the superior court or by a special majority of parliament. It is recommended that national law provide for well-defined circumstances in which these protections may be lifted in accordance with fair and transparent procedures.[322]

In its justification, the SCA emphasized the necessity of this provision:

> Providing members of the NHRI's decision-making body and staff protection from both criminal and civil liability for actions undertaken in good faith in their official capacity—often referred to as functional immunity—protects them from individual legal proceedings from anyone who objects to a decision or action of the NHRI.
>
> It is now widely accepted that the entrenchment of these protections in law is necessary for the reason that this protection, being one that is similar to that which is granted to judges under most legal systems, is an essential hallmark of institutional independence.
>
> It is recognized that in some national contexts, functional immunity is not part of the legal tradition and it may therefore be unrealistic or inappropriate for the NHRI to request that formal legal provisions be adopted. In such exceptional circumstances, the NHRI under review should provide sufficient information to explain why this is the case given its particular national context. This information will be reviewed in line with other guarantees provided at the national level to ensure independence, security of tenure, and the ability to engage in critical analysis on human rights issues.
>
> It is understood that these protections should not be absolute and should not cover circumstances where NHRI members or staff abuse their official functions or act in bad faith. In well-defined circumstances, the democratically-elected authority, such as the legislature, to which the NHRI is accountable, should have the power to lift these protections in accordance with a fair and transparent process.
>
> Excerpt from the Paris Principles
>
> B) Composition and guarantees of independence and pluralism—3. In order to ensure a stable mandate for the members of the national institution, without which there can be no real independence, their appointment shall be effected by an official act which shall establish the specific duration of the mandate. This mandate may be renewable, provided that the pluralism of the institution's membership is ensured.

[322] SCA, 'General Observations' (February 2018) (n 2) GO 2.3, 37.

> C) Methods of operation—
>
> Within the framework of its operation, the national institution shall: (a) Freely consider any questions falling within its competence, whether they are submitted by the Government or taken up by it without referral to a higher authority, on the proposal of its members or any petitioner.[323]

Functional immunity should be included as a provision in the NHRI enabling law.[324] In March 2014, in its assessment of the NHRI of the Netherlands (Netherlands Institute for Human Rights (NIHR)), the SCA explained the importance of immunity:

> Although the NIHR considers that the general law and jurisprudence provide its members with sufficient immunity to perform its duties, the SCA strongly recommends that express provisions be included in national law to protect the members of the NIHR's decision-making body from legal liability for the actions and decisions that are taken in good faith in their official capacity.[325]

The SCA also requires that sufficient and clear provision for immunity be provided for members in law.[326] For the NHRI of Thailand, the SCA was concerned that the NHRI was 'forced to rely on a variety of provisions in various laws to ensure its functional immunity and independence' and recommended the inclusion in the enabling law of a single, clear provision.[327] This was one of the areas of concern

[323] SCA, 'General Observations' (February 2018) (n 2) GO 2.3, 37–38.

[324] SCA, 'Accreditation Report—Chile (Instituto Nacional de Derechos Humanos (INDH))' (November 2012) 8; SCA, 'Accreditation Report—Denmark (DIHR)' (November 2012) 14; SCA, 'Accreditation Report—Malawi (MHRC)' (November 2012) 17–18; SCA, 'Accreditation Report—Oman (ONHRC)' (November 2013) 14; SCA, 'Accreditation Report—Thailand (NHRCT)' (November 2013) 27; SCA, 'Accreditation Report—Libya (NCCLHR)' (October 2014) 13–14; SCA, 'Accreditation Report—Korea (NHRCK)' (October 2014) 29–30 and SCA, 'Accreditation Report—Korea (NHRCK))' (March 2015) 41; SCA, 'Accreditation Report—Greece (GNCHR)' (March 2015) 32; SCA, 'Accreditation Report—Luxembourg (CCDH)' (November 2015) 26–27; SCA, 'Accreditation Report—Morocco (CNDH)' (November 2015) 34; SCA, 'Accreditation Report—Honduras (CONADEH)' (May 2016) 38, where an immunity provision had been repealed in 2004; SCA, 'Accreditation Report—Costa Rica (DHCR)' (November 2016) 19; SCA, 'Accreditation Report—Lithuania (SOO)' (March 2017) 11; SCA, 'Accreditation Report—Norway (NNHRI)' (March 2017) 16; SCA, 'Accreditation Report—Egypt' (March 2017) 36; SCA, 'Accreditation Report—Denmark (DIHR)' (November 2017) 40.

[325] SCA, 'Accreditation Report—Netherlands (NIHR) (March 2014) 7–8. This is the language subsequently included in the 2017 General Observations, noted above. See also, SCA, 'Accreditation Report—Slovakia (SNCHR)' (March 2014) 10; SCA, 'Accreditation Report—Korea (NHRCK)' (March 2014) 15–16.

[326] SCA, 'Accreditation Report—Thailand (NHRCT)' (March 2014) 17–18: 'the NHRCT suggested that section 15 of the enabling law and sections 130 and 257(1) of the Constitution provide its members with immunity. However, on the assumption that these protections apply, the SCA is of the view that they would only provide protection in limited circumstance'. Similarly, the SCA recommended to the NHRI of Egypt that even though Article 2.14 of the Constitution, guaranteed the independence of the NCHR, there should still be explicit protections in law for civil and criminal liability for official actions taken in good faith. SCA, 'Accreditation Report—Egypt' (May 2018) 22.

[327] SCA, 'Accreditation Report—Thailand (NHRCT)' (October 2014) 33: 'The NHRCT provided information to suggest that provisions in a number of laws may provide immunity from prosecution.

expressed by the SCA when the Thailand NHRI was downgraded to B-status in 2015.[328] Provision in the enabling law of the German NHRI that 'personal liability of the Board of Directors towards the Association is restricted to acts of intent or gross negligence' was also considered insufficiently clear.[329]

The SCA particularly considers that immunity for members of the NHRI should be closely aligned with that of the judiciary. In commenting on the NHRI of Finland (FNHRI) in 2014, it stated:

> Section 115 of the Constitution provides that the Ombudsman can be held liable for official acts in the same manner as Members of the Government, that being through a hearing by the High Court of Impeachment. While the FNHRI reports that there are no judicial immunities in Finland and that it is content with this state of affairs, the SCA notes that the Constitution provides for immunity for Members of Parliament. It strongly recommends that provisions be included in national law to protect relevant office holders of the FNHRI from legal liability for actions and decisions that are taken in good faith in their official capacity.[330]

It expressed concern about the Ombudsman law of Tajikistan, for example, as while the law 'ostensibly provides the Ombudsman with immunity from arrest, detention, bringing by force, search or imposition of administrative penalty by a court, these actions are permissible upon the approval of the President or the Prosecutor General'.[331] It continued that while no office holder should be above the law, 'the decision to [lift immunity] should not be exercised by an individual, but rather by an appropriately constituted body such as the superior court or by a special majority of Parliament'.[332]

Where the legislature is involved in issues related to immunity, the provisions which enable administrative sanction of the NHRI leadership should also not depend on overly simplified or potentially political decisions.[333] Thus, the SCA was

These laws included the Public Law, the Penal Code, Section 59, Paragraph 1, and Section 329; the NHRCT Act, 1999, Section 33, the Civil Code, Section 420; the Act on Liability for Wrongful Act of Official, B.E. 2539 (1996), Section 5.'

328 SCA, 'Accreditation Report—Thailand (NHRCT)' (November 2015) 40.
329 SCA, 'Accreditation Report—Germany (GIHR)' (November 2015) 18.
330 SCA, 'Accreditation Report—Finland (FNHRI)' (October 2014) 7.
331 SCA, 'Accreditation Report—Tajikistan (HROT)' (March 2012) 16.
332 ibid.
333 SCA, 'Accreditation Report—Latvia (OORL)' (March 2015) 10: 'In accordance with section 4 of the Law, an administrative sanction of the Ombudsman is permitted in relation to breaches of the Administrative Code when sanctioned by the Saeima. The Ombudsman advises that the Constitution provides that the Saiema may sit if at least half (50) of the members participate therein and that a decision may be taken by an absolute majority vote of the members present at the sitting. As a result, the SCA understands that a decision to administratively sanction the Ombudsman could be undertaken with the support of only 26 members of the Saeima.' (Under the heading 'administrative sanction'.)

concerned that the immunity of the Ombudsman of Serbia could be lifted by majority vote of the National Assembly.[334]

Even where the NHRI has primarily an advisory role, as with the Greek NHRI, the SCA still considers that immunity is appropriate for members to prevent external influence through initiation of or threat of legal proceedings.[335] The issue of lack of immunity was one of those listed by the SCA as an area of concern in recommending the NHRI be downgraded to B-status.[336] However, it was not the primary reason for downgrading. The SCA similarly did not accept assurances from Denmark's NHRI that immunity provisions were 'not relevant in the context of Denmark' as it 'failed to provide sufficient explanations to justify the reason why such a provision is neither relevant nor appropriate, given the specific context where it operates'.[337] However, the SCA did recognize that it can be problematic for some NHRIs to seek immunity provisions in their national contexts:

> It is recognised that in some national contexts, functional immunity is not part of the legal tradition and it may therefore be unrealistic or inappropriate for the NHRI to request that formal legal provisions be adopted. In such exceptional circumstances, the NHRI under review should provide sufficient information to explain why it would be both unnecessary and inappropriate to introduce such provisions given its particular national context. This information will be reviewed in line with other guarantees provided at the national level to ensure independence, security of tenure and the ability to engage in critical analysis on human rights issues.[338]

It has also recognized where there are domestic challenges to such immunity, such as in the case of the NHRI of Honduras (*Comisionado Nacional de los Derechos Humanos de Honduras* (CONADEH)):

> The SCA acknowledges that the CONADEH explained the reasons why the provision on immunity for all public officials, including the Commissioner of the CONADEH, was repealed by Legislative Decree No. 105-2004. It further acknowledges that the CONADEH considers that immunity should not apply to any of its members in order to avoid undermining the fight against corruption and impunity that is currently taking place in Honduras. Finally, the SCA notes that the CONADEH reports that the Constitution has been modified to provide that the Supreme Court of Justice resolves all processes initiated against High Officials of the State, including the Commissioner of the CONADEH.[339]

334 SCA, 'Accreditation Report—Serbia (PCRS)' (March 2015) 20.
335 SCA, 'Accreditation Report—Greece (GNCHR)' (May 2016) 35–36.
336 ibid.
337 SCA, 'Accreditation Report—Denmark (DIHR)' (November 2017) 40.
338 ibid.
339 SCA, 'Accreditation Report—Honduras (CONADEH)' (October 2019) 14–15.

However, the SCA was still of the view that it would be preferable for immunity provisions to be included in the law.[340] They further considered that this should extend to former Commissioners of the NHRI.[341]

NHRIs should make efforts to improve its enabling law as regards immunity, as can be seen in the following recommendation to the Philippines, welcoming efforts made by the NHRI as regards proposed amendments:[342]

> The Constitution and Executive Order 163 (EO 163) are silent on whether and how members and staff enjoy functional immunity for actions taken in their official capacity in good faith. The SCA acknowledges that provision described in Section 27 of the proposed CHR Act adequately addresses this concern by providing for the functional immunity of the members and staff of the CHRP.[343]

Immunity provisions should include immunity from civil liability as well as criminal.[344]

Although first mentioned in 2007,[345] and 2012,[346] since 2017, the SCA has increasingly recommended that immunity should also apply to the deputy leadership and staff of the NHRI.[347]

4.8 Staffing: Recruitment, Retention, and Secondment

Two parts of the 2009 SCA General Observations specifically dealt with issues of staffing at the NHRI: 2.4 staffing by secondment,[348] and 2.7 staff of the NHRI.[349] These were expanded and elaborated significantly in the 2013 General Observations under 'practices that directly promote Paris Principles compliance',[350] and were further elaborated in the 2018 General Observations combined into one observation. As these two issues are closely interlinked, and often discussed jointly by the

340 ibid.

341 ibid.

342 SCA, 'Accreditation Report—Korea (NHRCK)' (March 2015) 39. Where the SCA commended NHRI for putting forward proposals including a clause on immunity.

343 SCA, 'Accreditation Report—Philippines (CHRP)' (March 2017) 33.

344 SCA, 'Accreditation Report—Bosnia and Herzegovina (IHROBH)' (November 2016) 16.

345 SCA, 'Accreditation Report—Malawi (MHRC)' (March 2012) 20.

346 SCA, 'Accreditation Report—Poland (HRD)' (November 2012) 22.

347 SCA, 'Accreditation Report—Philippines (CHRP)' (March 2017) 33; SCA, 'Accreditation Report—Egypt (NHRC)' (March 2017) 36, noting that the draft law would provide immunity for members and staff and adequately address the SCA's concern; SCA, 'Accreditation Report—Panama (DPRP)' (November 2017) 26; SCA, 'Accreditation Report—Poland (CHRP)' (November 2017) 28.

348 In order to guarantee the independence of the NHRI, the Sub-Committee notes, as a matter of good practice, the following: (i) Senior level posts should not be filled with secondees; (ii) The number of seconded should not exceed 25 per cent and never be more than 50 per cent of the total workforce of the NHRI.

349 As a principle, NHRIs should be empowered to appoint their own staff.

350 They remained unchanged in the 2017 General Observations.

SCA, they are discussed together in this section. In its 2018 General Observation 2.4, the SCA recommended as follows:

> General Observation 2.4 Recruitment and retention of NHRI staff
>
> NHRIs should be legislatively empowered to determine the staffing structure and the skills required to fulfil the NHRI's mandate, to set other appropriate criteria (for example, to increase diversity), and to select their staff in accordance with national law.
>
> Staff should be recruited according to an open, transparent and merit-based selection process that ensures pluralism and a staff composition that possesses the skills required to fulfil the NHRI's mandate. Such a process promotes the independence and effectiveness of, and public confidence in, the NHRI.
>
> A fundamental requirement of the Paris Principles is that an NHRI is, and is perceived to be, able to operate independent of government interference. The SCA highlights that this requirement should not be seen to limit the capacity of an NHRI to hire a public servant with the requisite skills and experience. However, the recruitment process for such positions should always be open to all, clear, transparent, merit-based and at the sole discretion of the NHRI. Where an NHRI is required to accept staff assigned to it by the government, and in particular where this includes those at the highest levels in the NHRI, it brings into question its capacity to function independently.
>
> NHRIs must be provided with sufficient resources to permit the employment and retention of staff with the requisite qualifications and experience to fulfil the NHRI's mandate. Such resources should allow for salary levels, and terms and conditions of employment, equivalent to those of other independent of State agencies.
>
> JUSTIFICATION
>
> Pursuant to section B.2 of the Paris Principles, an NHRI is required to be provided with adequate funding, the purpose of which is 'to enable it to have its own staff . . . in order to be independent of the Government'. The Sub-committee interprets this provision to mean that:
>
> (i) NHRIs should possess the legislative authority to hire their own staff according to written recruitment guidelines based on merit and conducted through a transparent selection process using published criteria.
>
> (ii) NHRIs should be resourced in such a manner as to permit the employment and retention of staff with the requisite qualifications and experience to fulfil the NHRI's mandate. Additionally, such resources should allow for salary levels, terms and conditions of employment applicable to the staff of the NHRI to be equivalent to those of similarly independent State agencies and members of the public service undertaking similar work and with similar qualifications and responsibilities.

In this way, the SCA recognizes that fulfilling the requirements of Paris Principle B.2 is fundamental to ensuring the independence and efficient functioning of an NHRI. Where the NHRI lacks either adequate resources or the legislative ability to recruit its own staff, particularly at the senior-level—and these are instead appointed by the Executive—this undermines the principle of institutional independence.

Restrictions on the capacity of an NHRI to hire its own staff, or requirements to hire or accept assigned personnel from government agencies, except in exceptional or relevant circumstances, impacts on the real and perceived independence of an NHRI and may impede its ability to conduct its own affairs in an autonomous manner, free from government interference. This situation is particularly compounded where senior staff members, who set the direction and foster the culture of the NHRI, are seconded.

The SCA highlights that this requirement should not be seen to limit the capacity of an NHRI to hire a public servant with the requisite skills and experience, and indeed acknowledges that there may be certain positions within an NHRI where such skills are particularly relevant. However, the recruitment process for such positions should always be open to all, clear, transparent, merit based and at the sole discretion of the NHRI.

Excerpt from the Paris Principles

B) Composition and guarantees of independence and pluralism—

2. The national institution shall have an infrastructure which is suited to the smooth conduct of its activities, in particular adequate funding. The purpose of this funding should be to enable it to have its own staff and premises, in order to be independent of the Government and not be subject to financial control which might affect its independence.[351]

In relation to secondment from government or state bodies, which is an issue that frequently arises for NHRIs because they are state bodies, the SCA has not ruled out the use of seconded staff but rather placed limitations on the extent to which the NHRI can be staffed by secondees from other parts of the civil or public service. A previous specific observation on staffing of the NHRI by secondment was merged into the 2018 General Observations.[352]

From 2008 to 2012, the SCA raised the issue of staffing in the following terms: NHRIs should be able to recruit their own staff[353] to fulfil their requirements.[354] This power should be set out in legislation.[355] It also required NHRIs

[351] SCA, 'General Observations' (February 2018) (n 2) 39–40.

[352] SCA, 'General Observations' (March 2017) (n 62) 47.

[353] SCA, 'Accreditation Report—Mauritius (NHRC)' (April 2008) 6; SCA, 'Accreditation Report—Chad (CNDH)' (November 2009) 7; SCA, 'Accreditation Report—Senegal (CSDH)' (October 2011) 21.

[354] SCA, 'Accreditation Report—Korea (NHRCK)' (November 2008) 10.

[355] SCA, 'Accreditation Report—Algeria (CNCPPDH)' (March/April 2010) 7; SCA, 'Accreditation Report—Algeria (CNCPPDH)' (October 2010) 10; SCA, 'Accreditation Report—Namibia (Ombudsman)' (May 2011) 16.

to have 'the authority to appoint all staff and to determine the required skills and human rights expertise'.[356] Senior staff should not be appointed by the government.[357] Secondment from government ministries is not considered appropriate,[358] nor secondment from the public service,[359] and the majority of staff overall should not be secondees.[360] NHRI staff should also not be redeployed from other branches of the public service.[361] NHRIs with a high number of seconded staff, particularly in senior positions, should aim to reduce these.[362] The SCA expressed concern with the use of secondees in the NHRI of Thailand:

> A fundamental requirement of the Paris Principles is that a National Human Rights Institution is, and is perceived to be, independent of government interference... The secondment of staff brings into question the capacity of the National Institution to function independently.[363]

As with other areas of Paris Principles compliance, the SCA has required that the NHRI take initiatives to improve the situation in relation to the independence of its staff as can be seen in these recommendations to India (NHRCI):

> At the time of the NHRCI's re-accreditation in 2006, the SCA recommended that 'consideration be given to strengthening the consultation process regarding the selection and appointment of the Secretary General and staff under section 11(1) of the enabling law of the Commission in order to strengthen the independence of the staff appointed'.

356 SCA, 'Accreditation Report—Belgium (CEOOR)' (March/April 2010) 11.

357 SCA, 'Accreditation Report—Belgium (CEOOR)' (March/April 2010) 11; SCA, 'Accreditation Report—Algeria (CNCPPDH)' (October 2010) 10.

358 SCA, 'Accreditation Report—Thailand (NHRC)' (November 2008) 11; SCA, 'Accreditation Report—Mauritania (CNDH)' (May 2011) 16; SCA, 'Accreditation Report—Mali (CNDH)' (March 2012) 13–14.

359 SCA, 'Accreditation Report—Bangladesh (NHRCB)' (May 2011) 7.

360 SCA, 'Accreditation Report—Congo (CNDH)' (October 2010) 4, where 23 of 27 staff were seconded, including at the highest level.

361 SCA, 'Accreditation Report—Tanzania (CHRAGG)' (November 2016) 52; SCA, 'Accreditation Report—Bolivia (DPB)' (March 2017) 20–21: 'The SCA notes that the DPB reports in its Statement of Compliance that a high percentage of its staff are seconded. It does appear, however, that the DPB is legislatively empowered to determine the staffing structure, the skills required to fulfil the NHRI's mandate, set other criteria (such as diversity), and select their staff in accordance with their enabling law.'

362 SCA, 'Accreditation Report—Ukraine (UPCHR)' (October 2019) 20.

363 SCA, 'Accreditation Report—Thailand (NHRCT)' (November 2013) 29. The SCA noted that 'The 2007 Constitution [Section 256(6)] capacitates the Office of the NHRCT to autonomously administrate the personnel of the NHRCT, and Section 19 of the Act designates officials of the Office as "ordinary officials of the NHRCT under the law on parliamentary official service". In this connection, the President of the Commission is in charge of the personnel administration in the Office of the NHRCT. The NHRCT did not report on steps it has taken to address the concerns raised by the Sub-Committee on Accreditation in November 2008 about its permanent staff members being seconded from various government ministries.'

> Section 11 of the founding legislation requires that the Central Government second to the NHRCI a civil servant with the rank of Secretary to take the role of Secretary General of the Commission, and a police officer of the rank of Director General of Police or above to take the post of Director (Investigations). Email correspondence dated 30 November 2006, and re-submitted on 23 May 2011, further indicates that the posts of Joint Secretary, Chief Coordinator (Training), Director, Deputy Inspector General Police and Senior Superintendent Police are also seconded from the government.
>
> The SCA is not satisfied that the NHRCI has sufficiently addressed the recommendation it made in 2006. The SCA recommends that the NHRCI advocate to amend the PHRA 2006 to remove the requirement that the Secretary General and Director of Investigations be seconded from the Government, and to provide for an open, merit-based selection process. The SCA also remains concerned about the practice of having police officers and former police officers involved in the investigation of human rights violations, particularly in circumstances where the alleged perpetrators are the police. This practice has adverse implications for the actual and perceived independence of the NHRCI.[364]

The SCA raised concerns again in its 2016 review of India's NHRI; it raised particular concerns about the presence of former police officers as investigators, as well as the composition of senior management:

> Also in May 2011, the SCA expressed its concern about the practice of having police officers and former police officers involved in the investigation of human rights violations, particularly in circumstances where the alleged perpetrators are the police. It noted that this practice has adverse implications for the actual and perceived independence of the NHRCI.
>
> The SCA acknowledges the NHRCI's position that:
>
> - As concerns the Secretary General, the fact that this individual is seconded from the senior levels in the civil service means that they have wide knowledge of government functioning and standing among various levels of government. However, the SCA notes that, in the past five (5) years, the position has been held by a variety of people and has been vacant for a substantial period of time.
> - As concerns the Director General (Investigation) and the practice of using former police officers to investigate complaints, these individuals know how the system works and, as a result, are unable to unearth truth in cases where others could not. However, for victims of abuses by police, there is a real or perceived conflict of interest, and this may impact the ability of such persons to access human rights justice.

[364] SCA, 'Accreditation Report—India (NHRCI)' (May 2011) 13–14.

Notwithstanding the justifications provided, the SCA remains concerned that these practices have a real impact on the perceived independence of the NHRCI. The SCA therefore recommends that:

- the Secretary General be recruited through an open, merit-based selection process; and
- the NHRCI consider policy options to address the perceived independence issue created by having former police officers investigate complaints, for example, by providing for civilian oversight of these activities.[365]

In its 2017 examination of the NHRCI, the SCA emphasized its concerns that:

> for victims of abuses by police, there may be a real or perceived conflict of interest in having police officers engaged in the investigation of human rights violations, particularly those committed by the police, and this may impact on the ability to conduct impartial investigations as well as the ability of victims to access human rights justice.[366]

Since the 2013 revisions of the general observations, the SCA has continued and gradually strengthened its recommendations. Senior level posts should not be seconded, and there should not be more than 25 per cent seconded staff, barring 'exceptional circumstances'.[367] NHRIs should also not have to seek approval before hiring additional staff, particularly where that position is included in the budget of the NHRI, and funds secured.[368]

Issues relating to staffing can also impact the NHRI's effectiveness. In its 2013 review of Nepal, the SCA raised concerns over the lack of qualified staff:

> The SCA received correspondence, which was subsequently shared with the NHRC, questioning the NHRC's effectiveness due to an inability to hire and retain a sufficient number of staff. It was suggested that this arose in part due to delays in passing a law to allow for the appointment of staff outside the normal public service employment processes conducted by the Public Service Commission.[369]

[365] SCA, 'Accreditation Report—India (NHRCI)' (May 2011) 13–14. These concerns were reiterated in the 2016 and 2017 reviews of the NHRCI.

[366] SCA, 'Accreditation Report—India (NHRCI)' (November 2017) 20.

[367] SCA, 'Accreditation Report—Mauritius (NHRC)' (October 2014) 24. 'In accordance with Section 5(1) of the Act, the Secretary to the Cabinet shall make available to the Commission an officer of the rank of Principal Assistant Secretary who shall be the Secretary of the Commission and such other administrative and other staff as the Commission and any Division may require. The SCA notes with appreciation the NHRC's efforts to recruit its own staff. However, the NHRC reports that 50% of its staff are seconded.' A specific reference to a limit on the percentage of seconded staff was contained in the 2017 General Observations, but not retained in the 2018 revisions. SCA, 'General Observations' (March 2017) (n 62) 47.

[368] SCA, 'Accreditation Report—Serbia (PCRS)' (March 2015) 21–22.

[369] SCA, 'Accreditation Report—Nepal (NHRC)' (May 2013) 24. The review was deferred in order to provide the NHRI time to provide additional information. In the November 2013 review, it was noted

While it is essential that an NHRI can recruit its own staff,[370] this does not mean that the NHRI cannot use a national recruitment system per se. The SCA has found in relation to the NHRI of Tanzania (CHRAGG) that

> the use of a whole of government recruitment process for public servants is not inherently problematic provided that process is independent and objective, and ensures merit-based selection, and the CHRAGG is able to specify the requisite criteria for selection. However, it would be preferable that the CHRAGG be able to undertake its own recruitment.[371]

This is even the case where senior NHRI members participate as members of the interview panel.[372] However, such a process should not result in a high number of secondees. In reviewing the NHRI of Côte d'Ivoire (La Commission Nationale des Droits de l'Homme de Côte d'Ivoire (CNDHCI)), the SCA commented:

> The SCA notes that staff recruitment is conducted through the Integrated System of Civil Servants and State Agents Management Authority of the Ministry of Public Services. While the CNDHCI reports that it has the power to evaluate candidates and request their release from their entity of origin, the SCA expresses concern about the high percentage of civil servants employed on the basis of secondment among its staff, including officials at the most senior levels such as the Secretary General, the Director of the Cabinet, the heads of departments, and various other senior managers.
>
> Further, in accordance with article 42, administrative, financial and technical staff are provided to the CNDHCI by the government through secondment. Overall, the CNDHCI reports that 19 of its 43 staff, or 44%, are seconded.[373]

Such a system must also not undermine the autonomy of the NHRI, and the use of technical administrative or budgetary restrictions to limit the NHRI's ability to

that there had been a 'recent decision of the Supreme Court that allows the NHRC to recruit its own staff, and that the NHRC expects that it would soon recommence recruiting staff.' SCA, 'Accreditation Report—Nepal (NHRC)' (November 2013) 33. See also, SCA, 'Accreditation Report—Namibia (Ombudsman)' (October 2018) 14, where the NHRI was staffed 'by Public Service Officers that have been made available to it'.

[370] For example, SCA, 'Accreditation Report—Cyprus (CAHR)' (November 2015) 9; SCA, 'Accreditation Report—Namibia (Office of the Ombudsman (Ombudsman))' (November 2016) 41.

[371] SCA, 'Accreditation Report—Tanzania (CHRAGG)' (November 2016) 52. In its 2017 review of Tanzania, the SCA added the requirement of transparency: 'The use of a whole of government recruitment process for public servants is not inherently problematic so long as the process is *transparent* and objective, and ensures merit-based selection.' (Emphasis added.) SCA, 'Accreditation Report—Tanzania (CHRAGG)' (November 2017) 36.

[372] SCA, 'Accreditation Report—Tanzania (CHRAGG)' (November 2017) 36.

[373] SCA, 'Accreditation Report— Côte d'Ivoire (CNDHCI)' (May 2016) 13–14.

manage its own staff are viewed negatively by the SCA. In reviewing Montenegro's Protector of Human Rights and Freedoms (PHRF), it recommended:

> The SCA notes that the PHRF has not recruited its full staff complement of 33, and that the NHRI has plans to recruit more staff in 2017. The recruitment is conducted by the Human Resources Management Authority, including the advertising of vacancies and the evaluation of candidates. The Protector has indicated that these requirements undermine its autonomy and independence.
>
> Further, the PHRF reports that it may only staff positions after obtaining a certificate from the Ministry of Finance certifying that funds are available for salaries, despite the fact that the necessary funds have been approved in the budget.[374]

In addition, the terms and conditions of staff should also be equivalent to those of similarly independent state agencies and members of the public service undertaking similar work and with similar qualifications and responsibilities.[375]

Closely connected to the issue of secondment is that of the process for selection and appointment of staff. As noted in the General Observation 2.4 above, staff are to be recruited by an 'open, transparent and merit-based selection process'. Where a recruitment process has a limited pool, such as being limited to civil servants, this does not meet the relevant requirement.[376] Similarly, where the (staff) head of an organization is appointed by the government, this is unlikely to be compliant with the Paris Principles.[377] Staff should also have security of tenure. For example, the NHRI of Spain (DPS) had a practice whereby all staff member positions ended when a new head (*Defensor*) was elected. While no longer the practice by the 2018 review of the DPS, the SCA nonetheless recommended 'to ensure the ongoing and effective fulfilment of its mandate by guaranteeing staff security of tenure. This could be achieved through an amendment to the law that explicitly provides for such security of tenure regardless of the election of the Defensor.'[378]

Also closely related here are issues of funding, where the NHRI cannot afford to retain its staff, dealt with in Chapter 5.

374 SCA, 'Accreditation Report—Montenegro (PHRF)' (May 2016) 18.

375 SCA, 'Accreditation Report—Slovenia (HRORS)' (March/April 2010) 9.

376 SCA, 'Accreditation Report—Uruguay (National Human Rights and Ombudsman Institution of Uruguay (NHROI))' (March 2015) 27–28. Ten of the NHRI's seventeen staff were seconded.

377 SCA, 'Accreditation Report—Cameroon (NCHRF)' (November 2017) 16–17: 'Section 11.1 of the Law provides that the Secretary-General is appointed by a decree of the President. The SCA emphasizes that a fundamental requirement of the Paris Principles is that an NHRI is, and is perceived to be, able to operate independent of government interference. The SCA is of the view that this practice has the potential to impact on the perceived independence of the NHRI. It recommends that the law provides that the Secretary-General be recruited through an open, merit-based selection process. Until such time as an amendment to this effect can be adopted, the SCA encourages the NCHRF to pursue policy and/or administrative measures to provide the NCHRF with greater control over the process, including by setting the selection criteria and by participating in the evaluation of candidates.'

378 SCA, 'Accreditation Report—Spain (DPS)' (May 2018) 33.

4.9 Comment

This chapter has considered a range of issues that relate to the critical question of 'who runs NHRIs'. From how representative the institution is, seen in the requirements for pluralism, to the detail of the selection and appointment process, to tenure and dismissal, and the ability to recruit qualified staff, it covers areas that are fundamental to the independent functioning and legitimacy of the institution.

As noted in Chapter 2, the SCA first developed General Observations in 2006 which were said to be on 'common or important interpretative issues'.[379] Of the six initial General Observations, three dealt with issues discussed in this chapter: Ensuring pluralism; Selection and appointment of the governing body; and Government representatives on National Institutions. As seen in this chapter, these issues have been and continue to be significant areas of criticism and frequent areas of recommendation by the SCA. The general observations on these issues have been further developed, refined, and expanded, as in the case, for example, of government representatives (now entitled Political representatives on NHRIs). This continuous refinement of the General Observations reflects the further experience of the SCA and its desire to continue to strengthen the accreditation process and also to ensure that the General Observations are able to be applied to all NHRIs regardless of the political and legal system in which they operate. An example of this latter point can be seen in the renaming and revision of the General Observation on 'Guarantee of functional immunity', now entitled 'Protection from criminal and civil liability for official actions and decisions undertaken in good faith'.

The SCA has also, over the years, made efforts to clarify and explain what its main focus and concern is on each of the issues identified. For example, in the selection and appointment of the governing body, it has been made clear that the SCA is particularly concerned with the *process* by which selection and appointments are made, and not who ultimately appoints the members. That is, provided the process meets the requirements of the General Observation, then who selects/appoints the members of the decision-making body.

A number of international organizations have emphasized the importance of the selection process for leadership of NHRIs and other independent state-based bodies. The European Commission for Democracy Through Law (Venice Commission) has recommended that 'the way according to which an Ombudsman is appointed is of the utmost importance as far as the independence of the institution is concerned and the independence of the Ombudsman is a crucial corner stone of this institution'.[380] The Parliamentary Assembly of the Council of Europe

[379] SCA, 'Accreditation Report' (October 2006) 2.

[380] Venice Commission, 'Opinion on the Draft Law on the Public Attorney of "the former Yugoslav Republic of Macedonia"' (Venice 14–15 March 2003) CDL-AD(2003)007, B.II, Art 5.1.

(PACE) has recommended that an ombudsperson institution should have, 'exclusive and transparent procedures for appointment and dismissal by Parliament by a qualified majority of votes sufficiently large as to imply support from parties outside government, according to strict criteria which unquestionably establish the ombudsman as a suitably qualified and experienced individual of high moral standing and political independence'.[381] The European Commission against Racism and Intolerance (ECRI) has similarly recommended that 'the persons holding leadership positions in equality bodies should be selected and appointed by transparent, competency-based and participatory procedures'.[382] Clear and well-defined dismissal processes are similarly important.[383]

Closely connected to the issue of security of tenure, and the ability of the leadership to undertake fully its promotion and protection role, is the question of immunity. The SCA has been increasingly concerned about this. This is in keeping with the approach of international organizations. The Venice Commission, for example, has emphasized the need for functional immunity for independent human rights bodies. In its opinion on the draft law on the Protector of Human Rights of Montenegro it commented:

> Not only the Protector and his/her Deputies, but also his/her staff should have immunity 'from legal process in respect of words spoken or written and acts performed by them in their official capacity.' Such immunity shall continue to be accorded even after the end of the Protector's mandate or after the members of staff cease their employment with the Protector's institution. This immunity should also include baggage, correspondence and means of communication belonging to the Protector.[384]

ECRI has stated that 'persons holding leadership positions should benefit from functional immunity, be protected against threats and coercion and have

[381] Parliamentary Assembly, 'Strengthening the institution of ombudsman in Europe' Res 1959 (2013) (4 October 2013), para 7.3.

[382] European Commission against Racism and Intolerance (ECRI), 'ECRI General Policy Recommendation No. 2: Equality Bodies to Combat Racism and Intolerance at National Level' (7 December 2017) CRI(2018)06, para 23.

[383] Venice Commission, 'Opinion on the draft law on prevention and protection against discrimination' (19 March 2018) CDL-AD(2018)001, para 69 <https://www.venice.coe.int/webforms/documents/default.aspx?pdffile=CDL-AD(2018)001-e> accessed 25 February 2021: 'In order to be in conformity with the [European Court of Human Rights] case law, the draft law should spell out that the loss of capacity should be established before a competent authority on the basis on the basis of objective medical expertise.' See amongst many others, *Shtukaturov v Russia*, App no 44009/05, 27 March 2008, para 114; and *Winterwerp v the Netherlands*, App no 6301/73, 24 October 1979, para 39.

[384] Venice Commission, 'Opinion on the draft amendments to the law on the Protector of Human Rights and Freedoms of Montenegro' (Venice 9–10 October 2009) CDL-AD(2009)043, paras 12, 27, and 29.

appropriate safeguards against arbitrary dismissal or the arbitrary non-renewal of an appointment where renewal would be the norm'.[385]

The next chapter examines an equally critical area for NHRI functioning, and one that has been the focus of a considerable proportion of SCA recommendations since its establishment: funding and administrative regulation.

[385] ECRI, 'ECRI General Policy Recommendation No. 2: Equality Bodies to Combat Racism and Intolerance at National Level' (7 December 2017) CRI(2018)06, para 24.

5
National Human Rights Institutions Relationship with the State
Funding and Administrative Autonomy

5.1 Introduction

Funding is a significant point of concern for the Sub-Committee on Accreditation (SCA). Almost half of the SCA recommendations from 2008 to 2019 included reference to the need for adequate funding, with an additional forty-three including reference to financial autonomy. The issue of adequate funding is also closely connected to the National Human Rights Institution's (NHRI) coverage by administrative regulation, and thus is included later in this chapter. Whether or not an NHRI has sufficient budgetary resources to undertake its operations is fundamental to the ability of the institution to fulfil its mandate as an independent human rights body. The UN Paris Principles refer explicitly for the need for the NHRI to have 'adequate funding', particularly underlining its connection to independence:

> B) Composition and guarantees of independence and pluralisms
>
> 2. The national institution shall have an infrastructure which is suited to the smooth conduct of its activities, in particular adequate funding. The purpose of this funding should be to enable it to have its own staff and premises, in order to be independent of the Government and not be subject to financial control which might affect its independence.[1]

The SCA has elaborated considerably on what this means in practice. Centred on the core issue of NHRI independence, the requirement for adequate funding means that the NHRI must be able to determine its own priorities and have enough funds to undertake its mandate. The SCA's recommendations are set out in detail in General Observation 1.10 (2018):

> To function effectively, an NHRI must be provided with an appropriate level of funding in order to guarantee its independence and its ability to freely determine

[1] Principles relating to the Status of National Institutions, UNGA Res 48/134 (20 December 1993) UN Doc A/RES/48/134 (The Paris Principles) B.2.

National Human Rights Institutions. David Langtry and Kirsten Roberts Lyer, Oxford University Press. © David Langtry and Kirsten Roberts Lyer 2021. DOI: 10.1093/oso/9780198829102.003.0006

its priorities and activities. It must also have the power to allocate funding according to its priorities. In particular, adequate funding should, to a reasonable degree, ensure the gradual and progressive realisation of the improvement of the NHRI's operations and the fulfilment of its mandate.

Provision of adequate funding by the State should, as a minimum, include the following:

a) the allocation of funds for premises which are accessible to the wider community, including for persons with disabilities. In certain circumstances, in order to promote independence and accessibility, this may require that offices are not co-located with other government agencies. Where possible, accessibility should be further enhanced by establishing a permanent regional presence;
b) salaries and benefits awarded to its staff comparable to those of civil servants performing similar tasks in other independent institutions of the State;
c) remuneration of members of its decision-making body (where appropriate);
d) the establishment of well-functioning communications systems including telephone and internet;
e) the allocation of a sufficient amount of resources for mandated activities. Where the NHRI has been designated with additional responsibilities by the State, additional financial resources should be provided to enable it to assume the responsibilities of discharging these functions.

Funding from external sources, such as from international development partners, should not compose the core funding of the NHRI, as this is the responsibility of the State. However, the SCA recognizes the need for the international community, in specific and rare circumstances, to continue to engage and support an NHRI in order to ensure it receives adequate funding until such time when the State will be able to do so. In such unique cases, an NHRI should not be required to obtain approval from the state for external sources of funding, as this requirement may detract from its independence. Such funds should not be tied to donor-defined priorities but rather to the pre-determined priorities of the NHRI.

Government funding should be allocated to a separate budget line item applicable only to the NHRI. Such funding should be regularly released and in a manner that does not impact adversely on its functions, day-to-day management and retention of staff.

While an NHRI should have complete autonomy over the allocation of its budget, it is obliged to comply with the financial accountability requirements applicable to other independent agencies of the State.[2]

[2] SCA, 'General Observations of the Sub-Committee on Accreditation' (adopted on 21 February 2018) 28 (hereafter SCA, 'General Observations' (February 2018)).

In its justification, the SCA quotes Paris Principles section B.2 and elaborates on the connection between adequate funding and issues of NHRI accessibility, staffing and membership, communications, and operations:

> While the provision of 'adequate funding' is determined in part by the national financial climate, States have the duty to protect the most vulnerable members of society, who are often the victims of human rights violations, even in times of severe resource constraints. As such, the SCA believes that it is nevertheless possible to identify certain aspects of this Paris Principles requirement that must be taken into account in any particular context. They include the following:
>
> a) *Accessibility to the public*—This is particularly important for the most vulnerable sections of society, who would otherwise have particular difficulty bringing attention to any violation of their human rights.
>   - As many vulnerable persons may be geographically remote from the major cities where most NHRIs are located, establishing a regional presence increases the accessibility of NHRIs, giving them as wide a geographical reach as possible, and enabling them to have full national coverage for the receipt of complaints. It is essential that, where regional offices exist, they be adequately resourced to ensure their effective functioning.
>   - Another means of increasing the accessibility of NHRIs to vulnerable groups is to ensure that their premises are neither located in wealthy areas nor in or nearby government buildings. This is particularly important where government buildings are protected by military or security forces. Where an NHRI's offices are too close to government offices, this may not only compromise the perceived independence of the Institution but also risk deterring complainants.
>
> b) *NHRI staff*—Salaries and benefits awarded to NHRI staff should be comparable to those of civil servants performing similar tasks in other independent institutions of the State.
>
> c) *NHRI members*—Where appropriate, members of the NHRI's decision-making body should receive remuneration equivalent to those individuals with similar responsibilities in other independent institutions of the State.
>
> d) *Communications infrastructure*—The establishment of communications systems, including telephone and internet, is essential for the public to access the NHRI's office. A well-functioning communications structure, including simplified complaints-handling procedures which may include the receipt of complaints orally in minority languages, increases the reach of vulnerable groups to the NHRI's services.
>
> e) *Allocation for activities*—NHRIs should receive adequate public funding to perform their mandated activities. An insufficient budget can render an NHRI ineffective or limit it from reaching its full effectiveness. Where the NHRI has been designated with additional responsibilities by the State, such

as the role of National Preventive or Monitoring Mechanism pursuant to an international human rights instrument, additional financial resources should be provided to enable it to discharge these functions.[3]

The SCA further elaborates on the areas of donor funding and financial accountability:

Donor funding
As it is the responsibility of the State to ensure the NHRI's core budget, the SCA takes the view that funding from external sources, such as from international development partners, should not constitute the NHRI's core funding. However, it recognizes the need for the international community, in specific and rare circumstances, to continue to engage and support an NHRI in order to ensure it receives adequate funding until such time when the State will be able to do so. This is particularly applicable in post-conflict States. In these circumstances, NHRIs should not be required to obtain approval for external sources of funding, as this requirement may pose a threat to its independence.

Financial systems and accountability
Financial systems should be such that the NHRI has complete financial autonomy as a guarantee of its overall freedom to determine its priorities and activities. National law should indicate from where the budget of the NHRI is allocated and should ensure the appropriate timing of release of funding, which is particularly important in ensuring an appropriate level of skilled staff. This should be a separate budget line over which the NHRI has absolute management and control. The NHRI has the obligation to ensure the coordinated, transparent and accountable management of its funding through regular public financial reporting and a regular annual independent audit.[4]

The following sections will examine the questions of 'adequate' or 'appropriate' funding. This chapter begins by considering NHRIs' funding requirements. It then discusses that while the SCA emphasizes the importance of state funding for NHRIs, it also stresses that NHRIs must have sufficient financial autonomy over their own budgets, as well as to seek and receive external funding. Finally, the chapter discusses the related issues of the NHRIs' control over their administrative regulations and functioning as well as their ability to establish regional offices.

[3] ibid 29 (emphasis in original).
[4] SCA, 'General Observations' (February 2018) (n 2) 29–30 (emphasis in original).

5.2 Adequate Funding

In examining whether a budget is indeed adequate in keeping with the Paris Principles, the SCA has been consistent in its approach even from its earliest assessments, requiring that funding must cover all aspects of NHRI operations. The SCA's 2009 General Observations already set out the requirements for funding by the state that 'at a minimum' included:

a) the allocation of funds for adequate accommodation, at least its head office;
b) salaries and benefits awarded to its staff comparable to public service salaries and conditions;
c) remuneration of Commissioners (where appropriate); and
d) the establishment of communications systems including telephone and internet.[5]

In addition, the SCA considered that adequate funding 'to a reasonable degree' should 'ensure the gradual and progressive realization of the improvement of the organization's operations and the fulfilment of their mandate'.[6] Further, external funding 'should not compose the core funding of the NHRI as it is the responsibility of the state to ensure the NHRI's minimum activity budget in order to allow it to operate towards fulfilling its mandate'. The NHRI should have 'complete financial autonomy'.[7] This fits with the findings of the SCA in assessing NHRI budgets prior to the publication of the 2009 General Observations, which included calls for 'adequate funding',[8] the need for additional resources,[9] sufficient and sustainable funding,[10] funding for adequate accommodation, and gradual and progressive realization of operations and mandate,[11] as well enabling the NHRI to hire staff and for regional offices,[12] and that members should be remunerated, provision for which should be set out in legislation or internal regulations.[13]

[5] SCA, 'ICC Sub-Committee on Accreditation General Observations' (adopted in June 2009) GO 2.6, 2–3 (hereafter SCA, 'General Observations' (June 2009)).
[6] ibid 3.
[7] ibid.
[8] SCA, 'Report and Recommendations of the Session of the Sub-Committee on Accreditation—Mongolia (National Human Rights Commission (NHRC))' (November 2008) (hereafter SCA, 'Accreditation Report') 9; SCA, 'Accreditation Report—Paraguay (Defensoría del Pueblo (DP))' (November 2008) 9.
[9] SCA, 'Accreditation Report—Niger (Commission Nationale des Droits de l'Homme et des Libertés Fondamentales (CNDHLF)' (April 2008) 6.
[10] SCA, 'Accreditation Report—Croatia (Ombudsman of the Republic of Croatia (ORC))' (April 2008) 7.
[11] SCA, 'Accreditation Report—Timor-Leste (Provedoria for Human Rights and Justice (PDHJ))' (April 2008) 8–9.
[12] SCA, 'Accreditation Report—Kenya (National Commission on Human Rights (NCHR))' (November 2008) 8.
[13] SCA, 'Accreditation Report—Switzerland (Commission fédérale pour les questions féminines (CFQF))' (March 2009) 6.

The SCA has rarely referred to specific figures in its comments on budgeting. One example where it did this was for Luxembourg in 2008, noting that the 'annual budget for non-post expenditures has been set for the past 3 years at 12,500 EUR'.[14] While it did not elaborate on this recommendation, it is understood from the context of the SCA's report that the level was considered insufficient and stagnant. The NHRI was accredited with B-status. It is a challenge to identify where funding issues may become fatal to compliance with the Paris Principles. In the case of the NHRI of Switzerland (Federal Commission against Racism (FCR)), one of the few institutions to be given the now discontinued C-status (see Chapter 2.1), the SCA noted the significant insufficiency of funding. However, overall, the SCA's concerns were more connected to the institution being a non-independent governmental body, rather than an NHRI, than purely there being a funding problem:

> The FCR receives an annual budget from the Government to support its activities. The FCR has fewer than three full time staff positions and does not have its own premises. The FCR holds its meetings at the premises of the Federal Administration and the Secretariat's offices are seated in the premises of the General Secretariat of the FDI. The SCA refers to the Paris Principles which state that a national institution should be able to have its own staff and premises in order to ensure its independence.[15]

Between 2009 and 2011, the SCA continued to recommend the following:

- Adequate (or 'appropriate')[16] funding to effectively perform its functions,[17] implement its programmes and activities,[18] and carry out its mandated activities.[19]
- State provision of adequate *core* funding[20] that is adequate to ensure ongoing and effective fulfilment of its mandate,[21] 'sufficient to allow for core

[14] SCA, 'Accreditation Report—Luxembourg (Commission Consultative des Droits de l'Homme of Luxembourg (CCDH))' (November 2008) 9.

[15] SCA, 'Accreditation Report—Switzerland (FCR)' (March/April 2010) 12.

[16] SCA, 'Accreditation Report—Haiti (Office for the Protection of Citizens (OPC))' (November 2013) 9.

[17] SCA, 'Accreditation Report—Algeria (Commission Nationale Consultative de Promotion et de Protection des Droits de l'Homme (CNCPPDH))' (March/April 2010) 7; SCA, 'Accreditation Report—Bangladesh (National Human Rights Commission of Bangladesh (NHRCB))' (May 2011) 7.

[18] SCA, 'Accreditation Report—Congo (Commission Nationale des Droits de l'Homme (CNDH))' (October 2010) 4.

[19] SCA, 'Accreditation Report—Honduras (National Commissioner for Human Rights (CONADEH))' (May 2016) 39.

[20] SCA, 'Accreditation Report—Philippines (The Commission on Human Rights of the Philippines (CHRP))' (March 2012) 26; SCA, 'Accreditation Report—Rwanda (The National Commission for Human Rights of the Republic of Rwanda (NCHR))' (March 2012) 28.

[21] SCA, 'Accreditation Report—Burundi (Independent National Human Rights Commission of Burundi (INHRCB))' (November 2012) 8.

programming in protection and promotion of human rights and to sustain the required staff compliment'.[22]
- Funding should include not just core funding but also resources to undertake projects that help the NHRI fulfil its mandate.[23]

In reviewing the Scottish NHRI in 2010, the SCA noted that even at its establishment it had low funding that may be insufficient to ensure proper functioning, and that 'limitations on the staffing and resources of the SHRC in its establishment period may be such as to restrict its operations in the future'.[24]

The SCA is also concerned where—barring exceptional circumstances, such as shall be seen in Section 5.3 on donor funding—the government is not providing adequate funds for the NHRI. The SCA recommended the downgrading of the Senegal NHRI from A- to B-status in 2012, in part because of concerns over the 'lack of concrete support from the State in providing adequate funding'.[25]

Many NHRIs raise concerns to the SCA during the accreditation process about insufficient funding.[26] Others have highlighted that they would benefit from additional funding.[27] The SCA had generally not been specific in identifying what are the precise funding gaps that raise concern. One example of a specific early reference to funding is where the SCA also expressed concern that the NHRI of Iraq was 'required to operate without funding for the first half of 2013'.[28] However, in more recent assessments, the SCA reports have become somewhat more detailed

[22] SCA, 'Accreditation Report—Malawi (Malawi Human Rights Commission (MHRC))' (November 2012) 19.

[23] SCA, 'Accreditation Report—El Salvador (Procuraduría para la Defensa de los Derechos Humanos of El Salvador (PDDH))' (May 2011) 12; SCA, 'Accreditation Report—South Africa (South African Human Rights Commission (SAHRC))' (November 2012) 30.

[24] SCA, 'Accreditation Report—Scotland (Scottish Human Rights Commission (SHRC))' (March/April 2010) 4.

[25] SCA, 'Accreditation Report—Senegal (Comité Sénégalais des Droits de l'homme (CSDH))' (October 2011) 21; SCA, 'Accreditation Report—Senegal (CSDH)' (November 2012) 26. It may be noted that the NHRI did not provide documentation supporting its compliance with the Paris Principles within the time frame established by the ICC Statute for the consideration of downgrades in status. ibid.

[26] See for example, SCA, 'Accreditation Report—Democratic Republic of Congo (The National Human Rights Commission (CNDH))' (May 2018) 13; SCA, 'Accreditation Report—Guatemala (The Procurador de Derechos Humanos of Guatemala (PDH))' (May 2018) 25; SCA, 'Accreditation Report—Moldova (The Office of the People's Advocate of Moldova (OPA))' (May 2018) 26; SCA, 'Accreditation Report—Spain (The Defensor del Pueblo of Spain (DPS))' (May 2018) 35; SCA, 'Accreditation Report—Sri Lanka (The Human Rights Commission of Sri Lanka (SLHRC))' (May 2018) 38; SCA, 'Accreditation Report—Uganda (The Uganda Human Rights Commission (UHRC))' (May 2018) 40; SCA, 'Accreditation Report—Paraguay (DPP)' (March 2019) 12. See also, SCA, 'Accreditation Report—Timor-Leste (PDHJ)' (October 2018) 17, where 'the SCA received information' that the NHRI would benefit from additional funding.

[27] SCA, 'Accreditation Report—Bulgaria (Ombudsman of the Republic of Bulgaria (ORB))' (March 2019) 17; SCA, 'Accreditation Report—Croatia (ORC)' (March 2019) 19; SCA, 'Accreditation Report—Armenia (The Human Rights Defender of the Republic of Armenia (HRDA))' (March 2019) 15.

[28] SCA, 'Accreditation Report—Iraq (High Commission for Human Rights (HCHR))' (March 2015) 8.

in terms of identifying specific problems. In its March 2017 review of the NHRI of Colombia (DPC), the NHRI reported that its funding was insufficient to carry out its mandate 'in particular taking into consideration the recent signature of the Peace Agreements and the additional responsibilities mandated to the DPC as a result. Consequently, it faces a situation of understaffing and difficulties in retaining staff with the requisite skills.'[29]

As has been seen in other areas of SCA recommendations, the SCA expects that the NHRI will advocate for an improvement in its budget,[30] including where donor funding or raising funds are undertaken.[31] It encourages NHRIs to seek budget increases from the state.[32] Repeatedly throughout its assessments, the SCA has recommended to the NHRI to engage with the government to seek improved funding and financial autonomy.

5.2.1 Funding for Staff

The SCA is concerned where funding is insufficient to ensure proper staffing. It expressed concern regarding the salary levels of staff, impacting the Serbian NHRI's 'future capacity to employ and retain staff'.[33] It was also concerned that these salary levels may affect the capacity of the institution to employ and retain staff.[34] It considered that the NHRI 'should be resourced in such as [*sic*] manner as to permit the employment and retention of staff with the requisite qualifications and experience to fulfil its mandate. Their terms and conditions should be equivalent to staff with similar responsibilities and qualifications employed in other independent agencies of the state.'[35] This issue had not been resolved by 2015, with the NHRI reporting that its staff members were 'underpaid compared to other independent entities in the country', resulting in continuing issues with retention of qualified staff.[36] However, while a point of concern, the NHRI was not threatened with

[29] SCA, 'Accreditation Report—Colombia (The Defensoria Del Pueblo of Colombia (DPC))' (March 2017) 21–22. See also, SCA, 'Accreditation Report—Sierra Leone (Human Rights Commission (HRCSL))' (May 2016) 49.

[30] SCA, 'Accreditation Report—Haiti (OPC)' (March 2019) 27; SCA, 'Accreditation Report—Nepal (National Human Rights Commission of Nepal (NHRCN))' (March 2019) 29; SCA, 'Accreditation Report—Honduras (CONADEH)' (October 2019) 13.

[31] SCA, 'Accreditation Report—Sierra Leone (SLHRC)' (May 2011) 9. The SCA uses two different acronyms for this same NHRI in its reports: SLHRC and HRCSL.

[32] SCA, 'Accreditation Report—Ghana (Commission on Human Rights and Administrative Justice (CHRAJ))' (March 2014) 13; SCA, 'Accreditation Report—Tanzania (The Commission for Human Rights and Good Governance of Tanzania (CHRAGG))' (November 2017) 35.

[33] SCA, 'Accreditation Report—Serbia (Protector of Citizens of the Republic of Serbia (PCRS))' (March/April 2010) 5.

[34] ibid.

[35] ibid.

[36] SCA, 'Accreditation Report—Serbia (PCRS)' (March 2015) 21. See also, SCA, 'Accreditation Report—Malawi (MHRC)' (November 2016) 31.

downgrading. A similar concern was raised in relation to the NHRI of Hungary (CFR) in 2019.[37] The SCA also raised concerns where the NHRI of Zambia was understaffed due to funding. The SCA noted the NHRI's reports that:

> of the 131 positions in its organizational structure, 57 are filled, representing only 43% of its staffing needs ... budgetary constraints have inhibited its full recruitment of staff, and that it engages interns on a regular basis to fill the shortfall. Further, the HRCZ reports that, while funding allocated for staff has remained consistent during the review period, the budget allocated for other expenses was cut by 50% in 2016.[38]

Low salaries for NHRI staff compared to the private sector may also result in high turnover of staff, impacting the ability of the institution to implement its objectives.[39] Sufficient funding should also be provided for training staff.[40]

5.2.2 Gradual and Progressive Increase in Funding

Funding provided to NHRIs should be gradual and progressive. As noted in the previous section, in examining the NHRI of Scotland, the SCA had expressed concern in 2010 about the low level of funding provided on establishment. By the time of the NHRI's re-accreditation in 2015 there had been no improvement, with the NHRI continuing 'to employ the same number of staff at present as it did in 2010'; moreover, it had 'experienced a 15% reduction in its budget over the last 3 years'.[41] The SCA is particularly concerned where no financial improvements have been made after a number of years.[42] Slight improvements are also unlikely to be sufficient to meet the requirement of gradual and progressive funding.[43]

[37] SCA, 'Accreditation Report—Hungary (CFR)' (October 2019) 26. The SCA noted that: '[t]he CFR reported that salaries of its staff are much below the average salary of staff in comparable to institutions with constitutional status in Hungary'.

[38] SCA, 'Accreditation Report—Zambia (Human Rights Commission (HRCZ))' (November 2016) 57. A 2018 review saw an improvement in this situation: SCA, 'Accreditation Report—Zambia (HRCZ)' (October 2018) 20.

[39] SCA, 'Accreditation Report—Ethiopia (Ethiopia Human Rights Commission (EHRC))' (November 2012) 10.

[40] SCA, 'Accreditation Report—Ukraine (Ukrainian Parliament Commissioner for Human Rights (UPCHR))' (October 2019) 22.

[41] SCA, 'Accreditation Report—Scotland (SHRC)' (March 2015) 19.

[42] SCA, 'Accreditation Report—Cameroon (National Commission on Human Rights and Freedoms (NCHRF))' (March/April 2010) 8: 'The NCHRF continues to face financial constraints that hamper its capacity to fulfil its mandate.' This concern was reiterated in the March 2015 review of the NHRI. SCA, 'Accreditation Report—Cameroon (NCHRF)' (March 2015) 36–37.

[43] SCA, 'Accreditation Report—Uruguay (Institución Nacional de Derechos Humanos Defensoría del Pueblo (NHROI))' (May 2016) 21.

Funding should be increased where additional functions are added or the mandate expanded, particularly where the National Preventative Mechanism (NPM) under the Optional Protocol to the Convention Against Torture (OPCAT)[44] or National Monitoring Mechanism (NMM) under the Convention on the Rights of Persons with Disabilities is added.[45] See further on this point Section 5.2.4, regarding expansion of mandate, and more broadly Chapter 8 on NHRIs with these treaty-mandated functions. Funding must cover more than just staffing, hence the SCA's concern that 90 per cent of the budget for Bolivia's NHRI was directed towards personnel costs from 2013 to 2016.[46] Further, funding should allow for the strengthening of existing programmes and creation of new ones.[47]

5.2.3 Economic Downturns and Significant Budget Cuts

Particularly since the global economic downturn of 2008, the SCA has been faced with the issue of funding for the NHRI where there is a financial crisis or broad public sector cutbacks in the state. This raises a particular challenge to the general requirement of the SCA that NHRI funding from the state be increased gradually and progressively. A further challenge for the SCA is identifying where funding cuts are part of legitimate and multi-sector remedial actions or where the excuse of budgetary challenges is used to cut NHRI funding.

The NHRI in Ireland (Irish Human Rights Commission (IHRC)) faced a particularly severe funding cut following a financial crisis in 2008, with the SCA expressing 'deep concern about plans to significantly reduce the IHRC's budget for 2009. This would undermine the IHRC's capacity to carry out its mandate effectively and threatens its financial autonomy.'[48] However, as this was a planned reduction for the future budget, the SCA did not recommend a downgrade. By the time of the next re-accreditation, the state had created a 'new' NHRI by merging the existing NHRI with the national equality body. This was assessed as a newly accredited NHRI and accredited with A-status.[49] In 2013, the SCA noted that the funding for the NHRI in Croatia was cut to the extent that the NHRI was required to raise funds to undertake its activities. However, this was not fatal to A-status.[50]

[44] Optional Protocol to the Convention against Torture and other Cruel, Inhuman or Degrading Treatment or Punishment (adopted on 18 December 2002, entered into force on 22 June 2006) 2375 UNTS 237 (hereafter OPCAT).

[45] Convention on the Rights of Persons with Disabilities (adopted on 13 December 2006, entered into force on 3 May 2008) 2515 UNTS 3 Art 33 (hereafter CRPD). See SCA, 'Accreditation Report—Cyprus (Commissioner for Administration and Human Rights (CAHR))' (November 2015) 8–9.

[46] SCA, 'Accreditation Report—Bolivia (Defensoría del Pueblo (DPB))' (March 2017) 19–20.

[47] SCA, 'Accreditation Report—El Salvador (PDDH)' (November 2016) 21–22.

[48] SCA, 'Accreditation Report—Ireland (Irish Human Rights Commission (IHRC))' (November 2008) 8.

[49] SCA, 'Accreditation Report—Ireland (Irish Human Rights and Equality Commission (IHREC))' (March 2015) 41.

[50] SCA, 'Accreditation Report—Croatia (ORC)' (May 2013) 8–9.

Where cuts to funding are experienced across public bodies in a state, the SCA seems to be less concerned—most likely because it is not a targeted reduction in the budget of the NHRI. For example, while noting challenges faced by the NHRI of Finland, the SCA did not express particular concern at the lack of increase overall in the NHRI budget as this was due to the financial situation in the country.[51] Likewise, the NHRI of Bosnia Herzegovina had experienced 'significant' budget cuts but reported that other institutions in the country were facing similar challenges.[52] For the NHRI of Zimbabwe, a significant decrease in budget was a result of 'critical financial problems affecting Zimbabwe'.[53] The Northern Ireland NHRI had reported to the SCA that its government funding was 'not sufficient to effectively carry out its mandate'.[54] The NHRI had experienced 'a significant cut in its budget since 2009 … in line with other non-departmental public bodies, it will continue to have budgetary cuts until 2019'.[55] While the SCA recommended that the NHRI advocate for 'an appropriate level of funding', it did not downgrade the NHRI.

For the NHRI of Australia, the SCA repeatedly expressed its concern over a number of years that annual efficiency measures by the government were negatively impacting the NHRI, and gradually eroding the budget.[56] However, these measures were not targeted at the NHRI nor had they yet undermined its ability to carry out its functions. Similar concerns were raised for the NHRI of Kenya, which was taking steps to address the challenges it was facing in maintaining an adequate level of funding to fulfil its staffing needs and additional functions under the CRPD.[57] This reflects an approach by the SCA where legitimate national budgetary constraints, coupled with either an effort by the NHRI and/or some efforts by the state to improve or reduce limitations on the budget will not result in a downgrade, even where the funding is considered insufficient to ensure the proper functioning of the institution, unless it directly impacts its effectiveness.[58]

[51] SCA, 'Accreditation Report—Finland (Finnish National Human Rights Institution (FNHRI))' (October 2014) 8–9. See also, SCA, 'Accreditation Report—Namibia (Office of the Ombudsman (Ombudsman))' (October 2018) 13: 'The SCA notes that the Ombudsman's budget has increased regularly for the exception of 2018–19 due to the application of austerity measures to all public bodies.'

[52] SCA, 'Accreditation Report—Bosnia and Herzegovina (Human Rights Ombudsmen of Bosnia and Herzegovina (IHROBH))' (November 2016) 15.

[53] SCA, 'Accreditation Report—Zimbabwe (Human Rights Commission (ZHRC))' (May 2016) 22–23.

[54] SCA, 'Accreditation Report—Northern Ireland (Northern Ireland Human Rights Commission (NIHRC))' (May 2016) 46–47.

[55] ibid.

[56] SCA, 'Accreditation Report—Australia (Australian Human Rights Commission (AHRC))' (May 2011) 11; SCA, 'Accreditation Report—Australia (AHRC)' (November 2016) 12.

[57] SCA, 'Accreditation Report—Kenya (National Commission on Human Rights (NCHR))' (October 2019) 16–17.

[58] See also in this regard, SCA, 'Accreditation Report—Tanzania (CHRAGG)' (November 2016) 52; SCA, 'Accreditation Report—Peru (Defensoría del Pueblo (DPP))' (March 2017) 28–29.

An example of a threatened downgrading connected to funding occurred in relation to the NHRI of Greece (Greek National Commission for Human Rights (GNCHR)). The NHRI had faced substantial reductions in its funding since the 2008 economic downturn in the country. The budget of the NHRI was decreased in 2013, to around one-third of its 2009 budget.[59] While the SCA noted that the budget allocation had increased in 2014, it remained concerned that the NHRI did 'not have sufficient funds to effectively carry out its duties'.[60] Re-accreditation was deferred to May 2016, where downgrading to B-status was recommended, with multiple issues noted, including the budgetary provision. While the budget had increased in 2016, the SCA remained concerned that the NHRI did not have sufficient funds to effectively carry out its mandate.[61] In March 2017, re-accreditation with A-status was recommended, with the SCA applauding the 'continuing efforts of the GNCHR to implement the recommendations made in May 2016'.[62] In relation to funding it noted:

> The SCA notes that it received detailed information regarding the financial situation in which the GNCHR is operating, and in particular the social and other consequences of the program of austerity currently in effect in Greece. The SCA acknowledges that this situation limits the GNCHR's ability to advocate for increased funding ... The SCA encourages the GNCHR to continue to advocate for an appropriate level of funding to carry out its mandate including, where appropriate, the establishment of regional offices.[63]

Thus, in this instance, despite a significant cut to the NHRI's funding, the explanation and efforts of the NHRI were sufficient to allow for A-status re-accreditation of the institution.

The SCA does expect that as soon as possible the state will resume adequate funding of the NHRI. The NHRI of Latvia had its funding significantly reduced, with a 25% reduction in staff 'as a result of the economic crisis' since 2008, and an overall reduction in budget 'by almost half' in 2010, and while some increase had taken place subsequently, the SCA expressed concern in its March 2015 review that there had been no increase in funding in 2014 or 2015.[64]

The SCA has particularly welcomed where governments have protected the NHRI's budget—at least insofar as not applying any cuts—in spite of financial

[59] SCA, 'Accreditation Report—Greece (GNCHR)' (March 2015) 32–33.
[60] ibid 32.
[61] SCA, 'Accreditation Report—Greece (GNCHR)' (May 2016) 36–37.
[62] SCA, 'Accreditation Report—Greece (GNCHR)' (March 2017) 23.
[63] ibid 24.
[64] SCA, 'Accreditation Report—Latvia (Ombudsman of the Republic of Latvia (OORL))' (March 2015) 10–11.

austerity measures.[65] Also receiving SCA praise are gradual increases in an NHRI's budget.[66]

The SCA has recognized that as state-funded institutions, NHRIs may be vulnerable to budget cuts as a means of limiting the activities of the NHRI or its independence. As noted above, the SCA expressed serious concern where NHRIs receive large cuts to their budget that may impact their ability to fulfil their mandate.[67] When the SCA reviewed Malaysia's NHRI in 2015, it was concerned that it was at risk of receiving a 50% budget cut 2016, however, similarly to the case of Ireland noted above, this was a possible reduction for future years and thus not a reason for a downgrade and the SCA expressed support for the NHRIs efforts to avoid this budget cut.[68] The SCA noted that the NHRI of Niger had seen its budget repeatedly decreased and the disbursement of the budget slow down, thus 'limiting its ability to effectively respond to issues as they arise'.[69]

The NHRI of Great Britain (Equality and Human Rights Commission (EHRC)) received cuts to its funding, as had most public bodies, however, the SCA was concerned 'that the EHRC has experienced a cut in funding, equivalent to approximately seventy percent (70%) of its 2010 budget. The SCA also noted that the number of staff had been reduced from 500 in 2010, to 204 in 2015'.[70] The SCA was similarly concerned that the NHRI of Panama (The Defensoría del Pueblo de la República de Panamá (DPRP)) reported that its budget was 'the lowest of any institution in Panama and is not sufficient to discharge its mandate effectively, including its requirements related to staffing and infrastructure'.[71] More worryingly, it reported that:

> its budget has been decreased as a political punishment due to malpractices of the former administration. The DPRP reports to have requested four (4) reviews on its projected budget due to the insufficient allocation of funds. Furthermore, the DPRP informs that its offices are not accessible to persons with disabilities. The SCA acknowledges that the DPRP's financial situation is critical, as it is not allowing the DRPR [*sic*] to recruit and retain its technical employees or to improve its premises. Further, due to financial constraints, the DPRP has not been able to establish its [National Preventative Mechanism under the UN Optional

65 SCA, 'Accreditation Report—New Zealand (New Zealand Human Rights Commission (NZHRC))' (May 2011) 17; SCA, 'Accreditation Report—Albania (Peoples' Advocate (PA))' (October 2014) 18–19.

66 SCA, 'Accreditation Report—Georgia (Office of the Public Defender (OPD))' (November 2012) 17.

67 SCA, 'Accreditation Report—Côte d'Ivoire (La Commission Nationale des Droits de l'Homme de Côte d'Ivoire (CNDHCI))' (May 2016) 12–13; SCA, 'Accreditation Report—Ireland (IHRC)' (November 2008) 7–8.

68 SCA, 'Accreditation Report—Malaysia (Human Rights Commission of Malaysia (SUHAKAM))' (November 2015) 30.

69 SCA, 'Accreditation Report—Niger (CNDH)' (March 2017) 13–14.

70 SCA, 'Accreditation Report—Great Britain (EHRC)' (November 2015) 21.

71 SCA, 'Accreditation Report—Panama (DPRP)' (November 2017) 25.

Protocol to the Prevention on Torture] structure despite having been designated as the NPM.[72]

Thus, while the SCA acknowledged the DPRP's financial situation was critical, it re-accredited the institution with A-status and encouraged the DPRP to continue to advocate for an appropriate level of funding to carry out its mandate. Despite significant funding deficiencies and reductions, the DPRP's efforts to have its budget reviewed and increased were sufficient to allow for A-status re-accreditation

5.2.4 Expansion of Mandate—Funding Requirements

Where an NHRI is tasked with additional functions, there must be a corresponding increase in the budget to allow it to effectively undertake these functions. This additional funding should not be a 'one off' when new powers are allocated, but an ongoing increase in the budget.[73]

Of particular concern to the SCA is ensuring additional funding for the NPM under the OPCAT,[74] and the NMM under the Convention on the Rights of Persons with Disabilities (CRPD).[75] This issue is dealt with in more detail in Chapter 8 on treaty-mandated functions. Additional functions added to the NHRI's mandate such as responsibility for children's rights,[76] gender equality,[77] anti-discrimination,[78] data protection,[79] analysing situations of armed conflict,[80]

[72] ibid.

[73] SCA, 'Accreditation Report—Maldives (Human Rights Commission of The Maldives (HRCM))' (March/April 2010) 6. See also, SCA, 'Accreditation Report—Argentina (Defensoria del Pueblo de la Nación Argentina (DPNA))' (November 2016) 9–10: 'The SCA notes that the DPNA has experienced a reduction in funding and an increase in functions.'

[74] OPCAT (n 44). See SCA, 'Accreditation Report—Azerbaijan (The Human Rights Commissioner (Ombudsman) of the Republic of Azerbaijan (HRCA))' (March 2012) 31; SCA, 'Accreditation Report—Georgia (OPD)' (November 2012) 17; SCA, 'Accreditation Report—Finland (FNHRI)' (October 2014) 8–9; SCA, 'Accreditation Report—Ukraine (UPCHR)' (October 2014) 36; SCA, 'Accreditation Report—Serbia (PCRS)' (March 2015) 21; SCA, 'Accreditation Report—Montenegro (Protector of Human Rights and Freedoms (PHRF))' (May 2016) 17; SCA, 'Accreditation Report—Georgia (OPD)' (October 2018) 11; SCA, 'Accreditation Report—Togo (La Commission Nationale Des Droits De L'homme Du Togo (CNDH))' (October 2019) 18–19.

[75] CRPD (n 45). See SCA, 'Accreditation Report—Finland (FNHRI)' (October 2014) 8; SCA, 'Accreditation Report—Luxembourg (CCDH)' (November 2015) 27–28; SCA, 'Accreditation Report—Peru (DPP)' (March 2017) 27–28; SCA, 'Accreditation Report—Georgia (OPD)' (October 2018) 11.

[76] SCA, 'Accreditation Report—Albania (PA)' (October 2014) 19; SCA, 'Accreditation Report—Germany' (November 2015) 16–17.

[77] SCA, 'Accreditation Report—Mongolia (National Human Rights Commission of Mongolia (NHRCM))' (November 2013) 23; SCA, 'Accreditation Report—Mongolia (NHRCM)' (October 2014) 25–26.

[78] SCA, 'Accreditation Report—Ukraine (UPCHR)' (October 2014) 36; SCA, 'Accreditation Report—Montenegro (PHRF)' (May 2016) 17; SCA, 'Accreditation Report—Georgia (OPD)' (October 2018) 11.

[79] SCA, 'Accreditation Report—Ukraine (UPCHR)' (October 2014) 36.

[80] SCA, 'Accreditation Report—Germany (German Institute for Human Rights (GIHR))' (November 2015) 16.

human trafficking,[81] undertaking a national human rights report,[82] and business and human rights,[83] also require a corresponding increase in funding. This funding should be sufficient for the additional functions.[84]

Funding must be sufficient to cover all parts of an NHRI's mandate, whether they are added or existing at the time of accreditation. For example, the Ghana NHRI (the Commission on Human Rights and Administrative Justice (CHRAJ)) served as NHRI, Ombudsperson, and Anti-Corruption Agency. The SCA noted:

> The CHRAJ reports that funding in respect of its programmes and development has not kept pace with the broad mandate that it has been given and the network of offices spread throughout the country which require a substantial outlay of resources.[85]

Where additional functions are not state assigned but arise as a result of an assessment of needs by the NHRI due to the situation in the country, such as for the Nigeria NHRI which expanded its activities 'to address the repercussions of the civil unrest', adequate funding should also be provided.[86] Funding for additional mandates should form part of core NHRI funding.[87]

5.2.5 Funding Concerns Raised by UN Human Rights Bodies

There is a significant overlap in the extent of SCA and UN Treaty Body recommendations regarding NHRI funding, and the SCA has referred to Treaty Body concluding observations in its accreditation assessments. For Slovakia's NHRI, which was recommended to be accredited with B-status in March 2014, the SCA noted that several UN Treaty Bodies had expressed concerns regarding the funding of the institution.[88] While referring to the General Observations, the SCA did not

[81] SCA, 'Accreditation Report—Luxembourg (CCDH)' (November 2015) 27–28.

[82] SCA, 'Accreditation Report—Germany (GIHR)' (November 2015) 16.

[83] SCA, 'Accreditation Report—Finland (FNHRI)' (October 2019) 10.

[84] SCA, 'Accreditation Report—Costa Rica (DHCR)' (November 2016) 18–19; SCA, 'Accreditation Report—France (Commission Nationale Consultative des Droits de l'Homme (CNCDH))' (March 2019) 21, noting that the CNCDH reported a 25 per cent increase of its budget over a five-year period but that it had been 'vested with significant additional responsibilities' during that time for which the increase may not be sufficient.

[85] SCA, 'Accreditation Report—Ghana (CHRAJ)' (March 2019) 24.

[86] SCA, 'Accreditation Report—Nigeria (National Human Rights Commission (NHRC))' (November 2016) 49.

[87] SCA, 'Accreditation Report—Poland (Human Rights Defender (HRD))' (November 2012) 24. See also, SCA, 'Accreditation Report—Armenia (HRDA)' (May 2013) 8: 'sufficient and sustainable State funding ... should include adequate funding for the continued operation of its regional offices and the NPM'.

[88] SCA, 'Accreditation Report—Slovakia (National Centre for Human Rights (SNCHR))' (March 2014) 9. The SCA noted: '[t]he SCA notes the concerns expressed by the Committee on the Elimination of Racial Discrimination (CERD/C/SVK/CO/9-10), the Committee on Economic, Social and Cultural

otherwise detail the nature of its concern. However, the three Treaty Bodies concerned, the Committee on the Elimination of Racial Discrimination (CERD), the Committee on Economic, Social and Cultural Rights (CESCR), and the Human Rights Committee (HRC), made the following recommendations regarding the NHRI, the National Centre for Human Rights (NCHR) in the three years prior to the SCA review, and formed the basis for the SCA's concerns:

- CERD (2013): 'regrets the lack of adequate financial and human resources to empower the NCHR with necessary means in disseminating the Anti-Discrimination Act and assisting victims of racial discrimination (art. 2) . . . the Committee recommends that the State party strengthen the NCHR's independence and mandate and provide it with financial and human resources in order to efficiently fight against discrimination.'[89]
- CESCR (2012): 'is also concerned by the insufficiency of the financial and human resources placed at the Centre's disposal. The Committee recommends that the State party . . . endow it with the financial and human resources it needs in order to function in full conformity with the Paris Principles.'[90]
- HRC (2011): was concerned that the NHRI 'has not been provided with adequate resources to carry out its functions . . . The State party should also take concrete measures to ensure that the NCHR is provided with adequate financial and human resources in line with the Paris Principles.'[91]

The SCA also noted that Treaty Bodies had expressed concern about the budgets of the B-status NHRI of Kazakhstan,[92] and the NHRI of Nicaragua.[93] In its 2017 review of the NHRI of South Africa, it noted that the Committee on the Rights of the Child and the CERD Committee had both expressed concern about the level of resources available to the NHRI.[94] The expression of concern by the SCA and Treaty Bodies can be considered mutually reinforcing. The level of adherence to Treaty Bodies concluding observations may also provide future evidence for the

Rights (E/C.12/SVK/CO/2) and the Human Rights Committee (CCPR/C/SVK/CO/3) regarding the adequacy of the SNCHR's funding'.

[89] CERD, 'Concluding observations on the ninth to the tenth periodic reports of Slovakia' (17 April 2013) UN Doc CERD/C/ SVK/CO/9-10, para 15.

[90] CESCR, 'Consideration of reports submitted by States parties in accordance with articles 16 and 17 of the Covenant: Concluding observations of the Committee on Economic, Social and Cultural Rights—Slovakia' (8 June 2012) UN Doc E/C.12/SVK/CO/2, para 7.

[91] HRC, 'Consideration of reports submitted by States parties under article 40 of the Covenant: Concluding observations of the Human Rights Committee—Slovakia' (20 April 2011) UN Doc CCPR/C/SVK/CO/3, para 5.

[92] SCA, 'Accreditation Report—Kazakhstan (The Commissioner for Human Rights (CHR))' (March 2012) 9.

[93] SCA, 'Accreditation Report—Nicaragua (PDDH)' (November 2017) 46: 'The SCA notes that the Committee on Migrant Workers has expressed concern over the lack of adequate funding of the PDDH.'

[94] SCA, 'Accreditation Report—South Africa (SAHRC)' (November 2017) 33.

SCA as to the level of genuine commitment on the part of the state to properly fund the NHRI. It may also be noted here that recommendations from UN Special Procedures Mandate Holders may prompt an SCA recommendation for additional funding.[95]

5.3 External or Donor Funding

As state bodies, the SCA expects that NHRIs will be funded by the state. As seen in General Observation 1.10 (2018) set out in the introduction to this chapter, the SCA does however, allow for the possibility of donor funding ('funding from external sources'). This should not constitute core funding of the NHRI except in 'rare circumstances' where the international community needs to support the NHRI until the state is able to do so, this arises particularly in post-conflict situations.[96]

A number of NHRIs have been largely reliant on international funding. In particular, the Afghanistan NHRI (Afghanistan Independent Human Rights Commission (AIHRC)), which received just 4 per cent of its funding from the state in 2013.[97] Even with this level of external funding, the SCA emphasized that the NHRI 'should ensure the coordinated, transparent and accountable management of funding'.[98] The level of funding to the AIHRC had increased by the NHRI's 2019 review.[99] A similar situation existed for the Palestine NHRI, which the SCA noted in 2009 was 'nearly totally' funded through international donors.[100] The extent of external funding was specified in the 2015 review of the NHRI, with just 5 per cent of the NHRI budget coming from the state. While the special circumstances were noted by the SCA, it was also clear that the SCA considered that the state was not properly funding the NHRI even at this minimal level:

> While the SCA acknowledges that the State is itself reliant on funding from external sources and therefore has limited capacity to fully fund the budget of the PICHR, it remains the obligation of the State to fund its NHRIs. The SCA notes

[95] SCA, 'Accreditation Report—Nigeria (NHRC)' (November 2016) 49–50. The SCA further noted: '[t]he SCA also makes reference to the recommendations contained in the report of the Special Rapporteur on Minority issues (A/HRC/28/64) that recommended that sufficient resources are allocated to enable the Commission to carry out its work and ensure adequate and dedicated attention to issues of minorities in each region'.

[96] SCA, 'General Observations' (February 2018) (n 2) GO 1.10, 27. See also, SCA, 'Accreditation Report—Haiti Citizens (OPC)' (November 2013) 9–10.

[97] SCA, 'Accreditation Report—Afghanistan (AIHRC)' (November 2013) 18.

[98] SCA, 'Accreditation Report—Afghanistan (AIHRC)' (November 2008) 11; SCA, 'Accreditation Report—Afghanistan (AIHRC)' (November 2013) 18.

[99] SCA, 'Accreditation Report—Afghanistan (AIHRC)' (October 2019) 8. No precise figure of for the increase in state funding is given in the report.

[100] SCA, 'Accreditation Report—Palestine (Palestine Independent Commission for Human Rights (PICHR))' (March 2009) 7.

that the State has regularly failed to provide the five percent that it is expected to contribute.[101]

Barring such exceptional circumstances, the SCA takes the view that core funding should always come from the state, and expresses concern where this is not the case, for example, the Bangladesh NHRI received just 25 per cent of its funding from the state and 75 per cent from donors.[102] The Bolivia NHRI was 50 per cent funded by donors, including this funding being used for 50 per cent of its staff salaries.[103] Donor funding at 40 per cent of an NHRI's budget was also too high.[104] For Uruguay (NHROI), all its staff positions were funded by donors. The SCA was concerned that 'the NHROI appears to be, at present, substantially reliant on donor funding to ensure an adequate level of resources to carry out its mandate'.[105] The SCA has also expressed concern where an NHRI is obliged to seek donor funding in an effort to be able to carry out its mandate. The SCA has also expressed concern when the extent of donor funding appears to make up a significant amount of the project funding for the NHRI.[106] Where the level of reliance on donor funding is reduced, the SCA has welcomed it.[107]

Where the NHRI does seek external funding support it should not have to obtain government approval, in keeping with its independence.[108] The SCA has expressed particular concern where legislative provisions restrict the ability of the NHRI to seek external funding. In 2016, the SCA recommended that the Zimbabwe NHRI seek legislative change to a provision requiring ministerial approval of external funding, as it impacted the NHRI's ability to ensure sufficient funding.[109] Even

[101] SCA, 'Accreditation Report—Palestine (PICHR)' (November 2015) 35.

[102] SCA, 'Accreditation Report—Bangladesh (NHRC)' (March 2015) 14.

[103] SCA, 'Accreditation Report—Bolivia (DPB)' (March 2012) 17.

[104] SCA, 'Accreditation Report—Tajikistan (The Human Rights Ombudsman of the Republic of Tajikistan (HROT))' (March 2012) 14.

[105] SCA, 'Accreditation Report—Uruguay (NHROI)' (March 2015) 28 (accreditation deferred).

[106] SCA, 'Accreditation Report—Jordan (National Centre for Human Rights (NCHR))' (October 2010) 11. At the re-accreditation of the Jordan NHRI in November 2015, the SCA noted that an amendment to the law was being proposed 'to enable the NHRC to exercise its functions and implement its programs and activities in a satisfactory manner'. SCA, 'Accreditation Report—Jordan (JNCHR)' (November 2015) 24.

[107] SCA, 'Accreditation Report—Jordan (JNCHR)' (November 2015) 25. See also in the case of Malawi's NHRI, where the SCA report stated: 'The MHRC notes that its funding is not sufficient to effectively carry out its mandate. Consequently, it faces a situation of understaffing and difficulties in retaining staff with the requisite skills. The MHRC reports having advocated for an increase of its budget as well as having sought donor funding.' SCA, 'Accreditation Report—Malawi (MHRC)' (November 2016) 31.

[108] SCA, 'General Observations' (February 2018) (n 2) GO 1.10, 27. See also, SCA, 'Accreditation Report—Jordan (NCHR)' (November 2016) 31; SCA, 'Accreditation Report—Northern Ireland (NIHRC)' (May 2011) 19; SCA, 'Accreditation Report—Northern Ireland (NIHRC)' (May 2016) 46–47; SCA, 'Accreditation Report—Jordan (JNCHR)' (November 2015) 25; SCA, 'Accreditation Report—Iraq (HCHR)' (March 2015) 9; SCA, 'Accreditation Report—Nepal (NHRCN)' (March 2019) 29.

[109] SCA, 'Accreditation Report—(ZHRC)' (May 2016) 22.

where approval is not required in practice there should not be such provisions in legislation.[110]

Where donor funding is received it should also not be tied to donor priorities. The SCA outlined these concerns in its deferred review of the Danish NHRI in November 2017:

> The SCA notes that the DIHR receives 18.4 million USD for international work and 4.6 million USD for national work. The SCA understands that, outside of its core budget provided by the State, the DIHR receives funding from various and diverse sources to carry out specific projects. At the session, the DIHR reported that it receives funding, for example, from the Ministry of Foreign Affairs and development agencies. The SCA notes that where, an NHRI receives funding from external sources, such funds should not be tied to donor-defined priorities but rather to the pre-determined priorities of the NHRI. The SCA is of the view that to do otherwise has the potential to impact on the real or perceived independence of the NHRI. Accordingly, the SCA encourages that the DIHR to provide [*sic*] additional information about the sources of funding it receives, how it determines its priorities in relation to this funding, and what safeguards it has put in place to ensure that the receipt of this funding does not impact on its real or perceived independence and the ability to freely determine its own priorities.[111]

5.4 Financial Autonomy

A major issue for the financing of NHRIs, because of its potential to impact their independence, is the level of autonomy they have over their budget. Autonomy in this regard covers two areas: what entity ultimately decides on the NHRI's budget, and how that budget is distributed and controlled.

As noted at the outset of this chapter, the SCA, in its General Observation 1.10 (2018), requires that the NHRI should have 'complete financial autonomy' so that it has freedom to determine its priorities and activities. This provision is also clearly stated in the Paris Principles; 'funding should be to enable it to have its own staff and premises, in order to be independent of the Government and not be subject to financial control which might affect its independence'.[112] The SCA considers that to support financial autonomy, national laws should identify the source of the funds to be used for the NHRI's budget.[113] Funding must also be by way of a separate

[110] SCA, 'Accreditation Report—Zambia (HRCZ)' (October 2018) 20. The SCA also noted that an amendment bill proposed to remove the requirement for presidential approval.

[111] SCA, 'Accreditation Report—Denmark (Danish Institute for Human Rights (DIHR))' (November 2017) 43. See also, SCA, 'Accreditation Report—Malawi (MHRC)' (November 2016) 31–32.

[112] Paris Principles (n 1) B.2.

[113] SCA, 'Accreditation Report—Namibia (Office of the Ombudsman (Ombudsman))' (November 2016) 42: 'In accordance with section 9 of the existing Act, the budget of the Ombudsman is paid from

(dedicated) budget line. National laws should ensure that there is provision for appropriate timing for the release of funding. In managing the money allocated to it, the NHRI should have 'absolute management and control'.[114] NHRIs should 'should not be subject to financial control which might affect its independence'.[115] Any steps taken to improve financial autonomy are welcomed by the SCA.[116]

The NHRI has responsibility to ensure it complies with proper accountability practices 'through regular public financial reporting and a regular annual independent audit'. However, accountability requirements should 'not compromise the capacity of the NHRI to function independently and effectively'.[117]

5.4.1 Government Control over the Budget

A significant question in assessing budgetary autonomy is to what extent the executive, particularly in practice through a government ministry, has control over the budget of the NHRI. It may be noted that the SCA has on occasion discussed this issue under its General Observation on administrative regulation (Chapter 5.5) rather than under the General Observation on financial autonomy, as these issues are closely linked. The SCA is concerned at any form of government interference, perceived or actual. Where the government appoints a member of the board who has control over the budget, this will impact on the assessment of the independence of the institution.[118] Unwarranted government interventions into the financial affairs of an NHRI are also a cause for concern.[119]

The NHRI should have independent access to and control over its budget. For the B-status NHRI of Mali, funds were contained in the budget of the Ministry

moneys appropriated for that purpose. The Act does not specify the source of the funds. The SCA notes that the draft proposed amendments to the Act provide that the budget of the Ombudsman is paid from monies appropriated by government for that purpose ... The SCA encourages the Ombudsman to advocate for appropriate amendments to its enabling law in order to ensure the adequacy of the Ombudsman's funding and safeguard its financial independence.' See also, SCA, 'Accreditation Report—Namibia (Ombudsman)' (May 2011) 16–17; SCA, 'Accreditation Report—Luxembourg (CCDH)' (November 2008) 9, where the SCA stated '[t]here is also no indication that the CCDH exercises budgetary autonomy'.

114 SCA, 'General Observations' (June 2009) (n 5) GO 2.6, 3.

115 SCA, 'Accreditation Report—Ukraine (UPCHR)' (March 2009) 7.

116 SCA, 'Accreditation Report—Denmark (DIHR)' (November 2017) 43, noting that 'the SCA welcomes that the DIHR reports that the Ministry of Finance has approved the transition from operating appropriations to reservation appropriations, and that this will enhance its financial autonomy and independence'.

117 SCA, 'Accreditation Report—Mali (Commission Nationale des Droits de l'Homme (CNDH))' (March 2012) 13; SCA, 'Accreditation Report—Côte d'Ivoire (CNDHCI)' (May 2016) 13.

118 SCA, 'Accreditation Report—Belgium (Centre for Equal Opportunities and Opposition to Racism (CEOOR))' (March/April 2010) 11.

119 SCA, 'Accreditation Report—Korea (National Human Rights Commission (NHRCK))' (November 2008) 10.

of Justice, and the NHRI did 'not appear to have full and independent access, or management and control over their dispersal'.[120] For the NHRI of Greece, regulations for operation were drawn up 'by a decision of the Prime Minister' that could impede the independence of the NHRI in funding and accounting.[121] The SCA has expressed concern where the funding for the NHRI has to go through the president's office for approval and funds were transferred from that office on a quarterly basis.[122] A similar concern was expressed for the NHRI of Togo whose budget was prepared by the Ministry of Finance and disbursed on a monthly basis, with the SCA noting that 'this arrangement may restrict the Commission's capacity to plan and carry out long-term projects, particularly where financial commitments may vary from month to month'.[123] A government minister should also not be responsible for proposing the NHRI's budget to parliament.[124] The budget of the NHRI must also be released by the government.[125] Neither in law nor in practice should the NHRI have to request disbursement of funds from a government ministry.[126]

One means of enhancing financial autonomy is through the submission of the budget to parliament.[127] The SCA supports the approach whereby the NHRI presents its budget directly to the parliament.[128] The NHRI of Côte d'Ivoire (La Commission Nationale des Droits de l'Homme de Côte d'Ivoire (CNDHCI)), the SCA noted that there were issues with the independence of the budget in this regard:

> While the SCA acknowledges that the CNDHCI reports that it has control over its budget, the budget adoption process requires the endorsement of the Ministry of Human Rights prior to its presentation to Parliament. Further, the CNDHCI reports that its spending is subject to oversight by an official of the Ministry of the Budget.[129]

The SCA also expressed its concern that the budget ministry had 'significant discretion' over the NHRI's funds that had 'the potential to impact on its effectiveness and independence'.[130]

120 SCA, 'Accreditation Report—Mali (CNDH)' (March 2012) 13.
121 SCA, 'Accreditation Report—Greece (GNCHR)' (March 2015) 29.
122 SCA, 'Accreditation Report—Myanmar (MNHRC)' (November 2015) 12.
123 SCA, 'Accreditation Report—Togo (CNDH)' (May 2013) 18.
124 SCA, 'Accreditation Report—Luxembourg (CCDH)' (November 2015) 27. See also, SCA, 'Accreditation Report—Luxembourg (CCDH)' (March 2009) 9, where the SCA expresses concern about its 'limited budgetary autonomy'.
125 SCA, 'Accreditation Report—Madagascar (Commission Nationale Indépendante des Droits de l'Homme (CNIDH))' (March 2019) 9.
126 SCA, 'Accreditation Report—Togo (CNDH)' (October 2019) 18–19.
127 SCA, 'Accreditation Report—Kenya (NCHR)' (November 2008) 8.
128 SCA, 'Accreditation Report—South Africa (SAHRC)' (November 2017) 33.
129 SCA, 'Accreditation Report—Côte d'Ivoire (CNDHCI)' (May 2016) 13.
130 ibid.

A similar concern was expressed by the SCA in 2015 over the NHRI in Ireland (IHREC), whose enabling law included a provision that gave a Minister 'significant discretion' over the allocation of funds:

> the Minister for Justice and Equality may, after consultation with the IHREC, advance funds which the Minister, with the consent of the Minister for Public Expenditure and Reform, considers to be reasonably sufficient for the purposes of the expenditure of the IHREC in the performance of its functions.[131]

The government should thus not retain discretion over the budget to be allocated to the NHRI. For example, for the Great Britain NHRI (EHRC) the SCA found:

> in accordance with paragraph 38 of Schedule 1 of the Act, the Secretary of State shall pay to the EHRC such funds as appear to the Secretary of State to be reasonably sufficient for the purpose of enabling it to perform its functions.
>
> The SCA is concerned that the Secretary of State has significant discretion over the allocation of funds to the EHRC, and that this has the potential to impact on its effectiveness and independence.[132]

For the Northern Ireland NHRI (Northern Ireland Human Rights Commission (NIHRC)), the SCA was concerned about a similar provision to the above, which allowed that 'in accordance with Schedule 7 (6) of the act, the Secretary of State may make grants to the NIHRC from the budget provided by the Parliament' afforded the state 'significant' level of discretion.[133]

NHRIs should also not be restricted in how they utilize their allocated budget. For example, in assessing the NHRI of Cyprus (CAHR), it found:

> while the CAHR has management and control of its budget provided that the limits for each category of expense are respected, amendments to cover expenses not foreseen must be approved by the Ministry of Finance. The SCA is concerned that this may restrict the ability of the CAHR to direct its budget to those areas it has determined are most important.[134]

For the NHRI of Indonesia, the SCA was concerned that despite funding being provided by the Parliament, the Ministry of Finance was not releasing the approved funds.[135]

131 SCA, 'Accreditation Report—Ireland (IHREC)' (November 2015) 10.
132 SCA, 'Accreditation Report—Great Britain (EHRC)' (November 2015) 21.
133 SCA, 'Accreditation Report—Northern Ireland (NIHRC)' (May 2016) 46.
134 SCA, 'Accreditation Report—Cyprus (CAHR)' (November 2015) 8.
135 SCA, 'Accreditation Report—Indonesia (Indonesian National Commission on Human Rights (Komisi Nasional Hak Asasi Manusia (Komnas HAM))' (March 2012) 20.

Procurement should also not be under the discretion of a government ministry.[136]

5.4.2 Separate Entry in the National Budget

The SCA requires that the NHRI's budget be listed under a separate section of the national budget in order to ensure financial security and autonomy.[137] The NHRI's budget should not come from a general state fund.[138] Even where there is a specific fund designated for the NHRI, this may not be sufficient, and provision should rather be made through a separate budget line item.[139]

Lack of separate budget line and the resulting level of government control over the budget of Greece's NHRI (GNCHR) was of particular concern for the SCA in 2015:

> In accordance with article 1(2) of the Law, the budget of the GNCHR shall be incorporated into the budget of the General Secretariat of the Council of Ministers. The GNCHR reports that the fact that it must seek approval for its expenses makes it difficult to plan its activities, to hire staff in a timely manner, and generally to function in a flexible and efficient manner. There is no separate line in the budget applicable to the GNCHR.[140]

For Bosnia and Herzegovina (Human Rights Ombudsmen of Bosnia and Herzegovina (IHROBH)), the SCA was concerned in 2016 that the budget for the NHRI was included in the budget of the presidency:

> in accordance with article 39 of the existing Law, the financial appropriation necessary for the functioning of the IHROBH is included in the budget of the

136 SCA, 'Accreditation Report—Montenegro (PHRF)' (May 2016) 17. The SCA noted, '[w]hile the PHRF reports that it has management and control of its budget, the public procurement process requires the approval of the Ministry of Finance each year. The SCA is concerned that this may restrict the ability of the NHRI to direct its budget to those areas it has determined are most important.'

137 SCA, 'Accreditation Report—Qatar (National Human Rights Committee (NHRC))' (March 2009) 4; SCA, 'Accreditation Report—Bosnia and Herzegovina (IHROBH)' (November 2012) 12.

138 SCA, 'Accreditation Report—Ghana (CHRAJ)' (March 2014) 13. In 2019, the SCA report notes that '[f]urther, the SCA noted in March 2014 that the budget of the CHRAJ is charged on the Consolidated Fund of the State. The SCA notes the Supreme Court's decision, which requires the budget of the Audit Service to be approved by Parliament and not by the Minister of Finance. The SCA also notes that the CHRAJ is of the view that application of this procedure to it as well would improve its financial autonomy. The SCA further notes that the CHRAJ has advocated for the creation of an independent constitutional body to ensure financial autonomy of independent institutions. It encourages the CHRAJ to continue these efforts at improving its financial autonomy.' SCA, 'Accreditation Report—Ghana (CHRAJ)' (March 2019) 24.

139 SCA, 'Accreditation Report—Bangladesh (NHRC)' (March 2015) 15.

140 SCA, 'Accreditation Report—Greece (GNCHR)' (March 2015) 32–33. The threat to downgrade the GNCHR, largely connected to financing issues, is covered in Chapter 10.3.1.

> Presidency of Bosnia and Herzegovina. The existing Law does not specify the process by which this budget allocation is made, does not specify whether it appears as a separate budget line, and does not provide for the financial autonomy of the IHROBH over the budget allocation. The SCA also notes that the IHROBH has indicated that its most recent audit report called for greater financial independence for the IHROBH.[141]

In its subsequent review in November 2017, proposed amendments that enhanced financial independence were noted:

> The SCA acknowledges that IHROBH reports that it enjoys financial autonomy and that, in practice, its budget appears in a separate budget line. The SCA notes further that article 3 of the proposed amendments to the Law expands upon the details of the budgetary process and enhances the independence of the IHROBH in respect of this budget.[142]

5.5 Administrative Regulation

One of NHRIs' most critical relationships is with the state, particularly with the executive. NHRIs are state-established but also maintain their independence. This section examines the question of administrative regulation and interference by the government in the operations of the NHRI.

The issue of control through administrative regulation is closely connected to the content and quality of the enabling law discussed (Chapter 3), as well as adequate funding discussed in this chapter. Administrative regulation can significantly influence the independence and operation of the institution. The SCA General Observation 2.7 (2018) differentiates between regulations made for all state agencies, and those that may compromise the NHRI:

> The classification of an NHRI as an independent State agency has important implications for the regulation of certain practices, including reporting, recruitment, funding and accounting. Where a State has developed uniform rules or regulations to ensure State agencies are properly accountable for their use of public funds, the application of such rules or regulations on an NHRI is not considered inappropriate provided they do not compromise the NHRI's ability to perform its role independently and effectively. The administrative requirements

[141] SCA, 'Accreditation Report—Bosnia and Herzegovina (IHROBH)' (November 2016) 15.
[142] SCA, 'Accreditation Report—Bosnia and Herzegovina (IHROBH)' (November 2017) 10.

> imposed on an NHRI must be clearly defined and should be no more onerous than those applicable to other independent of State agencies.[143]

In its justification, the SCA indicates that it has broadly interpreted the 'adequate funding' provision of the Paris Principles in the formulation of this observation:

> Section B.2 of the Paris Principles considers the 'adequate funding' of an NHRI as a necessary guarantee of its independence. The purpose of this funding is: 'in order to be independent of the Government and not to be subject to financial control which might affect its independence.' Such a provision is not, however, intended to limit the application of laws that require an appropriate level of financial accountability by public agencies. To ensure respect for the principle of independence in circumstances where certain aspects of the administration of an NHRI is regulated by the Government, the SCA cautions that such regulation must not compromise the NHRI's ability to perform its role independently and effectively. It may therefore be appropriate for the State to impose general regulatory requirements to promote:
>
> - fair, transparent and merit-based selection processes;
> - financial propriety in the use of public funds; or
> - operational accountability.
>
> Such regulation should not, however, extend to requiring an NHRI to seek government approval prior to carrying out its legislatively mandated activities, since this may compromise its independence and autonomy. Such practice is inconsistent with the exercise of the protection and promotion function that an NHRI is established to carry out in an independent and unfettered manner. For this reason, it is important that the relationship between the Government and the NHRI be clearly defined so as to avoid any undue Government interference.[144]

The SCA has identified a number of ways in which an NHRI could be compromised by the use of administrative regulations including the ability to publish its own materials independently,[145] the submission process for its annual report (Chapter 3), utilize its budget (Chapter 5.4), and select and appoint members and staff (Chapter 4.8).

[143] SCA, 'General Observations' (February 2018) (n 2). The numbering of this General Observation was changed from the original 2.10 in 2009 to 2.8 in 2013, to 2.7 as of the 2018 General Observations.

[144] SCA, 'General Observations' (February 2018) (n 2) GO 2.7.

[145] SCA, 'Accreditation Report—Tunisia (Comité Supérieur des Droits de l'Homme et des Libertés Fondamentales (SCHRFF))' (November 2009) 6, noting '[t]he institution is required to submit all its reports to the President of the Republic. Pursuant to article 6 of the law the SCHRFF undertakes investigations upon request of the President of the Republic and reports the results of the investigations to the President. This provision is not consistent with the exercise of the protection function that an NHRI is to carry out in an independent and unfettered manner.'

Excessive administrative regulations may indicate that an NHRI is not, in fact, an NHRI. In some rare instances early in the SCA's development, an institution that applied for accreditation was not an NHRI but rather a government agency in the strict sense, as in the case of Switzerland's CFQF. One of the reasons for the determination of lack of independence, and accreditation with C-status,[146] was the presence of excessive regulation. Notably, the SCA found that the institution 'must seek prior approval of the Swiss Federal Department of the Interior prior to publishing its communications, reports, recommendations, and propositions'.[147] Similarly for Switzerland's Federal Commission Against Racism (FCR), in 2010, the SCA found that it was subordinate to the Federal Department of the Interior.[148] The FCR was required to submit its annual report to the department, and get approval for the 'publication of reports, recommendations and proposals'.[149] The FCR's secretariat was also attached to the general secretariat of the department.[150]

Outside of this type of rare situation where an institution applying for accreditation was *part* of the executive structure, the SCA has also raised concerns about the extent to which an institution can be regulated by the executive.[151] NHRIs should be 'able to independently conduct [their] affairs without undue interference from the government'.[152] Indonesia's enabling law provided that the organizational structure would be set out in a presidential decree, rather than in the NHRI's own regulations and policies.[153] This issue had still not been resolved ten years after the SCA first expressed its concerns. However, the NHRI had taken some steps within its powers, through the issuance of a regulation for the organization and administration of its secretariat, although this regulation did not supersede the provisions in the national law.[154]

The position of the NHRI within the executive structure can also be problematic. The NHRI of Mauritania was under the Office of the Prime Minister, and reported to the head of state, which the SCA in its 2009 review found to be a problem.[155] The SCA is likely to be willing to overlook some administrative regulation where the NHRI is operating effectively, and such provision is common within national law. Thus, in its 2012 review of the Danish NHRI (DIHR), the SCA did not raise

146 See Chapter 2.1 on the discontinuation of C-status.

147 SCA, 'Accreditation Report—Switzerland (CFQF)' (March 2009) 6.

148 SCA, 'Accreditation Report—Switzerland (FCR)' (March/April 2010) 12.

149 ibid.

150 ibid.

151 For example, in reviewing the Great Britain NHRI in November 2008, the SCA noted 'the requirement for the Minister's consent in relation to the following issues: payment of Commissioners; the numbers, terms and conditions of staff appointments; and the appointment of investigating commissioners'. SCA, 'Accreditation Report—Great Britain (Equality and Human Right Commission (EHRC))' (November 2008) 5.

152 SCA, 'Accreditation Report—Ireland (IHRC)' (November 2008) 8.

153 SCA, 'Accreditation Report—Indonesia (Komnas HAM)' (March 2012)) 19. An additional issue raised by the SCA was the NHRI's failure to seek rectification of the issue to ensure improved compliance with the Paris Principles. ibid.

154 SCA, 'Accreditation Report—Indonesia (Komnas HAM)' (March 2017) 27.

155 SCA, 'Accreditation Report—Mauritania (Commission National des Droits de l'Homme (NHRC))' (November 2009) 4.

excessive concern about a requirement for the by-laws of the institution to be approved by the Minister for Foreign Affairs, as 'the DIHR advised that this provision is a formality and an ordinary requirement under Danish law, and does not compromise the DIHR's ability to perform its role independently and effectively'.[156] In contrast, the SCA expressed considerable concerns in relation to a regulation for the NHRI of Greece. In its 2015 review of the NHRI, the SCA, under the heading 'independence', noted that the law provided for regulations for the operation of the institution to be drawn up by a decision of the prime minister.[157]

Changes to NHRIs to bring them further within the administrative structure of the state will also raise concerns for the SCA. A proposal was put forward to place the NHRI of South Korea under the Office of the President, and there had been interventions in the financial and administrative affairs of the NHRI.[158] This was in addition to the institution being considered a 'central government institution' under the National Fiscal Act, rather than an 'independent institution', the lack of public consultation on appointments, and lack of autonomy in staffing.[159]

The SCA was particularly concerned about government interference with the NHRI of Libya, which received B-status accreditation. The NHRI itself had expressed its concerns about its independence, due to 'constant attempts by the Executive Authority to interfere in its financial performance by imposing the political controller's policy of the Financial Controllers Department of the Ministry of Finance, in clear violation of the law of its inception'.[160]

For the NHRI of Canada (Canadian Human Rights Commission (CHRC)), the SCA was concerned that two measures relating to its premises and its website could impact the perception of the institution as independent from the state:

> The SCA notes that measures introduced to provide security to the building have meant that individuals must request prior approval to access the Ottawa premises. The SCA encourages the CHRC to ensure that this security measure does not limit the accessibility of the Ottawa premises.
>
> The SCA also notes that the CHRC has a separate website, but the CHRC indicated that the government has proposed that the CHRC website be integrated into a whole of government web portal. The SCA is of the view that this may impact on the public perception of the CHRC's independence and has the potential to dissuade individuals from filing human rights complaints against government or from accessing the website to obtain information on human rights.[161]

[156] SCA, 'Accreditation Report—Denmark (DIHR)' (November 2012) 14.
[157] SCA, 'Accreditation Report—Greece (GNCHR)' (March 2015) 29.
[158] SCA, 'Accreditation Report—Korea (NHRCK)' (November 2008) 10.
[159] ibid.
[160] SCA, 'Accreditation Report—Libya (National Council for Civil Liberties and Human Rights (NCCLHR))' (October 2014) 15.
[161] SCA, 'Accreditation Report—Canada (CHRC)' (May 2016) 27. This was dealt with under the heading of 'accessibility' and the SCA referred to Paris Principle B.2 and to its General Observation 1.10 on 'Adequate funding'.

5.6 Regional Offices

Closely connected to the issue of adequate funding is the ability of the NHRI to establish regional offices. This was emphasized regularly by the SCA in its early reports as important to ensure accessibility.[162] Where an NHRI only has its office in the capital city, it may not be easily accessible to the wider population. As the SCA stated in its review of the B-status Bangladesh NHRI:

> The SCA underscores the importance of ensuring the NHRC is broadly accessible, including through premises that are accessible to the wider community, including persons with disabilities. Establishing a regional presence further enhances accessibility.[163]

Similarly, for the NHRI of Iraq, the SCA noted that the inability to open regional offices 'may be a concern in the context of Iraq, where vulnerable persons are often located in geographically remote parts of the country'.[164] NHRIs should also be provided with sufficient funding to open regional offices.[165]

However, this issue has not been addressed in more recent SCA reports. This may be as a result of increased funding pressures on NHRIs and the feasibility and effectiveness of having a small regional office and additionally, improved technology may also have reduced the need for regional offices.

5.7 Comment

This chapter has shown that funding is an area of critical concern for the SCA. That adequate funding is such a significant issue for the SCA is not surprising given that the state is primarily responsible for providing the funding, and governments the world over experience financial pressures, particularly since the economic downturn. The provision of adequate and sufficient state funding also underscores the commitment, or lack thereof, of the state to its NHRI. Further, funding is an area where the government can easily undermine the NHRI by restricting the activities it has the ability to undertake in practice. This can be done either directly or under

[162] SCA, 'Accreditation Report—Niger (CNDHLF)' (April 2008) 6; SCA, 'Accreditation Report—Croatia (ORC)' (April 2008) 8; SCA, 'Accreditation Report—Albania (PA)' (November 2008) 6; SCA, 'Accreditation Report—Mongolia (NHRC)' (November 2008) 9; SCA, 'Accreditation Report—Thailand (National Human Rights Commission (NHRC))' (November 2008) 10.

[163] SCA, 'Accreditation Report—Bangladesh (NHRC)' (March 2015) 14. See also, SCA, 'Accreditation Report—Jordan (JNCHR)' (November 2015) 26.

[164] SCA, 'Accreditation Report—Iraq (HCHR)' (March 2015) 8.

[165] SCA, 'Accreditation Report—Iraq (HCHR)' (March 2015) 8–9; SCA, 'Accreditation Report—Indonesia (Komnas HAM)' (March 2012) 20; SCA, 'Accreditation Report—Chile (Instituto Nacional de Derechos Humanos (INDH))' (November 2012) 9.

the guise of an economic downturn or financial streamlining. Finally, almost every NHRI would see a need for, and welcome, increased funding in order to carry out, fully and effectively, a broad mandate to promote and protect human rights. The approach the SCA takes is, therefore, to assess whether the existing funding is adequate for the NHRI to effectively fulfil its mandate, and to identify shortcomings that exist due to insufficient funding.

For this reason, and similarly to the SCA's approach on other issues such as where NHRIs operate in difficult national environments (see Chapter 9), the SCA does not 'punish' the institution for the lack of financial support given to it by downgrading it. Rather, encourages better financial provision and considers what the NHRI is doing within the resources available to it. As seen in the cases referred to throughout this chapter, the SCA has avoided downgrading NHRIs solely on the basis of inadequate funding, even where the SCA notes a concern that the NHRI is unable to effectively discharge its mandate. The SCA will acknowledge efforts made by the NHRI in advocating for increased funding, and/or acknowledge state budgetary constraints, and will encourage the NHRI to continue to advocate for adequate funding.

While budgetary provision and financial control by the state are of concern for the SCA, there are few specifics on the level of budget to be provided (ie what constitutes 'adequate' in real terms) or on the level of control that is permitted by the state. In this regard, Meuwissen has argued that 'it might be desirable for the SCA to determine a minimum percentage of an NHRIs' budget that should be provided by the state'.[166] It can also be understood that NHRIs should be financially accountable, but that they should not be subject to the government in the utilization of their budget.

The overall approach of the SCA is in line with other international bodies on this point. The European Commission against Racism and Intolerance (ECRI), for example, has made a similar recommendation regarding non-discrimination bodies, where an expanded mandate must be accompanied by 'appropriate additional funding'.[167] The European Commission for Democracy Through Law (Venice Commission) has made the following recommendations in relation to ombudspersons institutions:

> The Venice Commission has consistently recommended in its opinions that the budgetary allocation of funds for the operations of the institution of the Ombudsman should be adequate to the need to ensure full, independent and effective discharge of the responsibilities and functions of the institution. The

[166] Katrien Meuwissen, 'NHRIs and the State: New and Independent Actors in the Multi-layered Human Rights System?' (2015) 15 Human Rights Law Review 441, 457.

[167] ECRI, 'General Policy Recommendation No. 2: Equality Bodies to Combat Racism and Intolerance at National Level' (7 December 2017) CRI(2018)06, para 28.

> Commission has further recommended that given the exceptionally sensitive nature and particular significance of the finance provisions for the independence of the Ombudsman Institution, provision should be made in the relevant laws that the public authorities shall not use the budgetary process for allocating funds from the budget in a manner that interferes with the independence of the institution of the Ombudsman.[168]

A Council of Europe Committee of Ministers draft recommendation on NHRIs (due for adoption in 2021) also emphasizes the need for 'adequate, sufficient and sustainable resources' and autonomy in determination of priorities and activities.[169] The draft specifies that where NHRIs are given additional competencies, sufficient additional resources need to be in place.

Issues of NHRI funding have also been raised frequently by the UN Treaty Bodies in their concluding observations to states. On occasion, the Treaty Body has made more precise comments on the financial stability of the NHRI than the SCA has in its reports. For example, in reviewing Togo's NHRI (CNDH) in May 2013, the SCA expressed concern over that 'the [CNDH] budget is inadequate to allow the national institution to function effectively and fully carry out its core functions'.[170] The Committee Against Torture, issuing its concluding observations in December 2012, expressed concern that 'the budget of the [NHRI] has reportedly decreased by 20 per cent since 2008, preventing it from fully carrying out its functions'.[171] It recommended to the state to 'provide the [NHRI] with sufficient financial, human and material resources to fully carry out its functions in an independent, impartial and effective manner'.[172]

Finally, this chapter also considered administrative regulation of NHRIs, which is a related area of concern for the SCA. As stated in the justification of General Observation 1.9, 'the SCA acknowledges the value in developing and maintaining effective links with relevant ministers and government agencies, particularly where cooperation will assist in promoting the NHRI's mandate. However, it stresses that this must be done in a way that ensures both real and perceived independence of decision making and operation, and avoids a conflict of interest'.[173] Thus, while an

[168] Venice Commission, 'Republic of Moldova—Draft Opinion on Proposed New Article 37 of the Law on the People's Advocate Finance Provision' (5 December 2017) Opinion No 906/2017, 5.

[169] Council of Europe, 'Drafting Group on Civil Society and National Human Rights Institutions (CDDH-INST)' (19 March 2020) CDDH-INST(2019)R6, para 13 <https://rm.coe.int/steering-committee-for-human-rights-cddh-drafting-group-on-civil-socie/16809cf87f> accessed 7 February 2021. The recommendation when adopted will replace Recommendation No. R(97) 14.

[170] SCA, 'Accreditation Report—Togo (National Human Rights Commission (CNDH))' (May 2013) 17–18.

[171] Committee Against Torture, 'Concluding observations on the second periodic report of Togo, adopted by the Committee at its forty-ninth Session (29 October–23 November 2012)' (11 December 2012) UN Doc CAT/C/TGO/CO/2, para 14.

[172] ibid.

[173] SCA, 'General Observations' (February 2018) (n 2) GO 1.9, 25.

NHRI should strive to have a good and effective relationship with government, for example to have its advice and recommendations received, heard and considered by government, it must ensure that the relationship is not so close that it is no longer independent or seen to be independent.

The next chapter examines the NHRIs substantive powers as an institution for the promotion and protection of human rights.

6
Human Rights Mandate—Promotion and Protection Functions

6.1 Introduction

This chapter examines the mandate given to National Human Rights Institutions (NHRIs). There are several interconnected questions examined in this chapter. First, is the definition of human rights sufficiently broad in the enabling law? Secondly, are the NHRI's promotion and protection functions explicitly provided for in the enabling law, and are they being undertaken as functions in practice? Thirdly, does the NHRI have a sufficient mandate to encourage ratification of international instruments? Finally, if the NHRI has a complaints-handling function, is it compliant with the Paris Principles?[1]

The SCA examines NHRIs' human rights promotion and protection functions as part of its review of their overall mandate. Using the same General Observation (1.2), the SCA details how a mandate should be reflected in the enabling law and lists specific activities that correspond to promotion and protection functions. The SCA expects that NHRIs will have a broad mandate that explicitly provides them with the ability to cover all human rights issues that may arise in the country.

In its 2018 General Observation 1.2 on human rights mandate, the SCA provides:

> All NHRIs should be legislatively mandated with specific functions to both promote and protect human rights. The SCA understands 'promotion' to include those functions which seek to create a society where human rights are more broadly understood and respected. Such functions may include education, training, advising, public outreach and advocacy. 'Protection' functions may be understood as those that address and seek to prevent actual human rights violations. Such functions include monitoring, inquiring, investigating and reporting on human rights violations, and may include individual complaint handling. An NHRI's mandate should be interpreted in a broad, liberal and purposive manner to promote a progressive definition of human rights which includes all rights set

[1] Principles relating to the Status of National Institutions, UNGA Res 48/134 (20 December 1993) UN Doc A/RES/48/134 (The Paris Principles).

National Human Rights Institutions. David Langtry and Kirsten Roberts Lyer, Oxford University Press. © David Langtry and Kirsten Roberts Lyer 2021. DOI: 10.1093/oso/9780198829102.003.0007

out in international, regional and domestic instruments, including economic, social and cultural rights. Specifically, the mandate should:

- extend to the acts and omissions of both the public and private sectors;
- vest the NHRI with the competence to freely address public opinion, raise public awareness on human rights issues and carry out education and training programs;
- provide the authority to address recommendations to public authorities, to analyse the human rights situation in the country, and to obtain statements or documents in order to assess situations raising human rights issues;
- authorize unannounced and free access to inspect and examine any public premises, documents, equipment and assets without prior written notice;
- authorize the full investigation into all alleged human rights violations, including the military, police and security officers.[2]

The SCA provides the following justification:

According to sections A.1 and A.2 of the Paris Principles, an NHRI should possess, 'as broad a mandate as possible', which is to be, 'set forth in a constitutional or legislative text', and should include both, 'the promot[ion] and protect[ion] of human rights'. Section A.3 of the Paris Principles enumerates specific responsibilities the NHRI must, at a minimum, be vested with. These requirements identify two main issues which must necessarily be addressed in the establishment and operation of an NHRI:

(i) The mandate of the NHRI must be established in national law. This is necessary to guarantee the independence and autonomy with which an NHRI undertakes its activities in the fulfilment of its public mandate;
(ii) The NHRI's mandate to both promote and protect human rights must be defined as broadly as possible so as to give the public the protection of a wide range of international human rights standards: civil; political; economic; cultural; and social. This gives effect to the principle that all rights are universal, indivisible, and interdependent.

Excerpt from the Paris Principles

A. Competence and responsibilities—

1. A national institution shall be vested with competence to promote and protect human rights
2. A national institution shall be given as broad a mandate as possible, which shall be clearly set forth in a constitutional or legislative text, specifying its composition and its sphere of competence.

[2] SCA, 'General Observations of the Sub-Committee on Accreditation' (adopted on 21 February 2018) 7 (hereafter SCA, 'General Observations' (February 2018)).

3. A national institution shall, inter alia, have the following responsibilities:

a) To submit to the Government, Parliament and any other competent body, on an advisory basis either at the request of the authorities concerned or through the exercise of its power to hear a matter without higher referral, opinions, recommendations, proposals and reports on any matters concerning the promotion and protection of human rights; the national institution may decide to publicize them; these opinions, recommendations, proposals and reports, as well as any prerogative of the national institution, shall relate to the following areas:
   (i) Any legislative or administrative provisions, as well as provisions relating to judicial organizations, intended to preserve and extend the protection of human rights; in that connection, the national institution shall examine the legislation and administrative provisions in force, as well as bills and proposals, and shall make such recommendations as it deems appropriate in order to ensure that these provisions conform to the fundamental principles of human rights; it shall, if necessary, recommend the adoption of new legislation, the amendment of legislation in force and the adoption or amendment of administrative measures;
   (ii) Any situation of violation of human rights which it decides to take up;
   (iii) The preparation of reports on the national situation with regard to human rights in general, and on more specific matters;
   (iv) Drawing the attention of the Government to situations in any part of the country where human rights are violated and making proposals to it for initiatives to put an end to such situations and, where necessary, expressing an opinion on the positions and reactions of the Government;

b) To promote and ensure the harmonization of national legislation regulation and practices with the international human rights instruments to which the State is a party, and their effective implementation;

c) To encourage ratification of the above-mentioned instruments or accession to those instruments, and to ensure their implementation;

d) To contribute to the reports which States are required to submit to United Nations bodies and committees, and to regional institutions, pursuant to their treaty obligations and, where necessary, to express an opinion on the subject, with due respect for their independence;

e) To cooperate with the United Nations and any other organization in the United Nations system, the regional institutions and the national institutions of other countries that are competent in the areas of the promotion and protection of human rights;

f) To assist in the formulation of programmes for the teaching of, and research into, human rights and to take part in their execution in schools, universities and professional circles;

g) To publicize human rights and efforts to combat all forms of discrimination, in particular racial discrimination, by increasing public awareness, especially through information and education and by making use of all press organs.[3]

This chapter focuses on the mandate provided to the NHRI, including its human rights mandate, and its promotion and protection functions, while Chapter 7 will examine more closely the SCA's consideration of NHRI practice in implementing these powers and functions.

6.2 Definition of Human Rights in the Enabling Law

There must be a clear definition of human rights in NHRIs' enabling law.[4] This should be broad and not be limited to only human rights in conventions ratified by the state. In 2015, reviewing the Scottish NHRI, the SCA observed that the definition of human rights in its enabling law is 'restricted to conventions ratified by the UK'.[5] Acknowledging that the NHRI interpreted its mandate more broadly, it recommended that the SHRC advocate for amendments to its enabling law to 'include a more expansive definition of human rights'.[6]

The scope of human rights should also not be selectively applied between promotion and protection functions. For the Sri Lanka NHRI (the Human Rights Commission of Sri Lanka (SLHRC)), the SCA noted that:

> [t]he definition of human rights contained in Section 33 of the [enabling] law refers to both civil and political and economic, social, and cultural rights. However, the effect of section 10 (a) of the law is that the SLHRC is mandated to inquire into and investigate complaints relating only to fundamental rights, as opposed to human rights. Chapter 3 of the Constitution is entitled 'fundamental rights' and guarantees only a limited set of civil and political rights.[7]

The SCA recognized that the NHRI had a broad interpretation in practice and had also advocated for explicit inclusion of economic, social, and cultural rights in its enabling law.[8]

[3] ibid 7–8.
[4] SCA, 'Report and Recommendations of the Session of the Sub-Committee on Accreditation—Palestine (Palestine Independent Commission for Human Rights (PICHR))' (March 2009) 7 (hereafter SCA, 'Accreditation Report').
[5] SCA, 'Accreditation Report—Scotland (Scottish Human Rights Commission (SHRC))' (March 2015) 17.
[6] ibid.
[7] SCA, 'Accreditation Report—Sri Lanka (SLHRC)' (May 2018) 37.
[8] ibid.

Other restrictions to a broad human rights mandate have been commented on by the SCA. For the Ombudsperson of Namibia, the SCA noted that its mandate to protect constitutional rights and freedoms included some, but not all, recognized civil, political, economic, social, and cultural rights.[9] The SCA found that the Hungarian NHRI was mandated for the protection of constitutional rights only, and that the legislation 'does not provide for the promotion of human rights more broadly'.[10] It urged the NHRI to advocate 'for a wider mandate that includes all rights set out in international, regional and domestic instruments, covers all areas of discrimination, gives it the responsibility to protect and promote human rights, allows for its engagement with international mechanisms, and gives it explicit functions for human rights education and monitoring'.[11]

A limitation in the scope of economic, social, and cultural rights has been identified on several occasions as problematic by the SCA. In 2017, in its review of the NHRI in the Philippines (Commission on Human Rights of the Philippines (CHRP)), the SCA observed that while its enabling law provided it with protection functions and it undertook protection-related work in practice for all rights, its protection mandate did not extend to economic, social, and cultural rights, only to civil and political rights.[12] Referring to a proposed bill for amending the enabling law, the SCA commented:

> The SCA notes that the Constitution and EO 163 mandate the CHRP with various protection functions, including the mandate to investigate complaints and all forms of human rights violations, provide appropriate legal measures for the protection of human rights, recommend to the Congress to provide compensation to victims or their families, monitor the Government's compliance with international treaty obligations on human rights, and make recommendations to relevant bodies. The SCA acknowledges that the CHRP fulfills its protection mandate through these powers and also, for example, the establishment of a witness protection programme ... in accordance with Article XIII Section 18 (1) of the Constitution and Section 3 (i) of EO 163, the CHRP is mandated to investigate all forms of human rights violations involving civil and political rights. [However], it does not have an explicit mandate with respect to economic, social and cultural rights.

[9] SCA, 'Accreditation Report—Namibia (Office of the Ombudsman (Ombudsman))' (October 2018) 12; SCA, 'Accreditation Report—Namibia (Ombudsman)' (May 2011) 16. In its 2016 review of the NHRI, the SCA reiterated the same concerns, encouraging it to advocate for amendments to its enabling law to promote and protect all human rights. SCA, 'Accreditation Report—Namibia (Ombudsman)' (November 2016) 40.

[10] SCA, 'Accreditation Report—Hungary (Parliamentary Commissioner for Civil Rights (PCCR))' (May 2011) 8. The PCCR ceased to exist in January 2012 following the adoption of a new basic law which merged it with the existing Commissioner for Fundamental Rights.

[11] ibid.

[12] SCA, 'Accreditation Report—Philippines (CHRP)' (March 2017) 29.

> The SCA acknowledges that the CHRP interprets its mandate in a broad manner and conducts activities in this regard. It further notes that, by virtue of ratification of the Covenant on Economic, Social and Cultural Rights by the Philippines and CHRP's Omnibus Rules of Procedures 2012, the CHRP has also interpreted its mandate as including violations of economic, social and cultural rights. The SCA further notes that section 3 of the proposed CHR Act makes specific reference to the Covenant on Economic, Social and Cultural Rights as forming part of the definition of human rights.[13]

Similarly, the NHRI in Mauritius undertook activities for the promotion of the realization of economic, social, and cultural rights, but it did not have an express mandate for addressing them.[14] In 2016, the SCA found that the Australian Human Rights Commission's (AHRC) mandate did not explicitly refer to the Convention against Torture or the International Covenant on Economic, Social and Cultural rights. In line with this observation, the SCA urged the NHRI to advocate for an amendment of the definition of 'human rights' within its enabling law to include these, and thus all seven core human rights treaties ratified by Australia.[15]

6.2.1 Limited-mandate Institutions

Closely related to the definition of the human rights that can be addressed by the NHRI is the question of the assigned mandate. In keeping with its requirement that NHRIs have a broad mandate, almost exclusively the SCA will not give A-status to NHRIs that are established with the express purpose of focusing on a limited area of human rights, such as equality or anti-discrimination bodies with a correspondingly limited mandate. In its 2009 review of the Swiss Commission fédérale pour les questions féminines (CFQF), the SCA observed that its mandate focused only on research and investigation of the status of women's rights, and stressed the need for NHRIs to have a broad human rights mandate.[16] In its 2010 review of the Swiss Federal Commission against Racism (FCR), the SCA recommended that 'the mandate of the FCR should be broadened as it currently only focuses on the research and investigation of discrimination-related issues, and possessing only a consultative function, as a specialized body on issues of

[13] ibid.

[14] SCA, 'Accreditation Report—Mauritius (National Human Rights Commission of Mauritius (NHRC))' (October 2014) 21. A similar recommendation was made to the Office of the Ombudsman of Samoa in 2016: SCA, 'Accreditation Report—Samoa (Office of the Ombudsman (Ombudsman))' (May 2016) 19.

[15] SCA, 'Accreditation Report—Australia (Australian Human Rights Commission (AHRC))' (November 2016) 10–11.

[16] SCA, 'Accreditation Report—Switzerland (CFQF)' (March 2009) 6. This institution was accredited C-status.

discrimination'.[17] Accrediting the NHRI of the Netherlands with B-status in 2010, the SCA was concerned that its mandate was 'limited to issues regarding ... discrimination and equality only', and recommended that it should be 'vested with the legislative competence to freely address public opinion, raise public awareness on human rights issues and carry out education and training programs'.[18] Reviewing the Swedish NHRI in 2011, the SCA observed that it 'does not have a broad mandate to promote and protect human rights; [as its] mandate is restricted to matters of equality'.[19] In 2011, in its review of the Bulgarian Ombudsperson, the SCA noted that its mandate was limited to preventing and protecting 'against discrimination, and to promote equality of opportunity', and recommended the institution advocate for a wider mandate giving it explicit functions in the promotion and protection of all human rights.[20] Reviewing the Slovakian NHRI in 2014, and accrediting it with B-status, the SCA found that its enabling law provided a clear mandate 'but with an emphasis on areas of equality and discrimination' and encouraged it to seek legislative amendments to also have explicit powers to 'submit to the Government opinions, recommendations, proposals and reports on any matters concerning human rights'.[21] Reviewing the Belgian Inter-federal Centre for Equal Opportunity and Fight against Racism and Discrimination (UNIA), the SCA noted that it had a limited mandate focusing on efforts to combat racism and discrimination, and activities related to the Convention on the Rights of Persons with Disabilities.[22] The SCA noted that UNIA interpreted its mandate broadly in practice, however the institution was accredited B-status in part as the enabling law did not provide for a mandate to promote and protect all human rights.

6.3 Promotion Functions

6.3.1 Requirement for Promotion Functions in the Enabling Law

An NHRIs' assigned promotion and protection functions are closely connected to its human rights mandate in general. The SCA has placed a particular emphasis on the specific inclusion of promotion functions in the enabling law of NHRIs, which should seek amendments to their enabling law for the explicit inclusion of both

[17] SCA, 'Accreditation Report—Switzerland (FCR)' (March/April 2010) 12. This institution was accredited C-status.
[18] SCA, 'Accreditation Report—Netherlands (Equal Treatment Commission (ETC))' (March/April 2010) 10.
[19] SCA, 'Accreditation Report—Sweden (Equality Ombudsman of Sweden (EOS))' (May 2011) 9.
[20] SCA, 'Accreditation Report—Bulgaria (Ombudsman of the Republic of Bulgaria (ORB))' (October 2011) 7.
[21] SCA, 'Accreditation Report—Slovakia (National Centre for Human Rights (SNCHR))' (March 2014) 8.
[22] SCA, 'Accreditation Report—Belgium (UNIA)' (May 2018) 9.

functions, promotion and protection.[23] For example, the SCA urged the Croatian NHRI to broaden its mandate to include the promotion of human rights.[24] In 2010, the SCA had the same recommendation for the Slovenian NHRI.[25] In 2011, for the NHRI from Namibia, the SCA noted that its enabling legislation referred to the protection of human rights but not to promotion.[26] NHRIs thus should not have a mandate solely limited to protection. In its 2013 review of the NHRI in Oman—accrediting it with B-status—the SCA encouraged it to advocate for the inclusion of a broad promotion mandate, raising concerns that it did provide a clear mandate and appropriate powers to promote and protect human rights.[27]

The promotion mandate must be explicit. For the NHRI of Armenia (HRDA), the SCA that noted that 'the mandate provided to the HRDA in articles 191(1) of the Constitution, 2(1) of the law and chapter 5 of the law is primarily protective in nature, and does not contain an explicit responsibility to promote human rights'.[28] In 2014, the SCA encouraged the NHRI in Slovakia to advocate for legislative changes to include a more explicit mandate and with it powers to 'create awareness of human rights norms through teaching, research and addressing public opinion', while also acknowledging that in practice it interprets its mandate in a way that includes such activities.[29] Implicit provisions are not sufficient to meet the requirement of reflection in the enabling law.[30] Neither should such provisions be so overly broad as to be vague. For instance, in 2009, the SCA noted that the Ukrainian NHRI (UPCHR) had a mandate that 'refers to the parliamentary control over constitutional human and citizens' rights and freedoms and to the protection of every individual's rights within the jurisdiction of Ukraine' and stressed that NHRIs should be mandated with specific functions.[31] The promotion component of the NHRI's mandate should not be limited to one area of the NHRI's functions. While the UPCHR had a mandate under its enabling law to 'engage in the "promotion of the legal awareness of the population"', the SCA considered this was

[23] SCA, 'Accreditation Report—Egypt (National Council for Human Rights (NCHR))' (October 2011) 13; SCA, 'Accreditation Report—Peru (The Defensoria del Pueblo del Peru (DPP))' (March 2012) 23; SCA, 'Accreditation Report—Philippines (CHRP)' (March 2012) 25; SCA, 'Accreditation Report—Egypt (NCHR)' (November 2015) 43.

[24] SCA, 'Accreditation Report—Croatia (Ombudsman of the Republic of Croatia (ORC))' (April 2008) 7; SCA, 'Accreditation Report—Albania (People's Advocate (PA))' (November 2008) 6.

[25] SCA, 'Accreditation Report—Slovenia (Human Rights Ombudsman of the Republic of Slovenia (HRORS))' (March/April 2010) 9.

[26] SCA, 'Accreditation Report—Namibia (Ombudsman)' (May 2011) 16; SCA, 'Accreditation Report—Namibia (Ombudsman)' (November 2016) 40.

[27] SCA, 'Accreditation Report—Oman (Oman National Human Rights Commission (ONHRC))' (November 2013) 13.

[28] SCA, 'Accreditation Report—Armenia (The Human Rights Defender of the Republic of Armenia (HRDA))' (March 2019) 19.

[29] SCA, 'Accreditation Report—Slovakia (SNCHR)' (March 2014) 8.

[30] SCA, 'Accreditation Report—Argentina (Defensoria del Pueblo de la Nación Argentina (DPNA)) (October 2011) 11.

[31] SCA, 'Accreditation Report—Ukraine (Office of the Ukrainian Parliament Commissioner for Human Rights (UPCHR))' (March 2009) 7.

insufficient and emphasized that there should be an explicit mandate with specific functions to promote and protect human rights.[32]

The SCA has frequently emphasized that while an NHRI may carry out promotional activities in practice, the NHRI's enabling law should still include a specific mandate for these functions.[33] For example, the SCA recommended the Ecuadorian NHRI to seek amendments to its enabling law to make its promotional mandate more explicit, observing that it contained a limited mandate for such functions despite the fact that the NHRI undertook 'a wide range of promotional activities in practice'.[34]

6.3.2 Requirement to Undertake Promotion Activities in Practice

NHRIs are expected to engage fully with both their promotion and protection mandates in practice.[35] The SCA has, on occasion, highlighted specific areas where the NHRI needs to focus on additional activities. Reviewing the NHRI in Iraq (High Commission for Human Rights (HCHR)), and accrediting it with B-status, the SCA acknowledged in 2015 that the NHRI faced financial constraints but at the same time underlined that the range of its promotional activities had been limited, and encouraged it to undertake promotional functions such as 'education training, advising, public outreach and advocacy'.[36]

32 SCA, 'Accreditation Report—Ukraine (UPCHR)' (October 2019) 20–21.

33 SCA, 'Accreditation Report—Macedonia (Ombudsman of the Republic of Macedonia (ORM))' (October 2011) 9; SCA, 'Accreditation Report—Poland (Human Rights Defender (HRD))' (November 2012) 22. The SCA reiterated this recommendation in its 2017 review: SCA, 'Accreditation Report—Poland (The Commissioner for Human Rights (CHRP))' (November 2017) 27. See also, SCA, 'Accreditation Report—Rwanda (The National Commission for Human Rights of the Republic of Rwanda (NCHR))' (May 2013) 16; SCA, 'Accreditation Report—Ukraine (UPCHR)' (October 2014) 35; SCA, 'Accreditation Report—Cyprus (Commissioner for Administration and Human Rights (CAHR))' (November 2015) 8; SCA, 'Accreditation Report—Canada (Canadian Human Rights Commission (CHRC))' (May 2016) 25; SCA, 'Accreditation Report—Montenegro (Protector of Human Rights and Freedoms (PHRF))' (May 2016) 16; SCA, 'Accreditation Report—Bosnia and Herzegovina (Human Rights Ombudsmen of Bosnia and Herzegovina (IHROBH))' (November 2016) 13–14; SCA, 'Accreditation Report—Costa Rica (Defensoría de los Habitantes (DHCR))' (November 2016) 18; SCA, 'Accreditation Report—Lithuania (Seimas Ombudsmen Office (SOO))' (March 2017) 10; SCA, 'Accreditation Report—Peru (DPP)' (March 2017) 27; SCA, 'Accreditation Report—Bosnia and Herzegovina (IHROBH)' (November 2017) 8, noting that proposed amendments would remedy this issue; SCA, 'Accreditation Report—Argentina (DPNA)' (October 2018) 23; SCA, 'Accreditation Report—Namibia (Ombudsman)' (October 2018) 12.

34 SCA, 'Accreditation Report—Ecuador (Defensoría del Pueblo de Ecuador (DPE))' (March 2015) 16. See also, SCA, 'Accreditation Report—Argentina (DPNA)' (November 2016) 9; SCA, 'Accreditation Report—Argentina (DPNA)' (November 2017) 38.

35 SCA, 'Accreditation Report—Cameroon (National Commission on Human Rights and Freedoms (NCHRF))' (March/April 2010) 8; SCA, 'Accreditation Report—Cameroon (NCHRF)' (March 2015) 34.

36 SCA, 'Accreditation Report—Iraq (HCHR)' (March 2015) 7.

The SCA has raised concerns where NHRIs not only lack a mandate for promotion functions but also implement limited promotional activities in practice. In a review of the Hungarian NHRI in 2013, the SCA underscored that the NHRI lacked an express promotional mandate in its enabling law while also encouraging it to expand the range of its promotional activities in practice, with a focus on education in general and minorities in particular.[37] Likewise in 2013, reviewing Albania's NHRI, the SCA encouraged the NHRI 'to expand the range of its promotional activities including in relation to human rights education generally, and minorities in particular, and to advocate for the express inclusion of a promotion mandate in the amending legislation'.[38] In both reviews, the SCA noted that such changes may have staffing and resource implications and that the requisite funding would need to be provided by the state.[39]

6.3.3 Mandate over the Private Sector

NHRIs should be mandated to cover the activities of the private sector.[40] In its 2012 review of the Portuguese NHRI (*Provedor*), the SCA underlined that the enabling law did not provide it with jurisdiction 'over the activities of private enterprises' and recommended that it continue its efforts to advocate for legislative amendments to broaden this aspect of its mandate.[41]

Laws should also not limit the responsibilities of the private sector to engage with the NHRI. In 2018, in relation to the Public Defender of Georgia (OPD), the SCA made the following recommendation:

> The SCA acknowledges that the OPD has a broad mandate to promote and protect human rights, and that it exercises this mandate in practice.
>
> The SCA notes, however, that the Anti-discrimination Law obliges public agencies to provide information to the Public Defender while private entities and individuals provide information to the Public Defender only on voluntary basis, and that the UN Committee on the Elimination of Racial Discrimination expressed concern that this may impact the ability of the OPD to effectively examine cases of discrimination (CERD/C/GEO/CO/6-8).

[37] SCA, 'Accreditation Report—Hungary (CFR)' (November 2013) 10.

[38] SCA, 'Accreditation Report—Albania (PA)' (November 2013) 19.

[39] SCA, 'Accreditation Report—Hungary (CFR)' (November 2013); SCA, 'Accreditation Report—Albania (PA)' (November 2013) 19.

[40] SCA, 'Accreditation Report—Austria (Austrian Ombudsman Board (AOB))' (May 2011) 11; SCA, 'Accreditation Report—Hungary (PCCR)' (May 2011) 8; SCA, 'Accreditation Report—Bulgaria (ORB)' (October 2011) 7; SCA, 'Accreditation Report—Armenia (HRDA)' (March 2019) 19; SCA, 'Accreditation Report—Russia (High Commissioner for Human Rights in the Russian Federation (OCHR))' (October 2019) 29.

[41] SCA, 'Accreditation Report—Portugal (Provedor de Justiça (Provedor))' (November 2012) 24.

> The SCA encourages the OPD to continue to advocate for appropriate amendments to the Anti-discrimination Law to make mandatory the provision of information by private entities and individuals.[42]

The mandate of the NHRI must cover both acts and omissions of the private sector. In reviewing the Human Rights Defender of Armenia (HRDA) in 2019, the SCA emphasized the following:

> The HRDA reports that its jurisdiction extends to private sector entities operating in the field of public service where there is information about mass violations of human rights or freedoms, or if it is of public importance or is related to the protection of interests of persons who cannot benefit from legal remedies for protection of their rights and freedoms on their own. However, the SCA emphasizes that the mandate of an NHRI should extend to the acts and omissions of both the public and private sectors.[43]

Even where the NHRI interprets its mandate broadly, and thus in practice undertakes actions in relation to human rights violations committed by private entities, this mandate should be explicit in legislation.[44]

6.4 Encouraging Ratification of International Instruments

In its General Observations, the SCA emphasizes that NHRIs have a key role in encouraging the ratification of and accession to international human rights instruments by the state, and that the Paris Principles prescribe that NHRIs should promote ratifications and accessions, as well as harmonization with national legislation. In its 2018 General Observation 1.3, the SCA underlines:

> [e]ncouraging ratification of, or accession to international human rights instruments, and the effective implementation of international human rights instruments to which the state is a party, is a key function of an NHRI. The Paris Principles further prescribe that NHRIs should promote and encourage the harmonization of national legislation, regulations and practices with these instruments. The SCA considers it important that these duties form an integral part of the enabling legislation of an NHRI. In fulfilling this function, the NHRI is encouraged to undertake activities which may include the following:

[42] SCA, 'Accreditation Report—Georgia (OPD)' (October 2018) 9.

[43] SCA, 'Accreditation Report—Armenia (HRDA)' (March 2019) 19; See also, SCA, 'Accreditation Report—Haiti (OPC)' (March 2019) 25.

[44] SCA, 'Accreditation Report—Honduras (Comisionado Nacional de los Derechos Humanos de Honduras (CONADEH))' (October 2019) 11.

- monitoring developments in international human rights law;
- promoting state participation in advocacy for and the drafting of international human rights instruments; and
- conducting assessments of domestic compliance with and reporting on international human rights obligations, for example, through annual and special reports and participation in the Universal Periodic Review process.

NHRIs should, in encouraging their governments to ratify international human rights instruments, advocate that this be done without reservations.[45]

The SCA provides the following justification:

Sections A.3(b) and (c) of the Paris Principles require that NHRIs have the responsibility to 'promote and ensure the harmonization of national legislation, regulations and practices with the international human rights instruments to which the State is a party, and their effective implementation'. Additionally, the NHRI has the responsibility 'to encourage ratification of [these] instruments or accession to those instruments, and to ensure their implementation'.

In practice this requires NHRIs to review relevant national laws, regulations and policies to determine that they are compatible with the obligations arising from international human rights standards and propose the amendment or repeal of any legislation, regulations or policies that are inconsistent with the requirements of these standards. The SCA is of the view that the NHRI should be legislatively empowered to carry out these responsibilities.

The SCA notes the distinction between the state's own monitoring obligations as required by these instruments and the distinct role played by the NHRI in monitoring the state's compliance and progress towards implementing the instruments it ratifies. Where the NHRI undertakes to carry out its own activities in promoting and protecting the rights contained therein, it shall do so in an entirely autonomous fashion. This does not preclude the NHRI from undertaking joint action with the state on certain activities, such as reviewing compliance of existing domestic legislation and regulations with international human rights instruments.

Excerpt from the Paris Principles

A) Competence and responsibilities—

3. A national institution shall, inter alia, have the following responsibilities:

...

[45] SCA, 'General Observations' (February 2018) (n 2) GO 1.3, 10–11.

(b) To promote and ensure the harmonization of national legislation regulations and practices with the international human rights instruments to which the State is a party, and their effective implementation;
(c) To encourage ratification of the above-mentioned instruments or accession to those instruments, and to ensure their implementation ....[46]

Overall, the SCA referred to General Observation 1.3 and commented on these functions 48 times in its accreditation reviews between 2008 and 2019.

Encouraging ratification or accession to international human rights instruments should be explicitly included in NHRIs' enabling law.[47] For example, in 2014, the SCA reiterated its 2008 observation to the Kenyan NHRI (KNCHR), and detailed why it found the NHRI's mandate did not sufficiently provide for this function:

> During its 2008 review, the SCA stressed the need for the KNCHR to entrench in its mandate the power to encourage ratification of or accession to international human rights instruments. The SCA acknowledges that article 59, paragraph (2)(g), of the Constitution and Section 8, paragraph (f), of the KNCHR Act of 2011, establish the KNCHR as the principal organ of the State in ensuring compliance with obligations under international treaties and conventions in respect of human rights. However, the SCA urges the KNCHR to advocate for legislative amendment to provide for an explicit mandate to encourage ratification of or accession to international human rights instruments.[48]

Even where promoting the ratification of international instruments is undertaken by the NHRI in practice, the SCA still requires provision in the enabling law.[49] It

[46] ibid 10–11.
[47] See for example, SCA, 'Accreditation Report—Niger (Commission Nationale des Droits de l'Homme et des Libertés Fondamentales (CNDHLF))' (April 2008) 6; SCA, 'Accreditation Report—Kenya (National Commission on Human Rights (NCHR))' (November 2008) 8; SCA, 'Accreditation Report—Cameroon (NCHRF)' (March/April 2010) 8; SCA, 'Accreditation Report—Slovenia (HRORS)' (March/April 2010) 9; SCA, 'Accreditation Report—Romania (Romanian Institute of Human Rights (RIHR))' (May 2011) 21; SCA, 'Accreditation Report—Bulgaria (CPD)' (October 2011) 8; SCA, 'Accreditation Report—Bulgaria (ORB)' (October 2011) 7; SCA, 'Accreditation Report—Great Britain (Equality and Human Rights Commission)' (November 2015) 21; SCA, 'Accreditation Report—Ireland (IHREC)' (November 2015) 10; SCA, 'Accreditation Report—Cameroon (NCHRF)' (May 2016) 28; SCA, 'Accreditation Report—Northern Ireland (Northern Ireland Human Rights Commission (NIHRC))' (May 2016) 47; SCA, 'Accreditation Report—Bosnia and Herzegovina (IHROBH)' (November 2016) 17; SCA, 'Accreditation Report—Namibia (Ombudsman)' (November 2016) 44; SCA, 'Accreditation Report—Cameroon (NCHRF)' (November 2017) 16; SCA, 'Accreditation Report—Egypt (NCHR)' (May 2018) 20; SCA, 'Accreditation Report—Namibia (Ombudsman)' (October 2018) 12; SCA, 'Accreditation Report—Armenia (HRDA)' (March 2019) 19; SCA, 'Accreditation Report—Paraguay (Defensoría del Pueblo de Paraguay (DPP))' (March 2019) 12.
[48] SCA, 'Accreditation Report—Kenya (KNCHR)' (October 2014) 20.
[49] SCA, 'Accreditation Report—Tajikistan (The Human Rights Ombudsman of the Republic of Tajikistan (HROT))' (March 2012) 15; SCA, 'Accreditation Report—Denmark (Danish Institute for Human Rights (DIHR))' (October 2018) 8; SCA, 'Accreditation Report—Paraguay (DPP)' (March 2019) 12; SCA, 'Accreditation Report—Kenya (NCHR)' (October 2019) 16; SCA, 'Accreditation

does, however, welcome actions by the NHRI even where it does not have an implicit mandate. In reviewing the South African NHRI the SCA observed that although its enabling law does not provide a mandate for encouraging ratification and implementation of international human rights standards, it acknowledged that it interpreted its mandate in practice in broad terms and highlighted the 'proactive role undertaken by the SAHRC to encourage the State to ratify the ICESCR and other international human rights instruments'.[50]

NHRIs should actively encourage the ratification of international instruments.[51] Reviewing the Hungarian NHRI (CFR) in 2014, the SCA elaborated more in detail on questions regarding the NHRI's mandate but also encouraged it to undertake this work in practice:

> In accordance with article 2(2) of its enabling law, the CFR may make proposals for the amendment or making of laws affecting fundamental rights and / or the expression of consent to be bound by an international treaty.
>
> The SCA acknowledges the CFR's view that, as its Constitution is derived from the European Charter of Fundamental Rights, it does not often encounter the need for ratification of or accession to international instruments. The SCA also acknowledges the CFR's past efforts to carry out this activity. The SCA is of the view that encouraging ratification of, or accession to, international instruments is a key function of an NHRI.
>
> The CFR is encouraged to monitor developments in international human rights law, promote state participation in advocacy for and the drafting of international human rights instruments and take a strategic approach in recommending ratification of or accession to international instruments.[52]

NHRIs should also have the explicit mandate to harmonize national legislation with international human rights instruments and principles, in addition to the encouragement of their ratification and implementation.[53] Enabling laws should be clear about this function. In 2016, the SCA recommended to the Canadian NHRI

Report—Togo (La Commission Nationale des Droits de l'homme du Togo (CNDH))' (October 2019) 17; SCA, 'Accreditation Report—Ukraine (UPCHR)' (October 2019) 21.

[50] SCA, 'Accreditation Report—South Africa (South African Human Rights Commission (SAHRC))' (November 2012) 30. See also, SCA, 'Accreditation Report—Croatia (ORC)' (May 2013) 9; SCA, 'Accreditation Report—Bosnia and Herzegovina (IHROBH)' (November 2016) 17; SCA, 'Accreditation Report—Niger (CNDH)' (March 2017) 11; SCA, 'Accreditation Report—Norway (Norwegian National Human Rights Institution (NNHRI))' (March 2017) 14; SCA, 'Accreditation Report—Philippines (CHRP)' (March 2017) 29; SCA, 'Accreditation Report—Bosnia and Herzegovina (IHROBH)' (November 2017) 11; SCA, 'Accreditation Report—Denmark (DIHR)' (November 2017) 42.

[51] SCA, 'Accreditation Report—Venezuela (Defensoría del Pueblo (DP))' (April 2008) 7.

[52] SCA, 'Accreditation Report—Hungary (CFR)' (October 2014) 11.

[53] SCA, 'Accreditation Report—Great Britain (EHRC)' (November 2008) 4; SCA, 'Accreditation Report—Slovakia (SNCHR)' (March 2014) 8.

(Canadian Human Rights Commission (CHRC)) that its enabling law 'should enumerate its mandate and functions more clearly, as was noted by the CHRC in relation to the encouraging ratification and implementation of international standards and engagement with the international human rights system'.[54]

In some instances, the SCA has discussed General Observation 1.3 on the functions of encouraging ratifications together with the General Observation 1.4 on interaction with the international human rights system, which is covered in Chapter 7.4. For example, in its 2016 review of Montenegro (Protector of Human Rights and Freedoms (PHRF)), the SCA commented:

> The SCA acknowledges the PHRF is a member of various regional human rights organizations and has engaged with the international human rights system. However, there is no specific legal provision for the PHRF to engage with these systems, or to encourage ratification or accession to international human rights instruments.[55]

The SCA has also occasionally recommended that an NHRI support the ratification of a specific international instrument, such as the Second Optional Protocol to the International Covenant on Civil and Political Rights (ICCPR).[56]

6.5 Protection Functions

As noted above, the SCA discusses protection together with promotion functions under General Observation 1.2 (2018),[57] however, it does give specific detail on each. The SCA sets out the details of what specific activities should be included under the protection functions of NHRIs:

> 'Protection' functions may be understood as those that address and seek to prevent actual human rights violations. Such functions include monitoring, inquiring, investigating and reporting on human rights violations, and may include individual complaint handling.[58]

[54] SCA, 'Accreditation Report—Canada (CHRC)' (May 2016) 25.

[55] SCA, 'Accreditation Report—Montenegro (PHRF)' (May 2016) 18–19. See also, SCA, 'Accreditation Report—Zambia (Human Rights Commission (HRCZ))' (November 2016) 59; SCA, 'Accreditation Report—Lithuania (SOO)' (March 2017) 10; SCA, 'Accreditation Report—Zambia (HRCZ)' (October 2018) 18; SCA, 'Accreditation Report—Ghana (The Commission on Human Rights and Administrative Justice (CHRAJ))' (March 2019) 24.

[56] SCA, 'Accreditation Report—Egypt (NCHR)' (May 2018) 20.

[57] SCA, 'General Observations' (February 2018) (n 2) GO 1.2, 7.

[58] ibid.

This has not been an area of considerable focus by the SCA. Altogether, the SCA made observations about protection functions specifically thirteen times in its reviews between 2008 and 2017.

Similar to the recommendations on promotion functions discussed in the previous section, NHRIs should be mandated with specific protection functions,[59] and NHRIs should seek amendments to their enabling law to have a broad protection mandate.[60] The protection mandate should not be unduly limited.[61] Protection provisions should also be explicit, not implicit.[62]

The SCA has occasionally been specific in the areas in which an NHRI needs to enhance its protection functions. Reviewing the C-status institution in Romania in 2011, it found that there were no provisions in the institution's enabling law for human rights protection functions, noting that the NHRI 'does not have the authority to address recommendations to public authorities, to analyze the human rights situation in Romania, nor to obtain statements or documents in order to assess situations raising human rights issues'.[63] Reviewing the French NHRI (CNCDH) in 2013, the SCA acknowledged that it undertook activities such as 'review of and advice on draft legislation; publishing reports on national human rights issues; and interacting with international human rights mechanisms, including treaty body reporting and the submission of amicus curiae briefs to competent courts'.[64] At the same time, it found that these were not sufficiently broad and that the NHRI should 'advocate for amendments to its law that provide it with the powers necessary to fulfil a broad protection mandate',[65] noting that this may have resource and staffing implications for the institution. In its 2019 review, while recognizing the efforts made by the French NHRI to broaden its activities in relation to its protection mandate, the SCA also expressed concern at the addition of new legislative responsibilities for human trafficking, business and human rights, and 'anti-LGBT hate' which had been added without 'an explicit broad protection mandate'.[66]

As noted in the previous section, NHRIs must actively engage both with their promotion and protection functions. Reviewing the Danish NHRI in 2017, and

[59] SCA, 'Accreditation Report—Germany (German Institute for Human Rights (GIHR))' (November 2008) 7.

[60] SCA, 'Accreditation Report—Germany (GIHR)' (November 2013) 21.

[61] SCA, 'Accreditation Report—Germany (GIHR)' (November 2015) 16.

[62] SCA, 'Accreditation Report—Mali (Commission Nationale des Droits de l'Homme (CNDH))' (March 2012) 12.

[63] SCA, 'Accreditation Report—Romania (RIHR)' (May 2011) 20.

[64] SCA, 'Accreditation Report—France (National Consultative Commission on Human Rights (NCCHR))' (May 2013) 10–11.

[65] SCA, 'Accreditation Report—France (NCCHR)' (May 2013) 11. In its 2019 review of the French NHRI, the SCA noted that the CNCDH had undertaken efforts to implement this recommendation. SCA, 'Accreditation Report—France (Commission Nationale Consultative des Droits de l'Homme (CNCDH))' (March 2019) 20. The SCA reports alternate between the use of the French and English language names of the NHRI.

[66] SCA, 'Accreditation Report—France (CNCDH)' (March 2019) 20.

deferring its accreditation decision, the SCA observed that the NHRI 'indicated that its core mandate is promotion rather than protection', although its enabling law provided it with a mandate for protection functions and that in practice, it undertook some protection activities.[67] Noting that NHRI's protection activities could be broadened, the SCA encouraged the NHRI to 'interpret their protection mandate in a broad manner and to conduct a range of protection activities including monitoring, enquiring, investigating and reporting on human rights violations, and may include individual complaint handling'.[68] It also encouraged the DIHR to 'provide additional information regarding how it discharges its protection mandate'.[69] In its October 2018 review, the SCA acknowledged that the DIHR had provided details 'about a wide range of activities it understands that would be considered to be protection functions'.[70] While the SCA's report does not list these explicitly, the SCA encouraged the NHRI 'to continue to interpret its protection mandate in a broad manner and to conduct a range of protection actions, including monitoring, enquiring, investigating, and reporting'.[71]

Accrediting the Bahrain NHRI (NIHRB) with B-status in 2016, under the heading of 'human rights mandate', the SCA detailed what protection activities it undertook and highlighted areas for improvement:

> The SCA is concerned about the effective application of the NIHRB's protection mandate in certain circumstances. While the SCA noted that the NIHRB had conducted some inquiries and made some public statements, it notes that NHRIs are expected to promote and ensure respect for the human rights of all individuals in all circumstances and without exception. In this regard, an NHRIs actions may include monitoring, documenting, issuing public statements and releasing regular and detailed reports on human rights violations through the media, and that these should be provided in a timely manner. Furthermore, an NHRI should also undertake rigorous and systematic follow-up activities, and should advocate for the consideration and implementation of its findings and recommendations in order to ensure the protection of those whose rights have been violated. These actions, in particular the release of public reports, serve to combat impunity for human rights violations.[72]

In accrediting the NHRI in Austria with B-status in 2011, the SCA observed that the designation of the institution as a National Preventative Mechanism (NPM) under the Optional Protocol to the Convention for the Prevention of Torture

[67] SCA, 'Accreditation Report—Denmark (DIHR)' (November 2017) 41–42.
[68] ibid 42.
[69] ibid.
[70] SCA, 'Accreditation Report—Denmark (DIHR)' (October 2018) 8.
[71] ibid.
[72] SCA, 'Accreditation Report—Bahrain (NIHRB)' (May 2016) 9.

(OPCAT)[73] would not in and of itself provide the institution with an adequately broad mandate for the protection and the promotion of human rights.[74]

6.5.1 Complaints-handling Functions

Not all NHRIs are mandated with quasi-judicial or complaints-handling functions. As noted by the SCA, it is not a requirement of the Paris Principles, however it is included in the Paris Principles. Furthermore, a sufficient number of NHRIs have these functions, particularly Ombuds-type institutions, that is merits specific attention from the SCA. In its 2018 General Observation 2.9, the SCA sets out the requirements where NHRIs do have these functions:

> When an NHRI is provided with a mandate to receive, consider and/or resolve complaints alleging violations of human rights, it should be provided with the necessary functions and powers to adequately fulfil this mandate. Depending on its mandate, such powers and functions might include:
>
> - the ability to receive complaints against both public and private bodies in its jurisdiction;
> - the ability to receive complaints that are filed by persons on behalf of the alleged victim(s), where consent is given;
> - the ability to commence a complaint on its own initiative;
> - the ability to investigate complaints, including the power to compel the production of evidence and witnesses, and to visit places of deprivation of liberty;
> - the ability to protect complainants from retaliation for having filed a complaint;
> - the ability to protect witnesses from retaliation for having provided evidence in relation to a complaint;
> - the ability to seek an amicable and confidential settlement of the complaint through an alternative dispute resolution process;
> - the ability to settle complaints through a binding determination;
> - the ability to refer its findings to courts of law or specialized tribunals for adjudication;
> - the ability to refer complaints falling beyond its jurisdiction or in a concurrent jurisdiction to the appropriate decision-making body;
> - the ability to seek enforcement through the court system of its decisions on the resolution of complaints;

[73] Optional Protocol to the Convention against Torture and other Cruel, Inhuman or Degrading Treatment or Punishment (adopted on 18 December 2002, entered into force on 22 June 2006) 2375 UNTS 237 (OPCAT) Art 3 (hereafter OPCAT).

[74] SCA, 'Accreditation Report—Austria (AOB)' (May 2011) 11.

- the ability to follow up and monitor the implementation of its decisions on the resolution of complaints; and
- the ability to refer its findings to government in situations where a complaint provides evidence of a widespread or systematic violation of human rights.

In fulfilling its complaints-handling mandate, the NHRI should ensure that complaints are dealt with fairly, transparently, efficiently, expeditiously, and with consistency. In order to do so, an NHRI should:

- ensure that its facilities, staff, and its practices and procedures, facilitate access by those who allege their rights have been violated and their representatives; and
- ensure that its complaint-handling procedures are contained in written guidelines, and that these are publicly available.[75]

In its justification, the SCA provides:

The Paris Principles do not require that an NHRI have the ability to receive complaints or petitions from individuals or groups regarding the alleged violation of their human rights. However, where it is provided with this mandate, the Paris Principles suggest that certain functions should be considered (see excerpt below). In essence, NHRIs are expected to handle complaints fairly, speedily and effectively through processes which are readily accessible to the public. NHRIs may be empowered to carry out investigations into complaints and refer their findings to an appropriate authority. NHRIs should have the authority to deal with bodies against which complaints are made and may be authorised to seek compliance with its decisions through the judiciary.

Excerpt from the Paris Principles

'Additional principles concerning the status of commissions with quasijurisdictional [*sic*] competence'

A national institution may be authorized to hear and consider complaints and petitions concerning individual situations. Cases may be brought before it by individuals, their representatives, thirds parties, non-governmental organizations, associations of trade unions or any other representative organizations. In such circumstances, and without prejudice to the principles stated above concerning the other powers of the commissions, the functions entrusted to them may be based on the following principles:

(a) Seeking an amicable settlement through conciliation or, within the limits prescribed by the law, through binding decisions or, where necessary, on the basis of confidentiality;

[75] SCA, 'General Observations' (February 2018) (n 2) GO 1.2, 49–50.

(b) Informing the party who filed the petition of his rights, in particular the remedies available to him, and promoting his access to them;
(c) Hearing any complaints or petitions or transmitting them to any other competent authority within the limits prescribed by the law;
(d) Making recommendations to the competent authorities, especially by proposing amendments or reforms of the laws, regulations and administrative practices, especially if they have created the difficulties encountered by the persons filing the petitions in order to assert their rights.[76]

Between 2007 and 2017, the SCA made observations only nine times on quasi-judicial functions, making it one of the least commented aspects of Paris Principles compliance. In two cases, the SCA made short observations about NHRIs' complaints handling practices, or merely noted that that it undertakes such work.[77] Reviewing the Bahrain institution (NIHRB) and accrediting it with B-status, the SCA stated that it had 'received allegations that raised concerns about the responsiveness of the NIHRB to complaints and its willingness to support and protect human rights defenders', and that 'in response, the NIHRB indicated that it receives and responds to all complaints'.[78]

In most instances, the SCA commented on whether and how complaints handling functions were part of the mandate of an NHRI, and in some cases made recommendations. Reviewing the Great Britain NHRI (EHRC) in 2008, in the context of unifying anti-discrimination and equality legislation, the SCA recommended that 'the functions of the EHRC be expanded to give it an explicit mandate to protect human rights, including the power to receive and determine complaints on human rights violations'.[79] In its review of the German NHRI (GIHR) the same year, the SCA referred 'to the importance for the GIHR to further broaden its mandate to include complaint handling functions'.[80] In 2014, accrediting the Slovakian NHRI with B-status, the SCA encouraged it to seek changes to its legislation, among other things, to have explicit powers to 'effectively investigative complaints of human rights violations'.[81]

The NHRI should not be restricted in its ability to use its complaints-handling functions. The SCA expressed concern that the Zimbabwe NHRI was 'prevented from investigating complaints related to an action or omission that occurred prior to 13 February 2009',[82] and recommended that the NHRI's 'mandate should authorize the full investigation of all alleged human rights violations and should not

[76] SCA, 'General Observations' (February 2018) (n 2) 49–50.
[77] SCA, 'Accreditation Report—Tajikistan (HROT)' (March 2012) 14.
[78] SCA, 'Accreditation Report—Bahrain (NIHRB)' (May 2016) 9.
[79] SCA, 'Accreditation Report—Great Britain (EHRC))' (November 2008) 4.
[80] SCA, 'Accreditation Report—Germany (GIHR))' (November 2008) 6.
[81] SCA, 'Accreditation Report—Slovakia (SNCHR)' (March 2014) 8.
[82] SCA, 'Accreditation Report—Zimbabwe (ZHRC)' (May 2016) 23.

be unreasonably limited'.[83] In its 2016 review of the New Zealand Human Rights Commission (NZHRC), the SCA reflected on limitations on the submission of complaints to the NHRI. It noted that due to 'Section 392 of the Immigration Act 2009, the NZHRC is prevented from accepting complaints with respect to the contents or application of the Immigration Act, Regulations or any policy under that Act',[84] and encouraged it to seek the removal of this provision from the law.[85]

In reviewing the NHRI of India, the SCA elaborated in detail on its concerns on the institution's practices related to its complaints-handling function. In 2011, the SCA commented:

> The SCA notes that civil society groups allege that the NHRCI's complaint handling functions suffer from extended delays and that the NHRCI does not adequately address human rights violations that have occurred. Their concerns were reiterated by the Special Rapporteur on the situation of human rights defenders who, at the conclusion of her official visit to India in January 2011, stated: '*(A)ll the defenders that I met during the mission voiced their disappointment and mistrust in the current functioning of (the NHRC). They have submitted complaints related to human rights violations to the Commission, but reportedly their cases were either hardly taken up, or the investigation, often after a significant period of delay, concluded that no violations occurred. Their main concern lies in the fact that the investigations into their cases [were] conducted by the police, which in many cases are the perpetrators of the alleged violations*.'
>
> By contrast, the NHRCI has indicated that in recent years it has introduced changes to its complaint handling process to address the increasing number of complaints and delays in complaint handling. On the information available, the SCA is unable to determine the veracity of the allegations raised above, however it is clear that there is at least a perception that there are significant delays, as well as ongoing concerns about the use of former police to investigate complaints, including those against the police. The SCA encourages the NHRCI to address these concerns.[86]

Its subsequent 2016 review of the Indian NHRI, the SCA raised concerns again in relation to complaints handling practices:

> The SCA has received information from civil society groups alleging that the NHRCI's complaint handling functions suffer from extended delays. The SCA notes with concern that the NHRCI confirmed to have a substantial backlog of

[83] ibid.
[84] SCA, 'Accreditation Report—New Zealand (NZHRC)' (May 2016) 44.
[85] ibid.
[86] SCA, 'Accreditation Report—India (National Human Rights Commission of India (NHRCI))' (May 2011) 14–15 (emphasis in original).

40,000 cases. In fulfilling its complaint handling mandate, the NHRI should ensure that complaints are dealt with fairly, transparently, efficiently, expeditiously, and with consistency. In order to do so, a NHRI should:

- ensure that its facilities, staff, and its practices and procedures, facilitate access by those who allege their rights have been violated and their representatives; and
- ensure that its complaint handling procedures are contained in written guidelines, and that these are publicly available.

The SCA encourages the NHRCI to handle complaints in timely manner and permit all individuals, regardless of their legal status, to access to its complaint process.[87]

6.6 Limitation of Powers for National Security Reasons

While rarely invoked by the SCA, occasionally, the mandate or functions of NHRIs are limited for 'reasons of national security'. The SCA has elaborated the following General Observation 2.6 (2018):

> G.O. 2.6 Limitation of power of NHRIs due to national security
> The scope of the mandate of an NHRI may be restricted for national security reasons. While this limitation is not inherently contrary to the Paris Principles, it should not be unreasonably or arbitrarily applied and should only be exercised under due process.[88]

The SCA provides the following in its justification:

> According to section A.2 of the Paris Principles, an NHRI should possess, 'as broad a mandate as possible'. To give full effect to this Principle, the SCA recommends that this provision be understood in the widest sense. That is, the mandate of the NHRI should extend to protect the public from acts and omissions of public authorities, including officers and personnel of the military, police and special security forces. Where such public authorities, who may potentially have a great impact on human rights, are excluded from the jurisdiction of the NHRI, this may serve to undermine the credibility of the Institution.
>
> NHRIs, in their analysis of the human rights situation in the country, should be authorized to fully investigate all alleged human rights violations, regardless

[87] SCA, 'Accreditation Report—India (NHRCI)' (November 2016) 28.
[88] SCA, 'General Observations' (February 2018) (n 2) GO 2.6, 43.

> of which State officials are responsible. This should include the ability to have unannounced and unimpeded access to inspect and examine any public premises, documents, equipment and assets without prior written notice. Although the authority of NHRIs to undertake such an investigation may be restricted for national security reasons, such restriction should not be unreasonably or arbitrarily applied and should be exercised under due process.
>
> Excerpt from the Paris Principles
>
> A) Competence and responsibilities –
>
> 2. A national institution shall be given as broad a mandate as possible, which shall be clearly set forth in a constitutional or legislative text, specifying its composition and its sphere of competence.[89]

In one of the few invocations of this General Observation, the SCA repeatedly expressed concern regarding the law of the NHRI of Tanzania (CHRAGG), beginning in 2006, in relation to 'the constitutional power of the President to issue directives to the Commission on issues of national interest under article 130(3) of the Constitution has not been invoked but suggests that consideration be given to limiting the scope of this power as prescribed by the law'.[90] The SCA commented:

> The SCA recognises that at times States may have legitimate reasons to issue national interest directives. However, such power should be appropriately circumscribed, particularly in circumstances where their issue may lead to impunity for human rights violations. The SCA therefore notes with concern that the CHRAGG has not taken any steps to follow up on the recommendation While the CHRAGG stated that this provision has yet to be invoked, it is the view of the SCA that its recommendations ought to have been pursued and steps taken to seek to limit the scope of this power.

[89] ibid.

[90] SCA, 'Accreditation Report—Tanzania (Commission for Human Rights and Good Governance (CHRAGG))' (October 2006) 5. The relevant provisions of the Tanzanian Constitution Article 130 provide: '(2) The Commission shall be an autonomous department, and without prejudice to other provisions of this Article, in exercising its powers in accordance with this Constitution, the Commission shall not be bound to comply with directive or orders of any person or any department of government, or any opinion of any political party or of any public or private sector institution. (3) The provisions of subarticle (2) shall not be construed as restricting the President from giving directive or orders to the Commission, nor are they conferring a right to the Commission of not complying with directions or orders, if the President is satisfied that in respect of any matter or any state of affair, public interest so requires. (4) The Commission shall conduct inquiry in accordance with the provisions of this Article and of any law enacted in that behalf by the Parliament, and shall inquire into the conduct of any person concerned or of any institution concerned whenever the President directs to conduct inquiry; likewise, except as the President directs the Commission not to conduct investigation the Commission may conduct investigation whenever it deems necessary to inquire into the conduct of any person concerned, or any institution concerned with the provisions of this Article who is suspected or which is suspected to have abused the authority of his office, misused the authority of his office or the functions of such institution or for violation of human rights and principles of good governance.' The Constitution of the United Republic of Tanzania 1977, Art 130.

> The SCA further notes that article 130(4) provides that the President can order the CHRAGG to conduct an inquiry, or (of particular concern to the SCA) the President can order it not to conduct an inquiry. While this provision may not have been invoked by the President, the SCA is concerned that this provision may affect the independence and autonomy of the CHRAGG, and that its use may also result in impunity for human rights violations. The SCA encourages the CHRAGG to advocate for amendments to this provision.[91]

In deferring the re-accreditation of the NHRI in 2016, the SCA noted a further concern:

> Further, in accordance with section 16 of the Act, the President may direct the CHRAGG not to investigate a matter where he or she considers that there is a real and substantial risk that an investigation would prejudice national security.[92]

In the deferred review in November 2017, the SCA reiterated its concerns about Articles 130(3) and (4) of the Constitution and Section 16 of the Act:

> The CHRAGG indicates that it has advocated for the removal of article 130(4) of the Constitution and sections 16(3) and (4) of the Act in order to remove the power of the President to order the CHRAGG to conduct or not to conduct an inquiry. It has additionally advocated for a provision guaranteeing the independence of the CHRAGG in article 241(1) of the Constitution. These amendments, if passed, would substantially address the SCA's concerns regarding the CHRAGG's independence. The SCA encourages the CHRAGG to continue to advocate for passage of these amendments.
>
> It further encourages the CHRAGG to advocate for the removal of article 130(3) of the Constitution, which provides for the power of the President to issue directives to the CHRAGG on issues of national interest.[93]

National security limitations should not restrict NHRIs from investigating alleged human rights violations by the military, police, or security forces 'where these occur outside situations classified as international or internal armed conflicts'. Reviewing the NHRI of Bangladesh in 2015, the SCA expressed concern that the NHRC was not empowered to directly investigate alleged human rights violations by the military.[94]

[91] SCA, 'Accreditation Report—Tanzania (CHRAGG)' (October 2011) 17–18.
[92] SCA, 'Accreditation Report—Tanzania (CHRAGG)' (November 2016) 50.
[93] SCA, 'Accreditation Report—Tanzania (CHRAGG)' (November 2017) 34.
[94] SCA, 'Accreditation Report—Bangladesh (National Human Rights Commission of Bangladesh (NHRCB))' (March) 12.

Related, but not precisely on this question of limitation for national security reasons, the SCA has expressed concern where an NHRI's mandate expressly precludes certain segments of the national system. In reviewing the NHRI of Kazakhstan (CHR) in 2012, accrediting it with B-status, the SCA noted:

> Art 18 of the Provision on the Commissioner of Human Rights precludes the Commissioner from considering complaints against actions of the President, Parliament and its members, Government, Constitutional Council, Prosecutor General, Central Electoral Commission and the Courts. It is of the view that this provision may limit the CHR's ability to carry out its mandate in an independent manner.
>
> The SCA notes that while it may be justified to place certain acts of these bodies beyond the scope of review by the CHR, it encourages the CHR to advocate for the power to consider human rights violations where these are not currently the subject of review by a more appropriate independent body.[95]

6.7 Comment

The SCA has devoted considerable attention to the promotion and protection functions of NHRIs. It has consistently emphasized the need for these functions to be explicitly and clearly set out in their enabling laws, even if an NHRI undertakes promotion and protection activities in practice. The definition of human rights that the NHRI has the power to examine should be broad and based in international standards, reflecting the connection NHRIs are expected to make between the national and international systems (see Chapter 1.5 and Chapter 1.6). The requirement for NHRIs to encourage the ratification of international instruments also speaks to the connection between NHRIs and the UN human rights system.

The SCA seeks to ensure that the enabling law explicitly provides that NHRIs will have a broad mandate to promote and protect all human rights issues that may arise and will require NHRIs to advocate for inclusion of provisions that the SCA views are needed, or for removal of provisions that may unduly limit that mandate. As can be seen in the approach of the SCA to Tanzania's NHRI (CHRAGG) described in Section 6.6, the SCA required the NHRI to advocate for amendments or removal of legislative provisions which could limit the scope of its mandate even though such provisions had never been invoked. This is consistent with its requiring NHRIs to advocate for inclusion of a specific mandate to both promote and protect human rights even where the NHRI interprets its mandate broadly in practice.

95 SCA, 'Accreditation Report—Kazakhstan (The Commissioner for Human Rights (CHR))' (March 2012) 7–8.

The SCA's reviews in this chapter show that the human rights covered by NHRIs are clearly connected to the international human rights system, in keeping with NHRIs origins in, and continuing connection to the international level (see Chapter 1). Further, NHRIs are intended to be active in both the promotion and protection of human rights. With the SCA giving equal weight to the importance of each of these aspects.

While the SCA does not list them as such, quasi-judicial functions may be interpreted as a cross cutting function that overlap both with protection and promotion functions and activities. The Paris Principles do not include quasi-judicial functions or complaints-handling as an institutional *requirement* for NHRIs, and therefore the General Observations do not present this function as a requirement either, reflecting that they fit some of the NHRI types but not others. Thus, to require these functions would be to mandate a specific type of NHRI—a move that the Paris Principles, and the SCA, generally seek to avoid.

The lack of requirement by the Paris Principles for all NHRIs to have complaints-handling functions has been subject of debate in the academic literature. As Linos and Pegram note, 'few design features provoke as much debate as complaint handling powers'.[96] Analysing which specific institutional design features make NHRIs more effective, with a dataset from 107 countries, Linos and Pegram found that NHRIs with strong investigatory capabilities with a focus on complaints-handling mechanisms stand out as one of the most important institutional design features.[97] In contrast, they argue, the Paris Principles have not placed an emphasis on complaints-handling functions unlike Latin American NHRIs, that traditionally did regardless of the Paris Principles. The authors state that the UN Representative of the High Commissioner for Human Rights in Latin America, for instance, even argued against the adoption of the Paris Principles and in favour of regional models partially because of the lack of explicit requirements and standards for complaints-handling functions. They contend that complaints-handling functions, besides allowing NHRIs to address individual problems and through that broader human rights issues, also help build community support for these organizations and increase their resilience against budgets cuts and other challenges. In light of the current commenting practices of the SCA, Linos and Pegram argue that recommendations-focused change in its comments might work for mainstreaming complaints-handling functions and establishing standards in their application across NHRIs.[98] In another study on NHRIs the authors note that while some scholars view complaints-handling powers as essential, 'NHRI models which principally perform a research or advisory function may also serve an important role in domestic contexts defined by functional investigative and adjudicatory structures

[96] Katrina Linos and Tom Pegram, 'What Works in Human Rights Institutions?' (2017) 111(3) American Journal of International Law 628.

[97] ibid.

[98] ibid 687.

(Reif 2012)'.[99] While it is not within the scope of this book to detail all of the academic debate on this issue, it is worth re-emphasizing a point made above: the SCA does not require complaints-handling functions because these are not a requirement for NHRIs set out in the Paris Principles.

In only a handful of reviews under the General Observation covered in this chapter did the SCA comment on how specific human rights issues and violations were (or were not) addressed with promotion and protection function related activities. Rather, the SCA has focused under the above-discussed General Observations on the more formal aspects of the NHRI's mandate and the powers provided to the institution. When considering human rights promotion and protection as regards to what NHRIs actually do in practice, the SCA has utilized General Observation 1.6, discussed in Chapter 7 specifically and Part III of this book more broadly.

[99] Katerina Linos and Tom Pegram, *Interrogating Form and Function: Defining Effective National Human Rights Institutions* (The Danish Institute for Human Rights 2015) 12 (see also on complaints-handling powers, ibid 29–30). Citing International Council on Human Rights Policy, *Assessing the Effectiveness of National Human Rights Institutions* (International Council on Human Rights Policy 2005) on the former point and Linda Reif, 'The Shifting Boundaries of the NHRI Definition in the International System' in Ryan Goodman and Thomas Pegram (eds), *Human Rights, State Compliance, and Social Change: Assessing National Human Rights Institutions* (CUP 2012).

PART III

NATIONAL HUMAN RIGHTS INSTITUTIONS AS HUMAN RIGHTS PROMOTERS AND PROTECTORS

This book is divided into three parts. Part I comprised two chapters introducing the origins and establishment of NHRIs, and setting out in detail the process and practice of the SCA. Part II began the book's analysis of the SCA's reports, covering NHRIs' legal basis, who runs NHRIs, the relationship with the state, and their human rights mandate. This part considers NHRIs' practice as human rights promoters and protectors, which is a growing area of focus and concern for the SCA. It examines how the SCA deals with NHRIs who are failing to promote and protect human rights, or worse, actively undermining human rights. It considers the requirements where NHRIs are also treaty-mandated national prevention or monitoring mechanisms, how the SCA deals with challenging cases, and looks at specific cases where there has been a loss of A-status.

7
The Practice of National Human Rights Institutions as Human Rights Advocates and Defenders

7.1 Introduction

This chapter is the first in this book that primarily examines recommendations of the Sub-Committee on Accreditation (SCA) in relation to the activity of the National Human Rights Institution (NHRI) on the ground as a human rights actor. This is a growing area of concern for the SCA, as will be seen in this chapter as well as Chapter 9 (on challenging cases) and Chapter 10 (losing A-status). There is also some overlap between the chapters in this part of the book, with several NHRIs appearing in multiple chapters.

In its early reviews of NHRIs, the SCA focused much of its attention on adherence to the formal requirements of the Paris Principles,[1] such as those laid out in Part II of this book, and their impacts on the actual and/or perceived independence of the NHRI. In more recent years, as the SCA has developed its work, it has focused considerably more of its attention on the activities of NHRIs as human rights actors, that is, whether the NHRI is actually fulfilling its mandate to promote and protect human rights.

This chapter examines a number of different aspects of NHRIs as human rights advocates and defenders. Firstly, it discusses their cooperation with other national human rights actors, primarily non-governmental organizations (NGOs) and civil society under General Observation 1.5. It then looks at the SCA's use of General Observation 1.6. This General Observation has the heading 'recommendations from NHRIs' and, as will be seen, the actual content and use of it is to determine whether the NHRI has been responding to human rights violations at the national level utilizing its promotion and protection functions. This connection can easily be made because in order for the NHRI to be in a position to provide recommendations, it must be monitoring and investigating them in the first place.

[1] Principles relating to the Status of National Institutions, UNGA Res 48/134 (20 December 1993) UN Doc A/RES/48/134 (The Paris Principles).

National Human Rights Institutions. David Langtry and Kirsten Roberts Lyer, Oxford University Press. © David Langtry and Kirsten Roberts Lyer 2021. DOI: 10.1093/oso/9780198829102.003.0008

7.2 Cooperation with Other National Human Rights Bodies

As the main human rights institution in the country, the NHRI is expected to work with a range of national stakeholders. The SCA has long promoted the active engagement of NHRIs at the national level. In revising its General Observation on this point in 2008, for example, it set out the following on cooperation with other human rights institutions:

> NHRIs should closely cooperate and share information with statutory institutions established also for the promotion and protection of human rights, for example at the state level or on thematic issues, as well as other organizations, such as NGOs, working in the field of human rights and should demonstrate that this occurs in their application to the ICC Sub-Committee.[2]

The 2013, and subsequently 2018, General Observations provided significant elaboration and details on the form of this cooperation, including clarifying that it referred not just to other 'institutions' but to the broader range of human rights bodies at the national level. General Observation 1.5 (2018) provides as follows:

> G.O. 1.5 Cooperation with other human rights bodies
> Regular and constructive engagement with all relevant stakeholders is essential for NHRIs to effectively fulfil their mandates. NHRIs should develop, formalize and maintain working relationships, as appropriate, with other domestic institutions established for the promotion and protection of human rights, including sub-national statutory human rights institutions, thematic institutions, as well as civil society and non-governmental organizations.[3]

In its rationale, the SCA outlines the following justification:

> In prescribing the NHRI's methods of operation, sections C(f) and C(g) of the Paris Principles require NHRIs to: 'maintain consultation with the other bodies, whether jurisdictional or otherwise, responsible for the promotion and protection of human rights (in particular ombudsmen, mediators and similar institutions)'.
>
> The Principles specifically recognize 'the fundamental role played by the non-governmental organizations in expanding the work of the national institutions', and therefore encourage NHRIs to, 'develop relations with the non-governmental organizations devoted to promoting and protecting human rights, to economic

[2] SCA, 'Report and Recommendations of the Session of the Sub-Committee on Accreditation' (April 2008) 16 (hereafter SCA, 'Accreditation Report').

[3] SCA, 'General Observations of the Sub-Committee on Accreditation' (adopted on 21 February 2018) 15 (hereafter SCA, 'General Observations' (February 2018)).

and social development, to combating racism, to protecting particularly vulnerable groups (especially children, migrant workers, refugees, physically and mentally disabled persons) or to specialized areas'.

To give full effect to these Paris Principle requirements, the SCA recommends that NHRIs should develop, formalize and maintain regular, constructive and systematic working relationships with other domestic institutions and actors established for the promotion and protection of human rights. Interaction may include the sharing of knowledge, such as research studies, best practices, training programmes, statistical information and data, and general information on its activities. For the following reasons the SCA considers such cooperation necessary to ensure the full realization of human rights nation-wide:

- *National human rights framework*—The effectiveness of an NHRI in implementing its mandate to protect and promote human rights is largely dependent upon the quality of its working relationships with other national democratic institutions such as: government departments; judicial bodies; lawyers' organizations; non-governmental organizations; the media; and other civil society associations. Broad engagement with all stakeholders may provide a better understanding of: the breadth of human rights issues across the state; the impact of such issues based on social cultural, geographic and other factors; gaps, as well as potential overlap and duplication in the setting of policy, priorities and implementation strategies. NHRIs working in isolation may be limited in their ability to provide adequate human rights protections to the public.
- *Unique position of NHRIs*—The character and identity of an NHRI serves to distinguish it from both government bodies and civil society. As independent, pluralistic institutions, NHRIs can play an important role.
- *Improved accessibility*—The NHRI's relations with civil society and NGOs is particularly important in improving its accessibility to sections of the populations who are geographically, politically or socially remote. These organizations are likely to have closer relations with vulnerable groups as they often have a more extensive network than NHRIs and are almost always likely to be closer to the ground. In this way, NHRIs may utilize civil society to provide an outreach mechanism to engage with vulnerable groups.
- *Expertise of other human rights bodies*—As a result of their specialized mandates, other human rights bodies and civil society groups may provide an NHRI with valuable advice on the major human rights issues facing vulnerable groups across the nation. As such, NHRIs are encouraged to regularly consult with other human rights bodies and civil society at all stages of programme planning and implementation, as well as policy making, to ensure the NHRI's activities reflect public concerns and priorities. Developing effective relationships with the mass media, as a section of civil society, is a particularly important tool for human rights education.

- *Formalized relationships*—The importance of formalizing clear and workable relationships with other human rights bodies and civil society, such as through public memoranda of understanding, serves as a reflection of the importance of ensuring regular, constructive working relationships and is key to increasing the transparency of the NHRI's work with these bodies.

> Excerpt from the Paris Principles
> C) Methods of operation—
> Within the framework of its operation, the national institution shall:
> ...
> (f) Maintain consultation with the other bodies, whether jurisdictional or otherwise, responsible for the promotion and protection of human rights (in particular ombudsmen, mediators and similar institutions);
> (g) In view of the fundamental role played by the non-governmental organizations in expanding the work of the national institutions, develop relations with the nongovernmental organizations devoted to promoting and protecting human rights, to economic and social development, to combating racism, to protecting particularly vulnerable groups (especially children, migrant workers, refugees, physically and mentally disabled persons) or to specialized areas.[4]

The SCA generally encourages 'regular and constructive engagement with all relevant stakeholders' as being essential for NHRIs to fulfil their mandates effectively, recommending that:[5]

> NHRIs should develop, formalize and maintain working relationships, as appropriate, with other domestic institutions established for the promotion and protection of human rights.[6]

NHRIs have committed themselves to engagement with a range of stakeholders. In its 2018 Marrakech Declaration, GANHRI's NHRIs resolved to:

a) Interact with human rights defenders and civil society in a regular manner and include them in the planning and implementation of, as well as follow-up on, the NHRI's activities, in a gender and disability-sensitive manner;

[4] ibid 15–16 (emphasis and ellipsis in original).

[5] See for example, SCA, 'Accreditation Report—Slovakia (National Centre for Human Rights (SNCHR))' (March 2014) 11; SCA, 'Accreditation Report—Argentina (Defensoria del Pueblo de la Nación Argentina (DPNA))' (November 2016) 10; SCA, 'Accreditation Report—Costa Rica (Defensoría de los Habitantes (DHCR))' (November 2016) 21; SCA, 'Accreditation Report—Tanzania (The Commission for Human Rights and Good Governance of Tanzania (CHRAGG))' (November 2017) 37.

[6] SCA, 'Accreditation Report—Slovakia (SNCHR)' (March 2014) 11. See also, SCA, 'Accreditation Report—Tanzania (CHRAGG)' (November 2017) 37.

b) Look for ways to cooperate with organisations including human rights organisations, the media, academia, business organisations, trade unions, national statistics offices, and local, national, regional and international intergovernmental and non-governmental organisations and institutions;
c) Support the development of national and regional defenders' networks and strengthen existing ones, in coordination with human rights defenders. Specifically support networks of women human rights defenders.[7]

This section examines the SCA recommendations to NHRIs in relation to General Observation 1.5, and particularly its comments on NHRI engagement with NGOs and Civil Society.

7.2.1 NGOs and Civil Society

The SCA has long encouraged NHRIs to develop and strengthen their engagement with civil society.[8] This cooperation should be 'close',[9] and consistent.[10] The SCA gradually developed its advice to promote formalized NHRI engagement with civil society,[11] that is regular and systemic,[12] and constructive.[13]

Enabling laws should provide for interaction with civil society.[14] Enabling laws should not just mandate the NHRI to cooperate with national bodies working on

[7] GANHRI, The Marrakech Declaration 2018: Expanding the civic space and promoting and protecting human rights defenders with a specific focus on women: The role of national human rights institutions (adopted on 12 October 2018) <https://www.forum-asia.org/uploads/wp/2019/10/GANHRI_Marrakech-Declaration_Oct-2018_EN-2.pdf> accessed 15 February 2020.

[8] For example, SCA, 'Accreditation Report—Ecuador (Defensoría del Pueblo (DP))' (April 2008) 4; SCA, 'Accreditation Report—Venezuela (Defensoría del Pueblo (DP))' (April 2008) 7; SCA, 'Accreditation Report—Luxembourg (Commission Consultative des Droits de l'Homme of Luxembourg (CCDH))' (November 2008) 9; SCA, 'Accreditation Report—Russia (High Commissioner for Human Rights in the Russian Federation (OCHR))' (November 2008) 5; SCA, 'Accreditation Report—Azerbaijan (The Human Rights Commissioner (Ombudsman) of the Republic of Azerbaijan (HRCA))' (March 2012) 30.

[9] SCA, 'Accreditation Report—Algeria (Commission Nationale Consultative de Promotion et de Protection des Droits de l'Homme (CNCPPDH))' (March/April 2010) 7; SCA, 'Accreditation Report—Algeria (CNCPPDH)' (October 2010) 11; SCA, 'Accreditation Report—Malaysia (National Human Rights Commission of Malaysia (SUHAKAM))' (October 2010) 12.

[10] SCA, 'Accreditation Report—Paraguay (Defensoría del Pueblo (DP))' (November 2008) 9.

[11] SCA, 'Accreditation Report—Hungary (Parliamentary Commissioner for Civil Rights (PCCR))' (May 2011) 8; SCA, 'Accreditation Report—Tanzania (CHRAGG)' (November 2017) 37.

[12] SCA, 'Accreditation Report—Austria (Austrian Ombudsman Board (AOB))' (May 2011) 11; SCA, 'Accreditation Report—Timor-Leste (Provedoria dos Direitos Humanos e Justica (PDHJ))' (October 2018) 16.

[13] SCA, 'Accreditation Report—France (National Consultative Commission on Human Rights (NCCHR))' (May 2013) 12; SCA, 'Accreditation Report—Iraq (High Commission for Human Rights (HCHR))' (March 2015) 9; SCA, 'Accreditation Report—Malaysia (SUHAKAM)' (November 2015) 31; SCA, 'Accreditation Report—Namibia' (November 2016) 44; SCA, 'Accreditation Report—Egypt (National Council of Human Rights (NCHR))' (March 2017) 34.

[14] SCA, 'Accreditation Report—Serbia (Protector of Citizens of the Republic of Serbia (PCRS))' (March/April 2010) 5.

the promotion and protection of human rights, it should formalize the relationship with civil society organizations specifically.[15] Where there is a structure such as an advisory council, it should meet regularly in line with the requirements set out in the enabling law.[16]

During the accreditation process, NHRIs must provide the SCA with sufficient details on its work with civil society.[17] Lack of engagement has been a cause for concern for the SCA.[18] The SCA will raise particular concerns where civil society indicates there are issues regarding the level of engagement of the NHRI. For example, in relation to the NHRI of Honduras:

> The SCA notes the concerns raised by the Special Rapporteur on the situation of human rights defenders in his 2019 report that some civil society organizations indicated that they did not trust the institution, particularly in relation to its political independence. The report further noted that some civil society actors did not have access to the NHRI's facilities in the country, and that some individuals had been turned away from regional offices.[19]

In reviewing the NHRI of Ukraine in 2019, the SCA noted that it had received information that the extent of cooperation with civil society could be improved and encouraged it to strengthen cooperation.[20]

The SCA has raised concerns with India's NHRI (the National Human Rights Commission of India NHRCI)) since 2011, that its 'Core/Expert Groups' through which it indicated it 'complies with the Paris Principles' requirement for pluralism and engagement with civil society and other human rights defenders' were 'not functioning effectively as a means of engagement and cooperation between the NHRCI and civil society'.[21] It is notable that this information on the ineffectiveness of these groups came from civil society directly to the SCA. In its November 2017 review of the NHRCI, the SCA expressed its concerns as follows:

[15] SCA, 'Accreditation Report—Bahrain (National Institution for Human Rights (NIHRB))' (May 2016) 10.

[16] SCA, 'Accreditation Report—Timor-Leste (PDHJ)' (November 2013) 30–31.

[17] SCA, 'Accreditation Report—Mali (Commission Nationale des Droits de l'Homme (CNDH))' (March 2012) 13; SCA, 'Accreditation Report—Korea (National Human Rights Commission of Korea (NHRCK))' (October 2014) 30.

[18] SCA, 'Accreditation Report—Kyrgyz Republic (The Ombudsman of the Kyrgyz Republic (OKR))' (March 2012) 11.

[19] SCA, 'Accreditation Report—Honduras (Comisionado Nacional de los Derechos Humanos de Honduras (CONADEH))' (October 2019) 12. The SCA noted that CONADEH had taken some steps to respond to the concerns, including establishing a network of human rights defenders. ibid.

[20] SCA, 'Accreditation Report—Ukraine (Ukrainian Parliament Commissioner for Human Rights (UPCHR))' (October 2019) 23.

[21] SCA, 'Accreditation Report—India (NHRCI)' (November 2016) 27; See also, SCA, 'Accreditation Report—India (NHRCI)' (May 2011) 14.

prior to its November 2017 session, the SCA received extensive information from various civil society organizations which indicated that the relationship between the NHRCI and civil society is not effective or constructive, particularly with respect to ongoing dialogue and follow-up on issues raised.

In describing its engagement with civil society, the SCA notes that the NHRCI relies to a substantial degree on its Core/Expert Groups as the mechanism for engagement. However, the SCA has received information from civil society at both its November 2016 session and its November 2017 session that these mechanisms are not functioning effectively as a means of engagement and cooperation between the NHRCI and civil society.[22]

Similarly to the India case, in its review of Mauritania in November 2016, deferring its decision, the SCA had also received information that the NHRI 'did not engage with a broad range of civil society organizations, particularly those who were critical of government'.[23]

The SCA has 'note[d] with appreciation' formalization of engagement through efforts such as memoranda of understandings and consultation meetings.[24] The SCA made a series of recommendations to the NHRI of Bosnia and Herzegovina over a number of years to improve its formal working relationship with civil society. This culminated in a proposed amendment to the enabling law that 'would include a new Article 36 (a) providing for 'regular and thematic consultations with civil society organizations, international organizations and bodies of the profession and the academic community'.[25] It also welcomes clear recognition by NHRIs of the crucial role of civil society.[26]

7.2.2 Other National Level Human Rights Institutions

In addition to their engagement with civil society organizations, NHRIs should develop relationships with other national human rights bodies.[27] There should be

[22] SCA, 'Accreditation Report—India (NHRCI)' (November 2017) 20.

[23] SCA, 'Accreditation Report—Mauritania (Commission Nationale des droits de l'homme (CNDH))' (November 2016) 35.

[24] SCA, 'Accreditation Report—Bahrain (NIHRB)' (May 2016) 10; See also, SCA, 'Accreditation Report—Moldova (The Office of the People's Advocate of Moldova (OPA))' (May 2018) 25.

[25] SCA, 'Accreditation Report—Bosnia and Herzegovina (The Institution of Human Rights Ombudsman of Bosnia and Herzegovina (IHROBH))' (November 2017) 11. See also, SCA, 'Accreditation Report—Bosnia and Herzegovina (IHROBH)' (November 2016) 17.

[26] SCA, 'Accreditation Report—Honduras (CONADEH)' (May 2016) 40.

[27] SCA, 'Accreditation Report—Russia (OCHR)' (November 2013) 25–26; SCA, 'Accreditation Report—Namibia (Office of the Ombudsman (Ombudsman))' (November 2016) 44; SCA, 'Accreditation Report—Nicaragua (Procuradoría para la Defensa de los Derechos Humanos (PDDH))' (November 2016) 45; SCA, 'Accreditation Report—Tanzania (CHRAGG)' (November 2016) 55; SCA, 'Accreditation Report—Zambia (Human Rights Commission (HRCZ))' (November 2016) 60; SCA, 'Accreditation Report—Lithuania (Seimas Ombudsmen Office (SOO))' (March 2017) 10; SCA, 'Accreditation Report—Norway (Norwegian National Human Rights Institution (NNHRI))' (March

cooperation with domestic institutions similar to the NHRI 'to ensure coherence and effectiveness of the national human rights protection system'.[28] These include bodies such as a public defender of rights,[29] Ombuds-institutions,[30] and regional bodies.[31] Cooperation between national bodies may also be operationalized under specific human rights treaties such as Optional Protocol to the Convention Against Torture (OPCAT).[32] The SCA has acknowledged cooperation for example for the French NHRI with the Defender on Human Rights 'to which it transmits individual petitions'.[33] This General Observation has also been used by the SCA in relation to the unique situation of the NHRIs in the United Kingdom where there is more than one accredited NHRI in one UN Member State, where the SCA has mandated that there should be cooperation.[34]

The SCA has also commended NHRIs from countries in conflict where they cooperate across divisions. In 2014, it noted 'with particular appreciation' the cooperation between the Ukraine NHRI and its counterpart in Russia.[35]

7.3 Investigation and Reporting by NHRIs

A critical area for NHRIs' Paris Principles compliance is their engagement with the human rights situation on the ground. Based on the requirement for NHRIs to possess and utilize both their promotion and protection functions, the SCA has

2017) 14–15; SCA, 'Accreditation Report—France (Commission Nationale Consultative des Droits de l'Homme (CNCDH))' (March 2019) 19.

[28] SCA, 'Accreditation Report—Croatia (Ombudsman of the Republic of Croatia (ORC))' (April 2008) 7.

[29] SCA, 'Accreditation Report—Slovakia (SNCHR)' (March 2014) 11.

[30] SCA, 'Accreditation Report—Lithuania (SOO)' (March 2017) 10; SCA, 'Accreditation Report—Norway (NNHRI)' (March 2017) 14–15.

[31] SCA, 'Accreditation Report—Russia (OCHR)' (November 2013) 25–26.

[32] Optional Protocol to the Convention against Torture and other Cruel, Inhuman or Degrading Treatment or Punishment (adopted on 18 December 2002, entered into force on 22 June 2006) 2375 UNTS 237 (hereafter OPCAT). See SCA, 'Accreditation Report—Mexico (Comisión Nacional de los Derechos Humanos of México (CNDH))' (October 2011) 15, noting that '[t]he SCA recognizes that Mexico is a federal state, with 32 State Human Rights Institutions, and notes that the CNDH has entered into agreements with 15 sub-national human rights institutions within the framework of the CNDH's role as National Preventative Mechanism'.

[33] SCA, 'Accreditation Report—France (NCCHR)' (May 2013) 12. See also, SCA, 'Accreditation Report—France (CNCDH)' (March 2019) 19. The SCA reports use both the French and English language titles and acronyms for the French NHRI.

[34] SCA, 'Accreditation Report—Great Britain (Equality and Human Rights Commission (EHRC))' (November 2008) 4. This situation for NHRIs of having three in one Member State is due to the unique governance structure of the United Kingdom. In its 2008 Report accrediting the EHRC, the SCA noted, 'The Sub-Committee acknowledges the EHRC met all of the mandatory requirements set out in General Observation 6.6 "More than one National Institution in a State". It emphasizes the importance of further developing cooperation between the EHRC, the Northern Ireland Human Rights Commission and the Scottish Human Rights Commission.'

[35] SCA, 'Accreditation Report—Ukraine (UPCHR)' (October 2014) 35.

expanded on General Observation 1.6 (2018) and gradually increased the application of this observation to focus on NHRIs' role as a human rights body. The General Observation provides:

> G.O. 1.6 Recommendations by NHRIs
> Annual, special and thematic reports of NHRIs serve to highlight key national human rights concerns and provide a means by which these bodies can make recommendations to, and monitor respect for, human rights by public authorities.
>
> NHRIs, as part of their mandate to promote and protect human rights, should undertake follow up action on recommendations contained in these reports and should publicize detailed information on the measures taken or not taken by public authorities in implementing specific recommendations or decisions.
>
> In fulfilling its protection mandate, an NHRI must not only monitor, investigate and report on the human rights situation in the country, it should also undertake rigorous and systematic follow up activities to promote and advocate for the implementation on its recommendations and findings, and the protection of those whose rights were found to have been violated.
>
> Public authorities are encouraged to respond to recommendations from NHRIs in a timely manner, and to provide detailed information on practical and systematic follow-up action, as appropriate, to the NHRI's recommendations.[36]

The SCA sets out the following justification:

> The Paris Principles are not only explicit in their direction that NHRIs have the responsibility to make recommendations to public authorities on improving the national human rights situation, but also that NHRIs ensure their recommendations are widely publicized. Specifically, section A.3(a) of the Paris Principles requires NHRIs to 'submit to the Government, Parliament and any other competent body, ... recommendations ... on any matters concerning the promotion and protection of human rights', and enumerates the three areas that these recommendations shall relate to:
>
> 1. The creation or amendment of any legislative or administrative provisions, including bills and proposals;
> 2. Any situation of violation of human rights within a state;
> 3. Human rights in general and on more specific matters.

[36] SCA, 'General Observations' (February 2018) (n 3) GO 1.6, 17.

In prescribing its methods of operation, section C(c) of the Paris Principles requires NHRIs to, '... publicize its opinions and recommendations', '... directly or through any press organ ...'.

Finally, section D(d) of the Principles, requires NHRIs with quasi-judicial competence, that is, with the ability to hear and consider complaints, to 'mak[e] recommendations to the competent authorities, especially by proposing amendments or reforms of the laws, regulations and administrative practices, especially if they have created the difficulties encountered by the persons filing the petitions in order to assert their rights.'

The SCA is of the view that the three-fold reinforcement of the obligation to make and publicize recommendations is indicative that the drafters of the Paris Principles considered that NHRIs would be more effective when provided with the authority to monitor the extent to which public authorities follow their advice and recommendations. To give full effect to this principle, the SCA encourages governments to respond to advice and requests from NHRIs, and to indicate, within a reasonable time, how they have complied with their recommendations.

NHRIs should monitor the implementation of recommendations from annual and thematic reports, inquiries and other complaint handling processes.

Excerpt from the Paris Principles

A) Competence and responsibilities—

3. A national institution shall, inter alia, have the following responsibilities:

   (a) To submit to the Government, Parliament and any other competent body, on an advisory basis either at the request of the authorities concerned or through the exercise of its power to hear a matter without higher referral, opinions, *recommendations*, proposals and *reports on any matters concerning the promotion and protection of human rights*; the national institution may decide to publicize them; these opinions, *recommendations*, proposals and reports, as well as any prerogative of the national institution, *shall relate to the following areas*:

      (i) Any legislative or administrative provisions, as well as provisions relating to judicial organizations, intended to preserve and extend the protection of human rights; in that connection, the national institution shall examine the legislation and administrative provisions in force, as well as bills and proposals, and *shall make such recommendations as it deems appropriate* in order to ensure that these provisions conform to the fundamental principles of human rights; it shall, if necessary, recommend the adoption of new legislation, the amendment of legislation in force and the adoption or amendment of administrative measures;

      (ii) Any situation of violation of human rights which it decides to take up;

      (iii) The preparation of reports on the national situation with regard to human rights in general, and on more specific matters;

(iv) Drawing the attention of the Government to situations in any part of the country where human rights are violated and making proposals to it for initiatives to put an end to such situations and, where necessary, expressing an opinion on the positions and reactions of the Government;

C) Methods of operation—
Within the framework of its operation, the national institution shall:
…
(c) Address public opinion directly or through any press organ, particularly in order to *publicize its* opinions and *recommendations*;
…
D) Additional principles concerning the status of commissions with quasi-jurisdictional competence—
A national institution may be authorized to hear and consider complaints and petitions concerning individual situations. Cases may be brought before it by individuals, their representatives, third parties, non-governmental organizations, associations of trade unions or any other representative organizations. In such circumstances, and without prejudice to the principles stated above concerning the other powers of the commissions, the functions entrusted to them may be based on the following principles:
…
(d) *Making recommendations to the competent authorities*, especially by proposing amendments or reforms of the laws, regulations and administrative practices, especially if they have created the difficulties encountered by the persons filing the petitions in order to assert their rights.[37]

The following sections examine how the SCA has been applying this General Observation in practice.

7.3.1 Reporting on Human Rights Violations

The SCA is increasingly focused on the practical activities of NHRIs in implementing their mandate. It is clear that as part of their role, NHRIs must publish reports (annual and thematic) highlighting key human rights concerns.[38] Addressing the point under General Observation 1.6, in its 2011 review of Romania, the SCA recalled the language now contained in General Observation 1.11 (2018) (see Chapter 3.2) that:

[37] SCA, 'General Observations' (February 2018) (n 3) GO 1.6, 17–19 (emphasis and ellipsis in original).
[38] This is a regular recommendation to NHRIs. See for example, SCA, 'Accreditation Report—Haiti (Office de la Protection du Citoyen (OPC))' (March 2019) 27; SCA, 'Accreditation Report—Madagascar

> annual and thematic reports serve to highlight key human rights concerns in the country and provide a means by which a NHRI can make recommendations to, and monitor respect for, human rights by government. Furthermore, annual and thematic reports provide a public account, and therefore public scrutiny, of the effectiveness of an NHRI.[39]

NHRIs are expected to make regular reports in relation to ongoing human rights violations. This can be seen also in Chapter 9 where the SCA criticized the inaction of the NHRI of Burundi, and in the cases set out in Chapter 10.2, including the NHRI's in Azerbaijan, Mauritania, Nicaragua, and Paraguay. As well as in the following situations in Sri Lanka, Honduras, Mexico, Thailand, and Venezuela.

Accrediting the Sri Lankan NHRI (SLHRC) with B-status in 2009, the SCA stated its concerns regarding its human rights engagement:

> SLHRC does not appear to have released regular and detailed reports or statements in relation to killings, abductions and disappearances stemming from the human rights crisis in Sri Lanka. While the SCA acknowledges the work of the SLHRC's regional offices in extremely difficult circumstances, it reemphasises the need for the SLHRC to carry out its core protection mandate to demonstrate its vigilance and independence during the ongoing state of emergency.[40]

NHRIs must show that they are actively working to implement their mandate, evidenced through substantive human rights reporting. For example, in examining the NHRI of Honduras (CONADEH) in 2010, the SCA found as follows:

> Although the CONADEH has a broad mandate to promote and protect human rights (Articles 1 and 9 of the Organic Law 153-1995), no documentary evidence on the performance of the CONADEH was submitted. According to the UN High Commissioner's report, the CONADEH failed to fulfil its protection mandate. In this regard, the 2009 Annual Report describes some actions taken by the CONADEH during the coup d'état, however its content is weak and does not provide detailed and substantive information on the alleged human rights violations and how the CONADEH addressed those violations. The Annual Report does not provide details such as numbers of victims subsequent to the coup d'état, the violations committed, the complaints received or cases investigated. There is also no

(Commission Nationale Indépendante des Droits de l'Homme (CNIDH))' (March 2019) 9; SCA, 'Accreditation Report—Bulgaria (Ombudsman of the Republic of Bulgaria (ORB))' (March 2019) 17–18.

[39] SCA, 'Accreditation Report—Romania (Romanian Institute of Human Rights (RIHR))' (May 2011) 21.

[40] SCA, 'Accreditation Report—Sri Lanka (The Human Rights Commission of Sri Lanka (SLHRC))' (March 2009) 5.

indication in the Report on the monitoring activities, recommendations or advice provided to the Government.[41]

In reviewing the NHRI of Mexico (CNDH) in 2016, the SCA expressed concern that the institution's output did not match the level of complaints made to it:

> The SCA has received information that the number of recommendations issued by the CNDH is substantially lower than the number of complaints of human rights violations received. The SCA acknowledges that there are a number of reasons for this, including the high percentage of complaints that are resolved through a conciliation process. However, the SCA encourages the CNDH to review its processes to ensure that its current methods of operations do not result in a failure to address systemic human rights violations.[42]

The SCA has expressed particular concerns where the NHRI is slow at inquiring into and reporting on serious human rights violations. For example, in examining the NHRI in Thailand (NHRCT) in November 2013, it noted 'substantial delays in inquiring into and reporting on serious human rights violations. In particular, [the SCA] noted the report on civil disturbances in 2010 was not released until 2013.'[43] This concern was again raised by the SCA in March 2014:

> In response, the NHRCT referred to the difficulties it faced in investigating and documenting these civil disturbances, in part due to the polarisation of parties and society since 2006. It noted however that its experiences in 2010 had helped it to deal in a more efficient manner with the similar incidents that occurred in late 2013 and in on-going demonstrations. In particular it highlighted the establishment of an Ad Hoc Working Group tasked with media monitoring, news clipping and on-site observation with daily reporting and recommendations submitted to the NHRCT for further action. As a result of this approach, the NHRCT indicated that it expected to release a report on these events in early 2014. The SCA noted however that the NHRCT has yet to release this report and the NHRCT was unable to indicate when it would be completed.[44]

[41] SCA, 'Accreditation Report—Honduras (Comisionado Nacional de los Derechos Humanos de Honduras (CONADEH))' (October 2010) 9. See also, SCA, 'Accreditation Report—Rwanda (The National Commission for Human Rights of the Republic of Rwanda (NCHR))' (October 2018) 14–15.

[42] SCA, 'Accreditation Report—Mexico (Comisión Nacional de los Derechos Humanos (CNDH))' (November 2016) 37.

[43] SCA, 'Accreditation Report—Thailand (National Human Rights Commission of Thailand (NHRCT))' (November 2013) 28.

[44] SCA, 'Accreditation Report—Thailand (NHRCT)' (March 2014) 19.

In its October 2014 review, the SCA expanded on its concerns as follows:

> In 2010, violent demonstrations and civil unrest resulted in a significant number of deaths and injuries as a result of alleged violations of human rights by law enforcement agencies. Despite the serious nature of these violations, the NHRCT took three years to complete and publish a report into the alleged human rights violations that occurred in 2010.
>
> In late 2013, further demonstrations also resulted in a significant number of deaths and injuries. The NHRCT provided the SCA with a summary of actions taken in response to the ongoing unrest. While these show that the NHRCT is operating in extremely difficult circumstances and has taken some steps to improve its monitoring operations, the SCA notes that the NHRCT is yet to complete and publish a report into alleged serious human rights violations that occurred in 2013.[45]

Recalling a number of its General Observations,[46] the SCA emphasized what was required of the NHRI:

> The SCA notes that in the situation of a coup d'état or a state of emergency, NHRIs are expected to conduct themselves with a heightened level of vigilance and independence, and to promote and ensure respect for human rights, democratic principles and the strengthening of the rule of law in all circumstances and without exception. Their actions may include monitoring, documenting, issuing public statements and releasing regular and detailed reports on human rights violations through the media in a timely manner. Furthermore, an NHRI should also undertake rigorous and systematic follow up activities and advocate for the consideration and implementation of its findings and recommendations in order to ensure the protection of those whose rights have been violated. These actions, in particular the release of public reports, serve to combat impunity for human rights violations.[47]

The NHRI was downgraded in 2014, in part because the NHRI had 'not been addressing serious human rights violations in a timely manner'.[48] The situation of the Thailand NHRI is addressed in further detail in Chapter 9.2 on NHRIs in situations of coups d'état.

The SCA deferred the re-accreditation of the NHRI of Egypt (NCHR) for an extended period from 2011 to 2018, including because of delays in reform of its

[45] SCA, 'Accreditation Report—Thailand (NHRCT)' (October 2014) 33–34.
[46] SCA, 'ICC Sub-Committee on Accreditation General Observations' (adopted in May 2013) GO 2.5, GO 1.6.
[47] SCA, 'Accreditation Report—Thailand (NHRCT)' (October 2014) 34.
[48] ibid 33.

enabling law as a result of the situation in the country during that time. In October 2011, it commended the NCHR for its ongoing documentation of human rights violations even in challenging circumstances.[49] At the third deferral in May 2013, it recognized the NCHR's continued efforts as a human rights institution:

> Despite the challenging context in which the NCHR is functioning, the SCA encourages it to continue its activities in a manner which reflects its independence, in law and in practice, as required by Paris Principles B.1 and B.3. This pertains especially to the investigation of alleged human rights violations, particularly torture, forced disappearances and violence.[50]

However, by 2018, the SCA noted challenges with the engagement of the NCHR with human rights violations:

> The SCA received information which raises concerns regarding the effectiveness of the NCHR in dealing with serious human rights issues, including torture, enforced disappearances and the protection of human rights defenders. The SCA notes that the NCHR reports to undertake various actions to address serious human rights issues in Egypt, including with respect to enforced disappearances and the closure of media outlets.
>
> The SCA encourages the NCHR to strengthen its efforts to address all human rights violations. The SCA further encourages the NCHR to ensure that its positions on these issues are publicly made available, as this will contribute to the credibility and accessibility of the institution for all people in Egypt.[51]

Reviewing the Defensoria del Pueblo (DP) of Paraguay at both its sessions in 2014, the SCA reported that it received and 'considered a submission from civil society that raised serious concerns as to the effective performance of the DP', it noted in its October 2014 session that the institution had responded to some of the points, but continued to express its concerns over the effectiveness of the NHRI, including as follows:

- providing recommendations to the State to ensure a clear and effective mandate to provide assistance to victims of human rights violations, including those arising from the Dictatorship;
- interpreting its mandate in a broad, liberal and purposive manner;
- proactively providing information and assistance to victims of the Dictatorship; and

[49] SCA, 'Accreditation Report—Egypt (National Council for Human Rights NCHR))' (October 2011) 13.
[50] SCA, 'Accreditation Report—Egypt (NCHR)' (May 2013) 10.
[51] SCA, 'Accreditation Report—Egypt (NCHR)' (May 2018) 20.

- advocating strongly for the appointment of a new Defensor, given that the current Defensor's fixed term ended in 2008.[52]

In line with these observations, the SCA underscored that the NHRI 'should effectively monitor, investigate and report on alleged human rights violations in a timely manner' and that it should 'take active steps to ensure that all relevant information to help victims of human rights violations is easily accessible and, where relevant, provide strong recommendations to the State in order to address human rights concerns'.[53] In March 2014, the SCA had warned the DP that if it did not address these concerns it would be recommended for re-accreditation with B-status. In October 2014, the DP withdrew its application for re-accreditation.[54] The institution re-applied for accreditation in March 2019, when a new *Defensor* was appointed, and was re-accredited B-status.[55] The situation in Paraguay is also examined in Chapter 10.2.4 on NHRIs failing to promote and protect human rights.

7.3.1.1 Venezuela

Venezuela's was the first NHRI to be downgraded to B-status by the SCA solely on the basis of its poor performance as a human rights actor, rather than for legal or structural issues or a combination of factors. It is thus worth examining the situation of that NHRI in some additional detail in this sub-section.

In 2013, the SCA expressed concerns over the failure by the Venezuela NHRI, the Defensoría del Pueblo de Venezuela (DPV, Venezuelan Office of the Ombudsman), to take a strong position in relation to human rights concerns, particularly, the continued detention of Judge Maria Lourdes Afiuni, the withdrawal of Venezuela from the American Convention on Human Rights, and the Uriban prison incident.[56] However, the NHRI was re-accredited with A-status in that review. The SCA then initiated a special review of the DPV in 2014.[57] The following year it recommended the DPV be downgraded to B-status. In accordance with Article 18.1 of the GANHRI Statute, the DPV was permitted one year in which to respond to the SCA recommendation.[58]

[52] SCA, 'Accreditation Report—Paraguay (Defensoría del Pueblo de Paraguay (DP))' (October 2014) 27. Bullet points per original.

[53] SCA, 'Accreditation Report—Paraguay (DP)' (March 2014) 16.

[54] SCA, 'Accreditation Report—Paraguay (DP)' (October 2014) 27.

[55] SCA, 'Accreditation Report—Paraguay (DPP)' (March 2019) 10. The SCA uses an alternative acronym in this report.

[56] SCA, 'Accreditation Report—Venezuela (DPV)' (May 2013) 22.

[57] SCA, 'Accreditation Report—Venezuela (DPV)' (October 2014) 23. The SCA only looked at events and issues that had arisen after the re-accreditation of May 2013, considering that it would be wrong to examine matters that could have been brought to the attention of the SCA at the time of that re-accreditation. This practice is set out in GANHRI, 'A Practical Guide to the Work of the Sub-Committee on Accreditation' (2018) 42, 45 <https://nhri.ohchr.org/EN/AboutUs/GANHRIAccreditation/Documents/GANHRI%20Manual_online(1).pdf> accessed 6 February 2021 (hereafter GANHRI Guide).

[58] GANHRI State (adopted on 15 March 2019). This provision was the same in the version in force in 2014.

Initially, the SCA recommended a special review of the DPV at its first sitting in 2014. This followed the receipt of information that the DPV may no longer be in full compliance with the Paris Principles, including the following points:

- actions taken or not taken, and statements made or not made by the DPV during the current volatile situation and protests in Venezuela; and
- tweets made from both the DPV's and the *Defensora's* personal Twitter accounts.[59]

These two points of concern were connected both to the fraught political context in Venezuela; following the death of Hugo Chávez in March 2013, Nicolás Maduro assumed the presidency, notably under difficult economic conditions, as well as to the personal conduct of the head of the DPV.

In its review, the SCA noted that several tweets and public statements by the head of the institution, the *Defensora*, aligned the DPV with the figure of Chávez and with the regime and actions of Maduro.[60] Among the three Tweets referred to by the SCA was one from 9 October 2013, in which the *Defensora* wrote, 'Our Human Rights Institution supports the defence undertaking [*sic*] Nicolas Maduro of our conquests'.[61] Such statements of support were accompanied by a partisan view of contemporary human rights issues. For example, the SCA took note that 'during an 8 March 2014 interview which was widely reported on by news outlets including El Nacional and El Universal, the *Defensora* provided a definition of torture, stating that torture was used for the sole purpose of obtaining information'.[62] Furthermore, when urged in February 2014 by the UN Secretary-General and UN High Commissioner for Human Rights to ensure that freedom of expression and assembly were respected, the DPV responded that 'there are reasonable grounds for believing that the majority of those arrests were conducted in situations of violence and those arrested have been caught *in flagrante delicto* in the commission of crimes'.[63]

The SCA added that the DPV was 'silent on critical domestic human rights issues' in Venezuela, including:

- trials of civilians in military courts;
- criminal trials of trade union leaders for exercising their constitutional right to strike and protest;
- threats by President Nicolas Maduro to initiate criminal procedures against trade union leaders;

[59] SCA, 'Accreditation Report—Venezuela (DPV)' (March 2014) 23.
[60] SCA, 'Accreditation Report—Venezuela (DPV)' (March 2015) 24–27.
[61] ibid 24.
[62] ibid 25.
[63] ibid.

- the withdrawal of Venezuela from the American Convention on Human Rights;
- the non-compliance of protection measures ordered by the Inter-American Court on behalf of victims of human rights violations in Venezuela;
- the continued detention of Judge Maria Lourdes Afiuni;
- the continued detention of Leopoldo Lopez and his allegations of being tortured;
- the statement of United Nations High Commissioner for Human Rights, of February 2014, urging the Government of Venezuela to ensure respect for freedom of expression and peaceful assembly and guarantee that law enforcement officers act according to international standards, in line with the statement of the Secretary General issued a few days before;
- the concerns expressed by the current United Nations High Commissioner for Human Rights in October 2014 in respect of the detention of protestors including Leopoldo Lopez, whose detention was considered as arbitrarily by the Working Group on Arbitrary Detention.[64]

The DPV, under a new head, responded to these concerns by releasing a report that summarized its activities, but this was not enough to satisfy the SCA. While the SCA acknowledged that the impetus for the review were public statements by former *Defensora* Ramirez, it asserted that these undermined the DPV's ability 'to effectively carry out its mandate to promote and protect human rights'.[65] The SCA remained concerned after the appointment of a new head of the DPV at the end of 2014, and officially recommended the NHRI be downgraded to B-status in March 2015.

At its May 2016 session, the SCA deemed the actions taken by the DPV to correct their operations as insufficient. In addition to the existing concerns, the SCA noted four other worrying issues: (i) the state of emergency situation and the deportation of Colombians at the Venezuela/Colombia border, (ii) the case of students Lorent Saleh and Gabriel Valle and their conditions of detention, (iii) cooperation with civil society, and (iv) attacks on human rights defenders. The SCA detailed these as follows:

- The state of emergency situation and the deportation of Colombians at the Venezuela/Colombia border: The United Nations Office for the Coordination of Humanitarian Affairs, in its progress report of 15 October 2015, reports that 22,342 persons have returned from Venezuela to Colombia and that 1,925 have been deported. The Spokesperson for the United Nations High Commissioner for Human Rights publicly raised concern on 28 August 2015,

[64] ibid 25–26 (bullet points in original).
[65] ibid 26.

about the situation at the border between Colombia and Venezuela and urged the Venezuelan authorities to ensure that the human rights of all affected individuals were fully respected, particularly in the context of any deportations. However, the DPV stated that it has not received information or specific allegations of human rights violations relating to the affected persons in the border region.

- The case of Lorent Saleh and Gabriel Valle: various credible sources of information described the conditions of detention at the prison known as 'la Tumba' ('the Grave'), and that this includes being held in cells approximately 2 × 3 meters with no access to sunlight or proper ventilation, in violation of international standards. The SCA was informed that two students, Lorent Saleh and Gabriel Valle, have been held in pre-trial detention in these conditions for more than 20 months, and have made allegations that they have been tortured and subject to inhuman and degrading treatment. In relation to detainee Lorent Saleh, the SCA was informed that he has received inadequate medical attention. The SCA noted that, in response to questions about the action the DPV has taken in relation to these serious allegations, it stated in its comments on the report received from NGOs that 'Lorent Saleh and Gabriel Valle asked through their relatives not being transferred to another detention centre, confirming that they were in good conditions of detention.' The SCA is concerned that this statement does not demonstrate that the DPV is taking appropriate action in relation to the allegations before it.
- Cooperation with civil society: While the DPV has indicated that it meets regularly with civil society organizations, the SCA has received a report from different credible civil society organizations that there has been little meaningful cooperation and that the DPV is not prepared to address their concerns.
- Attacks on human rights defenders: While the DPV has provided information on its activities in relation to the protection of human rights defenders, the SCA remains concerned that the DPV has not taken action in all cases to protect these defenders.[66]

In view of the instability surrounding the Maduro regime, the SCA allowed that 'the DPV is currently operating in a highly polarized context'.[67] This did not excuse the DPV's failure to address serious human rights issues, however. Thus, the SCA concluded:

Based on these cases, and all of the information that has been provided, the SCA is of the view that the DPV is not prepared to speak out in a manner that promotes respect for human rights in response to credible allegations of serious human

66 SCA, 'Accreditation Report—Venezuela (DPV)' (May 2016) 54–55 (bullets points in original).
67 ibid 54.

> rights abuses having been committed by government authorities. The failure to do so demonstrates a lack of independence. Therefore, the SCA is of the view that the DPV is not operating in full compliance with the Paris Principles.[68]

7.3.1.2 Ethiopia

It is also illustrative to mention the application by the NHRI of Ethiopia in this section, as the accreditation of the Ethiopian NHRI (Ethiopia Human Rights Commission (EHRC)) in 2012/13, shows the SCA both taking a firmer stance on accrediting new applicants (see Chapter 2.4.1), and in its focus on the institution's substantive human rights work.

The EHRC applied for accreditation in November 2012. The SCA expressed considerable concern about its activities under the heading of 'effectiveness':

> The SCA notes that various public reports by United Nations Treaty Bodies and other organisations have raised concerns about the independence and effectiveness of the EHRC. Notably, the Human Rights Committee (July 2011) refers to the EHRC undertaking 'very few investigations into alleged human rights violations', and to its failure to make 'any recommendations on existing and new laws' that impact on the enjoyment of human rights. The Committee against Torture also made recommendations to enhance the mandate of the EHRC to ensure 'an effective independent national system to monitor and inspect all places of deprivation of liberty'.
>
> During its interview with the EHRC, the SCA sought additional information, in particular seeking advice on whether the EHRC had provided advice to government on recent contentious legislation. The EHRC indicated that it had not provided the government with advice on either:
>
> - The Charities and Societies Proclamation law notwithstanding that it has been in operation for several years and has been identified by both national and international human rights organisations as having a serious impact on the rights to freedom of expression and association; or
> - The Anti Terrorism legislation, notwithstanding that it too has been in operation for several years and has been identified by national and international human rights organisations, and United Nations human rights experts, as having had a serious impact on freedom of speech and other rights.
>
> While the EHRC indicated that it intended to undertake studies into each of these laws, the SCA highlights the importance of NHRI's responding within a reasonable time responding within a reasonable time to alleged human rights

[68] ibid 55.

concerns, noting that the delay in so doing impacts adversely on the perceived independence of, and public's confidence in, the EHRC.[69]

In accrediting the EHRC with B-status in November 2013, the SCA noted that:

> While the EHRC indicated that it intended to undertake studies into each of these laws, and that it has dealt with some negative repercussions of this law by providing funding support to NGOs affected by the Charities and Societies Proclamation law, and by handling cases of persons affected by the Anti-terrorism legislation, the SCA highlights the importance of EHRC responding within a reasonable time to alleged human rights concerns, noting that the delay in so doing impacts adversely on the perceived independence of, and the public's confidence in, the EHRC.[70]

7.3.2 NHRI Human Rights Activities

Closely related to the approach by the SCA in the above examples, NHRIs are increasingly asked by the SCA to demonstrate concrete human rights actions. For example, in examining the re-accreditation application of Algeria's NHRI (CNDH) in May 2018, and recommending re-accreditation with B-status, the SCA noted with concern that:

> [d]uring the session, the SCA asked the CNDH to provide information about the actions it has taken in relation to torture, enforced disappearances and the expulsion of migrants. While the SCA acknowledges that the CNDH did provide some information, the SCA was concerned that the actions described were limited and did not demonstrate that the CNDH was taking adequate steps to address these human rights violations. The SCA encourages the CNDH to undertake actions to address all human rights violations.[71]

The SCA will also challenge the NHRI where the NHRI's views appear out of line with the reality of the situation in the country. In recommending that the NHRI of Nicaragua (PDDH) be downgraded to B-status in May 2018, the SCA noted with concern that it had found issues with independence and effectiveness in November 2016 and November 2017, when the NHRI had been provided with the opportunity

[69] SCA, 'Accreditation Report—Ethiopia (Ethiopia Human Rights Commission (EHRC))' (November 2012) 9–10.
[70] SCA, 'Accreditation Report—Ethiopia (EHRC)' (November 2013) 7. Citing then-General Observation 1.2 on 'Human Rights Mandate'.
[71] SCA, 'Accreditation Report—Algeria (The National Human Rights Council of Algeria (CNDH))' (May 2018) 17.

to respond to these issues. The SCA found that the NHRI was 'not prepared to adequately speak out in a manner that promotes respect for all human rights.[72] This case is covered in more detail in Chapter 10.2.3.

The SCA will also examine the specific recommendations made by the NHRI in certain cases to determine whether they are sufficient to demonstrate that it is fulfilling its mandate. For example, in relation to the National Human Rights Commission of Nepal (NHRCN), the SCA commented as follows:

> The SCA received information that raises concerns regarding the effectiveness of the NHRCN in dealing with serious human rights issues, particularly those relating to civil and political rights. This includes in relation to the March 2017 demonstrations in Rajbiraj where a number of persons were killed by police. The SCA received a report on this incident from the NHRCN that included general recommendations in relation to the actions of police and security forces. Notwithstanding that response, the SCA is of the view that, in cases like these, it is important that an NHRI clearly identifies human rights violations and takes steps to hold perpetrators to account.
>
> . . .
>
> The SCA encourages the NHRCN to strengthen its efforts to address all human rights violations. The SCA further encourages the NHRCN to ensure that its positions on these issues are publicly made available, as this will contribute to the credibility and accessibility of the institution for all people in Nepal.[73]

The SCA has occasionally encouraged NHRIs to engage on specific human rights issues. For example, in its review of Mexico's NHRI in October 2011, it encouraged the CNDH to tackle the issue of pre-trial detention:

> The SCA encourages the CNDH to continue to publicly express its concern with regard to 'arraigo' (sui generis pre-trial preventative detention) and to call for an amendment to the Constitution of Mexico to remove the provision allowing 'arraigo', given that it violates international human rights standards, including human rights treaties to which Mexico is a party.
>
> The SCA acknowledges and appreciates the efforts made by the CNDH regarding 'arraigo' to date, including its intervention in a case of 119 ex-police officers deprived of their liberty in an 'arraigo' detention centre, and issuing an academic report and opinion on this issue.[74]

[72] SCA, 'Accreditation Report—Nicaragua (Procuraduría para la Defensa de los Derechos Humanos (PDDH))' (May 2018) 28. See also, SCA, 'Accreditation Report—Nicaragua (PDDH)' (November 2017) 28.

[73] SCA, 'Accreditation Report—Nepal (NHRCN)' (March 2019) 29–30.

[74] SCA, 'Accreditation Report—Mexico (CNDH)' (October 2011) 15.

The SCA also made a specific recommendation in relation to the Egyptian NHRI's work on the death penalty, reflecting wording from General Observation 2.5 on NHRIs during a coup d'état or state of emergency (discussed further in Chapter 9):

> With respect to the NCHR position on the death penalty, the SCA encourages it to promote the abolition of death penalty in line with the requirements of the Second Optional Protocol to the International Covenant on Civil and Political Rights. The SCA further encourages the NCHR to advocate for the ratification of the Second Optional Protocol.
>
> NHRIs are required to promote and ensure respect for all human rights, democratic principles and the strengthening of the rule of law in all circumstances, and without exception. Where serious violations of human rights are imminent, NHRIs are expected to conduct themselves with a heightened level of vigilance and independence.[75]

For the Côte d'Ivoire's NHRI, the SCA recommended that the NHRI increase its investigations on violence against women and post-conflict violence.[76]

The SCA has commended NHRIs, like that in Afghanistan (AIHRC), where they have clearly demonstrated their work as a human rights body, particularly where the NHRI is operating in a difficult national environment (discussed further in Chapter 9):

> The SCA acknowledges that the AIHRC has been an effective national human rights institution, carrying out a broad range of activities to promote and protect human rights while operating in a particularly difficult and volatile political and security environment.
>
> The SCA commends the AIHRC for the recent inquiries and reports, which detail human rights violations in times of conflict, and human rights violations experienced by women and girls. In documenting such violations, the AIHRC's actions help to address impunity for past violations and promote a culture that is receptive to human rights.[77]

Where an NHRI fails to respond to specific concerns raised by the SCA in relation to addressing human rights violations, it is likely to see its A-status at risk. In deferring a decision on the Commissioner for Fundamental Rights of Hungary (CFR) in October 2019, the SCA requested additional information from the CFR on a range of issues, including concerns raised by CERD that it lacked information

75 SCA, 'Accreditation Report—Egypt (NCHR)' (May 2018) 20.

76 SCA, 'Accreditation Report—Côte d'Ivoire (La Commission Nationale des Droits de l'Homme de Côte d'Ivoire (CNDHCI))' (May 2016) 15.

77 SCA, 'Accreditation Report—Afghanistan (Afghanistan Independent Human Rights Commission (AIHRC))' (November 2013) 16. Afghanistan is also addressed below in Chapter 9.3.

on the CFR's work to prevent racial discrimination and xenophobia, and concerns raised by the Special Rapporteur on the situation of human rights defenders.[78] This case is also discussed in Chapter 9.6.1. Specifically, regarding addressing human rights violations, the SCA expressed serious concerns:

> [T]he SCA provided an opportunity for the CFR to respond to specific issues of concern. It acknowledges that the CFR did provide some information as follows:
>
> - With respect to the issue of vulnerable ethnic minorities, the CFR provided information about its work with Roma communities, its visits to detention centres for migrants and asylum seekers. It further indicated that it intervened before the Constitutional Court on the relocation of asylum seekers across EU Member States;
> - With respect to petitions to the Constitutional Court on cases deemed political and institutional, the CFR indicated that it has submitted 45 petitions between 2012 and 2019, some of which the CFR indicated were related to sensitive issues;
> - With respect to the 'Foreign Funded Organizations Act' and human rights defenders, the CFR reported that it made comments on the draft law, but that it has not taken public or legal action. The CFR further reported that it closely cooperates with civil society organizations, including those that are affected by the Act.
>
> The SCA is of the view that the information provided by the CFR does not demonstrate adequate efforts in addressing all human rights issues, nor has it spoken out in a manner that promotes and protects all human rights.[79]

Illustrating the increasing emphasis and attention to this General Observation, the SCA placed similar emphasis on the activities Russian Federation Office of the Commissioner for Human Rights (OCHR) in its 2019 review:

> [T]he SCA provided the OCHR with an opportunity to respond to specific issues of concern. It acknowledges that the OCHR did provide some information as follows:
>
> - With respect to the low number of complaints relating to civil and political rights, the OCHR indicated that this is due to the existence of other mechanisms in the Russian Federation to address complaints in this area such as the courts and the prosecutor's office;

78 SCA, 'Accreditation Report—Hungary (CFR)' (October 2019) 23–24.
79 ibid 25–26.

- With respect to allegations of torture received by the institution, the OCHR confirmed that it is correct that the majority of allegations of torture received are deemed unconfirmed. It also provided examples of other actions it had taken to address such cases, including cooperating with public monitoring commissions and regional ombudspersons, conducting visits to places of deprivation of liberty, providing alternative reports to the Committee against Torture, and advocating for the ratification of the OPCAT;[80]
- With respect to the protection of human rights defenders, the OCHR reports that it advocated for the review of the 'Foreign Agents Law', and that it worked to reduce the number of civil society organizations that are covered by the law.

It further indicated that its Advisory Council includes representatives of associations impacted by this Law;
- With respect to the statement that there are 'no tensions, national or religious conflicts' in the Russian Federation, the OCHR reported that, since the original report, it has received an increased number of applications in the area of freedom of religion; and
- With respect to discrimination against specific groups, including LGBTIQ [lesbian, gay, bisexual, transgender, intersex, queer and questioning] communities, Roma, migrants and ethnic minorities, the OCHR reports it conducted special monitoring activities to assess the human rights situation of vulnerable groups, such as during the FIFA World Cup 2018, and that it receives applications for such groups, including from the LGBTI community.

The SCA is of the view that the information provided by the OCHR to date is insufficient to satisfy it that the OCHR has made adequate efforts in addressing all human rights issues, and that it has spoken out in a manner that promotes and protects all human rights.[81]

Both the approach and level of detail in the Venezuela, Hungary, and Russia examples illustrate the increased level of scrutiny given to the specific actions of NHRIs as human rights actors.

7.3.3 Monitoring and Visiting Places of Deprivation of Liberty

The SCA has made recommendations on a specific area of NHRI human rights actions, namely, visiting places of deprivation of liberties. There are a wide range

[80] Optional Protocol to the Convention against Torture and other Cruel, Inhuman or Degrading Treatment or Punishment (adopted on 18 December 2002, entered into force on 22 June 2006) 2375 UNTS 237 (hereafter OPCAT).

[81] SCA, 'Accreditation Report—Russia (OCHR)' (October 2019) 27–28.

of places of deprivation of liberty that may be covered by NHRIs. The NHRI of Jordan, for example, reported that it conducted announced and unannounced visits to 'correction and rehabilitation centres (prisons), temporary detention centres, police station holding areas, and other institutions including the detention centre of the General Intelligence Department, as well as juvenile centres, elderly centres and centres for persons with disabilities'.[82]

NHRIs should have an explicit mandate to monitor places of detention, even where it does this in practice.[83] The SCA encourages NHRIs to use their powers to monitor places of deprivation of liberty and carry out visits.[84] These visits should be unannounced. As noted in relation to the B-status Myanmar National Human Rights Commission (NHRC) November 2015:

> Section 44(3) of the Law provides for the NHRC to visit all places of confinement upon prior notification. While the SCA notes that, in some circumstances, it may be necessary to provide notice for security reasons, it encourages the NHRC to conduct 'unannounced' visits as this limits opportunities for detaining authorities to hide or obscure human rights violations and facilitates greater scrutiny.[85]

Visits should be unannounced.[86] Enabling laws should be clear about the power for unannounced visits.[87] For example, the SCA noted that in relation to the B-status institution (National Institution for Human Rights (NIHRB)) of Bahrain:

> Article 12 of the [enabling] Law provides for the NIHRB 'to conduct field visits, in accordance with the applied rules in order to monitor human rights status in correction institutions, detention centres, labour gatherings, health and education centres, or any other public place in which it is suspected that human rights violations are committed'. While, the law is silent on unannounced visits, the NIHRB confirmed the need for prior notice to conduct these visits.[88]

[82] SCA, 'Accreditation Report—Jordan (National Centre for Human Rights (JNCHR))' (November 2015) 25.

[83] SCA, 'Accreditation Report—Ethiopia (EHRC)' (November 2013) 7; SCA, 'Accreditation Report—South Africa (South African Human Rights Commission (SAHRC))' (November 2017) 33; SCA, 'Accreditation Report—Ghana (The Commission on Human Rights and Administrative Justice (CHRAJ))' (March 2019) 25.

[84] SCA, 'Accreditation Report—Cameroon (NCHRF)' (March/April 2010) 8; SCA, 'Accreditation Report—Cameroon (NCHRF)' (May 2016) 32.

[85] SCA, 'Accreditation Report—Myanmar (MNHRC)' (November 2015) 13. See also, SCA, 'Accreditation Report—Egypt (NCHR)' (November 2015) 42; SCA, 'Accreditation Report—Jordan (JNCHR)' (November 2015) 25.

[86] SCA, 'Accreditation Report—Northern Ireland (NIHRC)' (May 2016) 48.

[87] SCA, 'Accreditation Report—Egypt (NCHR)' (March 2017) 34–35, referring to proposed amendments to the enabling law. See also, SCA, 'Accreditation Report—Ghana (CHRAJ)' (March 2019) 25.

[88] SCA, 'Accreditation Report—Bahrain (NIHRB)' (May 2016) 9.

Where the enabling law does not provide for unannounced visit, the SCA still encourages the NHRI to monitor, investigate and report pending amendments.[89]

Where NHRIs have the function of visiting places of detention, the SCA has expressed concern if the power of an NHRI to visit certain places of detention is restricted. For example, in relation to the NHRI of Afghanistan, it noted that the 'power to visit certain prisons and detention facilities, or to monitor the human rights of non-nationals held in detention in certain circumstances, may be restricted'.[90]

> While noting the circumstances under which these restrictions may have occurred, the SCA stresses that an NHRI should continue to seek access to all places of detention in order to effectively monitor, investigate and report on the human rights situation in a timely manner.[91]

Limits should not be placed on this power. So, while by 2019 the AIHRC had been given the power to visit all places of detention without prior notification, the SCA noted that there remained an exception for centres operated by the Directorate of National Security.[92]

NHRIs should not have to obtain authorization for visits. In reviewing the Northern Ireland Human Rights Commission (NIHRC), the SCA stated:

> In accordance with section 69(C) of the Justice and Security Act 2007, the NIHRC must be authorized to enter a specified place of detention.
>
> While the SCA notes that, in some circumstances, it may be necessary to provide notice for security reasons, it encourages the NIHRC to conduct 'unannounced' visits as this limits opportunities for detaining authorities to hide or obscure human rights violations and facilitates greater scrutiny.
>
> Reiterating its previous concern, the SCA encourages the NIHRC to continue to access all places of deprivation of liberty to effectively monitor, investigate and report on the human rights situation in a timely manner, and to undertake systematic follow-up activities and advocate for the consideration and implementation of its findings and recommendations in order to ensure the protection of those detained.[93]

89 SCA, 'Accreditation Report—Egypt (NCHR)' (May 2018) 22–23; SCA, 'Accreditation Report—Guatemala (The Procurador de Derechos Humanos of Guatemala (PDH))' (May 2018) 25.

90 SCA, 'Accreditation Report—Afghanistan (AIHRC)' (October 2014) 17.

91 ibid 17–18; See also, SCA, 'Accreditation Report—Afghanistan (AIHRC)' (October 2019) 7.

92 SCA, 'Accreditation Report—Afghanistan (AIHRC)' (October 2019) 7. This issue was raised by the SCA under General Observation 1.2 'Human Rights Mandate'.

93 SCA, 'Accreditation Report—Northern Ireland (NIHRC)' (May 2016) 48.

Neither should the NHRI be required to provide prior notice to authorities before visiting places of deprivation of liberty either in principle or in practice.[94] This is even where the authorization is from a judge.[95] The NHRI should also make its reports on monitoring of detention facilities public.[96]

7.3.4 State Responses to NHRI Recommendations

Since the earliest reports, the SCA has recommended that NHRIs publish information on how the public authorities have responded to its recommendations on substantive human rights violations.[97] While not a matter within the control of the NHRI, the SCA has raised concerns where the government complies only to a limited extent with the NHRI's recommendations.[98] It has commended institutions who have established mechanisms to ensure the implementation of its recommendations by competent ministries[99] or otherwise undertaken actions to follow up on implementation.[100] For the NHRI of Timor-Leste, the SCA 'noted with appreciation' the NHRI's initiative to establish a department responsible for following up on its recommendations.[101]

The SCA places emphasis on the responsibility of NHRIs for monitoring and publicizing 'detailed information on responses to and implementation of NHRI recommendations or decisions by public authorities'.[102] In reviewing the B-status NHRI of Libya (NCCLHR) in 2014, the SCA noted that 'to date, the NCCLHR has had limited success in having the Legislature and the Executive respond to its requests and recommendations' it nonetheless commended the institution for 'continuing to produce reports and recommendations in spite of the limited co-operation it has received to date'.[103]

[94] SCA, 'Accreditation Report—Egypt (NCHR)' (March 2017) 34–35; SCA, 'Accreditation Report—Egypt (NCHR)' (May 2018) 22–23. The SCA noted that 'Article 3(16) of the Law mandates the NCHR to visit prisons and all places of detention and interview inmates, as well as to submit its reports to Public Prosecutor and House of Representatives. The law is silent on whether or not prior notice is required in conducting these visits. The NCHR confirmed that such prior notice is necessary.'

[95] SCA, 'Accreditation Report—Guatemala (PDH)' (May 2018) 25.

[96] SCA, 'Accreditation Report—Bahrain (NIHRB)' (May 2016) 9.

[97] SCA, 'Accreditation Report—Sierra Leone (Human Rights Commission of Sierra Leone (SLHRC))' (May 2011) 21; SCA, 'Accreditation Report—Georgia Office of the Public Defender (OPD))' (May 2013) 13.

[98] SCA, 'Accreditation Report—Malawi (Malawi Human Rights Commission (MHRC))' (March 2012) 23. This was noted again in the periodic review in November 2016.

[99] SCA, 'Accreditation Report—Sierra Leone (HRCSL)' (May 2016) 49; SCA, 'Accreditation Report—Moldova (OPA)' (May 2018) 27–28.

[100] SCA, 'Accreditation Report—Georgia (OPD)' (October 2018) 9–10.

[101] SCA, 'Accreditation Report—Timor-Leste (PDHJ)' (November 2013) 30.

[102] SCA, 'Accreditation Report—Russia (OCHR)' (November 2013) 26.

[103] SCA, 'Accreditation Report—Libya (National Council for Civil Liberties and Human Rights (NCCLHR))' (October 2014) 14.

The SCA looks for NHRI enabling laws to provide for formal responses by the government and public bodies to the NHRI's recommendations and reports.[104] Authorities are also encouraged to respond 'in a timely manner'.[105] NHRI recommendations to authorities should be implemented and given 'serious follow-up'.[106]

7.4 NHRIs' Regional and International Engagement

Closely related to NHRIs practice as human rights actors is their substantive engagement with international and regional human rights bodies. The requirement that NHRIs interact with the UN human rights system is easily understood in the context of their emergence and development, discussed in Chapter 1. NHRIs are often described as a bridge[107] between the international and national levels of human rights protection, and this direct interaction with the UN human rights mechanisms is one of the critical areas in which this displays itself. In addition to engaging at the UN-level, the SCA has also encouraged engagement with the regional human rights system, where one exists.

International and regional engagement has long been a particular focus of SCA recommendations. General Observation 1.4 (2018) provides considerable detail on the extent of the expected means of NHRI engagement with the international system:

> G.O. 1.4 Interaction with the International Human Rights System
> The Paris Principles recognise that monitoring and engaging with the international human rights system, in particular the Human Rights Council and its mechanisms (Special Procedures and Universal Periodic Review) and the United Nations Human Rights Treaty Bodies, can be an effective tool for NHRIs in the promotion and protection of human rights domestically.
>
> Depending on existing domestic priorities and resources, effective engagement with the international human rights system may include:
>
> - submitting parallel or shadow reports to the Universal Periodic Review, Special Procedure mechanisms and Treaty Bodies Committees;
> - making statements during debates before review bodies and the Human Rights Council;

[104] SCA, 'Accreditation Report—South Africa (SAHRC)' (November 2012) 31.
[105] SCA, 'Accreditation Report—Russia (OCHR)' (November 2013) 26; SCA, 'Accreditation Report—Georgia (OPD)' (May 2013) 13.
[106] SCA, 'Accreditation Report—Thailand (NHRC)' (November 2008) 11.
[107] See for example, Nicola Jägers, 'National Human Rights Institutions: The Missing Link in Business and Human Rights Governance?' (2020) 14(3) ICL Journal 289, 295; Richard Carver, 'A New Answer to an Old Question: National Human Rights Institutions and the Domestication of International Law' (2010) 10(1) Human Rights Law Review 1.

- assisting, facilitating and participating in country visits by United Nations experts, including special procedures mandate holders, treaty bodies, fact finding missions and commissions of inquiry; and
- monitoring and promoting the implementation of relevant recommendations originating from the human rights system.

While it is appropriate for governments to consult with NHRIs in the preparation of a state's reports to human rights mechanisms, NHRIs should neither prepare the country report nor should they report on behalf of the government. NHRIs must maintain their independence and, where they have the capacity to provide information to human rights mechanisms, do so in their own right. NHRIs should not participate as part of a government delegation during the Universal Periodic Review, during periodic reviews before the Treaty Bodies, or in other international mechanisms where independent participation rights for NHRIs exist. Where independent participation rights for NHRIs do not exist in a particular fora and an NHRI chooses to participate in proceedings as part of a state delegation, the manner of their participation must clearly distinguish them as an independent NHRI.

In considering their engagement with the international human rights system, NHRIs are encouraged to actively engage with the Office of the United Nations High Commissioner for Human Rights (OHCHR), GANHRI, their Regional Network and other NHRIs, as well as international and national NGOs and civil society organizations.[108]

In its justification, the SCA sets out the following rationale:

Sections A.3(d) and A.3(e) of the Paris Principles give NHRIs the responsibility to interact with the international human rights system in three specific ways. That is, NHRIs are required:

1. To contribute to country reports submitted to United Nations bodies and committees, and to regional institutions, in line with the States' treaty obligations;
2. To express an opinion on the subject, where necessary, with due respect for their independence; and
3. To cooperate with the United Nations and any other organization in its system, as well as with regional human rights institutions and the NHRIs of other countries.

[108] SCA, 'General Observations' (February 2018) (n 3) GO 1.4, 12.

The SCA is of the view that NHRI engagement with international bodies is an important dimension of their work. Through their participation, NHRIs connect the national human rights enforcement system with international and regional human rights bodies. Domestically, NHRIs play a key role in raising awareness of international developments in human rights through reporting on the proceedings and recommendations of treaty-monitoring bodies, special procedures mandate holders and the Universal Periodic Review. Their independent participation in human rights mechanisms through, for example, the production of parallel reports on the State's compliance with treaty obligations, also contributes to the work of international mechanisms in independently monitoring the extent to which states comply with their human rights obligations.

Moreover, NHRI participation in regional and international coordination bodies serves to reinforce their independence and effectiveness, overall. Through exchanges, NHRIs are provided with an opportunity to learn from shared experiences. This may lead to collectively strengthening each other's positions and contributing to resolving regional human rights issues.

NHRIs are encouraged to monitor the states' reporting obligations under the Universal Periodic Review and the international treaty bodies, including through dialogue with the relevant treaty body committees.

While it is appropriate for governments to consult with NHRIs in the preparation of a state's reports to human rights mechanisms, NHRIs should neither prepare the country report nor should they report on behalf of the government. NHRIs must maintain their independence and, where they have the capacity to provide information to human rights mechanisms, do so in their own right.

The SCA wishes to clarify that an NHRI's contribution to the reporting process through the submission of stakeholder or shadow reports under relevant international instruments should be done independently of the state, and may draw attention to problems, issues and challenges that may have been omitted or dealt with inadequately in the state report.

The SCA recognizes the primacy of an NHRI's domestic mandate, and that its capacity to engage with the international human rights system must depend on its assessment of domestic priorities and available resources. Within these limitations, NHRIs are encouraged to engage wherever possible and in accordance with their own strategic priorities. In so doing, the SCA highlights that NHRIs should:

- avail themselves of the assistance offered by OHCHR, which provides technical assistance and facilitates regional and global cooperation and exchanges among NHRIs; and
- engage with GANHRI, their respective regional SCA representative and Regional Network.[109]

[109] ibid 12–13.

The SCA's justification cites the following parts of the Paris Principles:

> A) Competence and responsibilities—
> 3. A national institution shall, inter alia, have the following responsibilities: …
> (d) To contribute to the reports which States are required to submit to United Nations bodies and committees, and to regional institutions, pursuant to their treaty obligations and, where necessary, to express an opinion on the subject, with due respect for their independence;
> (e) To cooperate with the United Nations and any other organization in the United Nations system, the regional institutions and the national institutions of other countries that are competent in the areas of the promotion and protection of human rights.[110]

In recommending that NHRIs should interact with the international human rights system, the SCA has encouraged effective,[111] consistent engagement,[112] that is systematic[113] and constructive.[114] Particularly, interaction has been encouraged with the UN Treaty Body system and in following up on UN human rights recommendations at the national level.[115] The SCA has strongly encouraged NHRIs to offer input and participate in the human rights mechanisms,[116] and has expressed concern where such input is limited.[117]

NHRIs' enabling law should explicitly provide for interaction with the international human rights system.[118] It should be a specific part of the mandate of

[110] ibid 13–14.

[111] SCA, 'Accreditation Report—Algeria (CNCPPDH)' (April 2008) 4; SCA, 'Accreditation Report—Croatia (ORC)' (April 2008) 8; SCA, 'Accreditation Report—Maldives (Human Rights Commission (HRC))' (April 2008) 8; SCA, 'Accreditation Report—Timor-Leste (PHRJ)' (April 2008) 8; SCA, 'Accreditation Report—Ecuador (Defensoría del Pueblo de Ecuador (DPE))' (March 2009) 9; SCA, 'Accreditation Report—Netherlands (ETC)' (March/April 2010) 10.

[112] SCA, 'SCA, 'Accreditation Report—Qatar (National Human Rights Committee (NHRC))' (March 2009), March 2009 5.

[113] SCA, 'Accreditation Report—Russia (OCHR)' (November 2008) 5; SCA, 'Accreditation Report—Albania (People's Advocate (PA))' (November 2008) 6.

[114] SCA, 'Accreditation Report—Moldova (HRCM)' (November 2009) 5. Many early SCA reports simply noted the General Observation without further comment. For example, SCA, 'Accreditation Report—Guatemala (PDHG)' (April 2008) 5; SCA, 'Accreditation Report—Malaysia (SUHAKAM)' (April 2008) 5; SCA, 'Accreditation Report—Niger Commission Nationale des Droits de l'Homme et des Libertés Fondamentales (CNDHLF))' (April 2008) 6.

[115] SCA, 'Accreditation Report—Algeria (CNCPPDH)' (April 2008) 4; SCA, 'Accreditation Report—Ecuador (DP))' (April 2008) 7; SCA, 'Accreditation Report—Venezuela (DP)' (April 2008) 7.

[116] SCA, 'Accreditation Report—Ecuador (DP))' (April 2008) 4; See also, SCA, 'Accreditation Report—Venezuela (DPV)' (May 2013) 22.

[117] SCA, 'Accreditation Report—Paraguay (DPP)' (March 2019) 13. See also, SCA, 'Accreditation Report—Democratic Republic of Congo (The National Human Rights Commission (CNDH))' (May 2018) 14–15, noting that the NHRI had not submitted parallel reports to UN Treaty Bodies since its establishment in 2015.

[118] SCA, 'Accreditation Report—Serbia (Protector of Citizens of the Republic of Serbia (PCRS))' (March/April 2010) 5; SCA, 'Accreditation Report—Montenegro (Protector of Human Rights and Freedoms (PHRF))' (May 2016) 18–19, noting that while the B-status NHRI was 'a member of various

NHRIs.[119] The mandate should cover both encouraging ratification or accession to international human rights instruments and interaction with the international human rights system.[120] This is the case even where the NHRI undertakes these functions in practice.[121]

However, the requirement to engage at the international level is not absolute. The SCA has long recognized that as *national*-level institutions, NHRIs must give priority to national level work, thus it notes that the international or regional engagement is 'depending on the NHRIs assessment of priorities'.[122]

Where NHRIs do participate at the international level, their engagement must be done in a 'fully independent manner',[123] with the UN Treaty Bodies, Special Procedures Mandate Holders, and the UN Human Rights Council including the Universal Periodic Review (UPR).[124] Contribution to the state report is not

regional human rights organizations and has engaged with the international human rights system. However, there is no specific legal provision for the PHRF to engage with these systems, or to encourage ratification or accession to international human rights instruments.' See also, SCA, 'Accreditation Report—Zambia (HRCZ)' (November 2016) 59 and, SCA, 'Accreditation Report—Zambia (HRCZ)' (October 2018) 18, where the SCA noted that proposed amendments were considered sufficient to remedy the concerns, if adopted; SCA, 'Accreditation Report—Bosnia and Herzegovina (IHROBH)' (November 2016) 17 and SCA, 'Accreditation Report—Bosnia and Herzegovina (IHROBH)' (November 2017) 11–12, where proposed amendments were considered sufficient to remedy the concerns, if adopted; SCA, 'Accreditation Report—Costa Rica (DHCR)' (November 2016) 19–20; SCA, 'Accreditation Report—Nicaragua (PDDH)' (November 2016) 46; SCA, 'Accreditation Report—Lithuania (Seimas Ombudsmen Office (SOO))' (March 2017) 10; SCA, 'Accreditation Report—Belgium (The Interfederal Centre for Equal Opportunity and fight against racism and discrimination (UNIA))' (May 2018) 10.

119 SCA, 'Accreditation Report—Kazakhstan (The Commissioner for Human Rights (CHR))' (March 2012) 4–5; SCA, 'Accreditation Report—Poland (Human Rights Defender (HRD))' (November 2012) 23.

120 SCA, 'Accreditation Report—Zambia (HRCZ)' (November 2016) 59; SCA, 'Accreditation Report—Zambia (HRCZ)' (October 2018) 18, where the SCA noted that 'section 5(2) of the Amendment Bill explicitly mandates the HRCZ to both interact with the international human rights system and encourage ratification or accession to international human rights instruments. The SCA is of the view that these amendments, if passed in their present form, would address the previously stated concerns. The SCA therefore encourages the HRCZ to continue to advocate for the passage of the amendments.'

121 SCA, 'Accreditation Report—Lithuania (SOO)' (March 2017) 10; SCA, 'Accreditation Report—Bosnia and Herzegovina (IHROBH)' (November 2017) 11–12; SCA, 'Accreditation Report—Egypt (NCHR)' (May 2018) 23; SCA, 'Accreditation Report—Denmark (Danish Institute for Human Rights (DIHR))' (October 2018) 8.

122 SCA, 'Accreditation Report—Kazakhstan (CHR)' (March 2012) 8.

123 SCA, 'Accreditation Report—Ukraine (UPCHR)' (April 2008) 9. See also, SCA, 'Accreditation Report—Algeria (CNCPPDH)' (March 2009) 8; SCA, 'Accreditation Report—Bosnia (IHROBH)' (November 2009) 7.

124 SCA, 'Accreditation Report—Slovenia (Human Rights Ombudsman of the Republic of Slovenia (HRORS))' (March/April 2010) 9; SCA, 'Accreditation Report—Mauritius (National Human Rights Commission of Mauritius (NHRC))' (October 2014) 23; SCA, 'Accreditation Report—Cameroon (NCHRF)' (March 2015) 38 (noting with concern that the NHRI did not submit a parallel report during the 2013 UPR); SCA, 'Accreditation Report—Serbia (PCRS)' (March 2015) 23, noting that the NHRI had not provided a parallel report during the 2013 UPR of Serbia. See also SCA, 'Accreditation Report—Cameroon (NCHRF)' (May 2016) 32; SCA, 'Accreditation Report—Zambia (HRCZ)' (November 2016) 59 and SCA, 'Accreditation Report—Zambia (HRCZ)' (October 2018) 18; SCA, 'Accreditation Report—Democratic Republic of Congo (CNDH)' (May 2018) 14–15, where the SCA noted that the NHRI reported it was preparing a parallel report as part of the third cycle of the UPR.

sufficient.[125] As specified by the SCA, '[w]hile it is appropriate for NHRIs to provide information to the government in the preparation of the State report, NHRIs must maintain their independence and where they have the capacity to provide information to human rights mechanisms should do so in their own right'.[126] The information provided by the NHRI should be provided independently of the government.[127] The NHRI's participation should not be limited to contributing to the government report.[128] It should also not participate as part of the government delegation as this 'compromises the independence, and/or perception of the independence' of the NHRI.[129]

Where the enabling law provides that the NHRI has to prepare the state's report to a Treaty Body, the SCA will raise particular concerns.[130] In its examination of the (B-status) NHRI of Libya in October 2014, for example, the SCA noted that:

> Article 3(8) of the Law provides that the NCCLHR will participate 'within the Libyan delegation, and in meetings of the regional and international concerned in protection of the General Freedoms and Human Right' [*sic*].
>
> The SCA recognizes that an NHRI may have a role to play in assisting the State in meeting its reporting obligations before international bodies. However, the SCA emphasizes the need for NHRIs to participate in these bodies in a manner independent of the government.
>
> The SCA encourages the NCCLHR to conduct its engagement with the international human rights system independently of government. It further encourages the NCCLHR to advocate for an amendment to the enabling law to clearly provide for independent participation.[131]

Similarly, in relation to the NHRI of Tanzania (CHRAGG), the SCA expressed concern regarding the wording of its enabling law:

> The SCA commends the CHRAGG for having submitted reports to the UPR and CEDAW. The CHRAGG also indicated that it is communicating with Special Procedures mandate holders.
>
> While acknowledging submission of reports to UPR and various treaty bodies, the SCA notes with concern that Article 6(1)(m) of the Law establishes that the

125 SCA, 'Accreditation Report—Mauritius (NHRC)' (October 2014) 23.

126 SCA, 'Accreditation Report—Serbia (PCRS)' (March 2015) 23. See also SCA, 'Accreditation Report—Myanmar (MNHRC)' (November 2015) 13–14.

127 SCA, 'Accreditation Report—Slovenia (HRORS)' (March/April 2010) 9.

128 SCA, 'Accreditation Report—Tajikistan (The Human Rights Ombudsman of the Republic of Tajikistan (HROT))' (March 2012) 16. See also, SCA, 'Accreditation Report—Mauritius (NHRC)' (October 2014) 23–24.

129 SCA, 'Accreditation Report—Tajikistan (HROT)' (March 2012) 14.

130 SCA, 'Accreditation Report—Belgium (Centre for Equal Opportunities and Opposition to Racism (CEOOR))' (March/April 2010) 11.

131 SCA, 'Accreditation Report—Libya (NCCLHR)' (October 2014) 15.

> Commission shall carry out the following function: 'under the auspices of the government, to cooperate with and agencies of the United Nations, the OAU, the Commonwealth and other bilateral, multilateral or regional and national institutions of other countries which are competent in the areas of the protection and promotion of human rights and administrative justice.' The SCA expresses concern that the reference to 'under the auspices of the government' may impact on CHRAGG's capacity to freely engage and cooperate with the UN and other bodies.[132]

Part of NHRIs interaction with international human rights bodies should be the promotion of ratification and implementation of international instruments, as discussed in Chapter 7.4.[133]

In addition to the UN system, NHRIs should engage with the 'international and national civil society organisations',[134] as well as regional human rights systems such as the Inter-American human rights system[135] and African human rights system.[136] However, NHRIs interaction should not be limited to regional systems.[137]

The SCA is particularly concerned where an NHRI expresses opinions against the international human rights system. For example, the SCA commented that the annual report of the Honduras NHRI (CONADEH) 'reflects the lack of interaction between the CONADEH and the International Human Rights system. In the Annual Report the CONADEH questioned and criticized the role and reports of international observers such as the Organization of American States (OAS) and the UN during the crisis in Honduras.'[138] The SCA is also concerned where it receives reports from UN entities that the NHRI is not actively engaging with them.[139]

In its reviews, the SCA regularly notes where the NHRI has made efforts to increase its engagement with the international system,[140] or at least expresses an

[132] SCA, 'Accreditation Report—Tanzania (CHRAGG)' (November 2016) 54–55. The SCA recommended the NHRI seek removal of the term 'under the auspices'.

[133] SCA, 'Accreditation Report—Malaysia (SUHAKAM)' (March 2009) 10.

[134] SCA, 'Accreditation Report—Bulgaria (ORB)' (October 2011) 7. See also, SCA, 'Accreditation Report—Macedonia (Ombudsman of the Republic of Macedonia (ORM))' (October 2011) 10; SCA, 'Accreditation Report—Poland (HRD)' (November 2012) 23.

[135] SCA, 'Accreditation Report—Costa Rica (DHCR)' (October 2011) 12; SCA, 'Accreditation Report—Nicaragua (PDDH)' (November 2017) 45.

[136] SCA, 'Accreditation Report—Tanzania (CHRAGG)' (October 2011) 18.

[137] SCA, 'Accreditation Report—Portugal (Provedor de Justiça (Provedor))' (November 2012) 25, noting that the NHRI was engaged with the Council of Europe but had limited engagement with the international system.

[138] SCA, 'Accreditation Report—Honduras (CONADEH)' (October 2010) 10. By 2019, the situation had changed significantly, with the SCA noting in October 2019 that CONADEH had enhanced its cooperation with regional and international human rights systems. SCA, 'Accreditation Report—Honduras (CONADEH))' (October 2019) 11.

[139] SCA, 'Accreditation Report—Mauritania (CNDH)' (November 2016) 34.

[140] SCA, 'Accreditation Report—Albania (PA)' (November 2013) 20; SCA, 'Accreditation Report—Hungary (CFR)' (November 2013) 11; SCA, 'Accreditation Report—Russia (OCHR)' (November

intention to do so.[141] Lack of practical engagement with the regional and international human rights system is a source of concern for the SCA.[142] The SCA also praises active engagement with the international system, and where the NHRI has made particular efforts, such as for Moldova's NHRI, which was in the processing of 'establishing a specialized unit to monitor the compliance by the State with its international human rights obligations'.[143]

NHRIs should bring issues of human rights concern to the supra-national level. In 2019, it encouraged the NHRI of Hungary to raise sensitive issues with the international and regional human rights system.[144]

7.5 Comment

This chapter examined a number of critical aspects of the functioning of NHRIs relating to their engagement on the ground and showed the SCA's increasing attention to this area. This has been a significant development in the SCA's reviews, illustrating a maturation of the SCA process as NHRIs themselves have become more well established. As the subsequent chapters in this part of the book will further illustrate, the SCA focuses increasingly on ensuring that NHRIs are effective human rights bodies. Where there are significant concerns regarding their activities as human rights promoters and protectors, they are at risk of losing their A-status if they are unable or unwilling to improve their approach or provide a credible justification for their inaction.

While Part III of this book examines the SCA's reviews of the activities of NHRIs, this chapter has shown that these cannot be artificially separated from the functioning of the institution discussed in Part II. As the Asian NGO Network on National Human Rights Institutions (ANNI) noted in its 2019 Annual Report:

> Challenges [for NHRIs in Asia] include structural problems such as functional deficiencies as well as a lack of adequate financial and human resources. However,

2013) 26; SCA, 'Accreditation Report—Timor-Leste (PDHJ)' (November 2013) 31; SCA, 'Accreditation Report—Hungary (CFR)' (October 2014) 10; SCA, 'Accreditation Report—Costa Rica (DHCR)' (November 2016) 19: 'The SCA commends DHCR's interaction with the international human rights system and encourages it to continue this interaction. It notes that the DHCR is a member of various regional organizations and has actively engaged with the international and regional human rights systems.' See also, SCA, 'Accreditation Report—Mexico (CNDH)' (November 2016) 39; SCA, 'Accreditation Report—Egypt (NCHR)' (March 2017) 34; SCA, 'Accreditation Report—Moldova (OPA)' (May 2018) 27; SCA, 'Accreditation Report—Spain (The Defensor del Pueblo of Spain (DPS))' (May 2018) 34.

[141] SCA, 'Accreditation Report—Liberia (Independent National Commission on Human Rights (INCHR))' (March 2017) 8.

[142] SCA, 'Accreditation Report—Paraguay (DPP)' (March 2019) 13.

[143] SCA, 'Accreditation Report—Moldova (OPA)' (May 2018) 27.

[144] SCA, 'Accreditation Report—Hungary (CFR)' (October 2019) 26.

> in many instances the main barrier to NHRI's effective promotion and protection of human rights is a lack of independence and political will from governments.[145]

The SCA is clear that being an NHRI is not just about meeting the criteria of the Paris Principles; NHRIs are expected to actively engage in the promotion and protection of human rights at the national level. In keeping with the international role of NHRIs discussed in Chapter 1, the SCA has placed considerable focus on the level of engagement by NHRIs with the international and regional human rights bodies. The SCA views this not only as a necessary element of the promotion and protection of human rights at the national level, but also as an indication of the independence of the institution. The SCA does however, recognize that this is not an absolute obligation—national priorities are the focus of NHRIs and they may not have the resources to actively engage at the international level. For that reason, GANHRI has developed practical means of supporting NHRIs, such as through the GANHRI Geneva Representative who may present statements on behalf of an NHRI, or by an NHRI presenting or otherwise engaging via video link.[146]

The SCA reviews in this chapter also show that the SCA requires NHRIs to cooperate actively with other national human rights actors. As discussed in Chapter 1, NHRIs occupy a fourth space at the domestic level. Engagement with other national organizations is critical. It is particularly essential that NHRIs have a strong relationship with NGOs and civil society, given the role these organizations play in providing support to and advocacy for victims of human rights violations, marginalized groups, and more. NGOs and civil society are also essential sources of information and expertise for NHRIs. They can be a crucial connection to the situation on the ground.

NGOs and civil society may often be critical of NHRIs. This may be because of inaction or perceived inaction by the NHRI, a lack of legitimacy or faith in the institution, or unmet expectations. In the Asia-Pacific region, ANNI is an active network of NGOs specifically focused on the work of NHRIs. Their reports on individual NHRIs come directly from NGOs within the country in which the NHRI operates. It has highlighted the challenges faced by NGOs working with NHRIs:

> In some instances, the relationship between NHRI and civil society is marked by antagonism and/or disengagement. Often, though, the crises in legitimacy and erosion of trust that NHRIs suffer from are not unfounded. NHRIs have

[145] ANNI, *Report on the Performance and Establishment of National Human Rights Institutions in Asia* (Asian Forum for Human Rights and Development 2019) 15.

[146] See for example, GANHRI, 'National Human Rights Institutions and UN Treaty Bodies: GANHRI Background Paper' (May 2016) 14 <https://nhri.ohchr.org/EN/IHRS/TreatyBodies/Annual%20Meeting%20of%20Chairpersons%20of%20Human%20Rights%20Tre/GANHRI%20background%20paper%20FINAL.pdf> accessed 16 February 2021.

been found to adopt problematic positions or acted in ways that contradict their human rights mandate.[147]

While it has been less of a focus for the SCA to date, NHRIs are also expected to cooperate closely with similar national bodies, in particular, general or specialized ombudspersons (where these are separate institutions) and specialized rights-focused organizations such as equality bodies (particularly in the EU).

The next chapter examines a specific aspect of the functioning of NHRIs where they are tasked with additional functions as international treaty-mandated prevention and monitoring mechanisms.

[147] ANNI, *Report on the Performance and Establishment of National Human Rights Institutions in Asia* (Asian Forum for Human Rights and Development 2014) 7.

8
National Human Rights Institutions as Treaty-mandated National Prevention and Monitoring Mechanisms

8.1 Introduction

This chapter reviews the recommendations of the Sub-Committee on Accreditation (SCA) on National Human Rights Institutions (NHRIs) that have an additional role as treaty-mandated national mechanisms. Specifically, as National Preventative Mechanisms (NPMs) under the Optional Protocol to the Convention Against Torture and Other Cruel, Inhuman or Degrading Treatment or Punishment (OPCAT)[1] and/or as National Monitoring Mechanisms (NMM)[2] under the Convention on the Rights of Persons with Disabilities (CRPD).[3] States are required to establish these national mechanisms shortly after ratifying the instruments, and as the Office of the High Commissioner for Human Rights (OHCHR) describes it for NPM's, 'compliance with the Optional Protocol includes not only the establishment of NPMs but also ensuring their effective functioning'.[4]

The national mechanisms under OPCAT and CRPD are novel innovations in the modern human rights architecture. The Subcommittee on Prevention of Torture and Other Cruel, Inhuman or Degrading Treatment or Punishment (SPT), which has responsibility for overseeing the NPMs within the Convention Against Torture implementation system at the United Nations (UN) level, described itself as a 'new type of United Nations treaty body'.[5] As Pegram has described the OPCAT and its mechanism:

[1] Optional Protocol to the Convention against Torture and other Cruel, Inhuman or Degrading Treatment or Punishment (adopted on 18 December 2002, entered into force on 22 June 2006) 2375 UNTS 237 (hereafter OPCAT).

[2] On the origins of NHRIs role in the CRPD mechanism, see Michael Ashley Stein and Janet E Lord, 'Monitoring the Convention on the Rights of Persons with Disabilities: Innovations, Lost Opportunities, and Future Potential' (2010) 32 Human Rights Quarterly 689.

[3] Convention on the Rights of Persons with Disabilities (adopted on 13 December 2006, entered into force on 3 May 2008) 2515 UNTS 3 (CRPD) Art 33 (hereafter CRPD).

[4] OHCHR, *Preventing Torture—The Role of National Preventive Mechanisms: A Practical Guide* (United Nations 2018) 1 (hereafter OHCHR, *Preventing Torture—The Role of National Preventive Mechanisms: A Practical Guide*).

[5] CAT Subcommittee on Prevention, 'First Annual Report of the Subcommittee on Prevention of Torture and Other Cruel, Inhuman and Degrading Treatment or Punishment' (14 May 2018) UN Doc CAT/C/40/2, 5.

National Human Rights Institutions. David Langtry and Kirsten Roberts Lyer, Oxford University Press. © David Langtry and Kirsten Roberts Lyer 2021. DOI: 10.1093/oso/9780198829102.003.0009

> Establishing non new norms or standards, OPCAT is instead focused on implementing a well-established normative framework prohibiting torture through innovative procedural obligations. For the architects of OPCAT, the SPT forms the centre-piece of a novel legislation of human rights architecture which obliges states to recognise the jurisdiction of a global monitoring structure, as well as an analogous domestic structure [the NPM].[6]

A considerable proportion of states have designated their NHRI as NPMs under OPCAT.[7]

NHRIs may be designated as NPMs and/or NMMs in their countries, or as part of a structure involving additional institutions. NPMs are established under OPCAT, which requires that State Parties shall set up and designate (or maintain) a domestic-level body (or bodies) for the prevention of torture and other cruel, inhuman, or degrading treatment or punishment.[8] Mandated for these ends and operating under this legal framework, NPMs are composed of one or more domestic independent bodies and fulfil visiting, advisory, educational, and cooperation functions when carrying out their activities.[9] For NMMs operating under the CRPD, the treaty sets out that '[s]tates have to establish or designate a framework that includes one or more independent mechanisms to promote, protect and monitor the Convention's implementation'.[10] NHRIs may be designated for this function. In this context, the treaty specifically requires that 'States Parties shall take into account the principles relating to the status and functioning of national institutions for protection and promotion of human rights'.[11] When designated as NPM and/or NMMs, NHRIs fulfil these mandates and functions in addition to their 'regular' NHRI functions of promotion and protection, for example as set out in detail in Chapter 6.

The SCA examines NHRIs acting as NPMs/NMMs under General Observation 2.8 (2018) 'Assessing NHRIs as National Preventive and National Monitoring Mechanisms', which provides:[12]

[6] Thomas Pegram, 'Governing Relationships: The New Architecture in Global Human Rights Governance' (2015) 43(2) Millennium—Journal of International Studies 618, 628.

[7] In 2018, NHRIs made up two-thirds of NPMs <https://www.apt.ch/en/news_on_prevention/first-global-meeting-nhris-npm-mandate> accessed 23 July 2021. The Association for the Prevention of Torture (APT) provides a list of NPMs by institution type. APT, 'List of Designated NPM by type' <http://tortureprevention.ch/en/by-type/> accessed 16 February 2021.

[8] OPCAT (n 1) Art 3.

[9] OHCHR, *Preventing Torture—The Role of National Preventive Mechanisms: A Practical Guide* (n 4).

[10] OHCHR, 'Monitoring the Convention on the Rights of Persons with Disabilities: Guidance for Human Rights Monitors' (2010) No. 17, HR/P/PT/17, 30.

[11] CRPD (n 3).

[12] SCA, 'General Observations of the Sub-Committee on Accreditation' (adopted on 21 February 2018) GO 2.8, 46–48 (hereafter SCA, 'General Observations' (February 2018)). In the 2013 General Observations, this was 2.9: SCA, 'ICC Sub-Committee on Accreditation General Observations' (adopted in May 2013) 53–55. Because of this, the SCA's observations in this chapter relate to GO 2.9 depending on the year of reviewing an NHRIs accreditation.

Where, pursuant to an international human rights instrument, an NHRI has been designated as, or as part of, a national preventive or monitoring mechanism, the SCA will assess whether the applicant has provided sufficient information to demonstrate that it is carrying out its functions in compliance with the Paris Principles.

Depending on the specific roles and functions ascribed to the NHRI, in undertaking this assessment, the SCA will consider, as appropriate:

- whether a formal legal mandate has been provided;
- whether the mandate has been appropriately defined to encompass the promotion and protection of all relevant rights contained in the international instrument;
- whether the staff of the NHRI possess the appropriate skills and expertise;
- whether the NHRI has been provided with additional and adequate resources;
- whether there is evidence that the NHRI is effectively undertaking all relevant roles and functions as may be provided in the relevant international instrument. Depending on the instrument and the mandate of the national human rights institution, such activities might include monitoring and investigation, the provision of constructive and/or critical advice to government and in particular, systematic follow up of its recommendations and findings on alleged human rights violations.

The SCA may also consider, as it thinks appropriate, any guidance that has been developed by the relevant treaty body.[13]

In its justification, the SCA provides:

In recent years, international human rights instruments have begun to incorporate a requirement that States Parties create, or designate an existing domestic agency (or agencies) with responsibility for monitoring and promoting the objectives of that instrument.

These international instruments often specify particular roles and functions to be carried out by the relevant domestic agency or agencies, which are variously referred to as national preventive or monitoring mechanisms.

In response, States have often chosen to designate their NHRI as, or as part of, its national preventive or monitoring mechanisms. In so doing, the State signals that the NHRI has a primary role to play in the promotion and protection of rights contained in those instruments.

In assessing whether an NHRI is carrying out these function [*sic*] in accordance with the Paris Principles, the SCA will consider a range of factors that impact

[13] SCA, 'General Observations' (February 2018) (n 12) GO 2.8, 46.

on the capacity of a NHRI to function independently and effectively. With regard to the requirement for a specific legal mandate, this may depend on the scope of a NHRI existing mandate and the breadth of any additional roles and functions ascribed to it as a national preventive or monitoring mechanisms. Where additional powers are proposed, such as specific powers to enter, monitor, investigate and report on places of detention, and these go beyond the powers currently available to the NHRI, a more clearly defined legal mandate may be required in order to ensure the NHRI is able to undertake its role effectively and free from interference.

In undertaking its assessment, the SCA will also consider any guidelines developed by the relevant treaty body. It notes, however, that its role is to assess a NHRI against the Paris Principles, whereas the relevant treaty body undertakes its assessment of a national preventive or monitoring mechanism against the relevant international instrument upon which it is based. Guidelines developed by the relevant treaty body have, in general, been drafted for the broad range of agencies that may be designated as national preventive or monitoring mechanisms, and may not always be directly applicable to an NHRI.[14]

The SCA also cites the following excerpt from the Paris Principles:

(A) Competence and responsibilities.

...

3. A national institution shall, inter alia, have the following responsibilities:

(a) To submit to the Government, Parliament and any other competent body ... opinions, recommendations, proposals and reports on ....
    ii. Any situation of violation of human rights which it decides to take up;

(b) To promote and ensure the harmonization of national legislation regulations and practices with the international human rights instruments to which the State is a party, and their effective implementation;

(c) To encourage ratification of the above-mentioned instruments or accession to those instruments, and to ensure their implementation;

(d) To contribute to the reports which States are required to submit to United Nations bodies and committees, and to regional institutions, pursuant to their treaty obligations and, where necessary, to express an opinion on the subject, with due respect for their independence;

(e) To cooperate with the United Nations and any other organization in the United Nations system, the regional institutions and the national institutions of other countries that are competent in the areas of the promotion and protection of human rights.[15]

[14] ibid 47–48 (ellipsis in original).

[15] ibid (ellipsis in original).

The following sections examine the areas most frequently raised by the SCA in this context: the enabling law and funding.

8.2 Enabling Law

Treaty-mandated roles should be explicitly and clearly enshrined in NHRI enabling laws. In a 2011 review, the SCA welcomed the designation of Mexico's NHRI as an NPM but underlined that it was appointed not through legislation but via correspondence between the Minister of Foreign Affairs and the President of the NHRI. In this context, the SCA advised that the NHRI seek for the NPM designation to be enshrined in its enabling law. The SCA also encouraged the institution to 'continue to enhance' its effectiveness as an NPM.[16] Reviewing the NHRI again in 2016, it reiterated that its role as an NPM has still not been formalized. The SCA noted that a law pending before the parliament would formally appoint the NHRI as an NPM. It also underlined that, once adopted, 'a more clearly-defined legal mandate is required' for the NHRI which 'provides for additional powers to enter, monitor, investigate and report on places of detention that go beyond the powers of the NHRI already available in the enabling law'.[17] Reviewing the NHRI in Hungary in 2013, the SCA observed that draft amendments to its enabling law would designate the institution as the NPM, and encouraged the NHRI to carry on advocating for those amendments.[18] Accrediting the Sri Lankan NHRI in 2018, the SCA noted that it had been appointed as the NPM under OPCAT, however it had not been 'provided with an explicit legislative mandate in this regard'. The SCA recognized that the NHRI's enabling law gave it a mandate to access all place of detention, and that the NHRI reported that it regards this as adequate for fulfilling its role as an NPM. However, the SCA gave its opinion that for the NHRI to undertake its NPM role, a legislative mandate specifically for its NPM role would assist it to fulfil this role 'effectively and free from interference' and encouraged the NHRI to seek the establishment of its NPM designation in legislation.[19]

[16] SCA, 'Report and Recommendations of the Session of the Sub-Committee on Accreditation—Mexico (Comisión Nacional de los Derechos Humanos (CNDH))' (October 2011) 15 (hereafter SCA, 'Accreditation Report').

[17] SCA, 'Accreditation Report—Mexico (CNDH)' (November 2016) 39.

[18] SCA, 'Accreditation Report—Hungary (Commissioner for Fundamental Rights of Hungary (CFR))' (May 2013) 10.

[19] SCA, 'Accreditation Report—Sri Lanka (The Human Rights Commission of Sri Lanka (SLHRC))' (May 2018) 37.

8.3 Funding for National Human Rights Institutions as Treaty-mandated Mechanisms

In its observations on NHRIs acting as NPMs and NMMs, the SCA has paid the most attention to the question of funding and resources. Generally, the SCA has emphasized the importance of additional resources, or noted where additional resources need to be provided for NHRIs taking on these roles, often advising them to seek extra funding.

Additional funding must be provided to cover the work required as the treaty-mandated mechanism, including sufficient funding for the necessary staff. In its accreditation of the Serbian NHRI in 2010, the SCA noted that the NHRI was in line to be appointed as NPM under OPCAT. Referring to the SPT's Preliminary Guidelines for NPMs[20] and to its own General Observations,[21] the SCA stated 'adequate resources should be provided for work associated with this [additional] role'.[22] In its subsequent review in 2015, the SCA noted that as the NPM, the NHRI was understaffed and that 'additional financial resources should be provided to enable it to assume the responsibilities of discharging these [NPM] functions', urging the NHRI to advocate for an appropriate level of funding.[23] Reviewing the Spanish NHRI in 2018, the SCA noted with appreciation the work of the institution as an NPM, and stressed that NHRIs should receive funding at a level that enables it 'effectively [to] fulfil' these additional functions.[24] Examining the Croatian NHRI the same year, it observed that while its funding situation had improved, it would benefit from additional resources including for its mandate as an NPM. The SCA also underlined that the NHRI has been designated with additional responsibilities as part of legislation aimed at whistle-blower protection, without funding being assigned for these new functions.[25] While this is not an NPM/NMM function, the SCA's advice clearly follows the same pattern in its comments on the additional functions; these must come with sufficient financial resources for effectively fulfilling responsibilities that come with it as was also seen in Chapter 5.2.4 (expansion of mandate).

Funding for a treaty-mandated role is not a one-off, but it must be provided annually. Accrediting the Human Rights Commission of the Maldives (HRCM) in 2010 with B-status, the SCA observed that it had not received additional funding

[20] Subcommittee on the Prevention of Torture, 'Guidelines on national preventative mechanism' (9 December 2010) UN Doc CAT/OP/12/5.

[21] SCA, 'ICC Sub-Committee on Accreditation General Observations' (adopted in June 2009) GO 2.6, 2–3.

[22] SCA, 'Accreditation Report—Serbia (Protector of Citizens of the Republic of Serbia (PCRS))' (March/April 2010) 5.

[23] SCA, 'Accreditation Report—Serbia (PRCS)' (March 2015) 20–23.

[24] SCA, 'Accreditation Report—Spain (Defensoría del Pueblo (DPS))' (May 2018) 32, 35.

[25] SCA, 'Accreditation Report—Croatia (Ombudsman of the Republic of Croatia (ORC))' (March 2019) 19.

for its NPM role that year, in contrast to previous years. Referring to its General Observation and the SPT Guidelines, it emphasized the importance of NHRIs receiving adequate resources when nominated as NPMs 'to ensure the gradual and progressive realization of the improvement of the organization's operations and the fulfilment of its mandate'.[26] Examining the Bulgarian Ombudsman and accrediting it with B-status in 2011, the SCA encouraged the institution to seek extra funding for assuming its newly adopted responsibilities as an NPM.[27] In its 2019 review, the SCA underlined that the institution reported improvements to its budget, but also reiterated that it would 'benefit from additional funding' including for both its NPM and NMM roles.[28]

Funding is also not merely an issue of resources; it is closely linked to the independent functioning of the NHRI as a treaty-mandated body. Reviewing the Azerbaijan NHRI in 2012, the SCA noted that the institution reported insufficient funding to carry out its NPM mandate. Emphasizing the importance of adequate funding for fulfilling this additional role, the SCA observed that such funding also promotes the independence of the institution, by enabling it to set priorities freely in order to fulfil its mandate.[29] NHRIs should also advocate for sufficient funding and resources for their mandate under OPCAT/CRPD.[30]

The NHRI itself must work to ensure its treaty-mandated functions are undertaken appropriately independently. Accrediting the NHRI in Rwanda in 2018, the SCA noted the institution's enabling law had been amended to include an NPM mandate. Observing that the NHRI was in the process of establishing its structure and starting to implement its activities as an NPM, it encouraged the NHRI to 'discharge this mandate in an independent, effective and functional manner and to ensure that it is effectively undertaking all relevant roles and functions provided under OPCAT'.[31] In addition, as in other observations, it highlighted the

[26] SCA, 'Accreditation Report—Maldives (HRCM)' (March/April 2010) 6.

[27] SCA, 'Accreditation Report—Bulgaria (Ombudsman of the Republic of Bulgaria (ORB))' (October 2011) 7.

[28] SCA, 'Accreditation Report—Bulgaria (ORB)' (March 2019) 17.

[29] SCA, 'Accreditation Report—Azerbaijan (The Human Rights Commissioner (Ombudsman) of the Republic of Azerbaijan (HRCA))' (March 2012) 31. See also, SCA, 'Accreditation Report—Georgia (Office of the Public Defender (OPD))' (November 2012) 17; SCA, 'Accreditation Report—Georgia (OPD)' (October 2018) 11; SCA, 'Accreditation Report—Moldova' (The Office of the People's Advocate of Moldova (OPA))' (May 2018) 26–27. The SCA also reviewed a B-status institution in Moldova in 2009, and in that case received input from the SPT: SCA, 'Accreditation Report—Moldova' (Parliamentary Advocates & Centre for Human Rights of Moldova (HRCM))' (November 2009) 1, 4–5.

[30] This is a frequent recommendation by the SCA, see for example: SCA, 'Accreditation Report—Poland (Human Rights Defender (HRD))' (November 2012) 24; SCA, 'Accreditation Report—Togo (National Human Rights Commission (CNDH))' (May 2013) 18; SCA, 'Accreditation Report—Finland (Finnish National Human Rights Institution (FNHRI))' (October 2014) 9; SCA, 'Accreditation Report—Madagascar (Commission Nationale Indépendante des Droits de l'Homme (CNIDH))' (March 2019) 9; SCA, 'Accreditation Report—Moldova (OPA)' (May 2018) 26–27.

[31] SCA, 'Accreditation Report—Rwanda (The National Commission for Human Rights of the Republic of Rwanda (NCHR))' (October 2018) 15.

importance of additional resources for effectively fulfilling these functions, and recommended that the NHRI advocate for additional resources.[32]

The SCA has made direct recommendations to governments on the need to provide the necessary levels of funding. In 2011, the SCA expressed concerns that after newly assuming an NPM role, the Macedonian NHRI was not provided with the necessary funding. It urged the government to make adequate funding available to the institution.[33] The SCA expressed the same concerns regarding the NHRI in Costa Rica, also urging the government to provide the institution with necessary funding.[34] Reviewing the NHRI again in 2016, the SCA reiterated its concern that while its expanded mandate involving NPM and NMM roles have 'been provided with some additional funding to discharge these mandates … it may not be sufficient to effectively carry out its mandate'.[35] The SCA urged the government to provide the NHRI with adequate financial resources 'to enable it to properly fulfil its obligations, including carrying out its mandate as NPM and NMM'.[36]

Additional resources should include staffing. Accrediting the NHRI in Cyprus with B-status in 2015, the SCA noted that its mandate had 'increased significantly over the past years, with no concurrent increase in allocated resources'.[37] Observing that the NHRI had been designated with both NPM and NMM functions, the SCA noted that it had not increased its budget or staff. In addition, two staff from the NHRI had been seconded to a governmental institution and three vacancies had been recalled in spite of being budgeted.[38]

8.4 Effectiveness as a Treaty-mandated Mechanism

The SCA will seek concrete examples of the role of the NHRI as a treaty-mandated national mechanism. Deferring its accreditation decision on the Armenian NHRI in 2011, the SCA observed that the institution's new head appointed in that year 'has not yet had the opportunity to provide examples of how it completely fulfils its obligations under the OPCAT as the NPM'. Referring to Article 19 of OPCAT, the SCA noted that under its NPM role the NHRI should:

32 ibid.
33 SCA, 'Accreditation Report—Macedonia (Ombudsman of the Republic of Macedonia (ORM))' (October 2011) 10.
34 SCA, 'Accreditation Report—Costa Rica (Defensoria de los Habitantes de Costa Rica (DHCR))' (October 2011) 12.
35 SCA, 'Accreditation Report—Costa Rica (DHCR)' (November 2016) 18.
36 ibid.
37 SCA, 'Accreditation Report—Cyprus (Commissioner for Administration and Human Rights (CAHR))' (November 2015) 8.
38 ibid.

(a) ... regularly examine the treatment of the persons deprived of their liberty in places of detention as defined in article 4, with a view to strengthening, if necessary, their protection against torture and other cruel, inhuman or degrading treatment or punishment;
(b) ... make recommendations to the relevant authorities with the aim of improving the treatment and the conditions of the persons deprived of their liberty and to prevent torture and other cruel, inhuman or degrading treatment or punishment, taking into consideration the relevant norms of the United Nations;
(c) ... submit proposals and observations concerning existing or draft legislation.[39]

In this context, the SCA requested that the NHRI provide it with the recommendation, proposals and observations it made to the authorities and in relation to existing or draft legislation, before its next review in 2012.[40] Examining the Armenian NHRI again in 2013, besides commenting on appropriate levels of funding including for its mandated NPM role and the operation of its regional offices, the SCA acknowledged 'the improvement in the work of the National Preventive Mechanism and encourages the HRDA to continue efforts to strengthen its relationship with civil society'.[41] In a subsequent 2019 review of the NHRI, the SCA acknowledged that its budget had 'significantly increased since the previous review', and advised that the institution continue to advocate for adequate levels of resources to effectively carry out its mandate including for its additional NPM functions.[42]

Accrediting the Human Rights Ombudsman of the Republic of Slovenia (HRORS), the SCA acknowledged the 'effective work' of the NHRI as NPM. Referring to Article 18(4) OPCAT, it highlighted that institutions appointed as NPMs ought to be developed in line with the Paris Principles.[43] The SCA has also expressed concern about the independent functioning of a number of NHRIs with an NPM mandate, for example Azerbaijan and Mauritania, as discussed further in Chapter 10.2.

8.5 Comment

This chapter has shown that for NHRIs also acting as NMMs and/or NPMs, the SCA has mostly focused its attention on structural issues of funding and other resources,

[39] SCA, 'Accreditation Report—Armenia (The Human Rights Defender of the Republic of Armenia (HRDA))' (October 2011) 11–12 (ellipsis in original).
[40] ibid.
[41] SCA, 'Accreditation Report—Armenia (HRDA)' (May 2013) 7.
[42] SCA, 'Accreditation Report—Armenia (HRDA)' (March 2019) 16.
[43] SCA, 'Accreditation Report—Slovenia (HRORS)' (March/April 2010) 8–9.

and the status of the treaty-mandated mechanism in the NHRI's enabling law. Where NHRIs do have these mandates in addition to their promotion and protection functions, they must be given additional and adequate resources so as not to impair the ability of the institution to carry out their broad mandate and functions as NHRIs, which may ultimately also reduce their ability to fulfil their responsibilities as NPMs and/or NMMs. The approach of the SCA is in keeping with the International Coordinating Committee (now GANHRI)'s 2008 Nairobi Declaration, which stated that NHRIs should 'consider their designation as national preventive mechanism ... only if the necessary powers and resources are made available to them'.[44]

The SCA has only commented to a limited extent on the implementation of NPM/NMM functions in practice. Even in those cases, its observations were general and did not reflect on the content, quality, or concrete impact of the NHRI's work, and made no references to substantive issues an NPM/NMM mechanism should work on in a specific country context. The approach of the SCA here may be to avoid overstepping into the work of the SPT, which has the responsibility for assessing the effectiveness of NPMs and has developed specialized expertise.[45] However, that is not to say that the SCA does not pay attention to the work of the NHRI as a treaty-mandated mechanism. The SCA will consider the work of an NHRI as NMM/NPM when assessing the institution's overall work as a human rights body (see for example, Azerbaijan, Chapter 10.2.1). The SCA has paid less attention to the role of NHRIs as NMMs under CRPD. This may in part be because of the activity of civil society and the SPT in relation to the structure, functioning, and effectiveness of NPMs.

The NGO, the Association for the Prevention of Torture (APT) is highly active in analysing NPM institutional set-ups. It has noted that while the OPCAT refers to the Paris Principles, inviting State Parties to consider them when establishing NPMs,[46] this 'has been interpreted as providing a source of inspiration rather than criteria for assessment'[47] and that although the SCA's accreditation process can strengthen NHRIs acting as NPMs, 'its role is also limited given that the Paris Principles are broad in nature and designed for general purpose human rights

[44] The Nairobi Declaration (adopted on 24 October 2008) paras 39–43.

[45] For examples of the detailed nature of SPT recommendations to NPMs see SPT, 'Report on the visit made by the Subcommittee on Prevention of Torture and Other Cruel, Inhuman or Degrading Treatment or Punishment for the purpose of providing advisory assistance to the national preventive mechanism of Honduras' (25 January 2013) UN Doc CAT/OP/HND/3; SPT, Visit to the former Yugoslav Republic of Macedonia undertaken from 23 to 29 April 2017: observations and recommendations addressed to the national preventive mechanism—Report of the Subcommittee' (26 March 2018) UN Doc CAT/OP/MKD/2.

[46] OPCAT, Art 18 (4) (n 1).

[47] APT, 'APT Briefing series: National Human Rights Institutions as National Preventative Mechanisms: Opportunities and challenges' (December 2013), 4–5 <https://www.apt.ch/sites/default/files/publications/apt-briefing-on-nhris-as-npms-en.pdf> accessed 17 February 2021 (hereafter APT, 'APT Briefing series: National Human Rights Institutions as National Preventative Mechanisms: Opportunities and challenges').

bodies.'[48] It has further noted that some of the Paris Principles are not relevant for OPCAT's own framework and others are overridden by its more detailed guidelines for NPMs.[49] In this context, the SPT in its third annual report also explicitly stated that NHRI 'accreditation should not be used as a procedure for accreditation of national mechanisms in general, since it is for the Subcommittee to make such assessments.'[50] The SPT's Guidelines detail basic principles for NPMs and issues related to their establishment and operation for states and the NPMs themselves.[51] The SCA focuses rather on the NHRIs role as, or as part of, the NPM more generally when accrediting the NHRI.

The APT has expressed a number of general concerns regarding NHRIs acting as NPMs under OPCAT. Referring to the SPT's Guidelines,[52] it recommends that NPM units/departments should be given budgetary and operational autonomy within the NHRIs themselves, allowing them to decide their programmatic work and use of resources as per their needs and own judgement.[53] It emphasized that even if an NHRI is well-resourced, it does not automatically ensure that its NPM activities are too, as the resources of the NPM are influenced by the NHRI's internal resource allocation decisions. In this context, arguing for internal autonomy of SPT units within NHRIs, the APT noted that the 'broad mandate of an NHRI can detract focus from the specialized and resource intensive NPM function.'[54] The SCA to date has not examined the allocation of resources within the NHRI for the NPM, in keeping with its overall approach that it is for NHRIs themselves to determine the allocation of their resources based on the needs within the country. This is in line with its approach seen in General Observations 1.9 (Chapter 4.3.1) and 1.10 (Chapter 5) that NHRIs should be free to determine their institutional priorities based on the needs in the state. However, the APT appears to highlight that this could potentially be problematic for the NPM mandate.

The APT's analysis of NHRIs acting as NPMs also extends to staffing, methodological, and other institutional design issues, which it argues arise from differences between the 'generic' institutional nature of NHRIs (with broad mandates) versus the specific nature of NPMs. On the issue of staffing, the APT has highlighted that NHRIs tend to staff their institutions with lawyers and persons with legal background, but NPMs ideally require staff from more diverse backgrounds such as medical staff, child and gender specialists, and psychologists.[55] On methodology/

[48] ibid.
[49] ibid.
[50] SPT, 'Third annual report of the Subcommittee on Prevention of Torture and Other Cruel, Inhuman or Degrading Treatment or Punishment' UN Doc CAT/C/44/2 (25 March 2010) 17.
[51] SPT, 'Guidelines on national preventative mechanism' (9 December 2010) UN Doc CAT/OP/12/5.
[52] ibid.
[53] APT, 'APT Briefing series: National Human Rights Institutions as National Preventative Mechanisms: Opportunities and challenges' (n 47) 10.
[54] ibid 12 The APT report notes that there are some NHRIs where the NPM mandate has a ring-fenced budget.
[55] ibid 13.

tools used for implementing the mandate of NPMs in practice, the APT observed that the focus of certain types of NHRIs (such as ombudsman offices) are often more reactive, driven by complaints-based work rather than preventative. This sits somewhat in contrast with the approach of NPMs, which should be preventative and deploy methodologies that explicitly advance their preventative mandate.[56] The APT argues that for some NHRIs with more 'legalistic' mandates, a preventative approach might be challenging, as it 'requires a multidisciplinary "policy" approach to issues of deprivation of liberty'.[57] Lastly, the APT underlines that the institutional set up of NHRIs (eg ombudsman, commission-style institutions, or consultative bodies) are also relevant for understanding how their characteristics influence or determine the set-up of NPM units within them.[58]

A 2012 joint publication by the APT, the OHCHR and the Asian Pacific Forum of National Human Rights Institutions (APF) on torture prevention echoed guidance and observations similar to the APT's own. They argued that besides additional financial resources and legislative changes to enabling law(s), which the SCA mostly focuses on, for NHRIs to effectively fulfil NPM roles they will need organizational restructuring and additional human and logistical resources.[59] The joint publication also stresses that NHRIs may need to adopt new working methods (from being reactive to preventive) in line with their new preventative mandate, recommends the establishment of a new separate NPM unit within NHRIs, and emphasized the need for a professional diversity of staff, not to have only lawyers but also medical staff, among others.[60]

Overall, the approach of the SCA appears to recognize that it does not have the specific expertise to assess the performance of NHRIs serving as NMMs, and especially NPMs. The SCA rather recognizes that the SPT has that expertise and mandate for the NPM, and the SCA will invariably cite comments made by them and other treaty bodies as to the NMM/NPM. The SCA appears to be aware that the desire would be to have the NPM or NMM as a separate unit or entity within the NHRI, with its own separate funding and staff, and, while the SPT has said funding for the NPM should be ring-fenced, the SCA does not require it to be a separate entity or unit, as the SCA believes the NHRI should have the independence and autonomy to determine where it will allocate its resources. There are situations also where the NHRI is only part of the NPM/NMM in such cases it would be even more difficult for the SCA to assess performance. Sufficiency of funding is a much

[56] ibid 17.
[57] ibid 21.
[58] ibid 15.
[59] OHCHR, APT and the Asia Pacific Forum of National Human Rights Institutions (APF) 'Preventing Torture: An Operational Guide for National Human Rights Institutions' (May 2010) HR/PUB/10/1, 100–02.
[60] ibid 102.

simpler and objective issue—and in practice the NHRI has often informed the SCA of funding shortfalls or failure of the state to provide any or adequate resources to enable it to carry out its functions.[61]

The next chapter will consider what we term 'challenging cases' where the SCA reviews NHRIs that operate in difficult national contexts such as situations of armed conflict or unrest, where there are gross violations of human rights, where they may be under threat, or where rule of law has seen significant decline.

[61] For example, in reviewing the NHRI in Panama in 2017, the SCA reaccredited it with A-status even though the NHRI reported insufficient funds to establish the NPM. SCA, 'Accreditation Report—Panama (The Defensoría del Pueblo de la República de Panamá (DPRP))' (November 2017) 25.

9
Challenging Cases

9.1 Introduction

This chapter examines how the Sub-Committee on Accreditation (SCA) has dealt with what we term 'challenging cases'. These are situations where the National Human Rights Institution (NHRI) is operating in a highly challenging national climate such as during a time of coup or armed conflict (such as Afghanistan), or where rule of law is under significant threat (such as Hungary), or where it or its members come under direct threat of harm (such as Togo). As will be seen, the SCA approaches these different types of situations in a similar manner. Relying on its General Observation on situations of coup or national emergency, set out below, it applies the same principles to a number of other situations where there is a national-level crisis that may impact the NHRI's ability to effectively function. These cases often come before the SCA by way of a special review (see Chapter 2.5), rather than periodic re-accreditation.

This chapter is structured somewhat differently to previous chapters in that it includes contextual information from external (non-SCA) sources when discussing the SCA reviews. While a detailed description of the relevant country contexts is beyond the limits of this book, a brief overview is provided in this chapter to help explain the circumstances of the particular country. This chapter necessarily therefore provides a limited overview of the selected cases, all of which presented the SCA with different national and institutional contexts, and thus, different challenges. The SCA itself does not currently include information on the circumstances relevant to the country in its reports, outside of the information that may come directly to it from civil society or United Nations (UN) mechanisms, as discussed in Chapter 2.6.

Occasionally, the SCA recognizes that an NHRI is operating in a challenging context without specifying further the nature of that context. For example, in the case of the Philippines' Commission on Human Rights (CHRP), in 2017 the SCA 'commend[ed] the CHRP for its continuing efforts to promote and protect human rights despite the challenging context in which it operates. The SCA acknowledges the efforts of the CHRP in advocating for a stronger legislative framework through the proposed CHR Act, and it encourages the CHRP to continue these efforts, and advocate for further amendments.'[1] In recommending re-accreditation of A-status

[1] SCA, 'Report and Recommendations of the Sub-Committee on Accreditation—Philippines (Commission on Human Rights of the Philippines CHRP)' (March 2017) 29 (hereafter SCA, 'Accreditation Report').

National Human Rights Institutions. David Langtry and Kirsten Roberts Lyer, Oxford University Press. © David Langtry and Kirsten Roberts Lyer 2021. DOI: 10.1093/oso/9780198829102.003.0010

for the Palestine Independent Commission for Human Rights (PICHR) in 2015, the SCA stated it 'acknowledges that the PICHR continues to be an effective national human rights institution, carrying out a broad range of activities to promote and protect human rights despite operating in a particularly difficult and volatile political and security environment'.[2]

9.2 NHRIs during a Coup or National Emergency

The SCA provides guidance for NHRIs that operate during a coup d'état or state of emergency, including on what they are expected to specifically monitor and how to conduct their activities. It has set this out in General Observation 2.5 (2018):[3]

> G.O. 2.5 NHRIs during the situation of a coup d'état or a state of emergency
> In the situation of a coup d'état or a state of emergency, it is expected that an NHRI will conduct itself with a heightened level of vigilance and independence, and in strict accordance with its mandate.
>
> NHRIs are expected to promote and ensure respect for human rights, democratic principles and the strengthening of the rule of law in all circumstances and without exception. In situations of conflict or a state of emergency, this may include monitoring, documenting, issuing public statements and releasing regular and detailed reports through the media in a timely manner to address urgent human rights violations.[4]

In its justification, the SCA provides the following rationale:

> The Paris Principles[5] do not explicitly give guidance on the expected conduct of an NHRI when its country is experiencing a state of emergency or coup d'état. However, Paris Principle A.1 clearly specifies that NHRIs shall have the responsibility to promote and protect human rights. Furthermore, Paris Principle A.3 specifies the powers and responsibilities of an NHRI including:

[2] SCA, 'Accreditation Report—Palestine (Palestine Independent Commission for Human Rights PICHR)' (November 2015) 34–35.

[3] SCA, 'General Observations of the Sub-Committee on Accreditation' (adopted on 21 February 2018) GO 2.5, 41 (hereafter SCA, 'General Observations' (February 2018)). This General Observation has seen multiple number changes over the years. It was initially General Observation number 5.1, which later changed to GO 2.6 in the 2013 version, and then to GO 2.5 in the 2018 version.

[4] ibid.

[5] Principles relating to the Status of National Institutions, UNGA Res 48/134 (20 December 1993) UN Doc A/RES/48/134 (The Paris Principles).

- reporting on human rights violations (Paris Principle A.3(a)(ii)–(iii));
- monitoring and reporting on government action or inaction (Paris Principle A.3(a)(iv)); and
- publicizing its views on any matters concerning the promotion and protection of human rights (Paris Principle A.3(a)). This responsibility is further elaborated in Paris Principle C(c), which provides the capacity to address public opinion directly or through any press organ, particularly in order to publicize its opinions and recommendations.

While the impact of emergency circumstances varies from one case to another, the SCA is aware that they almost always have a dramatic impact on the rights recognized in international human rights standards, particularly on vulnerable groups. Disruptions to peace and security in no way nullify or diminish the relevant obligations of the NHRI. As in other comparable situations, those obligations assume greater practical importance in times of particular hardship. In such circumstances, the protection of human rights becomes all the more important, and NHRIs must ensure that individuals have accessible and effective remedies to address human rights violations.

NHRIs, as independent and impartial bodies, play a particularly important role by investigating allegations of violations promptly, thoroughly and effectively. As such, NHRIs will be expected to promote and ensure respect for human rights, democratic principles and strengthening the rule of law in all circumstances without exception. This may include issuing public statements and releasing regular and detailed reports through the media in a timely manner to address urgent human rights violations.

In order to fulfil its obligations, it is necessary that the NHRI continue to conduct itself with a heightened level of vigilance and independence in the exercise of its mandate. The SCA will scrutinize the extent to which the NHRI concerned has taken steps to the maximum of its available resources to provide the greatest possible protection for the human rights of each individual within its jurisdiction.

Excerpt from the Paris Principles

A. Competence and responsibilities—

1. A national institution shall be vested with competence to promote and protect human rights.

3. A national institution shall, inter alia, have the following responsibilities:

(a) To submit to the Government, Parliament and any other competent body, on an advisory basis either at the request of the authorities concerned or through the exercise of its power to hear a matter without higher referral, opinions, recommendations, proposals and reports on any matters concerning the promotion and protection of human rights; the national institution may decide to publicize them; these opinions, recommendations, proposals and reports, as well as any prerogative of the national institution, shall relate to the following areas:

...

(ii) Any situation of violation of human rights which it decides to take up;
(iii) The preparation of reports on the national situation with regard to human rights in general, and on more specific matters;
(iv) Drawing the attention of the Government to situations in any part of the country where human rights are violated and making proposals to it for initiatives to put an end to such situations and, where necessary, expressing an opinion on the positions and reactions of the Government;

C. Methods of operation—
Within the framework of its operation, the national institution shall:

...

(c) Address public opinion directly or through any press organ, particularly in order to publicize its opinions and recommendations.[6]

NHRIs are expected to act as independent and impartial human rights bodies even during situations of coups d'état.[7] The SCA reviewed the Honduran NHRI (CONADEH) in 2010, by way of a special review.[8] It identified significant problems with the NHRI's activities following a military-led coup d'état that had taken place in 2009. Human rights groups had expressed concern about the human rights situation during and after the coup, including the failure of authorities to address serious human rights abuses such as torture, beatings, mass arrests of those opposed to the coup, sexual violence by security forces, killing of journalists, intimidation of opposition leaders and human rights activists, and the removal of judges who were critical of the coup.[9] In a report about human rights violations related to the coup, the UN High Commissioner for Human Rights made similar observations.[10] The SCA commented in some detail about its concerns on the activities of the NHRI during the coup situation. Referring to its 2009 General Observations on the human rights mandate, on recommendations by NHRIs and the NHRI annual report, the SCA set out the extent of the problematic nature of the NHRI:

[6] SCA, 'General Observations' (February 2018) (n 3) 41.

[7] SCA, 'Accreditation Report—Timor-Leste (Provedoria for Human Rights and Justice (PHRJ))' (April 2008) 8.

[8] SCA, 'Accreditation Report—Honduras (Comisionado Nacional de los Derechos Humanos de Honduras (CONADEH)' (October 2010) 9–10.

[9] See for example, Amnesty International, 'Press release: Honduras failing to tackle coup rights abuses' (28 June 2010) <https://www.amnesty.org/en/press-releases/2010/06/honduras-failing-tackle-coup-rights-abuses/> accessed 12 August 2020; Human Rights Watch, 'Honduras After the Coup: Ongoing Violence, Intimidation, and Impunity in Honduras' (December 2010) <https://www.hrw.org/sites/default/files/reports/honduras1210webwcover_0.pdf> accessed 12 August 2020.

[10] See OHCHR, 'Report of the United Nations High Commissioner for Human Rights on the violations of human rights in Honduras since the coup d'état on 28 June 2009' (3 March 2010) UN Doc A/HRC/13/66 <https://documents-dds-ny.un.org/doc/UNDOC/GEN/G10/117/00/PDF/G1011700.pdf?OpenElement> accessed 12 August 2020.

1. No documentary evidence was provided to address all the concerns raised by the UN High Commissioner in her report to the Human Rights Council on the violations of human rights in Honduras since the coup d'état (A/HRC/13/66). The CONADEH provided a letter to the SCA Chairperson as a response to the issues of concern, which states: 'the High Commissioner's Report was drafted in a malicious manner with a minimum part of proved facts'. In its report the CONADEH states to have sent [*sic*] a letter to the President of the Congress regarding the CONADEH's disagreement with the measures taken during the coup d'état.
2. …
3. Although the CONADEH has a broad mandate to promote and protect human rights (Articles 1 and 9 of the Organic Law 153-1995), no documentary evidence on the performance of the CONADEH was submitted. According to the UN High Commissioner's report, the CONADEH failed to fulfil its protection mandate. In this regard, the 2009 Annual Report describes some actions taken by the CONADEH during the coup d'état, however its content is weak and does not provide detailed and substantive information on the alleged human rights violations and how the CONADEH addressed those violations. The Annual Report does not provide details such as numbers of victims subsequent to the coup d'état, the violations committed, the complaints received or cases investigated. There is also no indication in the Report on the monitoring activities, recommendations or advice provided to the Government.[11]

Further, the SCA noted a number of problematic statements made by the NHRI:

4. The Annual Report contains statements made by the CONADEH that support the Government following the coup d'état, which brings into question the independence of the national institution.
5. The Annual Report reflects the lack of interaction between the CONADEH and the International Human Rights system. In the Annual Report the CONADEH questioned and criticized the role and reports of international observers such as the Organisation of American States (OAS) and the UN during the crisis in Honduras. The Report states the International Mission of Observers 'lied in its report on the human rights situation in Honduras' …
6. The Report of the UN High Commissioner on the Human Rights Violations in Honduras since the coup d'état on 28 June 2009, reflects the lack of co-operation between the CONADEH and the NGOs and other civil society

[11] SCA, 'Accreditation Report—Honduras (CONADEH)' (October 2010) 9.

organisations. Moreover, the CONADEH states in its letter that no NGOs exist in Honduras.[12]

The SCA recommended that the NHRI be downgraded to B-status, which took place in October 2011, following the failure by the institution to provide information on its conformity with the Paris Principles.[13]

During situations of coup d'état or national emergency, NHRIs must act independently, and be perceived as doing so. Reviewing the NHRI of Thailand (NHRCT) in March 2014, and deferring its accreditation, the SCA raised concerns about the institution's independence in the context of civil unrest taking place in the country.

In 2010, Thailand saw mass political mobilization, protests and eventually armed clashes between security forces and some armed anti-government protesters, which according to Amnesty International, resulted in several deaths and more than 2,000 people wounded.[14] Human Rights Watch reported that both state security forces and some factions of armed opposition groups committed serious human rights violations, however, mostly opposition-led groups were prosecuted while security forces were not held accountable for serious abuses, including for reportedly using live ammunition on peaceful protesters,[15] and for the alleged torture and mistreatment of detainees as part of government crackdown.[16] Political mobilization and protests continued in 2013, resulting in violence between pro and anti-government groups, leading again to some deaths, several injuries and clashes with security forces.[17] Reportedly, impunity for human rights violations committed by state security forces continued.[18]

In its March 2014 review, the SCA stated it had received 'reports that some NHRCT staff members display publicly their political affiliations whilst

[12] ibid 9–10.

[13] SCA, 'Accreditation Report—Honduras (CONADEH)' (October 2011) 20. CONADEH was accredited with B-status in May 2016. SCA, 'Accreditation Report—Honduras (CONADEH)' (May 2016) 37–40. While commending CONADEH for 'its continuing efforts to promote and protect human rights despite the challenging context in which it operates' the SCA highlighted concerns around selection and appointment, immunity, pluralism, adequate funding, cooperation with other human rights bodies, and interaction with the international human rights system.

[14] Amnesty International, 'Thailand: Time to end human rights violations—Amnesty International Submission to the UN Universal Periodic Review' (October 2011) <https://www.amnesty.org/download/Documents/28000/asa390012011en.pdf> accessed 24 February 2021; Human Rights Watch, 'Descent into Chaos: Thailand's 2019 Red Shirt Protests and the Government Crackdown' (3 May 2011) <https://www.hrw.org/report/2011/05/03/descent-chaos/thailands-2010-red-shirt-protests-and-government-crackdown> accessed 6 September 2020.

[15] ibid.

[16] United States Department of State, 'Country Reports on Human Rights Practices for 2011: Thailand' <https://2009-2017.state.gov/j/drl/rls/hrrpt/2011humanrightsreport/index.htm?dlid=186310#> accessed 6 September 2020.

[17] Human Rights Watch, 'World Report 2014: Thailand—Events of 2013' <https://www.hrw.org/world-report/2014/country-chapters/thailand> accessed 6 September 2020.

[18] Amnesty International, *The State of the World's Human Rights, Amnesty International Report 2014/2015* (Amnesty International 2015) 365.

undertaking their official functions'.[19] The SCA emphasized the problematic nature of this, because 'in situations of political unrest, such as currently exist in Thailand, victims of human rights violations may find it difficult to approach the NHRCT if it is clear that some staff are politically affiliated with the alleged violators'.[20] The SCA underlined that during civil unrest the NHRI is expected to maintain its independence.[21]

The substantive action undertaken by the NHRI during a situation of coup d'état is particularly relevant—as was seen in the case of Honduras, above. The SCA raised concerns in this regard in relation to the NHRI of Thailand. Referring to General Observation 1.6 on recommendations by NHRIs, and as noted above in Chapter 7 on reporting on human rights violations, the SCA expressed its concerns 'about the failure of the NHRCT to release a timely report on the violent demonstrations that occurred in 2010',[22] which was only released in 2013. Reviewing the NHRI again in October 2014, following the deferral decision in March the same year, the SCA recommended that the NHRI be downgraded from A to B-status. The SCA commented that the NHRI had not been addressing serious violations in a timely manner, taking three years to complete and publish a report.[23] Further, the NHRI had not produced a report on 2013 demonstrations that had resulted in significant deaths and injuries.[24]

Reviewing the Thailand NHRI again in November 2015, following the one-year period in which the NHRI had the opportunity to address the SCA's concerns, the SCA downgraded the institution to B-status. The SCA cited the same issues as it had previously, about the lack of timeliness of the NHRI's actions following demonstrations, violence and the excessive use of state force, with the NHRI taking 3 years to publish its report after unrest in 2010 and up to 2 years after unrest in 2013 and 2014 (the report was published in November 2015). The SCA reiterated 'its concern that the NHRCT has not been addressing human rights violations in a timely manner'.[25]

The substantive actions of the NHRI in continuing its reporting functions are thus particularly important for the SCA. Accrediting the Sri Lankan NHRI (The Human Rights Commission of Sri Lanka (SLHRC)) with B-status in 2009, the SCA stated its concerns that:

> The SLHRC does not appear to have released regular and detailed reports or statements in relation to killings, abductions and disappearances stemming from the

[19] SCA, 'Accreditation Report—Thailand (National Human Rights Commission of Thailand (NHRCT))' (March 2014) 19.
[20] ibid.
[21] ibid.
[22] ibid.
[23] SCA, 'Accreditation Report—Thailand (NHRCT)' (October 2014) 33.
[24] ibid 34.
[25] SCA, 'Accreditation Report—Thailand (NHRCT)' (November 2015) 40.

human rights crisis in Sri Lanka. While the SCA acknowledges the work of the SLHRC's regional offices in extremely difficult circumstances, it reemphasises the need for the SLHRC to carry out its core protection mandate to demonstrate its vigilance and independence during the ongoing state of emergency.[26]

In contrast, when accrediting Mongolia's NHRI with A-status in November 2008, the SCA appreciated the NHRI for 'having carried out its mandate in a difficult and volatile political and security related situation'.[27]

9.3 NHRIs in Conflict Zones

Several NHRIs operate, or have operated, in active conflict zones, including in environments with protracted armed conflicts and/or country contexts in which armed or non-armed groups are competing for control of territory with the government beyond the framework of sound democratic institutions and rule of law. This section examines a number of cases when the SCA reviews NHRIs in such country contexts, in order to illustrate the challenges for, and the approach taken by, the SCA.

Among all the accredited NHRIs, the NHRI of Afghanistan has operated in one of the most challenging environments over the lengthiest period. In 2008, observers reported that Afghanistan was experiencing heightened violence and conflict since the fall of the Taliban government in Kabul, ousted by US and NATO (North Atlantic Treaty Organization) military forces.[28] The ensuing conflict resulted in conflict-related civilian deaths,[29] and reportedly in violations of international human rights and humanitarian law with high levels of impunity.[30] In 2013 and 2014, there were reportedly thousands of civilian deaths, internally displaced persons, and elections marred by armed violence, followed by lack of accountability for forces involved in killing or mistreating civilians.[31] By 2019, the conflict had not

[26] SCA, 'Accreditation Report—Sri Lanka (SLHRC)' (March 2009) 5.

[27] SCA, 'Accreditation Report—Mongolia (National Human Rights Commission (NHRC))' (November 2008) 9.

[28] Human Rights Watch, 'World Report 2009: Afghanistan events of 2008' <https://www.hrw.org/world-report/2009/country-chapters/afghanistan> accessed 27 September 2020.

[29] United States Department of State, '2008 Country Reports on Human Rights Practices—Afghanistan, 2007' (25 February 2009) <https://www.refworld.org/docid/49a8f1b0c.html> accessed 27 September 2020.

[30] Amnesty International (n 18) 45.

[31] Human Rights Watch, 'Words Reports 2014: Afghanistan—Events of 2013' <https://www.hrw.org/world-report/2014/country-chapters/afghanistan> accessed 18 February 2021; United States Department of State, '2014 Country Reports on Human Rights Practices—Afghanistan' (25 June 2015) <https://www.refworld.org/docid/559bd58728.html>; Amnesty International, 'Amnesty International Report 2014/2015—Afghanistan, 2015' (25 February 2015) <https://www.refworld.org/docid/54f07e2215.html> accessed 21 February 2021.

abated and continued causing thousands of civilian deaths.[32] Armed groups specifically targeted members of Afghanistan's NHRI, resulting in the killing of two staff members in 2015, and in the abduction and killing of the acting head of the institution in 2019.[33]

At time of writing, the SCA had reviewed the NHRI on six occasions: in 2007 (twice), 2008, 2013, 2014, and 2019. Many of the challenges faced by the NHRI were not specific to it but were faced by institutions in the country as a whole, for example funding[34] and independent appointments.[35] In October 2007, the SCA accredited the NHRI with A-status, but emphasized that funding from external donors and development partners should not constitute the core income of the NHRI, as it is the responsibility of the state.[36] Reviewing this issue again in November 2008, the SCA stated it 'recognizes the need for the international community to continue to engage and support the AIHRC in order to ensure it receives adequate funding, until such time when the State will be able to cover the AIHRC's adequate funding'.[37] The SCA also expressed concerns over attempts to set budgetary constraints or amendments to the institution's legal structure including about its appointment process, which it stated could undermine the independence and the effectiveness of the institution.[38] The SCA noted that the NHRI carries out 'its mandate in a difficult and volatile political and security related context and [encouraged it] to continue its vigilant role in monitoring, promoting and protecting human rights'.[39]

A particular challenge the SCA has faced with the AIHRC is that while the institution made considerable efforts to be an active promoter and protector of human rights, it also faced significant government interference with its independence. Reviewing the institution in 2013, the SCA deferred its accreditation decision. The SCA reflected that the NHRI had been 'carrying out a broad range of activities to promote and protect human rights while operating in a particularly difficult and volatile political and security environment' and also praised the NHRI for 'recent inquiries and reports, which detail human rights violations in times of conflict,

[32] United Nations Assistance Mission in Afghanistan, 'Afghanistan: Protection of Civilians in Armed Conflict 2019' (February 2020) 34–35 <https://unama.unmissions.org/sites/default/files/afghanistan_protection_of_civilians_annual_report_2019.pdf> accessed 18 February 2021; Human Rights Watch, 'World Report 2020: Afghanistan—Events of 2019' <https://www.hrw.org/world-report/2020/country-chapters/afghanistan> accessed 27 September 2020.

[33] Amnesty International, 'Afghanistan: Human rights defenders under attack' (28 August 2019) <https://www.amnesty.org/en/latest/news/2019/08/afghanistan-human-rights-defenders-under-attack/> accessed 18 February 2021.

[34] SCA, 'Accreditation Report—Afghanistan (Human Rights Commission (AHRC))' (March 2007) 5.

[35] ibid.

[36] SCA, 'Accreditation Report—Afghanistan (Independent Human Rights Commission (AIHRC))' (October 2007) 8.

[37] SCA, 'Accreditation Report—Afghanistan (AIHRC)' (November 2008) 11.

[38] ibid.

[39] ibid.

and human rights violations experienced by women and girls … [which] help to address impunity for past violations and promote a culture that is receptive to human rights.'[40] However, the SCA also raised significant concerns about selection and appointment, staffing (particularly the gender imbalance of 81 per cent men to 19 per cent women) and adequate funding (the state provided just 4 per cent of the AIHRC's funding). Specifically, the SCA noted that members of the NHRI, including its chairpersons are 'appointed largely at the discretion of the President of the Republic',[41] and that the enabling law does not provide details on the criteria and process for selecting and appointment them. The SCA also noted national and international criticism regarding recent appointments,[42] including on the lack of requirements for experience in human rights for vacancies. Reflecting more in detail on the different aspects of a selection process that ensures pluralism promotes independence and are formalized in laws and regulations, the SCA encouraged the NHRI to 'engage with the President' and referred to the General Observation on selection and appointment.[43] On staffing, the SCA noted the significant gender imbalance, referring to General Observation 2.4 on the recruitment and retention of NHRI staff (see further Chapter 4.8), and commented extensively on adequate funding. It underlined that the majority of the NHRI's budget comes from international donors. While the SCA saw that as being critical for the moment for its effectiveness, it stressed that it is the responsibility of the state to provide core funding. The SCA recommended B-status accreditation for the NHRI unless and until these concerns they were addressed.[44] Reviewing the institution again in 2014, the SCA accredited it with A-status. It acknowledged again that the NHRI carried out a 'broad range of activities to promote and protect human rights despite operating in a particularly difficult and volatile political and security environment'.[45] Further, it noted the NHRI's 'response to SCA recommendations made in November 2013, including its successful advocacy for a Presidential Decree establishing a merit-based selection and appointment process for Commissioners,

[40] SCA, 'Accreditation Report—Afghanistan (AIHRC)' (November 2013) 16.

[41] ibid 17.

[42] For example, the President of the Republic did not fill various Commissioner vacancies at the NHRI between 2011 and 2013, and the NHRI also received criticism from the United Nations High Commissioner for Human Rights on the lack on inclusivity, transparency, or participation in for the process for appointing new Commissioners. See Human Rights Watch, 'World Report: Afghanistan—Events of 2014' <https://www.hrw.org/world-report/2014/country-chapters/afghanistan> accessed 18 February 2021. Human Rights Committee, 'Report of the United Nations High Commissioner for Human Rights on the situation of human rights in Afghanistan and on the achievements of technical assistance in the field of human rights in 2013' (10 January 2014) UN Doc A/HRC/25/41. See also, Committee on Elimination of Discrimination against Women, 'Concluding observations on the combined initial and second periodic reports of Afghanistan' (30 July 2013) UN Doc CEDAW/C/AFG/CO/1-2.

[43] SCA, 'Accreditation Report—Afghanistan (AIHRC)' (November 2013) 17.

[44] ibid 19.

[45] SCA, 'Accreditation Report—Afghanistan (AIHRC)' (October 2014) 16.

and increased funding from the government'.[46] At the same time, it encouraged the institution to continue 'vigilance in monitoring, promoting and protecting human rights in Afghanistan, and its pursuit of improvements to the structure and staffing of the Commission'.[47]

Referring to General Observation 1.6. on recommendations by NHRIs and General Observation 2.7 on limitation of power of NHRIs due to national security, it noted that the NHRI's access for monitoring may be restricted to some detention and prison facilities.[48] The SCA stressed that the 'NHRI should continue to seek access to all places of detention in order to effectively monitor, investigate and report on the human rights situation in a timely manner ... [and] undertake rigorous and systematic follow up activities and advocate for the consideration and implementation of its findings and recommendations in order to ensure the protection of those detained'.[49] Reviewing the NHRI again in 2019, the AIHRC was re-accredited with A-status. The SCA commended 'the efforts undertaken by the AIHRC to promote and protect human rights in the challenging context in which it operates, including by taking public stands on sensitive issues. The SCA encourages the AIHRC to continue to address human rights issues in an active manner.'[50] The SCA did note that the NHRI has not advocated for the abolition of death penalty (but had advocated for its limitation) and also commented on its concerns around monitoring places of deprivation of liberty by the NHRI, adequate funding, and the ambiguity of the term of office for commissioners.[51]

Overall, it is clear that the AIHRC acted in a manner that fully met the expectations of an NHRI operating for the promotion and protection of human rights. This is particularly the case for an NHRI that is operating not only in a highly volatile and challenging national environment but also with direct threats and attacks against its own personnel. The situation of the NHRI is a stark contrast to the actions of the NHRIs of Thailand, Honduras, and Burundi, also discussed in this chapter, where little concrete action was taken in response to human rights violations. It can be seen from its assessments of Afghanistan, that the SCA has been cognizant of national environment while not ignoring issues of concern regarding Paris Principles compliance.

[46] ibid.
[47] ibid.
[48] ibid 17–18.
[49] ibid.
[50] SCA, 'Accreditation Report—Afghanistan (AIHRC)' (October 2019) 7.
[51] ibid 7–8.

9.4 Situations of Gross Violations of Human Rights

A number of NHRIs operate in countries where there have been gross violations of human rights. The SCA expects that the NHRI will actively engage with these issues. At its May 2016 meeting, the SCA decided to initiate a special review of Burundi's NHRI (CNIDH). A wave of anti-government protests began in April 2015 in response to President Pierre Nkuruziza's announcement that he would seek a third term in office.[52] An attempted coup d'état in May failed and Nkuruziza initiated a series of reprisals and supported general suppression of oppositional activity.[53]

The SCA's report indicates that it 'received information which calls for it to initiate a special review to ensure that the CNIDH continues to operate in full compliance with the Paris Principles'.[54] Precisely what information was received is not specified by the SCA, as the May 2016 review was to determine whether or not to open a special review, and the NHRI had not been provided with the opportunity to respond. But in its November 2016 report, the SCA notes that civil society organizations allege that the CNIDH:

- Is perceived as having taken positions that do not demonstrate independence from government;
- Has not taken a position vis-à-vis abuses by security forces and militias in respect of certain gross human rights violations, including arbitrary detention and extrajudicial executions; and
- Has underreported instances of serious human rights violations, including with respect to incidences of torture and the existence of mass graves.[55]

Furthermore, the SCA took note of the UN Independent Investigation on Burundi:

> which asserts that the CNIDH has issued one report since the crisis erupted, and that 'The report downplays gross human rights violations by indicating minimal numbers. As an illustration, for the whole of 2015, the report refers to 27 cases of torture and ill-treatment in contrast to 250 cases of torture and ill-treatment documented by OHCHR between April 2015 and April 2016'.[56]

[52] Amnesty International, 'Amnesty International Report 2015/16—Burundi' (24 February 2016) <www.refworld.org/docid/56d05b6c15.html> accessed 19 February 2021.

[53] ibid.

[54] SCA, 'Accreditation Report—Burundi (Commission nationale indépendante des droits de l'homme (CNIDH))' (May 2016) 50.

[55] SCA, 'Accreditation Report—Burundi (CNIDH)' (November 2016) 61.

[56] ibid, citing Human Rights Council, 'Report on the independent investigation on Burundi carried out pursuant to Human Rights Council resolution S-24/1' (25 October 2016) UN Doc A/HRC/33/37.

In response to the SCA's concerns, the CNIDH provided information on its activities, including:

- Development of a strategy on the monitoring of human rights violations relating to the 2015 electoral period which defines CNIDH's role in the prevention, monitoring, and responses to human rights violations during the electoral period;
- Activities undertaken by the CNIDH during the electoral period to promote human rights, including organisation of training and advocacy workshops for a wide range of stakeholders i.e. local administration, judiciary and police, religious leaders, women and youth leaders of the province of Bujumbura;
- Visits to 13 places of detention including prisons and custody cells where coup leaders and demonstrators against the candidacy of the outgoing President were detained;
- Recommendations made to the Ministry of Justice on the situation of juvenile detainees; and
- Declarations and press releases issued throughout the electoral process.[57]

The CNIDH President also provided information on the following areas, according to the SCA report:

> the dissolution of the network of human rights observers; cooperation with civil society organisations; regularity of visits of place of detention; neutral position of CNIDH; actions undertaken to protect women victims of human rights violation and rape; downscaling of number of killings reported; number of complaints received; protection of internally displaced persons and refugees; cooperation with the international human rights mechanisms i.e. UN independent investigation on the situation of human rights in Burundi and military armed groups.[58]

The SCA review resulted in a recommendation to downgrade the CNIDH to B-status. Similar to the case of Venezuela, the SCA recognized and took account of the 'volatile' political situation and 'extremely difficult circumstances' in which the CNIDH was operating, and noted that it had 'taken this into account in arriving at this decision'.[59] Notwithstanding the NHRI's responses, the SCA concluded that the 'CNIDH has not spoken out in a manner that promotes protection for human rights in response to credible allegations of gross human rights violations having been committed by government authorities. The failure to do so demonstrates a lack of its independence.'[60] Accordingly, the SCA invoked Article 18.1 of the Global

[57] SCA, 'Accreditation Report—Burundi (CNIDH)' (November 2016) 61.
[58] ibid 62.
[59] ibid 61.
[60] ibid 62.

Alliance of NHRIs (GANHRI) Statute[61] and gave the CNIDH one year to provide evidence of continued compliance with the Paris Principles.

In finalizing its recommendation to downgrade the NHRI to B-status in November 2017, the SCA considered information from the CNIDH about its activities in 2016 and 2017. However, it also took into account the following information:

> The September 2017 report of the United Nations Commission of Inquiry on Burundi (A/HRC/36/54) which confirms the persistence of grave human rights violations, including extrajudicial executions, enforced disappearances, torture and cruel, inhuman or degrading treatment or punishment, and sexual violence. The report indicates that most of these violations are committed by members of the police, the army and the youth league of the ruling party. With respect to the CNIDH, the report notes is stating [*sic*] 'the lack of independence of the national institutions for monitoring the authorities' actions in the field of human rights, namely the Independent National Human Rights Commission'.[62]

The SCA also noted the finding of a UN Treaty Body about the NHRI:

> The November 2016 Concluding Observations of the Committee on the Elimination of Discrimination against Women (CEDAW/C/BDI/CO/5-6) which states: 'The Committee welcomes the statutory establishment of the Independent National Human Rights Commission in 2011, but is concerned that the independence of the National Commission may be jeopardized by its insufficient action taken to investigate and report on allegations of human rights violations, including acts of violence against women'.[63]

The CNIDH's responses to this information seem to have been of particular concern to the SCA:

> the Commission of Inquiry confirms the persistence of grave human rights violations, including extrajudicial executions, enforced disappearances, torture and cruel, inhuman or degrading treatment or punishment, and sexual violence. When asked to characterize the current human rights situation in Burundi, the CNIDH indicated that the situation has improved, that the number of formal requests they have received has decreased and the number of recorded human rights violations has also decreased. The SCA is of the view that this response is

[61] GANHRI Statute (adopted on 15 March 2019). This provision was the same in the statute in force in 2016.

[62] SCA, 'Accreditation Report—Burundi (CNIDH)' (November 2017) 49–50.

[63] ibid 50.

> inadequate and demonstrates an unwillingness to appropriately respond to credible allegations of serious human rights violations having been committed.[64]

While noting again the 'volatile and extremely difficult circumstances' in which the NHRI operates, the SCA concluded that, in its view:

> the CNIDH does not discharge its mandate in a manner that promotes respect for human rights in response to credible allegations of serious human rights violations having been committed by the authorities and has failed to demonstrate a willingness to speak out on all human rights issues. The failure to do so demonstrates a lack of independence . . . Given all the material before it, the SCA is of the view that Burundi is facing a sudden and dramatic change in the internal political order of a state, considering gross violations of human rights noted in particular by the Commission of Inquiry on Burundi, and this is accompanied by the fact that the CNIDH acts in a way that seriously compromises its compliance with the Paris Principles.[65]

In the initial application for accreditation by the NHRI of Myanmar (NHRC), the SCA noted reports from the UN Human Rights Council and civil society 'highlighting concerns about human rights violations occurring as a result of situations of armed conflict between the government and different ethnic groups, as well as internal unrest between different ethnic and religious groups'.[66] The SCA recognized that the MNHRC had 'conducted some inquiries and made some public statements' but emphasized the requirements of General Observation on human rights mandate and NHRIs during the situation of a coup d'état or a state of emergency, and accredited the institution with B-status.

9.5 NHRIs under Threat of Harm

The SCA has, on occasion, had to deal with the situation of NHRIs which come under direct threat from their own state. Following the publication of a report by the NHRI in early 2012 on allegations of torture by the security services in Togo during a period of unrest in 2009, the head of the NHRI had to flee the country with his family because of serious threats to his safety that were carried out to try to pressure him to change findings of the report.[67] In its 2012 review of the country,

[64] ibid 50.
[65] ibid 51.
[66] SCA, 'Accreditation Report—Myanmar (National Human Rights Commission (NHRC))' (November 2015) 12.
[67] This is referenced in Committee Against Torture, 'Concluding observations on the second periodic report of Togo, adopted by the Committee at its forty-ninth session (29 October–23 November 2012)' (11 December 2012) UN Doc CAT/C/TGO/CO/2, para 14.

the UN Committee Against Torture called on Togo to 'investigate the reasons that led [the NHRI head] to leave the country and take all the protection measures and provide all the guarantees that would allow the safe return to the country of [the NHRI head] and his family should he decide to come back'.[68] The head of the NHRI, Koffi Kounté, sought asylum in France with his family.[69] In assessing the re-accreditation application of the Togo NHRI in 2013, the SCA put particular emphasis on the efforts the institution had made:

> The SCA commends the CNDH for the steps it has taken to protect its independence in the wake of the threats and harassments received following the release of its investigative report into allegations of torture committed by the State's Intelligence Service. As investigation and reporting into human rights violations are considered to be core functions of the NHRI's protection function, it is expected that in a situation where the NHRI receives threats against its independence, it will continue to conduct itself with a heightened level of vigilance and in strict accordance with its mandate.
>
> The SCA remains concerned about the failure of the national authorities to protect and defend the independence of the CNDH through the issuance of public statements or by instituting criminal investigations into allegations of threats against and harassment of CNDH members.[70]

The SCA re-accredited the NHRI with A-status because of the continued efforts made by the institution to act independently for the promotion and protection of human rights in accordance with its mandate.

9.6 NHRIs where Rule of Law Is under Threat

A number of NHRIs operate in a national context where rule of law is under threat and democratic institutions are under pressure from authoritarian or undemocratic governments. This section reviews the SCA's observations on two NHRIs that operate in such environments: Hungary and Poland.

[68] ibid para 14(d).

[69] Koffi Kounté, 'Une conscience' (Amnesty International, France, 1 June 2012) <www.anctogo.com/koffi-kounte-une-conscience-8367> accessed 18 February 2021; Africa Rdv, '"Koffi Kounté peut rentre au Togo" (Officiel)' (29 July 2019) <https://www.africardv.com/societe/koffi-kounte-peut-rentrer-au-togo-officiel/> accessed 19 February 2019.

[70] SCA, 'Accreditation Report—Togo (National Human Rights Commission (CNDH))' (May 2013) 17.

9.6.1 Hungary

The Commissioner for Fundamental Rights of Hungary (CFR) has been operating in an environment where rule of law has been gradually and systematically eroded. Since 2010, Hungary has witnessed a gradual but steady democratic backsliding. Numerous domestic, European Union (EU), and international organizations and institutions have documented the country's rule of law crisis. Following elections in 2010, media independence and plurality[71] and the independence of the judiciary deteriorated,[72] while attacks on civil society organizations[73] and civil liberties[74] increased. The government also put pressure on the independence of courts,[75] attacked the independence of higher education institutions,[76] and undermined the fairness of elections creating an increasingly uneven playing field for opposition political parties,[77] leading both Freedom House[78] and the Varieties of Democracy Institute (V-dem),[79] to classify Hungary by 2020 as the first 'non-democracy' within the EU. In 2018, the European Parliament adopted a resolution stating that there was a clear risk of a serious breach of the EU founding values in Hungary including on issues of judicial independence, freedom of expression, and

[71] See for example, International Press Institute and Others, 'Joint International Press Freedom Mission to Hungary' (3 December 2019) <https://ipi.media/wp-content/uploads/2019/12/Hungary-Conclusions-International-Mission-Final.pdf> accessed 23 February 2021, and Centre for Media Pluralism and Media Freedom, 'Media Pluralism Monitor 2016, Country report: Hungary' 2016 <https://cadmus.eui.eu/bitstream/handle/1814/46799/Hungary_EN.pdf?sequence=1&isAllowed=y> accessed 23 February 2021.

[72] See for example, International Bar Association's Human Rights Institute, 'Still under threat: the independence of the judiciary and the rule of law in Hungary' (October 2015) <https://www.ibanet.org/Document/Default.aspx?DocumentUid=a00b5f64-4b05-4b25-81c6-5e507c45cc74> accessed 23 February 2021.

[73] Hungarian Civil Liberties Union and Others, 'Timeline of Governmental Attacks Against Hungarian Civil Society Organisations' (17 November 2017) <http://www.helsinki.hu/wp-content/uploads/Timeline_of_gov_attacks_against_HU_NGOs_17112017.pdf> accessed 23 February 2021.

[74] See for example, Venice Commission and Organisation for Security and Cooperation in Europe (OSCE)/Office for Democratic Institutions and Human Rights (ODIHR), 'Joint Opinion on the Provisions of the so-called "Stop Soros" draft legislative package which directly affects NGOs' (25 June 2018) CDL-AD(2018)013-e <https://www.venice.coe.int/webforms/documents/default.aspx?pdffile=CDL-AD(2018)013-e> accessed 23 February 2021.

[75] See for example Human Rights Watch. 'European Union: Events of 2019—Hungary' <https://www.hrw.org/world-report/2020/country-chapters/european-union#fa79c3> accessed 23 February 2021; Amnesty International, 'Hungary: 2019' <https://www.amnesty.org/en/countries/europe-and-central-asia/hungary/report-hungary/> accessed 23 February 2021.

[76] See for example, Venice Commission, 'Preliminary Opinion on Act XXV of 4 April 2017 On the Amendment of ACT CCIV of 2011 on National Tertiary Education' (11 August 2017) CDL-PI(2017)005-e <https://www.venice.coe.int/webforms/documents/default.aspx?pdffile=CDL-PI(2017)005-e> accessed 23 February 2021.

[77] See for example, OSCE/ODIHR, 'ODIHR Limited Election Observation Mission Final Report: Hungary Parliamentary Elections 8 April 2018' (27 June 2018) <https://www.osce.org/odihr/elections/hungary/385959?download=true> accessed 23 February 2021.

[78] Freedom House, 'Nations in Transit 2020: Hungary country report' <https://freedomhouse.org/country/hungary/nations-transit/2020> accessed 23 February 2021.

[79] V-Dem Institute, 'Autocratization Surges—Resistance Grows: Democracy Report 2020' (March 2020) 16–17 <https://www.v-dem.net/media/filer_public/de/39/de39af54-0bc5-4421-89ae-fb20dcc53dba/democracy_report.pdf> accessed 23 February 2021.

rights of minorities, among others.[80] The European Commission's first Rule of Law Report (2020) also underlined several aspects of demise of democratic institutions in Hungary.[81]

Over the course of this period (2010–2020), the SCA has reviewed Hungary's NHRI (CFR) three times. The case of Hungary's NHRI was also discussed in Chapter 7.3.2 on NHRI's human rights activities. Reviewing the CFR in 2013, and deferring its accreditation decision, the SCA commented on the CFR's human rights mandate, lack of functions to encourage ratification or accession to human rights instruments, interaction with the human rights system, selection and appointment procedures, pluralism of staff, and on limitations due to national security.[82] Specifically on its human rights mandate, the SCA encouraged the NHRI to expand the range of its promotional activities, 'including in relation to human rights education generally, and minorities in particular, and to advocate for the express inclusion of a promotion mandate in the amending legislation'.[83] The SCA also observed that 'vacancies in the posts of Commissioner and Deputies are neither widely advertised, nor is there broad consultation'.[84] The SCA also recommended to the NHRI that it develop 'policies and procedures to ensure that its staff is broadly representative of the society in which it operates'.[85] Referring to the General Observation on limitations due to national security, the SCA noted that such a limitation 'should not be unreasonably or arbitrarily applied and should only be exercised under due process ... [and recommended] that Section 23 of the CFR law be interpreted in such a way as to ensure that the CFR can carry out effective investigations into the relevant bodies'.[86] Accrediting the NHRI with A-status in 2014, the SCA referenced amendments that had been made to the NHRI's enabling law and found that they 'address the SCA's previously stated concerns with respect to the promotional mandate of the CFR'.[87] Comparing the SCA's recommendation made from 2014 to 2013, it repeated its concerns only about selection and appointment procedures.[88]

[80] European Parliament, 'Rule of Law in Hungary: Parliament calls on the EU to act' (12 September 2018) <https://www.europarl.europa.eu/news/en/press-room/20180906IPR12104/rule-of-law-in-hungary-parliament-calls-on-the-eu-to-act> accessed 23 February 2021.

[81] European Commission, '2020 Rule of Law Report: Country Chapter on the rule of law situation in Hungary' (30 September 2020) SWD(2020) 316 final <https://ec.europa.eu/info/sites/info/files/hu_rol_country_chapter.pdf> accessed 23 February 2021.

[82] SCA, 'Accreditation Report—Hungary (Commissioner for Fundamental Rights (CFR))' (November 2013) 10–12.

[83] ibid 10.

[84] ibid 11.

[85] ibid 12.

[86] ibid 12.

[87] SCA, 'Accreditation Report—Hungary (CFR)' (October 2014) 9.

[88] Apart from this, the SCA made observations about the importance of interaction with the international human rights system, noted that some of the publications of the NHRI are only available in English, encouraging it to make them available in the local language, and observed that under the amended enabling law it may encourage the ratification or accession to international human rights instruments. SCA, 'Accreditation Report—Hungary (CFR)' (October 2014) 10–11.

Democratic decline in Hungary accelerated following national elections in the country in 2014. The NHRI's next review took place in 2019, during which the SCA extensively commented on the grounds for deferral and referred to details of a telephone interview with the NHRI. It particularly highlighted concerns raised by UN Treaty Bodies and other UN human rights mechanisms about the CFR. These concerns included:

- Steps taken to implement the SCA's October 2014 recommendation regarding selection and appointment;
- The concerns expressed by the UN Committee on the Elimination of Racial Discrimination in 2019 that it lacked information about the work of the CFR to prevent racial discrimination and xenophobia against vulnerable ethnic minorities including migrants, refugees and asylum seekers;
- The concerns expressed by the Special Rapporteur on the situation of human rights defenders in 2017 that amendments to the CFR enabling law and the lack of enforceability of its recommendations have weakened its protection mandate in relation to certain rights;
- The further concerns expressed by the Special Rapporteur on the situation of human rights defenders in 2017 that, despite its mandate, the CFR has been reluctant to refer complaints to the Constitutional Court for review in cases that it deems political or institutional;
- The concerns expressed by the Special Rapporteur on the situation of human rights defenders, the Special Rapporteur on the promotion and protection of the right to freedom of opinion and expression, the UN Human Rights Committee and others regarding the 'Foreign Funded Organizations Act', and whether the CFR has taken any public position with respect to this law and what actions it has taken to promote and protect the rights of human rights defenders and civil society organizations.[89]

The SCA noted that the CFR had provided insufficient information and responses to these issues and deferred the accreditation decision on two key grounds. First, that the existing laws did not meet the standards required for the advertising of vacancies, criteria for assessing and selecting candidates and broad consultation and/or participation in the application and selection process.[90] In July 2019, the Hungarian Parliament appointed a new Ombudsperson leading the NHRI, without an open call or consultation for candidates.[91] The second ground for deferral the

[89] SCA, 'Accreditation Report—Hungary (CFR)' (October 2019) 23–24 (bullet points in original).
[90] ibid 24–25.
[91] According to reports, in 2019 a new Ombudsperson was appointed by the Parliament, where the ruling parties hold a constitutional supermajority. There was no open call for the vacancy, and consultations did not take place with civil society organization. The ruling party-appointed Ombudsperson has served in various governmental positions under the previous terms of the ruling party, including

SCA highlighted were a range of specific areas where the CFR had not engaged on human rights violations. These were noted previously in Chapter 7 and covered issues of vulnerable ethnic minorities, petitions to the Constitutional Court and the anti-civil society 'foreign funded organizations act'.[92] The SCA found that the information provided by the NHRI 'does not demonstrate adequate efforts in addressing all human rights issues, nor has it spoken out in a manner that promotes and protects all human rights'.[93] Implicitly referring to the well-documented deterioration of rule of law in Hungary, the SCA underlined the need for NHRIs to interpret their mandate in a 'broad, liberal and purposive manner' and that they are expected to promote and protect human rights, democratic principles and the strengthening of the rule of law 'in all circumstances'.[94]

As regards the SCA's review of Hungary, it can be seen that it has approached the situation of this NHRI in a country where the rule of law is under serious threat similarly to its review of NHRIs in conflict situations, highlighting the need for continued independence, for clear action by the NHRI on human rights violations as well as for public and active engagement to promote and protect international human rights standards. Where such active engagement does not take place, the institution's A-status is at risk.

9.6.2 Poland

In Poland, observers have raised concerns about the undermining of the rule of law particularly since 2015. However, in some contrast to the situation in Hungary, the NHRI in Poland used its position to continue to promote and protect human rights actively. The erosion of the independence of the judiciary was the most prominent issue among a range of setbacks to the country's democratic institutions. Since 2015, the governing party took steps to increase its control of the judiciary including through disciplinary proceedings, legislative changes, political appointments, and governmental takeover of key institutions. Undermining efforts included attempts to control the country's Constitutional Tribunal, the National

in the Ministry of Finance, Ministry of Justice and the Ministry of Interior. The Hungarian Helsinki Committee, 'Assessment of the Activities and Independence of the Commissioner for Fundamental Rights of Hungary in Light of the Requirements Set for National Human Rights Institutions' (September 2019) 4 <www.helsinki.hu/wp-content/uploads/Assessment_NHRI_Hungary_2014-2019_HHC.pdf> accessed 19 February 2021.

92 SCA, 'Accreditation Report—Hungary (CFR)' (October 2019) 25.>

93 ibid.

94 ibid. The SCA noted further issues that were not reasons for deferral but were nonetheless relevant to accreditation. These included concerns about adequate funding and about low levels of staff salaries at the NHRI and about interaction with the international human rights system, noting that the NHRI has made limited use of international and regional human rights mechanism in relation to sensitive issues. SCA, 'Accreditation Report—Hungary (CFR)' (October 2019) 26.

Council of the Judiciary, and the Supreme Court's Disciplinary Chamber, which launched proceedings against judges and prosecutors critical of the government's moves to weaken judicial independence.[95] In 2020, the European Court of Justice (ECJ) ordered the suspension of powers of the Disciplinary Chamber,[96] following infringement proceedings launched by the European Commission.[97] In 2017, the European Commission had triggered the Article 7(1) of the Treaty on European Union[98] procedure on the basis that there was a clear risk of serious breach of rule of law in Poland,[99] and launched infringement proceedings in relation to two other judicial independence-related issues in 2017 and 2018.[100] Extreme right-wing and anti-liberal discourse, and restrictive measures by government actors against lesbian, gay, bisexual, transgender/transsexual, intersex, and queer and questioning (LGBTIQ) and women's rights have been well-documented by observers as other contributing to the decline of civil and political rights in the country.[101]

In the context of decline of the rule of law, the NHRI in Poland has been also under pressure. It was the target of a smear campaign by public broadcasters.[102] Ruling party officials called for the dismissal of the head of the NHRI for addressing LGBTIQ rights, and the NHRI's budget was significantly cut, among other measures.[103] These promoted a statement of support from the European Network of National Human Rights Institutions (ENNHRI) together with the Global Alliance

[95] Freedom House, 'Poland, Nations in Transit 2020' <https://freedomhouse.org/country/poland/nations-transit/2020> accessed 3 August 2020.

[96] Court of Justice of the European Union, 'Order of the Court in Case C-791/19 R Commission v Poland: Poland must immediately suspend the application of the national provisions on the powers of the Disciplinary Chamber of the Supreme Court with regard to disciplinary cases concerning judges' (8 April 2020) Press release No 47/20 <https://curia.europa.eu/jcms/upload/docs/application/pdf/2020-04/cp200047en.pdf> accessed 3 August 2020.

[97] European Commission, 'Rule of Law: European Commission launches infringement procedure to safeguard the independence of judges in Poland' (29 April 2020) <https://ec.europa.eu/commission/presscorner/detail/en/ip_20_772> accessed 3 August 2020.

[98] Consolidated versions of the Treaty on European Union and the Treaty on the Functioning of the European Union (TFEU) [2016] OJ C202/1, Art 7(1).

[99] European Commission, 'Reasoned Proposal in Accordance with Article 7(1) of the treaty on European Union Regarding the Rule of Law in Poland: Proposal for a Council Decision on the determination of a clear risk of a serious breach by the Republic of Poland of the rule of law' (20 December 2017) COM (2017) 835 final <http://ec.europa.eu/newsroom/just/document.cfm?action=display&doc_id=49108> accessed 22 February 2021.

[100] For an overview about the history of EC infringement proceedings and related ECJ judgements about judicial independence in Poland, see for example the European Commission (n 97); Amnesty International, 'Country report: Poland 2019' <https://www.amnesty.org/en/countries/europe-and-central-asia/poland/report-poland/> accessed 22 February 2021.

[101] See for example: Human Rights Watch, 'Poland: Events of 2019—Part of the EU Chapter', <https://www.hrw.org/world-report/2020/country-chapters/poland> accessed 3 August 2020; United States State Department, 'Human Rights country reports: Poland 2019', <https://www.state.gov/wp-content/uploads/2020/02/POLAND-2019-HUMAN-RIGHTS-REPORT.pdf> accessed 3 August 2020; Freedom House, 'Freedom in the World 2020: Poland' <https://freedomhouse.org/country/poland/freedom-world/2020> accessed 3 August 2020.

[102] Freedom House (n 95).

[103] Human Rights Watch, 'Eroding Checks and Balances: Rule of Law and Human Rights Under Attack in Poland' (24 October 2017) <https://www.hrw.org/report/2017/10/24/eroding-checks-and-balances/rule-law-and-human-rights-under-attack-poland#_ftn35> accessed 4 August 2020.

of NHRIs (GANHRI) and other regional and international human rights bodies in 2016[104] and 2019.[105] There was also a joint visit of the Council of Europe, Office of the High Commission for Human Rights (OHCHR), OSCE, and ENNHRI, where they underlined that the NHRI was 'considered . . . by many actors as a model national human rights institution', and noted that they discussed with the NHRI the 'institutional landscape in Poland and the environment in which the Ombudsman's Office is currently operating'.[106]

The Polish NHRI, the Commissioner for Human Rights (CHRP), also referred to as the Polish ombudsperson, was reviewed and re-accredited with A-status by the SCA in 2017. Reflecting on the challenging context in which the NHRI was operating, the SCA commended 'the efforts of the CHRP in discharging its mandate effectively despite the challenging political context in which it operates and expresses appreciation to the current Commissioner, Dr. Adam Bodnar, for his continued commitment and good work in fulfilling his mandate'.[107]

The SCA noted some ongoing issues of concern including that the CHRP's mandate does not cover 'the full range of functions that a NHRI should undertake in exercising its promotional mandate'.[108] It also noted that the NHRI's enabling law does not require the pluralistic representation of various groups in its composition, that the NHRI provided information about gender balance and presence of staff with disabilities, and encouraged the institutions 'to advocate for amendments to its enabling legislation to require a pluralistic composition in its membership and staff'.[109] It expressed concern about functional immunity, noting that that Poland's Constitution provides that the head of the NHRI (Commissioner) 'shall not be subject to penal liability nor deprived of liberty without the earlier consent of Parliament',[110] but that 'officers, including Deputy Commissioners, and staff of the CHRP do not enjoy similar protection'.[111] In this context, the SCA highlighted the language of its 2013 General Observation 2.3 (guarantee of functional immunity)[112] on immunity that 'external parties may seek to influence the independent operation of an NHRI by initiating, or by threatening to initiate, legal

[104] ENNHRI, 'ENNHRI Statement of Support for Poland's Commissioner for Human Rights' (28 October 2016) <http://ennhri.org/wp-content/uploads/2019/09/General-Assembly-Statement-of-Support-for-Poland%E2%80%99s-Commissioner-for-Human-Rights.pdf> accessed 4 August 2020.

[105] ENNHRI, 'Joint Statement in Support of the Polish Commissioner for Human Rights' (June 2019) <www.ennhri.org/wp-content/uploads/2019/09/Joint-Statement-in-Support-of-the-Polish-Commissioner-for-Human-Rights.pdf> accessed 3 August 2020.

[106] Council of Europe and Others, 'Joint statement from meeting in Warsaw with the Office of the Polish Ombudsman' (1 March 2016) <https://www.ohchr.org/Documents/Issues/Defenders/JointStatementPolishCommissionerforHR.pdf> accessed 3 August 2020.

[107] SCA, 'Accreditation Report—Poland (The Commissioner for Human Rights (CHRP))' (November 2017) 26.

[108] ibid 27.

[109] ibid.

[110] ibid.

[111] ibid.

[112] SCA, 'General Observations of the Sub-Committee on Accreditation' (adopted in May 2013) GO 2.3.

proceedings against a member'.[113] The SCA encouraged the NHRI to 'advocate for amendments to its enabling legislation to protect the Deputy Commissioners and staff members of the CHRP from legal liability for actions undertaken by them in good faith in their official capacity'.[114] Finally, the NHRI reported to the SCA that it does not have 'adequate resources to effectively fulfil its mandate, including as the NPM [National Preventative Mechanism]'.[115]

9.7 Comment

It is clear from the reviews discussed in this chapter that in assessing NHRIs operating in challenging contexts, the SCA focuses on the acts of the institution. It places less attention on the context in which an institution operates, and how that may affect its work. This is understandable, because the grading and the observations of the SCA are about the institution itself, and the context in which it is operating is not the fault of the NHRI, nor is the SCA a monitoring body for the overall human rights situation in a country. Two of the examples above have particularly illustrated this approach. The Polish Ombudsperson continued to be an active and public defender of human rights in the face of serious efforts by the government to undermine human rights, thus, its A-status was not at risk. In contrast, the Hungarian NHRI appeared to be silent or have been silenced by the government, meaning its A-status may be lost (it was under review at time of writing). The SCA has taken a similar approach in reviewing the Russian Federation's NHRI (High Commissioner for Human Rights in the Russian Federation (OCHR)) over the course of its accreditations between 2014 and 2019. While the rule of law situation in Russia has been challenging for the entire period of the SCA's existence, a clear decline and corresponding rise in autocracy took place over that same period. The SCA has focused on the level of engagement undertaken by the NHRI as a promoter and protector of human rights. As was seen in Chapter 7.3.2, at time of writing the A-status of the NHRI was under threat due to the SCA's concerns regarding its activities. In particular, the SCA commented:

> The SCA is of the view that the information provided by the OCHR to date is insufficient to satisfy it that the OCHR has made adequate efforts in addressing all human rights issues, and that it has spoken out in a manner that promotes and protects all human rights.[116]

[113] SCA, 'Accreditation Report—Poland (The Commissioner for Human Rights (CHRP))' (November 2017) 27.
[114] ibid 28.
[115] ibid.
[116] SCA, 'Accreditation Report—Russia (High Commissioner for Human Rights in the Russian Federation (OCHR))' (October 2019) 27–28.

The examples in this chapter show the challenges for the SCA in assessing an NHRI in a country that has a national emergency or severely declining human rights situation. While an NHRI is not expected to be able to solve all the human rights issues in its country, the SCA's reviews show that it is expected to act in a particular way when serious human rights concerns arise. Primarily, it is expected to act as a promoter and protector of human rights when the state retreats from international human rights standards. The necessity of such action by an NHRI is summed up in the following paragraph by the Asian NGO Network on National Human Rights Institutions (ANNI) in its 2014 annual report:

> it is precisely in systematic and widespread incidents of human rights violations that NHRIs are expected to display integrity, moral courage and competence in the exercise of sound judgement and discharge of their duties as well as exhibit sufficient independence from executive influence to warrant any public credibility.[117]

The SCA takes the approach that even in a difficult national situation, such as a coup d'état, NHRIs are still expected to act in a manner that is consistent with their role as promoters and protectors of human rights. The SCA focuses on the institution, not the country, and the above examples of Afghanistan and Poland illustrate that in practice, an NHRI can indeed be a promoter and protector of human rights even in a non-human rights or rule of law respecting state.

The next chapter considers a number of situations where the NHRI has failed to act as a Paris Principles-compliant human rights body and has lost its A-status, further illustrating the approach of the SCA in scrutinizing the human rights activities of NHRIs.

[117] ANNI, *2014 ANNI Report on the Performance and Establishment of National Human Rights Institutions in Asia* (Asian Forum for Human Rights and Development, 2014) 9.

10
Losing A-status
Special Reviews and Downgrading

10.1 Introduction

In the period of work of the Sub-Committee on Accreditation (SCA) covered by this book, there have been a number of National Human Rights Institutions (NHRIs) who have lost their A-status accreditation following a special review or re-accreditation. That is, they have been 'downgraded' to B-status due to either their actions or their inaction. This chapter examines some of these instances in a case-study format. This chapter does not focus on one specific SCA general observation but looks overall at the situation of the discussed NHRIs and in what circumstances they lost their A-status accreditations. In that regard, this chapter aims to identify the combination of institutional gaps and engagement failures that may result in the loss of Paris Principles-compliant status.[1]

It may also be noted that not every instance where an NHRIs has been downgraded is included here. Other cases are provided elsewhere in this book. For example, in the case of Thailand (Chapter 7 and Chapter 9), its NHRI, the National Human Rights Commission of Thailand, was downgraded from A- to B-status in 2014/2015 for its failure to act in a Paris Principles-compliant manner during a situation of national emergency.

There are a number of SCA provisions which emphasize how NHRIs are the most likely to lose their A-status through the SCA procedure. SCA Practice Note 2 (2017) on special reviews indicates the type of situation where the SCA may have particular concerns about the continued Paris Principles compliance, and is at risk of downgrading:

> In accordance with Article 16.2 of the GANHRI Statute, the SCA may initiate a Special Review where it appears that the circumstances of any A-status NHRI may have changed in a way that affects compliance with the Paris Principles.
>
> In practice, this may include, but is not limited to, situations where:
>
> • the enabling law of the NHRI has been amended significantly;

[1] Principles relating to the Status of National Institutions, UNGA Res 48/134 (20 December 1993) UN Doc A/RES/48/134 (The Paris Principles).

National Human Rights Institutions. David Langtry and Kirsten Roberts Lyer, Oxford University Press. © David Langtry and Kirsten Roberts Lyer 2021. DOI: 10.1093/oso/9780198829102.003.0011

- there has been a significant political change that impacts adversely on the ability of the NHRI to fulfill its mandate;
- the conduct of the NHRI—such as a failure to respond adequately or in a timely manner to serious rights violations—call into question the institution's independence; or
- the SCA has received credible information from a third party that the circumstances of the NHRI have changed.[2]

Special reviews have been initiated relatively frequently by the SCA—see Table 10.1—because of the conduct of the institution. Other special reviews have been initiated because there has been a change to the mandate or enabling law of the NHRI (Nepal, 2012–14),[3] or dismissal of senior leadership (Ecuador, 2018–19,[4] Chile, 2018,[5] Panama 2019[6]). In these instances, A-status was retained. The SCA has also considered downgrading where there have been changes to internal regulations (Indonesia, 2013–14),[7]

SCA Practice Note 3 (2017) is also illustrative here in that it sets out the areas the SCA will review for accreditation of the institution:

> The SCA assesses compliance with the Paris Principles in both law and practice. When assessing applications for accreditation, re-accreditation and special or other reviews, it will consider:
>
> - Whether the organizational structure of the NHRI—including its staff complement and budget—lends itself to effective functioning.
> - Whether the provisions of the enabling law are sufficient to allow the institution to function effectively and independently.
> - Whether the NHRI is able to carry out its mandate effectively and without interference.
> - Whether the NHRI demonstrates independence in practice and a willingness to address the pressing human rights issues.
>
> ...

[2] SCA, 'Practice Note 2: Special Reviews' (6 March 2017).

[3] SCA, 'Report and Recommendations of the Session of the Sub-Committee on Accreditation—Nepal (National Human Rights Commission (NHRC))' (November 2012) 32 (hereafter SCA, 'Accreditation Report'); SCA, 'Accreditation Report—Nepal (NHRC)' (May 2013) 23–24; SCA, 'Accreditation Report—Nepal (NHRC)' (October 2014) 37–38.

[4] SCA, 'Accreditation Report—Ecuador (Defensoría del Pueblo de Ecuador (DPE))' (May 2018) 41; SCA, 'Accreditation Report—Ecuador (DPE)' (October 2018) 24; SCA, 'Accreditation Report—Ecuador (DPE)' (October 2019) 30.

[5] SCA, 'Accreditation Report—Chile (Instituto Nacional de Derechos Humanos (INDH))' (May 2018) 41–42; SCA, 'Accreditation Report—Chile (INDH))' (October 2018) 25.

[6] SCA, 'Accreditation Report—Panama (Defensoría del Pueblo de Panamá (DPP))' (October 2019) 30. The DPP's review was not finalized at time of writing.

[7] SCA, 'Accreditation Report—Indonesia (Komisi Nasional Hak Asasi Manusia (Komnas HAM))' (November 2013) 33; SCA, 'Accreditation Report—Indonesia (Komnas HAM)' (March 2014) 20.

The SCA notes that even an effective NHRI may be criticized by a variety of stakeholders for the way it undertakes its mandate, and that the SCA must independently assess whether those criticism are, or are not, well-founded.

Should the SCA wish to rely on information provided by a third party, the SCA will ensure that the NHRI under review is provided with that information and will provide an opportunity for the NHRI to respond to it.[8]

Finally, Practice Note 4 (2017) covers the siltation of NHRIs in transition, where A-status may be lost because a new institution has been formed, which needs to be re-accredited on its own merit, as follows.

In making this determination, the SCA will first and foremost consider the wording of the new enabling legislation, including whether it:

- changes the name of the existing institution;
- dissolves the previously-existing institution;
- provides that the newly-created institution is a continuation of the previously-existing institution; and
- contains appropriate continuation provisions.

The SCA will further consider whether the newly-created institution:

- maintains or expands its previous mandate; and
- maintains equivalent or strengthened protections in relation to its structure and functioning.

Where the SCA determines that a newly-created institution will be considered a new institution for the purposes of accreditation, it immediately ceases to hold status and cannot rely on the status of its predecessor institution.

General Observation 1.11 on 'Annual reports of NHRIs' requires that new institutions must be in operation for one (1) year prior to submitting their application for accreditation. It further requires that they submit a published annual report to the SCA. In relevant and exceptional circumstances, the SCA may consider accepting an alternate unpublished report from a new institution for the purposes of accreditation.[9]

As regards the practice of the SCA itself, the Global Alliance of NHRIs (GANHRI) Guide[10] on the work of the SCA aims to clarify how it sets out its recommendations where there is a risk an NHRI will lose A-status. The content of the Guide on this

[8] SCA, 'Practice Note 3: Assessing Performance' (6 March 2017) 1–2.

[9] SCA, 'Practice Note 4: NHRIs in Transition' (6 March 2017).

[10] GANHRI, 'A Practical Guide to the Work of the Sub-Committee on Accreditation (SCA)' (December 2017, updated in November 2018) (hereafter GANHRI Guide).

point is set out in detail in Chapter 2.6. However, it is worth briefly recalling here that the Guide provides the reasons for downgrading include where an NHRI has not taken steps to address a previous issue of concern, or because of the conduct of the NHRI 'either as a result of a single incident of sufficient severity or a pattern of conduct'.[11] As also noted in Chapter 2.6, a new paragraph was added to the preamble of the SCA's reports, beginning in May 2018, which indicates how the SCA reports are to be read to understand the reasons for downgrading, in particular with 'notes with concern' being the primary reason for a lack of A-status accreditation.[12]

The institutions that have been downgraded or threatened with downgrading are as follows:

Table 10.1 NHRIs downgraded or threatened with downgrading to B-status

Institution (country)	Year(s) of downgrade	Primary reason for downgrade	Obtained or regained A-status
Algeria	2009	Revisions to enabling law.	No
Bosnia and Herzegovina	2009 (threat)	Range of concerns. Not downgraded.	Avoided downgrading
Nepal	2010 (threat)	Range of concerns.	Avoided downgrading
Norway	2010/11	Creation of reformed/new institution.	New institution created
Senegal	2011–12	Concerns and failure to provide information.	No
Honduras	2011	Failure to address human rights violations.	No
Rwanda	2012 (threat)	Requirement for becoming a commissioner.	Avoided downgrading
Afghanistan	2013/14 (threat)	Range of concerns. Not downgraded.	Avoided downgrading
Paraguay	2013/14	Range of concerns.	Suspended. New accreditation with B-status
Thailand	2014/15	Failure to address human rights violations.	No
Venezuela	2015/16	Failure to address human rights violations.	No
Greece	2016 (threat)	Range of concerns. Not downgraded.	Avoided downgrading

[11] GANHRI Guide, 36–37 (bullet points in original).
[12] SCA, 'Accreditation Report' (May 2018) 5–6.

Table 10.1 Continued

Institution (country)	Year(s) of downgrade	Primary reason for downgrade	Obtained or regained A-status
Burundi	2016/17	Failure to address human rights violations.	No
Mauritania	2017/18	Independence & Failure to address human rights violations.	No
Azerbaijan	2011 (threat) 2017/18	Independence & Failure to address human rights violations.	Avoided downgrading No
Nicaragua	2018/19	Independence & Failure to address human rights violations.	No

The following sections provide an overview of those NHRIs who were downgraded or threatened with downgrading, and where the SCA's concerns were not previously examined as a whole in this book, namely for the NHRIs of Azerbaijan, Mauritania, Nicaragua, Paraguay, Greece, Senegal, and Norway.

10.2 Failure to Address Serious Human Rights Issues

10.2.1 Azerbaijan

The A-status of the Azerbaijan NHRI (HRCA) was in question for a considerable period. In 2009, the United Nations (UN) Committee Against Torture in its concluding observations on Azerbaijan expressed its concern that 'the Ombudsman lacks the requisite degree of independence to be the national institution responsible for investigating complaints of torture and other human rights violations, as well as to serve as the [NPM]'.[13] The Ombudsperson was also re-appointed by a change to the Constitution permitting a further term, rather than by an open appointments process as required under the Paris Principles.[14] These two issues resulted in a special review of the NHRI by the SCA that commenced in 2010. In 2011, the SCA recommended the NHRI be downgraded,

[13] Committee Against Torture, 'Consideration of reports submitted by States parties under article 19 of the Convention, Concluding observations of the Committee against Torture: Azerbaijan' (2 September 2011) UN Doc CAT/C.AZE/CO/3.

[14] SCA, 'Accreditation Report—Azerbaijan (Human Rights Commissioner of the Republic of Azerbaijan (HRCA))' (October 2010) 7. As regards the appointments issue, the Sub-Committee stated that 'pursuant to Constitutional law, the term of the Commissioner expired on 2 July 2009, and a new Commissioner was to be elected 30 days before the end of the Commissioner's term. The Constitutional

with one year to prove compliance. However, following receipt of evidence that it considered demonstrated conformity with the Paris Principles, the NHRI was re-accredited with A-status in 2012.[15]

Azerbaijan's already poor human rights record significantly deteriorated in the mid-2010s. A worsening of the situation for civil society and journalists culminated in 2014 in a heavy crackdown on human rights defenders.[16] The NHRI said little about this situation. In September 2014, the Subcommittee on Prevention of Torture (SPT) suspended its visit to Azerbaijan citing official obstruction.[17] Yet, in the same month the A-status NHRI stated at the Organization for Security and Cooperation in Europe (OSCE) 'as a result of democratic reforms carried out … new progressive laws serving to [*sic*] more efficient protection of human rights were adopted'.[18] It also reported a meeting with then-detained rights activist Leyla Yunus who 'did not complain' about the treatment she received in prison. This was despite publicly available statements from Ms Yunus about being attacked and beaten in her cell.[19] In March 2017, during its periodic re-accreditation, the SCA recommended that the HRCA be downgraded to B-status.[20] The SCA had received information that the HRCA was not operating in full compliance with the Paris Principles. It noted that the information:

> related to actions taken and not taken, and statements made and not made, by the HRCA indicating unwillingness to effectively engage on serious human rights violations, including those relating to torture and conditions of detention, arbitrary detention, freedom of expression, and the protection of human rights defenders.[21]

law at that time did not provide for the possibility of re-appointment of the Commissioner. The current Commissioner did not leave office following the expiration of her term, and on 26 November 2009, an amendment to the Constitutional law was passed which allowed the incumbent to be re-appointed for an additional 7-year term, and the current Commissioner was re-appointed for a second term on 5 March 2010. This process raised concerns with the SCA as to the independence regarding the transparency of the appointment procedures and the independence of the HRCA, which concerns were not sufficiently addressed by the HRCA.'

15 SCA, 'Accreditation Report—Azerbaijan (HRCA)' (March 2012) 28–29.

16 See for example, Human Rights Watch, 'World Report 2014: Azerbaijan Events of 2013' <https://www.hrw.org/world-report/2014/country-chapters/azerbaijan> accessed 20 February 2021, stating, '[t]he Azerbaijani government's poor record on freedom of expression, assembly, and association dramatically deteriorated during the year'.

17 OHCHR, 'Prevention of Torture: UN human rights body suspends Azerbaijan visit citing official obstruction' (17 September 2014) <www.ohchr.org/EN/NewsEvents/Pages/DisplayNews.aspx?NewsID=15047&LangID=E> accessed 16 February 2021.

18 OSCE, 'Human Dimension Implementation Meeting 22 September to 3 October Warsaw, Poland: Speech by Aydin Safikhanli, Head of the Office of the Commissioner for Human Rights (Ombudsman) of the Republic of Azerbaijan: Activity of the Azerbaijani Ombudsman as a National Preventative Mechanism against torture' Doc No HDIM.DEL/0127/14.

19 See for example, International Federation for Human Rights, 'Azerbaijan: Acts of violence in prison against Ms. Leyla Yunus' (12 September 2014) <https://www.fidh.org/en/region/europe-central-asia/azerbaijan/16031-azerbaijan-acts-of-violence-in-prison-against-ms-leyla-yunus> accessed 20 February 2021.

20 This decision was challenged by the NHRI. See SCA, 'Accreditation Report' (March 2017) 1.

21 SCA, 'Accreditation Report—Azerbaijan (HRCA)' (March 2017) 17.

In particular, the SCA considered the following concerns and responses of the NHRI:

- The 2015 Concluding Observations of the Committee against Torture in which it expressed concern that the HRCA, in its role as NPM, 'has not been effective in addressing the main problematic issues related to the prevention of torture and human rights violations in places of deprivation of liberty', as well as the Human Rights Committee in its 2016 Concluding Observations noted that it 'is concerned about the mechanism's effectiveness in preventing torture and ill-treatment and other violations in places of deprivation of liberty'.

  At the session, the SCA provided the HRCA with the opportunity to respond to these observations. The SCA acknowledges that it is the position of the HRCA that the concerns expressed represent the views of various NGOs rather than the Committee members themselves. However, the SCA was not satisfied with this response.
- Various statements of the UN High Commissioner for Human Rights expressing concern about the reported crackdown in Azerbaijan on journalists and human rights defenders, including a September 2015 statement.[22]

  At the session, the SCA provided the HRCA with an opportunity to outline the actions taken by the institution in response to these concerns, with reference to the specific cases of Khadija Ismayilova, Lyal and Arif Yunus, Intigam Aliyev, Anar Mammadli and Rasul Jafarov.

  The SCA acknowledges that the HRCA did provide some evidence about actions taken in relation to these concerns, including undertaking visits to the detained individuals and, in the case of Intigam Aliyev, making a request for the return of two books that had been seized. However, the SCA is of the view that the evidence provided does not establish that the HRCA has effectively responded to the concerns raised.
- A report from civil society organizations presenting concerns relating to the independence and effectiveness of the HRCA, and asserting that it is not viewed as an effective institution by civil society organizations as a result of its failure to respond to gross human rights violations, including by remaining silent in relation to government crackdowns on civil society, the jailing of leading human rights defenders, the closure of human rights NGOs, and the adoption of repressive NGO laws limiting the ability of these organizations to operate effectively. The submission references the specific cases of Bayram Mammadov and Giyas Ibrahimov and alleges that the HRCA failed

22 The SCA provides the following link—OHCHR, 'Zeid condemns civil society crackdown in Azerbaijan' (8 September 2015) <https://www.ohchr.org/EN/NewsEvents/Pages/DisplayNews.aspx?NewsID=16393&LangID%20=E> accessed 20 February 2021.

to promptly visit the youth activists in detention and, when they did, falsely reported that they had no complaints and had not been subject to torture.

The SCA received and considered a written response from the HRCA. It acknowledges that the HRCA disputes the veracity of the NGO submission and that it has provided some evidence of activities it has taken in response to these issues and specific cases, including visiting the two individuals in detention. However, the SCA is of the view that the evidence provided does not establish that the HRCA has effectively responded to the concerns raised.[23]

The SCA underscored the seriousness of the situation:

In view of all of the material before it, the SCA is of the view that the HRCA has not spoken out in a manner that promotes protection for human rights in response to credible allegations of serious human rights violation having been committed by government authorities. The failure to do so demonstrates a lack of its independence. Therefore, the SCA is of the view that the HRCA is acting in a way that has seriously compromised its compliance with the Paris Principles.[24]

While the NHRI's failure to engage with serious human rights violations was the cause of its downgrading, the SCA also noted a number of problematic structural issues. The law governing the election of the head of the HRCA, in which a two-thirds parliamentary majority elects one of three candidates proposed by the President, was 'not sufficiently broad and transparent'.[25] Deficiencies included the lack of a requirement to advertise vacancies and no specification of the 'process for achieving broad consultation and/or participation in the application, screening, selection and appointment process'.[26]

Following the mandated one year in which NHRIs are given the opportunity to respond to the recommendation to downgrade, in the May 2018 session of the SCA the HRCA provided records of submitted and accepted motions to the government, legislation and motions it has proposed to bolster respect for human rights, visits to detention facilities, and awareness-raising initiatives it organized for law enforcement officials and other stakeholders. The SCA also considered a 2017 report from the mission to Azerbaijan of the UN Working Group on Arbitrary Detention which expressed concerns over the absence of independent oversight in places of detention.[27] The SCA noted that the NHRI had not submitted contributions for the UPR or session of the Committee Against Torture.[28]

23 SCA, 'Accreditation Report—Azerbaijan (HRCA)' (March 2017) 17–18 (bullet points in original).
24 ibid 18.
25 ibid.
26 ibid.
27 SCA, 'Accreditation Report—Azerbaijan (HRCA)' (May 2018) 44.
28 ibid.

The SCA concluded that, 'the HRCA has not adequately spoken out in a manner that effectively promotes protection for all human rights, including in response to credible allegations of human rights violations having been committed by government authorities. The failure to do so demonstrates a lack of sufficient independence.'[29] Accordingly, the SCA confirmed its recommendation to downgrade the HRCA.

10.2.2 Mauritania

At its November 2017 meeting, the SCA recommended that Mauritania's Commission Nationale des droits de l'homme (CNDH, National Commission for Human Rights) be downgraded to B-status. The SCA had received information from civil society, and from the Special Rapporteur on extreme poverty and human rights in 2016 and 2017, that 'expressed concerns regarding the independence of the CNDH including in relation to its composition, the selection and appointment of its members, its working methods and its willingness to address all human rights issues'.[30] Further, the SCA reported that it 'also considered information available from [the] Committee against Torture that also expressed concerns regarding the independence of the CNDH'.[31]

The 2017 downgrade recommendation came after a year of deferred re-accreditation,[32] awaiting reform of the CNDH's enabling law. Though amendments were enacted, these were deemed by the Special Rapporteur on extreme poverty as 'not sufficient to address the substance of the concerns previously expressed'.[33] The SCA identified several enduring deficiencies in the enabling law: principally, a newly created committee to facilitate the selection of the head and members of the CNDH was formed on a somewhat arbitrary basis, and that the CNDH was not sufficiently independent from the selection committee and government bodies.[34]

The SCA also expressed concern that the CNDH was unwilling to 'effectively engage on serious human rights violations, including those relating to torture and conditions of detention, arbitrary detention and freedom of expression'.[35] The SCA referenced three substantive human rights issues in particular. First, it set out the following concerns on the prevention of torture:

[29] ibid.
[30] SCA, 'Accreditation Report—Mauritania (The Human Rights Commission of Mauritania (CNDH))' (November 2017) 21.
[31] ibid.
[32] SCA, 'Accreditation Report—Mauritania (CNDH)' (November 2016) 33.
[33] SCA, 'Accreditation Report—Mauritania (CNDH)' (November 2017) 22.
[34] ibid 21.
[35] ibid 22.

> The December 2016 Report of the Special Rapporteur on torture and other cruel, inhuman or degrading treatment or punishment on his mission to Mauritania (A/HRC/34/54/Add.1), reports 'a troubling lack of complaints being brought forward, even to institutions specifically mandated to assist in such cases, such as the National Bar Association and the National Human Rights Commission, both of which informed the Special Rapporteur that they had never received a complaint of torture'. The report further indicates that 'the National Human Rights Commission has a mandate to monitor all types of detention centres through unannounced visits and confidential interviews with inmates and their families, in accordance with its founding legislation (see Law No. 2010-031 of 20 July 2010, art. 4). However, allegedly owing to limited resources, the Commission has been unable to pursue such visits since 2012'.[36]

While the CNDH said that it had conducted activities in this area, and reports on this were contained in its 2017 annual report, the SCA noted that it was 'unable to locate these references'.[37]

Second, five private television stations were closed in 2017, 'allegedly for non-payment of taxes'.[38] The CNDH reported that it took no action, viewing this exclusively as a tax issue. The SCA considered this response 'insufficient', demonstrating inattention to free expression and the availability of public information.[39] Third, the SCA mentioned the case of an individual sentenced to death for apostasy, a capital crime in Mauritania's legal system. The CNDH had issued a statement supporting the death penalty for apostasy, although purportedly without the authorization of the CNDH President, it issued no retraction despite the application of the death penalty for apostasy being in contravention of international law. The CNDH asserted that it had expressed support for the abolition of the death penalty in its 2017 annual report, but again, the SCA could not locate such a reference.[40]

In light of these issues, the SCA invoked Article 18.1 of the GANHRI statute, giving the CNDH one year to respond to the recommendation to downgrade its status.[41] In the absence of sufficient evidence from the NHRI, the SCA gave the following reasons for recommending that the CNDH be downgraded in 2018:

[36] ibid.
[37] ibid.
[38] ibid 23.
[39] ibid.
[40] SCA, 'Accreditation Report—Mauritania (CNDH)' (November 2017) 23.
[41] The October 2018 report notes that '[a]s per the Record of Decisions of the Bureau of the Global Alliance of National Human Rights Institutions on the Human Rights Commission of Mauritania, "the Bureau decided to adopt the recommendation of the SCA relating to the NHRI of Mauritania of October 2018, both with regard to the accreditation status and to the recommendations."' SCA, 'Accreditation Report' (October 2018) 1.

In October 2018, the SCA reviewed the documentation and additional material made available by the CNDH, summarizing and reporting on all activities it has carried out to implement the previous recommendations of the SCA. The SCA also reviewed information received from civil society. During the session, the SCA conducted a telephone interview and gave the CNDH the opportunity to respond to the information received and provide its views on matters, including:

- the selection and appointment process of members;
- the involvement of civil society in the selection and appointment process;
- the rights of voting and non-voting members;
- the absence of publicly available reports on visits of places of detention;
- the lack of consideration of 'politically-sensitive' complaints;
- cases of enforced disappearances in the context of the 2018 elections;
- actions undertaken to protect the rights of marginalised groups such as the Haratines; and
- the public position taken by the CNDH on the amendments to the Mauritanian criminal code in 2018.

The SCA acknowledges that the CNDH has taken some steps to address the previously-stated concerns of the SCA.

However, the SCA remains concerned that the actual and perceived independence of the CNDH has not been established. In view of all the information provided, the SCA is not satisfied that the CNDH has adequately addressed the substance of its concerns.[42]

The SCA also noted further concerns on the human rights activities of the CNDH, in particular:

that the CNDH has reported in its submission to the Committee Against Torture that it has not found any cases of arbitrary detention. The SCA has received credible reports on the existence of arbitrary detention. Similarly, during the telephone interview during the session, the CNDH reported that there are no cases of extra-judicial executions in the country. Again, the SCA has received credible reports to the contrary. The SCA is of the view that these responses provided by the CNDH demonstrate an unwillingness to address these serious human rights violations.[43]

It also reported that the CNDH continued to fail to engage effectively on the abolition of the death penalty.[44] The SCA thus concluded, based on all the evidence,

[42] SCA, 'Accreditation Report—Mauritania (CNDH)' (October 2018) 25.
[43] ibid 28.
[44] ibid 29.

that the CNDH was failing to promote the protection of human rights, and that its failure to do so evidenced a lack of independence.[45]

10.2.3 Nicaragua

In November 2016, the SCA deferred re-accreditation of Nicaragua's NHRI (PDDH). It cited several areas of concern, but noted that a new head of the PDDH had just been appointed earlier in 2016.[46] A year later, the SCA again deferred re-accreditation, citing three areas of concern (independence, addressing human rights violations, and interaction with the international human rights system) and further noting four areas: selection and appointment of PDDH officers, adequacy of PDDH funding, term of office for PDDH officers, and pluralism within the PDDH.[47] The SCA invoked Article 18.1 of the GANHRI Statute and recommended the PDDH be downgraded to B-status at its May 2018 session, which would occur after one year.

The SCA noted that it had received information in its November 2016, November 2017, and May 2018 sessions, and had reviewed documentation and spoken to the PDDH by phone.

In its review, it detailed a range of concerns about the institution's engagement as a human rights body:

> In November 2017, the SCA noted that the May 2014 Universal Periodic Review outcome report recommended that Nicaragua to guarantee a safe and enabling environment for journalists and human rights defenders, and ensure that all cases of attacks against them are investigated by independent and impartial bodies. The SCA noted at that time that the PDDH had indicated that it has not received any complaints about attacks against human rights defenders and other human rights violations.
>
> The SCA encouraged the PDDH to provide information about the actions it has taken in relation to the protection of human rights defenders and reports of attacks against these individuals.
>
> The SCA acknowledges that the PDDH indicates that, 'in Nicaragua, there is a secure and suitable environment for journalists and defenders of human rights ... and that there have been no cases of harassment, persecution or assault due to their work against journalists, human rights defenders or anyone due to political, ideological or religious beliefs'. Further, the PDDH indicated that it has

[45] ibid.

[46] SCA, 'Accreditation Report—Nicaragua (Procuradoría para la Defensa de los Derechos Humanos (PDDH))' (November 2016) 44–47.

[47] SCA, 'Accreditation Report—Nicaragua (PDDH)' (November 2017) 43–48.

> 'an excellent and exemplary level of citizen security and an environment that enables the work of human rights defenders in Nicaragua, thanks to the accurate preventative police model . . . implemented by the national police'.[48]

It determined that the NHRI was not acting in compliance with the Paris Principles:

> The SCA acknowledges that the PDDH is currently operating in a complex and volatile context. However, the SCA is of the view that the response provided demonstrates an unwillingness to address fundamental human rights issues in a fulsome and independent way.[49]

It concluded:

> Based on all of the information that has been provided, the SCA is of the view that the PDDH is not prepared to adequately speak out in a manner that promotes respect for all human rights, including in response to credible allegations of serious human rights violations having been committed by government authorities. The failure to do so demonstrates a lack of sufficient independence. Therefore, the SCA is of the view that the PDDH is acting in a way that has seriously compromised its compliance with the Paris Principles.[50]

The SCA's report contains considerable detail on the problems relating to the PDDH. While it is not possible for reasons of space to detail these extensively here, these included concerns from the UN Committee on Migrant Workers about the independence and effectiveness of the NHRI.[51] In response to a November 2017 request from the SCA to provide reports on its human rights work, the PDDH provided 'a list of 99 publications' on its activities and public pronouncements. However, the SCA found insufficient evidence in the document that the PDDH had 'engaged in critical assessments of the human rights situation'.[52]

The downgrade recommendation's justification refers first to concerns about the independence of the PDDH. One notable criticism of the PDDH was the case of Maria Luisa Acosta before the Inter-American Court of Human Rights, where Nicaragua was found to have international responsibility for denying access to justice to the human rights defender, Maria Luisa Acosta. Nicaragua had failed to undertake diligent investigation into the murder of Acosta's husband for fifteen

[48] SCA, 'Accreditation Report—Nicaragua (PDDH)' (May 2018) 30.
[49] ibid. The NHRI was downgraded to B-status in March 2019. SCA, 'Accreditation Report—Nicaragua (PDDH)' (March 2019).
[50] SCA, 'Accreditation Report—Nicaragua (PDDH)' (May 2018) 28.
[51] ibid.
[52] ibid 29.

years at the time of the judgment.[53] The PDDH noted it had posted the judgment on its website:

> With respect to this specific case of Maria Luisa Acosta, the SCA acknowledges that the decision of the Inter-American Court specifically required the PDDH to post the decision on its website. However, the SCA is of the view that posting a decision on its website without accompanying critical commentary is an inadequate response of an NHRI to a finding of gross violations of human rights. Further, the SCA notes that the website of the PDDH has been and continues to be shut down, and that the PDDH is unable to indicate when it can again be accessed.[54]

Separately under the heading of human rights violations, the SCA raised the matter of guaranteeing 'a safe and enabling environment for journalists and human rights defenders, and ensur[ing] that all cases of attacks against them are investigated by independent and impartial bodies'.[55] The PDDH responded that it had received no complaints regarding attacks on journalists or human rights defenders and asserted that the environment in Nicaragua is 'secure and suitable'. The SCA took issue with the response of the PDDH, which claimed that 'there have been no cases of harassment, persecution or assault due to their work against journalists, human rights defenders or anyone due to political, ideological or religious beliefs' and praised the 'accurate preventative' model used by the police.[56]

Beyond these two main concerns, the SCA identified three institutional/procedural issues. First, the SCA found that the selection of PDDH officers was not sufficiently broad and transparent, failing to 'specify the process for achieving broad consultation and/or participation in the application, screening, selection and appointment process'.[57] Second, at the time of the review there was no limit on the number of five-year terms an individual could serve as the head of the PDDH. The SCA encouraged the imposition of term limits, preferably to a maximum of two.[58] Third, the SCA noted that the enabling law 'is silent on the requirement for pluralism and diversity in the composition of the PDDH'.[59]

When the PDDH was assessed again in March 2019, the SCA reaffirmed its recommendation to downgrade. In an interview with the PDDH, the SCA inquired about the following issues:

[53] Amnesty International, 'Public Statement—Nicaragua: the state must uphold, without delay, the judgment issued by the Inter-American Court of Human Rights' (3 May 2017) AMR 43/6173/2017.

[54] SCA, 'Accreditation Report—Nicaragua (PDDH)' (May 2018) 30.

[55] ibid.

[56] ibid.

[57] ibid 31.

[58] ibid 32.

[59] ibid.

- a statement made by the Sub-Procurador on behalf of the Government during the High Level Segment of the 40th Session of the Human Rights Council;
- a statement made by the UN High Commissioner for Human Rights expressing concern about a raid on the headquarters of an NGO coalition as a reprisal for having engaged with [the Office of the High Commissioner for Human Rights] OHCHR;
- actions taken in relation to incidents of violence in the context of an alleged 'failed coup d'état';
- the institution's engagement with the international human rights system;
- information regarding alleged reprisals against various female detainees following engagement with a visiting EU delegation; and
- the role of the PDDH in the national dialogue process.[60]

Despite the responses from the PDDH the SCA remained 'concerned that the actual and perceived independence of the PDDH has not been established', and 'that the PDDH continues to act in a manner contrary to the requirements of the Paris Principles'.[61]

The SCA considered that the PDDH had failed to adequately respond to the substance of its previously raised concerns regarding independence.[62] It added to its existing concerns about the PDDH's independence that it 'received information that the *Sub-Procurador* addressed the High-Level Segment of the 40th session of the Human Rights Council as the representative of the Government',[63] despite having been advised by OHCHR and GANHRI before making the statement that such participation was incompatible with its status as an independent NHRI. Further, the contents of the statement 'dismissed credible reports of human rights violations having been committed by the authorities'.[64]

In response to concerns about its work addressing human rights violations, the PDDH submitted records of 'issuing recommendations in respect of the penitentiary system; releasing reports in relation to violations of human rights in the context of a failed coup d'état; and participating in several sessions of the UN Human Rights Council'.[65] The SCA was not satisfied, however, again referencing the PDDH's statement to the 40th session of the Human Rights Council, specifically its expression of views putatively supporting the government, in contradiction of 'credible publicly-available information', stating 'that there are no political prisoners, that there is no evidence of torture or ill-treatment against persons deprived of their liberty, that there has been no excessive use force by police'.[66]

60 SCA, 'Accreditation Report—Nicaragua (PDDH)' (March 2019) 30 (bullet points in original).
61 ibid.
62 ibid 32.
63 ibid.
64 ibid.
65 ibid 33–34.
66 ibid 34.

Additionally, the SCA raised two other specific human rights matters. First, the SCA received a statement by the UN High Commissioner for Human Rights about a raid carried out on the headquarters of an NGO coalition, Red Nicaraguense para la Democracia y Desarrollo, 'which was considered by the High Commissioner to be a reprisal for the organizations' cooperation with OHCHR'.[67] The PDDH responded that 'this incident was not a raid, but rather a judicial procedure carried out against eight (8) NGOs presumably related to crimes, including money laundering'.[68] Second, the SCA raised allegations of reprisals against 'female detainees following their engagement with a visiting EU delegation'.[69] The PDDH denied the occurrence of any reprisals, pointed out that one detainee had been released, and asserted that it conducts visits to detention centres. The SCA considered both responses inadequate and demonstrating 'that the PDDH does not appropriately respond to credible allegations of serious human rights violations in the manner that would be expected of an independent NHRI'.[70]

The SCA concluded by reaffirming its concerns and asserting, 'the PDDH continues to act in a way that seriously compromises its compliance with the Paris Principles'.[71]

10.2.4 Paraguay

The SCA deferred re-accreditation of the A-status Paraguay Defensoria del Pueblo (DP) in November 2013, noting that the term of the NHRI had ended on 30 June 2008, but the legislature had failed to reach agreement on a new appointment. It noted the concerns of the UN Human Rights Committee in its 2013 Concluding Observations.[72] The SCA stated:

> The SCA received and considered a submission from civil society which raised serious concerns as to the effective performance of the DP. The SCA was of the view that the response of the DP to the civil society submission did not address the concerns.[73]

In March 2014, the SCA deferred the re-accreditation, noting that a new parliament had been inaugurated and the process for appointment of a new *Defensor* was

[67] ibid.
[68] ibid.
[69] ibid.
[70] ibid.
[71] ibid 35.
[72] SCA, 'Accreditation Report—Paraguay (DP)' (November 2013) 24–25.
[73] ibid 24.

to be undertaken, and noting that at its November 2013 session it had received a civil society submission that raised serious concerns, and that further:

> the SCA remains concerned about the DP's effectiveness in some areas, including:
>
> - providing recommendations to the State to ensure a clear and effective mandate to provide assistance to victims of human rights violations, including those arising from the Dictatorship;
> - interpreting its mandate in a broad, liberal and purposive manner;
> - proactively providing information and assistance to victims of the Dictatorship; and
> - advocating strongly for the appointment of a new Defensor, given that the current Defensor's fixed term ended in 2008.[74]

The SCA stressed 'the importance of the DP addressing the above noted concerns, failing which the SCA will recommend that the DP be accredited with B status at its second session in 2014'.[75]

In October 2014, the SCA recommended that the *Defensoria* be suspended.[76] Noting that it had previously stressed the need for the DP to respond to the concerns, and that failing which it would recommend the DP be accredited with B-status, the SCA stated that '[i]n response to this request for information on developments on implementation of the above recommendations, the DP withdrew its application for re-accreditation'.[77] The SCA therefore decided:

> Given the withdrawal of the DP's application for re-accreditation, the SCA recommends that the accreditation status of the DP be suspended in accordance with article 19 of the ICC Statute. In accordance with article 23 of the Statute, all rights and privileges conferred on the DP through accreditation would immediately cease.
>
> The SCA notes that pursuant to article 20 of the ICC Statute, the accreditation of the DP will lapse if it fails to submit an application for re-accreditation within one year (1) of the suspension of its accreditation status.[78]

The institution applied for accreditation in 2019, at which time it was accredited with B-status based on concerns with its selection and appointment and dismissal processes. In its report, the SCA stated:

[74] SCA, 'Accreditation Report—Paraguay (DP)' (March 2014) 16.
[75] ibid 17.
[76] SCA, 'Accreditation Report—Paraguay (DP)' (October 2014) 27.
[77] ibid.
[78] ibid.

The SCA recalls that the DPP was previously accredited by GANHRI before its status lapsed in November 2015. During the SCA's last review of the DPP in March 2014, it noted various concerns with respect to the effectiveness of the institution, including in relation to: providing recommendations to the state to ensure a clear and effective mandate to provide assistance to victims of human rights violations; and interpreting its mandate in a broad and purposive manner.

The SCA welcomes the appointment of the new Defensor. It commends the DPP for its efforts to strengthen its institutional capacity following a period during which the DPP was without a Defensor.

The SCA encourages the DPP to continue these efforts, and to seek assistance from OHCHR, GANHRI and the RINDHCA [Network of NHRIs of the Americas] in order to strengthen its compliance with the Paris Principles.[79]

10.3 Other Cases of Downgrading

In addition to cases where NHRIs have lost their A-status accreditation as Paris Principles-compliant institutions for failing to promote and protect human rights, a number of NHRIs have been downgraded to B-status, or threatened with downgrading, for 'structural' reasons of non-compliance. This section considers some of those cases in more detail.

10.3.1 Greece

The example of the Greek National Commission for Human Rights (GNCHR) represents a successful response to a downgrade recommendation. At its March 2015 meeting the SCA deferred re-accreditation of the GNCHR, citing concerns about (i) independence, (ii) selection and appointment of GNCHR officers, (iii) the presence of political representatives (with voting rights) within the GNCHR, (iv) a lack of clarity on grounds for dismissal, (v) the absence of any full-time members ('largely as a result of the significant financial constraints faced by the GNCHR'),[80] (vi) the lack of functional immunity (and hence independence) for GNCHR members, (vii) potential conflicts of interests of members, (viii) adequacy of funding and assurance of financial autonomy, and (ix) procedures for dissemination of GNCHR annual reports.[81] Several of these concerns stemmed from the

[79] SCA, 'Accreditation Report—Paraguay (DPP)' (March 2019) 10. Note: the institution's name had not changed, but the SCA referred to it here as 'DPP' rather than 'DP' as previously.

[80] SCA, 'Accreditation Report—Greece (Greek National Commission for Human Rights (GNCHR))' (March 2015) 31.

[81] SCA, 'Accreditation Report—Greece (GNCHR)' (March 2015) 29–34.

unique financial limitations faced by the Greek government and state following the European debt crisis.

In May 2016, the SCA commended 'GNCHR's efforts to address the concerns previously expressed' but noted that the measures taken did not fully address previous concerns.[82] Consequently, the SCA recommended that the GNCHR be downgraded to B-status.

On the selection and appointment of the GNCHR members, the SCA noted that various societal entities 'designate' members, but this did not address the concern that 'having each body make nominations may result in different processes being employed by each entity'.[83] Relatedly, the SCA noted that 'each entity, body or authority may replace the member or alternate member that it has designated in accordance with its statute and internal procedures'.[84] Notwithstanding the GNCHR's justification, the SCA recalled its General Observation on dismissals, and stated that:

> in order to address the requirement for a stable mandate, which is important in reinforcing independence, the enabling law of an NHRI must contain an independent and objective dismissal process similar to that accorded to members of other independent State agencies. This process should apply uniformly to all nominating entities.[85]

The SCA noted several issues concerning the GNCHR's membership and funding. First, the GNCHR confirmed that one representative from parliament had voting rights, which the SCA asserted is deleterious to NHRI independence.[86] The SCA also referred to General Observation 1.9 regarding government representatives on the board.[87] Second, the SCA again noted that the GNCHR had no full-time members. Though the GNCHR offered a justification, the SCA reiterated the General Observation on having full-time remunerated members in an NHRI's governing body.[88] Third, the SCA stated that members still lacked the security of functional immunity.[89] Provisions can be made, the SCA added in response to the GNCHR, to lift this immunity through 'the superior court or by a special majority of parliament'.[90] Fourth, the SCA stated its concern 'that the GNCHR may not have sufficient funds to effectively carry out its mandate'.[91] Finally, the SCA noted the lack

82 SCA, 'Accreditation Report—Greece (GNCHR)' (May 2016) 33.
83 ibid.
84 ibid 34.
85 ibid.
86 ibid.
87 ibid 35.
88 ibid.
89 ibid 35–36.
90 ibid 36.
91 ibid.

of a legal requirement to discuss the GNCHR's annual reports in parliament. It recommended this be explicitly enshrined in law.

Upon reviewing the GNCHR's work to make improvements, the SCA recommended re-accreditation with A-status in March 2017. It noted that amendments to the GNCHR's enabling law 'fully address the SCA's concerns with respect to political representatives on NHRIs, full-time members, and annual reports'.[92] Nevertheless, the SCA reaffirmed its criticism that the selection and appointment 'process enshrined in the enabling law is not sufficiently broad and transparent'.[93] It also reiterated the need for adequate funding, but acknowledged that 'it received detailed information regarding the financial situation in which the GNCHR is operating, and in particular the social and other consequences of the program of austerity currently in effect in Greece. The SCA acknowledges that this situation limits the GNCHR's ability to advocate for increased funding.'[94] Lastly, the SCA noted enduring concerns about the GNCHR's regulations surrounding dismissal of members.

10.3.2 Senegal

In October 2007, the NHRI of Senegal received A-status accreditation. The SCA expressed concern over funding (financial autonomy), full-time members, and staffing (power to appoint its own staff). The SCA said that it would come back to these issues in October 2010, that is, in three years rather than the usual five.[95] The consideration was deferred in October 2010 due to failure by the institution to submit its materials on time.[96] In May 2011, the SCA recommended downgrading to B-status and reiterated its 2007 concerns regarding budget, members, and staff.[97] In October 2011, the SCA noted that there was no response from the NHRI.[98] The NHRI had still not provided the SCA with documentation to consider on the points it had raised by November 2012, and was thus downgraded.[99] The SCA also noted two observations about the NHRI from UN Treaty Bodies:

> At its current session, the SCA noted the following observations made by the Committee on the Elimination of Racial Discrimination (CERD/C/SEN/CO/R.16-18) 31 August 2012:

[92] SCA, 'Accreditation Report—Greece (GNCHR)' (March 2017) 23.
[93] ibid.
[94] ibid 24.
[95] SCA, 'Accreditation Report—Senegal (Comité Sénégalais des Droits de l'homme (CSDH))' (October 2007) 7.
[96] SCA, 'Accreditation Report—Senegal (CSDH)' (October 2010) 13.
[97] SCA, 'Accreditation Report—Senegal (CSDH)' (May 2011) 23.
[98] SCA, 'Accreditation Report—Senegal (CSDH)' (October 2011) 20.
[99] SCA, 'Accreditation Report—Senegal (CSDH)' (November 2012) 25.

The Committee recommends that the State party take all necessary measures to ensure full compliance of the CSDH with Paris Principles in order to ensure functional independence. It also encourages the State party to implement its commitment to double the budget of the CSDH, as announced during the interactive dialogue, to ensure that the CSDH has the necessary human and financial resources and to inform the International Coordinating Committee (ICC) about the measures taken so that the CSDH avoids the loss of its 'A' status.

And further noted the following observations made by the Special Rapporteur on the human right to safe drinking water and sanitation (A/HRC/21/42/Add.1) 16 August 2012:

The Special Rapporteur reiterates the call for urgently increasing financial support for the Senegalese Committee for Human Rights, given its role in monitoring the situation of human rights in the country. Reinforcing the monitoring and technical capacity of the Committee could promote accountability and raise awareness of economic and social rights, including the rights to water and sanitation. This would also give a voice to alleged victims of these human rights.[100]

The SCA further noted problems with the operation of the NHRI:

The SCA, in its interview with a representative of the CSDH, was informed that the CSDH has not had any members in place since March 2011, and that despite the government's commitment in 2010 to increase the budget of the CSDH from 40 million francs to 70 million francs, no increase has been received.

Taken together, and given that the CSDH had not provided any documentation to support its compliance, the SCA downgraded the NHRI to B-status. At time of writing, it had not applied for re-accreditation since 2012.

10.3.3 Norway

In October 2011, the NHRI of Norway, the Norwegian Centre for Human Rights (NCHR) was informed that it would be re-accredited with B-status the following year, due to the transformation of the institution at the national level. The SCA noted the following:

The NCHR has a dual role as a department of the University of Oslo and a NHRI, and the SCA understands that the University of Oslo intends to terminate the

[100] ibid 27.

> NCHR's role as a NHRI by the end of 2012. The NCHR, in collaboration with the Norwegian Government, intends on developing a strategy for follow-up and establishment of a Paris Principle compliant NHRI.
>
> The SCA notes that the NCHR, as presently constituted, is not fully Paris Principle compliant, but given the stated intention of the NHRC to develop a strategy for the establishment of a Paris Principles compliant NHRI before the end of 2012, the SCA wishes to provide guidance to the NCHR and the Norwegian Government for matters to consider in developing the strategy.[101]

The SCA recommended both an inclusive process for the development of the NHRI and Paris Principles-compliant legislation, necessary resources, and a broad mandate.[102] Further, it recommended to the government to 'develop a strategy for the interim period with clear commitments to uphold as a minimum, the current level of NCHR work until a new NHRI has been established'. Further, it recommended that in this interim period, the NHRI should 'make every effort to continue its work 'particularly in relation to conducting human rights monitoring, documentation and advocacy, and to enhance its current knowledge base, work methods, and independent functioning'.[103] In confirming the downgrading in November 2012, the SCA noted that the government had established an inter-ministerial working group to 'consider whether changes should be made to the NHRI, including whether a new NHRI should be established on the basis of a different institutional model'.[104] The SCA commended the efforts of the NCHR but noted that it was not in its present form operating fully in compliance with the Paris Principles.[105] A reconstituted Norwegian NHRI was accredited with A-status in March 2017.[106]

10.4 Comment

This chapter, in conjunction with the other chapters in Part III of this book, illustrates the development of the SCA as a body that monitors not merely formal compliance with the structural requirements of the Paris Principles but as one that examines the specific human rights activities of NHRIs on the ground. The detailed assessments in the cases of the NHRIs in Nicaragua and Azerbaijan provide a particularly clear illustration of this.

[101] SCA, 'Accreditation Report—Norway (Norwegian Centre for Human Rights (NCHR))' (October 2011) 15–16.
[102] SCA, 'Accreditation Report—Norway (NCHR)' (October 2011) 16.
[103] ibid.
[104] SCA, 'Accreditation Report—Norway (NCHR)' (November 2012) 20.
[105] ibid.
[106] SCA, 'Accreditation Report—Norway (NCHR)' (March 2017) 14–16.

The increasing focus of the SCA on NHRI effectiveness in practice has necessitated a more detailed explanation and assessment being set out in the SCA reports. The SCA provides as much detail in its reports as it believes reasonably necessary to fully explain and justify whatever recommendation it may make, especially in those cases where the SCA is recommending a downgrade of an A-status institution. That detail may include responses made by the NHRI to the reports, as well as observations and conclusions of the international human rights system. The SCA also identifies the issues it 'notes with concern' and form the basis of its recommendation to accredit with other than A-status, and those which it 'notes' but are not part of the reason for the accreditation. The increased level of detail in the reports allows the NHRI to understand the reasons for the recommendation in full and is intended to be of considerable benefit to the GANHRI Bureau should it be called upon to consider a challenge to the recommendation (see Chapter 2.8).

The SCA's focus on effectiveness in practice has additionally necessitated increased attention to observations and recommendations of the international human rights system, including the Universal Periodic Review, Treaty Bodies, and Special Procedures mandate holders, as well as credible third party reports, including from civil society,[107] as these address issues relevant to the activities of an NHRI on the ground, rather than simply the formal structure of the NHRI, and provide a level of detail that assists the SCA in making its assessments. The SCA has stated that 'the importance given to information received from various sources is determined on a case-by-case basis by SCA members. In practice, if information provided by various sources are convergent, detailed and in-depth, and refer to verifiable facts, SCA members are more likely to give importance to them.'[108] At a practical level, NHRIs are given the chance to address the concerns raised in the information that comes before the SCA. As set out in Chapter 2, in its capacity as Secretariat, the OHCHR prepares a summary of all accreditation applications. This includes all information that is relevant to the accreditation under review, and the relevant information contained in the reports, recommendations, and observations of international human rights mechanisms. These summaries are reviewed by the NHRIs, and they are able to correct any factual errors, prior to their being shared with SCA members. The NHRIs are therefore aware of what information will be before the SCA when it considers the accreditation, and they have the opportunity to respond to any of that information.

The SCA will downgrade to B-status where there are a range of concerns about an institution's structure, effectiveness, and independence, or where is one concern that is so serious that the NHRI is clearly no longer Paris Principles compliant. For the NHRIs in Azerbaijan, Mauritania, and Nicaragua, the extent of

[107] Rules of Procedure for the GANHRI Sub-Committee on Accreditation (adopted on 4 March 2019) 8.1, lists these sources amongst others.

[108] GANHRI, 'Practice Note 5: Sources of information to assess NHRIs' (adopted on 18 May 2018).

these institutions' failures to address human rights violations—also seen in previous chapters in Part III in the cases of the NHRIs of Burundi and Thailand—were so serious as to warrant their downgrading. The SCA gave all institutions the opportunity to explain their actions and to justify the retention of A-status. However, it is clear that this will be a challenge for an institution that has clearly documented anti-human rights activities or rhetoric or one that has failed to act in the face of an evident need to do so. The SCA will also downgrade where the institution's structure no longer complies with the Paris Principles to such an extent that the institution is compromised, such as in the cases of Norway and Greece.

In the concluding chapter of the book, we provide some reflections on the work of the SCA, and the future for it and NHRIs more broadly.

11

Looking Forward—the Sub-Committee on Accreditation and National Human Rights Institutions

11.1 The Sub-Committee on Accreditation

Since its earliest published assessments of National Human Rights Institutions (NHRIs), the Global Alliance of NHRIs' (GANHRI) Sub-Committee on Accreditation (SCA) has developed a substantive body of work that has examined the operation and practice of institutions in countries from every part of the globe. Covering all aspects of structure and functioning, its assessments have created an important resource for scholars and practitioners as to how NHRIs, and more broadly, independent domestic institutions can and do function at the national level as well as what problems they face and, ultimately, how they can be protected. This final chapter of the book offers some reflections by the authors on the role of the SCA, the potential and risks for it, and the future for NHRIs.

This book illustrates the significant contribution that the SCA has made in enhancing our understanding of the implementation and application of the Paris Principles[1] in practice. As was seen in Chapter 1, the 1993 United Nations (UN) Paris Principles emerged from a long period of consideration of the establishment of national institutions for the promotion and protection of human rights. While an important framework on which to build, the Paris Principles lacked the detail necessary to secure independently functioning institutions. It is this gap that has been filled by the SCA since its establishment, as this book attests. The contents of this book also make it clear that the SCA is a steward of NHRIs, assisting in their strengthening while holding them to the standards expected both by the Paris Principles and their peers.

NHRIs can no longer be regarded as new institutions; they are an established part of the national and international human rights system. As was seen in Part III, the SCA has been cognizant of this, moving beyond assessments focusing on the institutional framework set out in the Paris Principles—those issues identified in Part II such as enabling laws, budgets, and leadership—to look at the actual work

[1] Principles relating to the Status of National Institutions, UNGA Res 48/134 (20 December 1993) UNGA Doc A/RES/48/134 (The Paris Principles).

National Human Rights Institutions. David Langtry and Kirsten Roberts Lyer, Oxford University Press. © David Langtry and Kirsten Roberts Lyer 2021. DOI: 10.1093/oso/9780198829102.003.0012

of NHRIs on the ground as human rights actors. This represents an important shift in the approach of the SCA reflecting the maturation of NHRIs and the Paris Principles.

The SCA's work has also matured since its establishment. It takes a nuanced approach to its reviews, recognizing the considerable differences between GANHRI member institutions. It does not view one type or size of institution as better than another, nor prefer one political or legal system over another. While A-status is defined as being in 'full compliance' with the Paris Principles, the SCA is clearly aware that no NHRI is 'perfect', and therefore in every instance of accreditation, there are recommendations made to enhance and improve the NHRI in law or in practice, or both. These recommendations address issues that do not so significantly adversely affect the NHRI's ability to act effectively and independently such that A-status is unwarranted. For example, as seen in Chapter 5, one of the most often cited areas of concern is that of 'adequate funding'. The SCA recognizes that while virtually all NHRIs it reviews would welcome additional funding, there are often considerable differences in the size and level of funding between NHRIs, and it must assess the performance of each NHRI with that in mind, by not expecting smaller, poorly funded NHRIs to do as much as larger NHRIs with greater funding and staffing are able to do. NHRIs, especially the smaller ones, must always be allowed to prioritize the areas of greatest need to devote their focus and attention, and the SCA must assess its performance and effectiveness in the context of the financial constraints the NHRI faces. At the same time, should the NHRI be so poorly funded that it cannot effectively fulfil its mandate the NHRI would not be accredited with A-status (for example, in the case of the NHRI of Greece, Chapter 10.3.1). Further, because the SCA itself is formed of one member from each of the four NHRI regions, and because the UN Office of the High Commissioner for Human Rights (OHCHR), as well as representatives of the four NHRI regional networks and the GANHRI head office are present at the SCA meetings as permanent observers, this allows for checks and balances to guard against biases towards different structures, mandates, conditions, contexts, and systems.

11.2 The SCA and NHRI Effectiveness and Independence

While the SCA takes a nuanced and context-specific approach, it does not ignore issues that may impact the compliance with the Paris Principles of NHRIs under review. It approaches A-status as both a 'reward' for properly functioning institutions, and the loss of this status as a 'punishment' for NHRIs who fail to act to the best of their ability. A critical question that often arises in relation to NHRIs is whether they are effective. Effective in this regard means that they advance the implementation of international human rights standards at the national level in order to improve the national human rights situation progressively. And that they undertake this by making reliable and impartial assessments of national human rights situations using a process that is accessible, accountable, transparent, open, and inclusive, and that takes into account the inputs of its stakeholders (even where its assessment ultimately differs from these inputs).

Effectiveness for NHRIs is vital to ensure that they can fulfil their role as promoters and protectors of human rights. An ineffective NHRI can negatively impact both the international monitoring of human rights implementation in its country, and the actual human rights situation on the ground. At the international level, the increasing recognition given to NHRIs, which was identified in particular in Chapters 1, 6, and 8, requires NHRIs to be worthy interlocutors. A-status NHRIs have a presumed legitimacy at the international level that they should collectively protect. Indeed, their ability to engage independently at the international level is a core feature of why they are unique institutions that can connect the national level with the international level. For NHRIs to be reliable partners of international and regional human rights organizations, they must be effective and trustworthy. It is this credibility which the accreditation process undertaken by the SCA has a significant role in conferring on NHRIs. At the national level, an ineffective NHRI has the potential to damage human rights by supporting the positions of a repressive government, failing to investigate or oversee human rights on the basis of international standards, and potentially squeezing the space in which civil society actors can engage.

Where NHRIs do not act in compliance with the Paris Principles, they have the potential to exacerbate a poor national human rights situation. NHRIs' prominent position nationally and internationally means that where they do not speak out on a human rights issue of national importance, or where they speak out on an issue but go against international human rights standards in doing so, it can have a serious impact for the rights of individuals and groups in their country. Examples of this were seen in Part III from the NHRIs of Azerbaijan, Burundi, Nicaragua, Thailand, Venezuela, and others. It must be clear that the only good NHRI is an effective one. This does not mean that the only effective NHRIs are A-status institutions; there may be both B-status and unaccredited NHRIs that are effective, however the SCA process does provide a robust means of assessing these bodies.

The activities of the SCA are critically important to ensuring that NHRIs are effective in their work. As was seen in particular in Part III, the SCA has developed both its procedure and its practice towards ensuring this effectiveness. The process of development of NHRIs set out in Chapter 1 showed that states were reluctant to give much power to national human rights bodies. Indeed, the proposals for establishing these institutions had moved slowly for thirty years before the 1978 Geneva Guidelines.[2] Nonetheless, the Paris Principles did not result in the creation

[2] United Nations Division of Human Rights, 'Seminar on National and Local Institutions for the Promotion and Protection of Human Rights' (18–29 September 1978) UN Doc ST/HR/SER.A/2,

of impotent institutions, they provided a framework through which a vibrant range of national bodies now work to promote and protect human rights, and this has created a new space for the advancement of human rights.

The question of NHRIs' independence is probably the most challenging one examined by the SCA. While it is commonly agreed among scholars and practitioners that independence is critical, it is also a nebulous concept (like effectiveness). The SCA clearly places independence at the centre of its reviews of NHRIs, both in terms of functional autonomy and, critically, in their effectiveness in practice. It recognizes that independence cannot be artificially separated from the question of effectiveness in any analysis of NHRIs.

Based on the SCA's assessments, we can say that there are two stages to determining independence. First, the NHRI must have the institutional and operational factors that help to ensure its independence, including establishment in the constitution/legislation, requisite mandate and powers, consultative, transparent and merit-based appointments, adequate human and financial resources, and pluralistic representation. These are the areas examined by the SCA in Part II of this book. Secondly, the NHRI must exercise its independence in practice through making timely, impartial assessments of the human rights situation and focusing their work on international human rights standards. These were the aspects of the NHRI's work examined by the SCA in Part III. It can be seen that the SCA places the highest premium on this latter aspect of NHRI operations: downgrading to B-status has almost exclusively come in response to the failure of the NHRI to engage with the human rights situation on the ground, particularly where there are significant human rights violations in the country. Independence, when understood in the context of effectiveness, thus requires looking at the operation of the NHRI as a whole, and not simply against a checklist of criteria from the Paris Principles. It is this approach that the SCA takes in its accreditations of NHRIs.

It is critical that the SCA undertake both these stages of review. A lack of functional independence is likely to lead to a lack of independence in practice. The SCA has placed particular emphasis on the appointment process (see Chapter 4). The presence of an improperly appointed leadership requires enhanced scrutiny of the NHRI's work, to ensure that the institution is effective in practice, and that the weakness in the decision-making body's appointment process is not impacting the NHRIs ability to improve the national human rights situation. As this book has shown, the SCA views NHRIs holistically, looking at their legislative and functional compliance with the Paris Principles, as well as their practice. Thus, the absence of one factor, even such a crucial one as an open appointments system, is unlikely to be fatal to A-status in and of itself, unless it impacts the independence in practice of the institution.

'Guidelines on the Structure and Functioning of National and Local Institutions for the Promotion and Protection of Human Rights', paras 184–185.

This leads to an interesting aspect of the increasing prominence of NHRIs, which is the types of state that have established an NHRI. Pegram notes that 'most adopting states [of NHRIs] present relatively hybrid forms of democracy'.[3] As Pegram asks, 'in highly unstable or autocratic contexts, the questions arise: what function does an NHRI serve, and is early creation always advisable?'[4] Moreover, a notable proportion of A-status NHRIs are in states that have poor human rights records, low rule-of-law compliance, or are authoritarian. It is a perennially challenging question as to whether a non-democratic regime can have an 'independent' rights organization, and the presence of A-status NHRIs in these types of states raises questions from many observers. The mere fact of an A-status NHRI being in an undemocratic state or one which does not respect human rights does not in itself warrant refusal of this status. However, additional scrutiny should certainly be applied to NHRIs in countries where the government routinely and openly violates human rights in order to ensure that the NHRI is taking the actions expected of it. While the SCA cannot influence which states establish NHRIs they are responsible for legitimizing that decision through the accreditation process.

11.3 Protecting the NHRI Name

In the context of NHRIs' increasing prominence in international fora, the growing reliance by international bodies on domestic implementation structures, and the role that they play at the national level, it is important to highlight some potential risks that may undermine the status and credibility of NHRIs overall. While NHRIs are intended to be 'independent bodies for the promotion and protection of human rights', merely designating or establishing an institution and labelling it as an 'NHRI', as clearly seen from the contents of this book, does not ensure that the institution is in fact going to meet the requirements of the Paris Principles. And NHRIs must carefully guard their legitimacy. If NHRIs become regarded as merely state mouthpieces or ineffectual for the improvement of human rights, they will lose their prominence at the international and regional level as partners that can support the implementation of international standards. Domestically, they will have little legitimacy even where they do seek to make change.

While those working with and for SCA-accredited NHRIs may have no issue with identifying the institutions to which the term 'NHRI' applies, this is not always the case more broadly. As was seen in the Introduction, scholars frequently disagree over the application of the term, and international organizations have not

[3] Thomas Pegram, 'Diffusion Across Political Systems: The Global Spread of National Human Rights Institutions' (2010) 32(3) Human Rights Quarterly 729, 730.

[4] Thomas Pegram, 'Global human rights governance and orchestration: National human rights institutions as intermediaries' (2015) 21 European Journal of International Relations 595, 608.

uniformly applied it. Lack of clarity around the use of 'NHRI' has its risks for all NHRIs. Where an institution presents itself as being an NHRI without having gone through the process of accreditation, it can damage the image of all A-status institutions. While GANHRI cannot police the usage of the term 'NHRI', it may need to consider the risk from institutions that use the term without seeking or gaining SCA accreditation and which are not compliant with the Paris Principles, by promoting a clear definition of what the designation 'NHRI' refers to, and encouraging uniform usage at the international and regional levels.

Of perhaps more concern than the existence of NHRIs in undemocratic states per se is the existence of NHRIs that are clearly problematic but that nonetheless obtain and retain A-status. As was seen in Chapter 10, Azerbaijan's NHRI maintained A-status for a period of four years following very serious accusations about its effectiveness as a human rights body, including from a UN Treaty Body. Nicaragua's NHRI retained its status as an A-status institution until 2019, despite serious concerns being raised first in 2016, and subsequently spoke before the Human Rights Council as a representative of the government despite being still accredited with A-status. As was seen in the case of Venezuela's NHRI, while the SCA recommended that the NHRI be downgraded to B-status for its actions and inaction in relation to the serious human rights situation in the country,[5] the Venezuelan NHRI retained A-status from the announcement of the re-examination of its status in March 2014 until October 2016. During this time, the UN Committee Against Torture expressed its grave concerns regarding the independence of the NHRI and its ability to deal with serious issues of torture and ill-treatment raised by the Committee.[6] Instances like these may bring the A-status accreditation into question for members of these expert committees and other observers. It also has serious potential consequences for international scrutiny of the domestic human rights situation. Particularly in countries with restricted civil society, A-status institutions may be the only bodies apart from the government that are able to provide an assessment of the situation on the ground to international monitoring bodies. Where that assessment is absent, inaccurate, partisan, or otherwise problematic, it can undermine international efforts to improve the situation. Measures to counteract this risk include the SCA using the rapid suspension clause in the GANHRI Statute,[7] and encouraging the submission of information from civil society where there are serious concerns about the effectiveness of an NHRI, so that the situation can be examined in the presence of all the facts.

Related to this is the matter of B-status institutions. As discussed in Chapter 2, B-status institutions are not subject to the same level of scrutiny as A-status, because

[5] See further on the case example of Venezuela in Chapter 7.3.1.1.

[6] UN Committee Against Torture, 'Concluding observations on the combined third and fourth periodic reports of the Bolivarian Republic of Venezuela' (12 December 2014) UN Doc CAT/C/VEN/CO/3-4, para 20.

[7] GANHRI Statute (adopted on 5 March 2019).

they are not required to apply for periodic re-accreditation. The review process for these institutions requires that they actively apply to the SCA, and the special review procedure set out in Article 16.2 of the GANHRI statute is only relevant to A-status institutions. Similarly, the provisions for suspension and lapse of status in Articles 18 and 19 of the GANHRI Statute also only apply to A-status institutions.

Some B-status institutions have gone for long periods with no SCA scrutiny. In its 2014 Universal Periodic Review (UPR) Report, Kazakhstan stated that although it held B-status, 'the Commissioner's activities are in full compliance with a number of the Paris Principles'.[8] The institutions in neighbouring Tajikistan and Kyrgyz Republic have also been accredited with B-status since 2012, but at time of writing none of these have applied for review or accreditation with A-status. Additionally, the wide application of B-status to a range of institutions may cause confusion as to what is a 'proper' NHRI, and result in international partnerships with inappropriate and ineffective institutions.[9] In particular, the SCA may have to reconsider its use of B-status accreditation if it is being applied to institutions that are NHRIs in name only, but subsequently present themselves as being 'GANHRI accredited'. While there may be a justifiable desire to have institutions inside the NHRI 'club' rather than outside, GANHRI must ensure that this does not undermine the legitimacy of NHRIs.

An additional risk is unaccredited or previously accredited C-status institutions, holding themselves out as Paris Principles institutions. For example, a human rights ombudsman was established in 1995 in Uzbekistan. Despite not having sought accreditation with the SCA, in its 2008 UPR, the government of Uzbekistan stated that this model 'fully complied with the Paris Principles'.[10]

11.4 The Future of the SCA

The trend towards domestic institutionalization for the implementation of international human rights standards has seen increased focus on the role and potential of NHRIs, further increasing the importance of ensuring their effective functioning as promoters and protectors of human rights. Furthermore, the Paris Principles are often utilized as a framework for the effective functioning of domestic mechanisms

[8] UN Human Rights Council, 'Working Group on the Universal Periodic Review Twentieth session 27 October–7 November 2014 National report submitted in accordance with paragraph 5 of the annex to Human Rights Council resolution 16/21: Kazakhstan' (16 September 2014) UN Doc A/HRC/WG.6/20/KAZ/1.

[9] However, Hafner-Burton has commented that A *and* B-status institutions are good places to start for governments in search of partnerships. Emilie M Hafner-Burton, *Making Human Rights A Reality* (Princeton University Press 2013) 173.

[10] OHCHR, 'Human Rights Council—Universal Periodic Review Highlights 11 December 2008 (morning)' <www.ohchr.org/EN/HRBodies/UPR/Pages/Highlights11December2008am.aspx> accessed 12 February 2021.

for the implementation of international human rights standards, meaning that it is important for the SCA's interpretation and elaboration of the Principles to become more well-known—a gap we aim to fill through this book.

The establishment of an NHRI indicates a general willingness on the part of the state to engage with international human rights standards. Furthermore, states have been prepared to make adjustments to their own domestic laws in order to ensure that their NHRI gains or retains its A-status, indicating that a level of prestige is attached to this status. It can be argued that an A-status institution, even in the most repressive of states, provides space for human rights that might not otherwise exist and thus underscores the importance of the NHRI as a potential human rights interlocutor even in countries where there may otherwise be little or no space for human rights. In this line of argumentation, the actions of the SCA in monitoring the compliance of NHRIs with the Paris Principles, as well as GANHRI as a forum for developing human rights standards and keeping NHRIs moving forward in their human rights work, clearly has great potential.

It cannot be omitted from a discussion on NHRIs, that many institutions operate under significant threat from the state, as summarized by the Asian Non-Governmental Organization (NGO) Network on National Human Rights Institutions (ANNI) in its 2019 Annual Report:

> In reality many NHRIs in the region are confronted with operational and practical impediments in implementing their mandate and performing their role meaningfully. There appears to be a recurring trend of governments actively trying to undermine the effective work and functioning of NHRIs. These attacks and reprisals may come in the form of amendments to the NHRIs' enabling law, restriction of their mandate and jurisdiction, imposition of arbitrary restrictions on funding, as well as recruitment of Commissioners who either refuse to criticise the authorities or seriously lack capacity in human rights. These have severely impeded the functional independence, effectiveness as well as credibility of many NHRIs.[11]

As has been seen throughout this book, it is the NHRI that is assessed and not the state within which it operates. That is, while the SCA considers the context in which an NHRI is operating, including factors such as political instability, conflict or unrest, and lack of state infrastructure,[12] the SCA assesses the NHRI's compliance with the Paris Principles in law and practice and not the state within which it is located. The SCA has endeavoured to reflect this distinction when recommending

[11] ANNI, *Report on the Performance and Establishment of National Human Rights Institutions in Asia* (Asian Forum for Human Rights and Development 2019) 18.

[12] Rules of Procedure for the GANHRI Sub-Committee on Accreditation (adopted on 4 March 2019) 8.4.

A-status for NHRIs operating in a 'volatile context', discussed in Chapter 9. As was seen in that chapter, the SCA has commended Afghanistan's Independent Human Rights Commission, as well as the Philippines Commission on Human Rights, the Palestine Independent Commission for Human Rights, and the Polish Commissioner for Human Rights, among others, for their ongoing efforts in spite of the challenging circumstances in which they operate.

There is a reason that NHRI board members and staff themselves are increasingly referred to as human rights defenders[13] and accept this title themselves,[14] because many have a demonstrated lifelong commitment to working for human rights. As members of NHRIs themselves, the SCA members are able to identify NHRIs that are not actively contributing to improving the national human rights situation. The SCA must also be cognizant—as its reviews show it to be—that the designation of A-status can legitimate the actions of a government as well as of an NHRI which does not respect human rights. It needs to be sure that promoting NHRIs is not an end in itself, but that it is promoting institutions that make a positive difference. NHRIs should not be seen to be unduly supporting each other to the detriment of the overall goal of NHRIs as human rights actors.

The SCA must maintain the legitimacy of its process and enhance it further. This includes by enhancing its capacity to seek submissions from reputable NGOs and civil society in the country of the NHRI under assessment (see Chapter 2.6). In addition, the SCA should ensure that it acts in a transparent manner. In the future, opening up the process and hearings to public scrutiny, and/or making the accreditation documents from applying institutions publicly available may also improve the transparency, legitimacy and robustness of the process. It is hoped that this compilation of 'case law' will also assist with clarity and understanding of the SCA's recommendations and standards.

13 See for example, Defend Defenders, 'Geneva: Special Rapporteur on HRDs Highlights Role of National Human Rights Institutions' (5 March 2013) <https://defenddefenders.org/geneva-special-rapporteur-on-hrds-highlights-role-of-national-human-rights-institutions/> accessed 22 February 2021; European Network of NHRIs, 'Germany launches protection programme for human rights defenders at risk' (11 December 2020) <http://ennhri.org/news-and-blog/germany-launches-protection-programme-for-human-rights-defenders-at-risk/> accessed 22 February 2021; Council of Europe, 'Declaration of the Committee of Ministers on Council of Europe action to improve the protection of human rights defenders and promote their activities' (6 February 2008) <https://wcd.coe.int/wcd/ViewDoc.jsp?id=1245887&Site=CM&BackColorInternet=9999CC&BackColorIntranet=FFBB55&BackColorLogged=FFAC75> accessed 24 February 2021.

14 GANHRI, The Marrakech Declaration 2018: Expanding the civic space and promoting and protecting human rights defenders with a specific focus on women: The role of national human rights institutions (adopted on 12 October 2018) <https://www.forum-asia.org/uploads/wp/2019/10/GANHRI_Marrakech-Declaration_Oct-2018_EN-2.pdf> accessed 22 February 2021.

11.5 Final Thoughts

To the authors, this book has once again underscored the importance of NHRIs and the SCA. The SCA is a unique mechanism within the international human rights system. Entrusted to assess NHRIs, with its judgments accepted by the international community, the SCA has worked to improve the functioning of these institutions around the world.

Do NHRIs improve human rights? There is certainly some evidence that they do, and moreover, it is clear that there is great potential for them to do so. Their unique position at the national and international level, their expertise, and their powers and functions mean that they can and do make a positive difference. But as institutions that rely almost exclusively on persuasion as a means of creating change, they are fragile,[15] and must individually and as a group carefully protect their legitimacy. It must be recognized that the existence of an NHRI is not a goal in and of itself; they must actually do something to improve the national human rights situation. Their continued legitimacy and future growth are likely to be dependent on their ability to add value. For this, NHRIs must be able to demonstrate that they are effective. Recognizing their value and potential, and the precarious position they occupy, the SCA has shifted its focus towards ensuring that NHRIs are effective human rights bodies. NHRIs were established after a long process of consideration at the UN. They have become widely accepted institutions that exist throughout the world. Furthermore, their voices on human rights are listened to both nationally and internationally. But there is considerable risk to NHRIs from loss of their legitimacy individually and as a group. The SCA's increasing focus on effectiveness will help to ensure this does not happen.

A-status institutions come under a high level of scrutiny and are accompanied by high expectations. A-status is the benchmark by which NHRIs are measured, as well as a statement by NHRIs themselves that this is the highest level of achievement for them. Where this status is attached to institutions that are clearly ineffective, or worse, act against international human rights standards, it calls into question the entire model. By refocusing on effectiveness, and clearly stating what that means, the SCA has been working to reinforce their importance and protect the designation of A-status.

This book has shown that the Paris Principles should be regarded as minimum standards. The work of the SCA makes it clear that they regard the Principles in this way. However, it is unclear whether the perception of the Paris Principles by all UN Member States that are establishing or developing an NHRI corresponds with this understanding. Given the extent of the recommendations and commentary

[15] See Ann Linnarsson and Vanessa Sedletzki, 'Independent Human Rights Institutions for Children: An Actor for the Protection of Children's Rights During Armed Conflict?' (2014) 36(2) Human Rights Quarterly 447.

provided by the SCA, set out in this book, it seems that many states rather regard the Principles as standards to be met. We hope that this book will assist in promoting an understanding of the need for the Paris Principles to be viewed as a set of minimum standards, as well as how much is additionally required of NHRIs above the Paris Principles, in particular, the necessary and increasing emphasis on their effectiveness as human rights actors.

Bibliography

Cases

Shtukaturov v. Russia, App no 44009/05, 27 March 2008.
Winterwerp v. the Netherlands, App no 6301/73, 24 October 1979.

Legislation

UN General Assembly (UNGA)

UNGA, National Institutions for the Promotion and Protection of Human Rights, UNGA Res 33/46 (14 December 1978) UN Doc A/RES/33/46.
UNGA, National Institutions for the Promotion and Protection of Human Rights, UNGA Res 48/134 (4 March 1994) UN Doc A/RES/48/134.
UNGA, National Institutions for the Promotion and Protection of Human Rights UNGA Res 50/176 (27 February 1996) UN Doc A/RES/50/176.
UNGA, National Institutions for the Promotion and Protection of Human Rights, UNGA Res no 70/163 (17 December 2015) UN Doc A/RES/70/163.
UNGA, National Human Rights Institutions, UNGA Res 74/156 (18 December 2019) UN Doc A/RES/74/156.
UNGA, Optional Protocol to the Convention against Torture and other Cruel, Inhuman or Degrading Treatment or Punishment (adopted on 18 December 2002, entered into force on 22 June 2006) 2375 UNTS 237.
UNGA, Principles relating to the Status of National Institutions, UNGA Res 48/134 (20 December 1993) UN Doc A/RES/48/134 (The Paris Principles).
UNGA, Role of the Ombudsman, Mediator and Other National Human Rights Institutions in the Promotion and Protection of Human Rights, UNGA Res 72/186 (19 December 2017) UN Doc A/RES/72/186.
Universal Declaration of Human Rights (adopted 10 December 1948 UNGA Res 217 A(III).
UNGA Res 32/123 (16 December 1977) UN Doc A/RES/32/123.
UNGA Res 34/49 (23 November 1979) UN Doc A/RES/34/49.
UNGA Res 36/134 (14 December 1981) UN Doc A/RES/36/134.
UNGA Res 38/123 (16 December 1983) UN Doc A/RES/38/123.
UNGA Res 39/144 (14 December 1984) UN Doc A/RES/39/144.
UNGA Res 40/123 (13 December 1985) UN Doc A/RES/40/123.
UNGA Res 41/129 (4 December 1986) UN Doc A/RES/41/129.
UNGA Res 60/251 (3 April 2006) UN Doc A/RES/60/251.
UNGA Res 62/207 (21 December 2010) UN Doc A/RES/65/207.
UNGA Res 63/169 (18 December 2008) UN Doc A/RES/63/169.
UNGA Res 63/172 (18 December 2008) UN Doc A/RES/63/172.
UNGA Res 64/161 (18 December 2009) UN Doc A/RES/64/161.
UNGA Res 172 (18 December 2008) UN Doc A/Res/63/172.

Human Rights Council (HRC)

National Human Rights Institutions, Human Rights Council Res 39/17 (28 September 2018) UN Doc A/HRC/RES/39/17.

National Institutions for the Promotion and Protection of Human Rights of the UN Human Rights Council, Human Rights Council Res 27/18 (7 October 2014) UN Doc A/HRC/RES/27/18.

Regional Arrangements for the Promotion and Protection of Human Rights, Human Rights Council Res 34/17 (11 April 2017) UN Doc A/HRC/RES/34/17.

Human Rights Council Res 5/1 (18 June 2007) UN Doc A/HRC/RES/5/1.

Human Rights Council Res 16/21 (12 April 2011) UN Doc A/HRC/RES/16/21.

Economic and Social Council (ECOSOC)

ECOSOC Commission on Human Rights, Res 1992/54 (3 March 1992) UN Doc E/CN.4/1992/L.11/Add.4.

ECOSOC Res 9(II) (21 June 1946).

ECOSOC Res 772(XXX)B (25 July 1960).

ECOSOC, 'Resolution on Future Work of the United Nations in the Field of Prevention of Discrimination and Protection of Minorities' (25 October 1951) UN Doc E/CN.4/641, Res I.

Organization of American States (OAS)

OAS, 'Strengthening of the National Human Rights Systems of the Member States and Support for the Work of Defenders of the People, Defenders of the Population, and Human Rights Attorneys or Commissioners (Ombudsmen)' General Assembly Res AG/RES. 2221 (XXXVI-O/06) (6 June 2006).

OAS, 'Strengthening of the National Human Rights Systems of the Member States and Support for the Work of Defenders of the People, Defenders of the Population, and Human Rights Attorneys or Commissioners (Ombudsmen)' General Assembly Res AG/RES. 2411 (XXXVIII-O/08) (3 June 2008).

OAS, 'Strengthening the Role of National Institutions for the Promotion and Protection of Human Rights in the Organization of American States' General Assembly Res AG/RES. 2421 (XXXVIII-O/08) (3 June 2008).

OAS, 'Strengthening the Role of National Institutions for the Promotion and Protection of Human Rights in the Organization of American States' General Assembly Res AG/RES. 2448 (XXXI X-O/09) (4 June 2009).

Council of Europe

Convention on Preventing and Combating Violence against Women and Domestic Violence (Istanbul Convention) (adopted on 11 May 2011, entered into force on 1 August 2014) CETS No 2010.

Parliamentary Assembly of the Council of Europe, 'Strengthening the Institution of Ombudsman in Europe' Res 1959 (2013).

African Union

ACHPR, 'Resolution on the Granting of Affiliate Status to National Human Rights Institutions in Africa' ACHPR/Res 370(LX)2017 (Niamey 22 May 2017).

ACHPR, 'Resolution on the Granting of Observer Status to National Human Rights Institutions in Africa' ACHPR/Res 31(XXIV)98 (Banjul 31 October 1998).

African Charter on Human and Peoples' Rights (adopted 27 June 1981, entered into force 21 October 1986) (1982) 21 ILM 58 (African Charter).

Protocol to the African Charter on Human and Peoples' Rights on the Establishment of an African Court (adopted on 10 June 1998, entered into force 25 January 2004) OAU Doc. OAU/LEG/EXP/AFCHPR/PROT(III).

Rules and Procedure of the African Commission on Human and People's Rights (adopted in May 2010).

European Council

Council Regulation (EC) No 168/2007 of 15 February 2007 establishing a European Union Agency for Fundamental Rights [2007] OJ L 53/1.

International Treaties and Conventions

Convention on the Rights of Persons with Disabilities (adopted on 13 December 2006, entered into force on 3 May 2008) 2515 UNTS 3 (CRPD).

International Covenant on Civil and Political Rights (adopted 16 December 1966, entered into force 23 March 1976) 999 UNTS 171.

UN Treaty Bodies

Committee Against Torture (CAT)

CAT, 'Guidelines on national preventative mechanisms' (9 December 2010) UN Doc CAT/OP/12/5.

Committee on Elimination of Racial Discrimination (CERD)

CERD, 'Rules of Procedure' (1 January 1989) UN Doc CERD/C/35/Rev3.

Authorities

Adamson B, 'NHRI and their European Counterparts: Scope for Strengthened Cooperation and Performance towards European Human Rights Institutions' in Jan Wouters and Katrien Meuwissen (eds), *National Human Rights Institutions in Europe: Comparative, European and International Perspectives* (Intersentia Publishing 2013).

Africa Rdv, 'Koffi Kounté peut rentre au Togo (Officiel)' (29 July 2019) <https://www.africardv.com/societe/koffi-kounte-peut-rentrer-au-togo-officiel/> accessed 19 February 2019.

African Commission on Human and Peoples' Rights, 'National Human Rights Institutions' <www.achpr.org/network> accessed 3 February 2021.

Amnesty International, 'Press release: Honduras failing to tackle coup rights abuses' (28 June 2010) <https://www.amnesty.org/en/press-releases/2010/06/honduras-failing-tackle-coup-rights-abuses/> accessed 12 August 2020.

Amnesty International, 'Thailand: Time to end human rights violations—Amnesty International Submission to the UN Universal Periodic Review' (October 2011) <https://www.amnesty.org/download/Documents/28000/asa390012011en.pdf> accessed 24 February 2021.

Amnesty International, *The State of the World's Human Rights, Amnesty International Report 2014/2015* (Amnesty International 2015).

Amnesty International, 'Amnesty International Report 2014/2015—Afghanistan, 2015' (25 February 2015) <https://www.refworld.org/docid/54f07e2215.html> accessed 27 September 2020.

Amnesty International, 'Amnesty International Report 2015/16—Burundi' (24 February 2016) <www.refworld.org/docid/56d05b6c15.html> accessed 19 February 2021.

Amnesty International, 'Public Statement—Nicaragua: the state must uphold, without delay, the judgment issued by the Inter-American Court of Human Rights' (3 May 2017) AMR 43/6173/2017.

Amnesty International, 'Afghanistan: Human rights defenders under attack' (28 August 2019) <https://www.amnesty.org/en/latest/news/2019/08/afghanistan-human-rights-defenders-under-attack/> accessed 18 February 2021.

Amnesty International, 'Hungary: 2019' <https://www.amnesty.org/en/countries/europe-and-central-asia/hungary/report-hungary/> accessed 23 May 2020.

Amnesty International, 'Country report: Poland 2019' <https://www.amnesty.org/en/countries/europe-and-central-asia/poland/report-poland/> accessed 22 February 2021.

Asia-Pacific Forum of NHRIs, 'NHRIs to be formally included in work of UN panel on Ageing' (5 January 2017) <https://www.asiapacificforum.net/news/nhris-be-formally-included-work-un-panel-ageing/> accessed 8 January 2021.

Asia-Pacific Forum of NHRIs, 'APF to advise on draft legislation to establish Cambodian NHRI' (21 October 2020) <https://www.asiapacificforum.net/news/apf-advise-draft-legislation-establish-cambodian-nhri/> accessed 15 January 2021.

Asia-Pacific Forum of NHRIs, '2019–20 Annual Report' (25 November 2020) 8–10 <https://www.asiapacificforum.net/resources/2019-2020-annual-report/> accessed 15 January 2021.

Asia-Pacific Forum of NHRIs, 'APF 15: UNDP Presentation on Engagement with NHRIs in the Asia Pacific' <www.asiapacificforum.net/resources/apf-15-undp-presentation-engagement-nhris-asia-pacific/> accessed 15 February 2021.

Asia Pacific Forum of National Human Rights Institutions and United Nations Development Programme, *Capacity Assessment Manual for National Human Rights Institutions* (Asia Pacific Forum of National Human Rights Institutions and United Nations Development Programme 2014).

Asian NGO Network on National Human Rights Institutions, *Report on the Performance and Establishment of National Human Rights Institutions in Asia* (Asian Forum for Human Rights and Development 2014).

Asian NGO Network on National Human Rights Institutions, *Report on the Performance and Establishment of National Human Rights Institutions in Asia* (Asian Forum for Human Rights and Development 2019).

Association for Prevention of Torture, 'APT Briefing series: National Human Rights Institutions as National Preventative Mechanisms: Opportunities and challenges' (December 2013) <https://www.apt.ch/sites/default/files/publications/apt-briefing-on-nhris-as-npms-en.pdf> accessed 17 February 2021.

Association for Prevention of Torture, 'List of Designated NPM by type' <http://tortureprevention.ch/en/by-type/> accessed 16 February 2021.

Brodie M, 'Progressing Norm Socialisation: Why Membership Matters. The Impact of the Accreditation Process of the International Coordinating Committee of National Institutions for the Promotion and Protection of Human Rights' (2011) 80 Nordic Journal of International Law 143.

Burdekin B and Naum J, *National Human Rights Institutions in the Asia-Pacific Region* (Martinus Nijhoff 2007).

Byrnes A, Renshaw C, and Durbach A, 'A Tongue but No Teeth: The Emergence of a Regional Human Rights Mechanism in the Asia Pacific Region' (2009) 31 Sydney Law Review 211.

Cardenas S, 'Emerging Global Actors: The United Nations and National Human Rights Institutions' (2003) 9(1) Global Governance 23.

Cardenas S, *Chains of Justice: The Global Rise of State Institutions for Human Rights* (University of Pennsylvania Press 2014).

Carver R, 'A New Answer to an Old Question: National Human Rights Institutions and the Domestication of International Law' (2010) 10(1) Human Rights Law Review 1.

Carver R, 'One NHRI or Many? How Many Institutions Does it Take to Protect Human Rights?—Lessons from the European Experience' (2011) 3(1) J Human Rights Practice 1.

Carver R, National Human Rights Institutions in Central and Eastern Europe: The Ombudsman as Agent of International Law' in Ryan Goodman and Thomas Pegram (eds), *Human Rights, State Compliance and Social Change: Assessing National Human Rights Institutions* (CUP 2012).

Centre for Media Pluralism and Media Freedom, 'Media Pluralism Monitor 2016, Country report: Hungary' 2016 <https://cadmus.eui.eu/bitstream/handle/1814/46799/Hungary_EN.pdf?sequence=1&isAllowed=y> accessed 23 May 2020.

Collins B and Fleischman L, 'Human Rights and Social Conflict in the Oil, Gas, and Mining Industries' (Oxfam America, 9 April 2013) <https://s3.amazonaws.com/oxfam-us/www/static/media/files/nhri-backgrounder.pdf> accessed 25 February 2021.

Committee Against Torture, 'Consideration of reports submitted by States parties under article 19 of the Convention, Concluding observations of the Committee against Torture: Azerbaijan' (2 September 2011) UN Doc CAT/C.AZE/CO/3.

Committee Against Torture, 'Concluding observations on the second periodic report of Togo, adopted by the Committee at its forty-ninth session (29 October–23 November 2012)' (11 December 2012) UN Doc CAT/C/TGO/CO/2.

Committee Against Torture, 'Concluding observations on the combined third and fourth periodic reports of the Bolivarian Republic of Venezuela' (12 December 2014) UN Doc CAT/C/VEN/CO/3-4.

Committee on Economic, Social and Cultural Rights, 'Draft General Comment No. 10: The role of national human rights institutions in the protection of economic, social and cultural rights' (10 December 1998) UN Doc E/C.12/1998/25.

Committee on Economic, Social and Cultural Rights, 'General Comment No. 16, The equal right of men and women to the enjoyment of all economic, social and cultural rights' (11 August 2005) UN Doc E/C.12/2005/4.

Committee on Economic, Social and Cultural Rights, 'General Comment No. 19, The right to social security (art.9)' (4 February 2008) UN Doc E/C.12/GC/19.

Committee on Elimination of Discrimination Against Women, 'General Recommendation No. 28 on the Core Obligations of States Parties under Article 2 of the Convention on the Elimination of All Forms of Discrimination Against Women' (19 October 2010) UN Doc CEDAW/C/2010/47/GC.2.

Committee on Elimination of Discrimination Against Women, 'Statement by the Committee on the Elimination of Discrimination against Women on its relationship with national human rights institutions' (11 February 2008) UN Doc E/CN.6/2008/CRP.1.

Committee on Elimination of Discrimination Against Women, 'Concluding observations on the combined initial and second periodic reports of Afghanistan' (30 July 2013) UN Doc CEDAW/C/AFG/CO/1-2.

Committee on Elimination of Racial Discrimination, 'General Recommendation No. 33, Follow-up to the Durban Review Conference' (29 September 2009) UN Doc CERD/C/GC/33.

Committee on Elimination of Racial Discrimination, 'Concluding observations on the ninth to the tenth periodic reports of Slovakia' (17 April 2013) UN Doc CERD/C/ SVK/CO/9-10.

Committee on Elimination of Racial Discrimination, 'Consideration of reports submitted by States parties in accordance with articles 16 and 17 of the Covenant: Concluding observations of the Committee on Economic, Social and Cultural Rights—Slovakia' (8 June 2012) UN Doc E/C.12/SVK/CO/2.

Committee on the Rights of the Child, 'General Comment No. 2 (2002), The Role of Independent National Human Rights Institutions in the Promotion and Protection of the Rights of the Child' (15 November 2002) UN Doc CRC/GC/2002/2.

Commonwealth Forum of National Human Rights Institutions, 'CFNHRI Communiqué to Commonwealth Heads of Government CHOGM 2013' (Colombo, Sri Lanka 2013) <https://thecommonwealth.org/sites/default/files/events/documents/CHOGM%202013%20Communique_0.pdf> accessed 20 January 2021.

Commonwealth Forum of National Human Rights Institutions, <https://cfnhri.org> accessed 22 February 2021.

Commonwealth Forum of National Human Rights Institutions, 'Strategic Plan 2019–2021' <https://cfnhri.org/wp-content/uploads/2020/01/CFNHRIStrategicPlanFinalDraft.pdf> accessed 23 February 2021.

Commonwealth Secretariat, *National Human Rights Institutions: Best Practice* (Commonwealth Secretariat 2001).

Conference on Security and Co-Operation in Europe, 'Report to the CSCE Council from the CSCE Seminar of Experts on Democratic Institutions, Oslo, November 15, 1991' (1992) 31 ILM 374, 385.

Council of Europe, Recommendation 1615 (2003).

Council of Europe, 'Declaration of the Committee of Ministers on Council of Europe action to improve the protection of human rights defenders and promote their activities' (6 February 2008) <https://wcd.coe.int/wcd/ViewDoc.jsp?id=1245887&Site=CM&BackColorInternet=9999CC&BackColorIntranet=FFBB55&BackColorLogged=FFAC75> accessed 24 February 2021.

Council of Europe, 'Drafting Group on Civil Society and National Human Rights Institutions (CDDH-INST)' (19 March 2020) CDDH-INST(2019)R6, para 13 <https://rm.coe.int/steering-committee-for-human-rights-cddh-drafting-group-on-civil-socie/16809cf87f> accessed 7 February 2021.

Council of Europe, Recommendation CM/Rec(2018)11 of the Committee of Ministers to Member States on the need to strengthen the protection and promotion of civil society space in Europe (adopted on 28 November 2020).

Council of Europe, 'Civil society and national human rights institutions' <https://www.coe.int/en/web/human-rights-intergovernmental-cooperation/human-rights-development-cddh/civil-society-and-human-rights-institutions> accessed 23 February 2021.

Council of Europe and others, 'Joint statement from meeting in Warsaw with the Office of the Polish Ombudsman' (1 March 2016) <https://www.ohchr.org/Documents/Issues/Defenders/JointStatementPolishCommissionerforHR.pdf> accessed 3 August 2020.

Council of Europe Commissioner for Human Rights, 'Co-operation with National Human Rights Structures' <www.coe.int/en/web/commissioner/co-operation-with-national-human-rights-structures> accessed 18 February 2021.

Council of the European Union, 'Council Conclusions on the Action Plan on Human Rights and Democracy 2015–2019' (20 July 2015) 10897/15RC/oza. 4. DGC 2B.

Council of the European Union, 'Council Conclusions on the Charter of Fundamental Rights after 10 Years: State of Play and Future Work' (20 September 2019) 12357/19.

Court of Justice of the European Union, 'Order of the Court in Case C-791/19 R Commission v Poland: Poland must immediately suspend the application of the national provisions on the powers of the Disciplinary Chamber of the Supreme Court with regard to disciplinary cases concerning judges' (8 April 2020) Press release No 47/20 <https://curia.europa.eu/jcms/upload/docs/application/pdf/2020-04/cp200047en.pdf> accessed 3 August 2020.

Defend Defenders, 'Geneva: Special Rapporteur on HRDs Highlights Role of National Human Rights Institutions' (5 March 2013) <https://defenddefenders.org/geneva-special-rapporteur-on-hrds-highlights-role-of-national-human-rights-institutions/> accessed 22 February 2021.

ECOSOC Commission on Human Rights, 'Draft Report of the Commission on Human Rights to the Economic and Social Council' (17 June 1948) UN Doc E/CN.4/148.

ECOSOC Commission on Human Rights, 'Further Promotion and Encouragement of Human Rights and Fundamental Freedoms, Including: (b)The Importance of National Institutions in the Field of Human Rights, Addendum to Report of the Secretary-General' (7 February 1979) UN Doc E/CN.4/1321/Add.2.

ECOSOC Commission on Human Rights, 'Local Human Rights Committees or Information Groups, Memorandum Submitted by the Secretary-General' (27 February 1951) UN Doc E/CN.4/519.

ECOSOC Commission on Human Rights, 'Local Human Rights Committees or Information Groups, Note by the Secretary-General' (10 March 1952) UN Doc E/CN.4/519/Add.1.

ECOSOC Commission on Human Rights, 'National Advisory Committees on Human Rights, Note by the Secretary-General' (23 November 1959) UN Doc E/CN.4/791.

ECOSOC Commission on Human Rights, 'National Advisory Committees on Human Rights, Report of the Secretary-General' (10 January 1962) UN Doc E/CN.4/828.

ECOSOC Commission on Human Rights, 'National Institutions for the Promotion and Protection of Human Rights, Updated Report of the Secretary-General' (16 December 1988) 45th Session UN Doc E/CN.4/1989/47.

ECOSOC Commission on Human Rights, 'Further promotion and encouragement of human rights and fundamental freedoms, including the question of the programme and methods of work of the Commission; Alternative approaches and ways and means within the United Nations system for improving the effective enjoyment of human rights and fundamental freedoms: National institutions for the protection and promotion of human rights' (9 January 1991) UN Doc E/CN.4/1991/23.

ECOSOC Commission on Human Rights, 'Report of the International Workshop on National Institutions for the Promotion and Protection of Human Rights (Paris 7–9 October 1991)' (16 December 1991) UN Doc E/CN.4/1992/43.

ECOSOC Commission on Human Rights, 'Report of the 3rd International Workshop on National Institutions for the Promotion and Protection of Human Rights' (18–21 April 1995) UN Doc E/CN.4/1996/8.

European Commission, Reasoned Proposal in Accordance with Article 7(1) of the treaty on European Union Regarding the Rule of Law in Poland: Proposal for a Council Decision on the determination of a clear risk of a serious breach by the Republic of Poland of the rule of law' (20 December 2017) COM (2017) 835 final <http://ec.europa.eu/newsroom/just/document.cfm?action=display&doc_id=49108> accessed 22 February 2021.

European Commission, 'Rule of Law: European Commission launches infringement procedure to safeguard the independence of judges in Poland' (29 April 2020) <https://ec.europa.eu/commission/presscorner/detail/en/ip_20_772> accessed 3 August 2020.

European Commission, '2020 Rule of Law Report: Country Chapter on the rule of law situation in Hungary' (30 September 2020) SWD(2020) 316 final <https://ec.europa.eu/info/sites/info/files/hu_rol_country_chapter.pdf> accessed 5 October 2020.

European Commission against Racism and Intolerance, 'ECRI General Policy Recommendation No. 2: Equality Bodies to Combat Racism and Intolerance at National Level' (7 December 2017) CRI(2018)06.

European Parliament, 'Rule of Law in Hungary: Parliament calls on the EU to act' (12 September 2018) <https://www.europarl.europa.eu/news/en/press-room/20180906IPR12104/rule-of-law-in-hungary-parliament-calls-on-the-eu-to-act> accessed 23 May 2020.

European Parliament, 'The establishment of an EU Mechanism on Democracy, the Rule of Law and Fundamental Rights' (7 October 2020) P9-TA(2020)0251.

European Network of NHRIs, 'Intervention of the European Group of National Human Rights Institutions at the Interlaken Ministerial Conference on the Future of the European Court of Human Rights' Interlaken 18–19 February 2010.

European Network of NHRIs, 'Submission to Council of Europe's Committee of experts on the reform of the European Court of Human Rights (DH-GDR) on the longer term future of the system of the European Convention on Human Rights, and the European Court of Human Rights' (27 January 2014) <www.ihmisoikeuskeskus.fi/@Bin/256832/ENNHRI%20sub%20obn%20Conv%20system%20270114%20Final.pdf> accessed 19 January 2021.

European Network of NHRIs, ENNHRI, 'ICC29 Highlights' (31 March 2016) <http://ennhri.org/news-and-blog/icc29-highlights/> accessed 22 February 2021.

European Network of NHRIs, 'ENNHRI Statement of Support for Poland's Commissioner for Human Rights' (28 October 2016) <http://ennhri.org/wp-content/uploads/2019/09/General-Assembly-Statement-of-Support-for-Poland%E2%80%99s-Commissioner-for-Human-Rights.pdf> accessed 4 August 2020.

European Network of NHRIs, 'Joint Statement in Support of the Polish Commissioner for Human Rights' (June 2019) <www.ennhri.org/wp-content/uploads/2019/09/Joint-Statement-in-Support-of-the-Polish-Commissioner-for-Human-Rights.pdf> accessed 3 August 2020.

European Network of NHRIs, 'Third Party Interventions Before the European Court of Human Rights: Guide for National Human Rights Institutions' (October 2020) <http://ennhri.org/wp-content/uploads/2020/10/Third-Party-Interventions-Before-the-European-Court-of-Human-Rights-Guide-for-NHRIs.pdf> accessed 25 February 2021.

European Network of NHRIs, 'Germany launches protection programme for human rights defenders at risk' (11 December 2020) <http://ennhri.org/news-and-blog/germany-launches-protection-programme-for-human-rights-defenders-at-risk/> accessed 22 February 2021.

European Network of NHRIs, 'About ENNHRI' <http://ennhri.org/about-us/> accessed 13 January 2021.

European Network of NHRIs, 'NHRI Academy' <http://ennhri.org/our-work/nhri-academy/> accessed 17 February 2021.

European Network of NHRIs, 'Oral Statement of the European Group of National Human Rights Institutions at the Izmir High-Level Ministerial Conference on the Future of the European Court of Human Rights, 26–27 April 2011'.

European Union Agency for Fundamental Rights, *National Human Rights Institutions in the EU Member States—Strengthening the Fundamental Rights Architecture in the EU* (European Union Agency for Fundamental Rights 2010).

European Union Agency for Fundamental Rights, *Strong and Effective National Human Rights Institutions—Challenges, Promising Practices and Opportunities* (European Union Agency for Fundamental Rights 2020).

Fairbanks II R, 'The Political Economic Gradient' in Ram Cnaan and Carl Milofsky (eds), *Handbook of Community Movements and Local Organisations* (Springer 2007).

Fellous G, *Les Institutions Nationales des Droits de l'Homme: Acteurs de Troisième Type* (Commission Nationale Consultative Des Droits de l'Homme 2006).

Freedom House, 'Freedom in the World 2020: Poland' <https://freedomhouse.org/country/poland/freedom-world/2020> accessed 3 August 2020.

Freedom House, 'Nations in Transit 2020: Hungary country report' <https://freedomhouse.org/country/hungary/nations-transit/2020> accessed 23 May 2020.

Freedom House, 'Poland, Nations in Transit 2020' <https://freedomhouse.org/country/poland/nations-transit/2020> accessed 3 August 2020.

Global Alliance of National Human Rights Institutions (GANHRI), Guidelines for Accreditation Applications, Compilation of the Rules and Working Methods of the SCA (February 2014) <https://nhri.ohchr.org/EN/ICC/GeneralMeeting/27/Theme%202%20ICC%20accreditation%20process/Compilation%20of%20the%20Rules%20and%20Working%20Methods%20of%20the%20SCA_Eng_February_2014.pdf> accessed 5 February 2021.

GANHRI, 'National Human Rights Institutions and UN Treaty Bodies: GANHRI Background Paper' (May 2016) 14 <https://nhri.ohchr.org/EN/IHRS/TreatyBodies/Annual%20Meeting%20of%20Chairpersons%20of%20Human%20Rights%20Tre/GANHRI%20background%20paper%20FINAL.pdf> accessed 16 February 2021.

GANHRI, 'Practice Note 1: Deferrals' (adopted on 6 March 2017).

GANHRI, 'Practice Note 2: Special Reviews' (adopted on 6 March 2017).

GANHRI, 'Practice Note 4: NHRIs in Transition' (adopted on 6 March 2017).

GANHRI, 'Practice Note 5: Sources of information to assess NHRIs' (adopted on 18 May 2018).

GANHRI, 'A Practical Guide to the Work of the Sub-Committee on Accreditation' (2018) <https://nhri.ohchr.org/EN/AboutUs/GANHRIAccreditation/Documents/GANHRI%20Manual_online(1).pdf> accessed 6 February 2021.

GANHRI, The Marrakech Declaration 2018: Expanding the civic space and promoting and protecting human rights defenders with a specific focus on women: The role of national human rights institutions (adopted on 12 October 2018) <https://www.forum-asia.org/uploads/wp/2019/10/GANHRI_Marrakech-Declaration_Oct-2018_EN-2.pdf> accessed 15 February 2021.

GANHRI, 'Accreditation Status as of 27 November 2019' <www.ohchr.org/Documents/Countries/Cooperation/StatusAccreditationChart.pdf> accessed 15 January 2021.

GANHRI, Guidelines for Accreditation Applications, Compilation of the Rules and Working Methods of the SCA (2019) <https://nhri.ohchr.org/EN/AboutUs/GANHRIAccreditation/Documents/Forms/DispForm.aspx?ID=172> accessed 8 February 2021.

GANHRI, Rules of Procedure for the GANHRI Sub-Committee on Accreditation (adopted on 4 March 2019).

GANHRI, Statute (adopted on 5 March 2019).

GANHRI, 'Compilation of the SCA Rules, Working Methods and Template for the Statement of Compliance' <https://nhri.ohchr.org/EN/AboutUs/GANHRIAccreditation/Documents/Forms/DispForm.aspx?ID=172> accessed 5 February 2021.

Goodman R and Pegram T (eds), *Human Rights, State Compliance and Social Change: Assessing National Human Rights Institutions* (CUP 2012).

Guo S, 'Effectiveness of National Human Rights Institutions in International Human Rights Law: Problems and Prospects' (2009) 14 Asian Yearbook of International Law 101.

Hafner-Burton EM, *Making Human Rights A Reality* (Princeton University Press 2013) 173.

Harrison ML and Shirom A, *Organizational Diagnosis and Assessment: Bridging Theory and Practice* (Sage 1999).

Herman RD and Renz DO, 'Doing Things Right: Effectiveness in local Nonprofit Organizations, a Panel Study' (November/December 2004) 64(6) Public Administration Review 694.

Herman RD and Renz DO, 'Advancing Nonprofit Organizational Effectiveness Research and Theory: Nine Theses' (2008) 18(4) Nonprofit Management and Leadership 399.

Human Rights Council, 'General Comment No. 31, The nature of the general legal obligation imposed on States Parties to the Covenant' (26 May 2004) UN Doc CCPR/C/21/Rev1/Add.13.

Human Rights Council, 'Process currently utilized by the International Coordinating Committee of National Institutions for the Promotion and Protection of Human Rights to accredit national institutions in compliance with the Paris Principles: Report of the Secretary-General' (18 January 2010) UN Doc A/HRC/13/45.

Human Rights Council, 'Consideration of reports submitted by States parties under article 40 of the Covenant: Concluding observations of the Human Rights Committee—Slovakia' (20 April 2011) UN Doc CCPR/C/SVK/CO/3.

Human Rights Council, 'Report of the United Nations High Commissioner for Human Rights on the situation of human rights in Afghanistan and on the achievements of technical assistance in the field of human rights in 2013' (10 January 2014) UN Doc A/HRC/25/41.

Human Rights Council, 'Working Group on the Universal Periodic Review Twentieth session 27 October–7 November 2014 National report submitted in accordance with paragraph 5 of the annex to Human Rights Council resolution 16/21: Kazakhstan' (16 September 2014) UN Doc A/HRC/WG.6/20/KAZ/1.

Human Rights Council, 'Summary prepared by the Office of the United Nations High Commissioner for Human Rights in accordance with paragraph 15(c) of the annex to Human Rights Council resolution 5/1 and paragraph 5 of the annex to Council Resolution 16/21: Rwanda' (August 2015) UN Doc A/HRC/WG.6/23RWA/317.

Human Rights Council, 'Report on the independent investigation on Burundi carried out pursuant to Human Rights Council resolution S-24/1' (25 October 2016) UN Doc A/HRC/33/37.

Human Rights Council, 'Working Methods' VIII. Participation of non-governmental organizations and national human rights institutions in the activities of the Committees <https://www.ohchr.org/EN/HRBodies/CCPR/Pages/WorkingMethods.aspx> accessed 19 January 2021.

Human Rights Watch, 'World Report 2009: Afghanistan events of 2008' (2009) <https://www.hrw.org/world-report/2009/country-chapters/afghanistan> accessed 27 September 2020.

Human Rights Watch, 'Honduras After the Coup: Ongoing Violence, Intimidation, and Impunity in Honduras' (December 2010) <https://www.hrw.org/sites/default/files/reports/honduras1210webwcover_0.pdf> accessed 12 August 2020.

Human Rights Watch, 'Descent into Chaos: Thailand's 2019 Red Shirt Protests and the Government Crackdown' (3 May 2011) <https://www.hrw.org/report/2011/05/03/descent-chaos/thailands-2010-red-shirt-protests-and-government-crackdown> accessed 6 September 2020.

Human Rights Watch, 'World Report 2014: Events of 2013' (2014) <https://www.hrw.org/world-report/2014 > accessed 20 February 2021.

Human Rights Watch, 'World Report: Afghanistan—Events of 2014' (2015) <https://www.hrw.org/world-report/2014/country-chapters/afghanistan> accessed 18 February 2021.

Human Rights Watch, 'Eroding Checks and Balances: Rule of Law and Human Rights Under Attack in Poland' (24 October 2017) <https://www.hrw.org/report/2017/10/24/eroding-checks-and-balances/rule-law-and-human-rights-under-attack-poland#_ftn35> accessed 4 August 2020.

Human Rights Watch, 'European Union: Events of 2019—Hungary' (2020) <https://www.hrw.org/world-report/2020/country-chapters/european-union#fa79c3> accessed 23 May 2020.

Human Rights Watch, 'Poland: Events of 2019—Part of the EU Chapter' (2020) <https://www.hrw.org/world-report/2020/country-chapters/poland> accessed 3 August 2020.

Human Rights Watch, 'World Report 2020: Afghanistan—Events of 2019' (2020) <https://www.hrw.org/world-report/2020/country-chapters/afghanistan> accessed 27 September 2020.

Hungarian Civil Liberties Union and others, 'Timeline of Governmental Attacks Against Hungarian Civil Society Organisations' (17 November 2017) <http://www.helsinki.hu/wp-content/uploads/Timeline_of_gov_attacks_against_HU_NGOs_17112017.pdf> accessed 23 May 2020.

International Bar Association Human Rights Institute, 'Still under threat: the independence of the judiciary and the rule of law in Hungary' (October 2015) <https://www.ibanet.org/Document/Default.aspx?DocumentUid=a00b5f64-4b05-4b25-81c6-5e507c45cc74> accessed 23 May 2020.

International Coordinating Committee, The Nairobi Declaration (adopted on 24 October 2008).

International Coordinating Committee, Statute (as amended 24 March 2009).

International Coordinating Committee, 'Guidelines for Accreditation & Re-Accreditation of National Human Rights Institutions to the International Coordinating Committee of National Human Rights Institutions' (June 2009).

International Coordinating Committee, Rules of Procedure (as amended on 14 April 2008) annexed to the ICC Statute (adopted on 23 March 2012).

International Coordinating Committee, 'Chart of the Status of National Institutions' (May 2012) <https://nhri.ohchr.org/EN/Documents/Chart%20of%20the%20Status%20of%20NIs%20(30%20May%202012).pdf> accessed 8 February 2021.

International Council on Human Rights Policy, *Assessing the Effectiveness of National Human Rights Institutions* (International Council on Human Rights Policy 2005).

International Federation for Human Rights, 'Azerbaijan: Acts of violence in prison against Ms. Leyla Yunus' (12 September 2014) <https://www.fidh.org/en/region/europe-central-asia/azerbaijan/16031-azerbaijan-acts-of-violence-in-prison-against-ms-leyla-yunus> accessed 20 February 2021.

International Ombudsman Institute, 'Bylaws' (adopted on 13 November 2012).

International Press Institute and others, 'Joint International Press Freedom Mission to Hungary' (3 December 2019) <https://ipi.media/wp-content/uploads/2019/12/Hungary-Conclusions-International-Mission-Final.pdf> accessed 23 May 2020.

Jägers N, 'National Human Rights Institutions: The Missing Link in Business and Human Rights Governance?' (2020) 14(3) ICL Journal 289.

Jensen SLB, Lagoutte S, and Lorion S, 'The Domestic Institutionalization of Human Rights: An Introduction' (2019) 37(3) Nordic Journal of Human Rights 165–76.

Kaplan T, 'Women's Rights as Human Rights: Women as Agents of Social Change' in Marjorie Agosín (ed), *Women, Gender & Human Rights: A Global Perspective* (Rutgers University Press 2001).

Kindiki K, 'On the Independence of the Kenya National Commission on Human Rights: A Preliminary Comment' (2004) 2 East African Journal Human Rights & Democracy 120.

Kounté K, 'une conscience' (Amnesty International, France, 1 June 2012) <www.anctogo.com/koffi-kounte-une-conscience-8367> accessed 18 February 2021.

Kumar CR, 'National Human Rights Institutions: Good Governance Perspectives on Institutionalization of Human Rights' (2003–04) 19(2) American University International Law Review 259.

L'Association francophone des commissions nationales des droits de l'Homme (AFCNDH) <http://afcndh.org> accessed 22 February 2021.

Link MG, 'The Role of National Human Rights Institutions (NHRI) in Promoting and Protecting Human Rights in the OSCE Area 2015: Opening speech by Michael Georg Link Director of the Office for Democratic Institutions and Human Rights' (2015 OSCE Human Dimension Seminar, Warsaw 1–3 June 2015) <www.osce.org/files/f/documents/e/5/161271.pdf> accessed 19 January 2021.

Linnarsson A and Sedletzki V, 'Independent Human Rights Institutions for Children: An Actor for the Protection of Children's Rights During Armed Conflict?' (2014) 36(2) Human Rights Quarterly 447.

Meuwissen K, 'NHRI Participation in United Nations Human Rights Procedures: International Promotion versus Institutional Consolidation' in Jan Wouters and Katrien Meuwissen (eds), *National Human Rights Institutions in Europe: Comparative, European and International Perspectives* (Intersentia Publishing 2013).

Meuwissen K, 'NHRIs and the State: New and Independent Actors in the Multi-layered Human Rights System?' (2015) 15 Human Rights Law Review 441.

Mertus J, *Human Rights Matters: Local Politics and National Human Rights Institutions* (Stanford University Press 2009).

Müller A and Seidensticker F, *The Role of National Human Rights Institutions in the UN Human Rights Treaty Body Process* (German Institute for Human Rights 2007).

Murray R, *The Role of National Human Rights Institutions at the International and Regional Levels: The Experience of Africa* (Hart Publishing 2007).

Murray R, 'National Human Rights Institutions: Criteria and Factors for Assessing Their Effectiveness' (2007) 25 Netherlands Quarterly of Human Rights 189.

Network of African National Human Rights Institutions <www.NANHRI.org> accessed 19 January 2021.

Office of the United Nations High Commissioner for Human Rights (OHCHR), 'Fact Sheet No. 19, National Institutions for the Promotion and Protection of Human Rights' (Geneva 1993).

OHCHR, 'A Handbook on the Establishment and Strengthening of National Human Rights Institutions for the Promotion and Protection of Human Rights' (New York/Geneva 1995).

OHCHR, 'Report of the United Nations High Commissioner for Human Rights on the violations of human rights in Honduras since the coup d'état on 28 June 2009' (3 March 2010) UN Doc A/HRC/13/66 <https://documents-dds-ny.un.org/doc/UNDOC/GEN/G10/117/00/PDF/G1011700.pdf?OpenElement> accessed 12 August 2020.

OHCHR, 'Survey on National Human Rights Institutions' (Geneva 2009).

OHCHR, 'Monitoring the Convention on the Rights of Persons with Disabilities: Guidance for Human Rights Monitors' (2010) No 17, HR/P/PT/17.

OHCHR, 'Information Note on National Human Rights Institutions (NHRIs) interaction with the UN Treaty Body System' (5 April 2011).

OHCHR, 'Prevention of Torture: UN human rights body suspends Azerbaijan visit citing official obstruction' (17 September 2014) <www.ohchr.org/EN/NewsEvents/Pages/DisplayNews.aspx?NewsID=15047&LangID=E> accessed 16 February 2021.

OHCHR, 'Summary prepared by the Office of the United Nations High Commissioner for Human Rights in accordance with paragraph 15(c) of the annex to Human Rights Council resolution 5/1 and paragraph 5 of the annex to Council Resolution 16/21: Rwanda' (August 2015) UN Doc A/HRC/WG.6/23/RWA/3.

OHCHR, 'Zeid condemns civil society crackdown in Azerbaijan' (8 September 2015)<https://www.ohchr.org/EN/NewsEvents/Pages/DisplayNews.aspx?NewsID=16393&LangID%20=E> accessed 20 February 2021.

OHCHR, 'Contribution of parliaments to the work of the Human Rights Council and its universal periodic review: Report of the Office of the United Nations High Commissioner for Human Rights' (17 May 2018) UN Doc A/HRC/38/25, Annex I.

OHCHR, *Preventing Torture—The Role of National Preventive Mechanisms: A Practical Guide* (United Nations 2018).

OHCHR, 'Human Rights Council—Universal Periodic Review Highlights 11 December 2008 (morning)' <www.ohchr.org/EN/HRBodies/UPR/Pages/Highlights11December2008am.aspx≥ accessed 12 February 2021.

OHCHR, 'NHRIs with an NPM Mandate' <https://nhri.ohchr.org/EN/ICC/GeneralMeeting/2018/Opening%20ceremony/NHRIs%20and%20NPMs%20Meeting%20Flyer.pdf≥ accessed 16 February 2021.

Office of the United Nations High Commissioner for Human Rights, Association for Prevention of Torture and the Asia Pacific Forum of National Human Rights Institutions, 'Preventing Torture: An Operational Guide for National Human Rights Institutions' (May 2010) HR/PUB/10/1.

Okafor OC, 'National Human Rights Institutions in Anglophone Africa' in Ryan Goodman and Thomas Pegram (eds), *Human Rights, State Compliance and Social Change: Assessing National Human Rights Institutions* (CUP 2012).

Organization of American States, 'IACHR Holds Successful Third Meeting on Best Practice for National Human Rights Institutions' (27 January 2008) Press release no 016/20 <https://www.oas.org/en/iachr/media_center/PReleases/2020/016.asp> accessed 15 January 2021.

Organization of American States, 'Permanent Council Report on Strengthening the Role of National Institutions for the Promotion and Protection of Human Rights in the Organization of American States' (29 April 2009) OEA/Ser.G CP/CG-1770/09 rev 2.

Organization of American States, 'IACHR and National Human Rights Institutions (NHRIs) sign Declaration of Commitment for Technical Cooperation' (19 November 2018) Press release no 246/18 <http://www.oas.org/en/iachr/media_center/PReleases/2018/246.asp> accessed 15 January 2021.

Organization for Security and Cooperation in Europe, 'Document of the Copenhagen Meeting of the Conference on the Human Dimension of the CSCE' (29 June 1990) <www.osce.org/files/f/documents/9/c/14304.pdf> accessed 19 January 2021.

Organization for Security and Cooperation in Europe, 'Ombudsman and Human Rights Protection Institutions in OSCE Participating States, OSCE Human Dimension Implementation Meeting October 1998 Background Paper 1' (21 September 1998).

Organization for Security and Cooperation in Europe, 'Conclusions of the International Roundtable on the Role of National Human Rights Institutions and Treaty Bodies, Berlin, 23 and 24 November 2006' (16 July 2007) PC.SHDM.IO/9/07/Corr.1.

Organization for Security and Cooperation in Europe, 'Supplementary Human Dimension Meeting on National Human Rights Institutions (ombudsinstitutions, commissions, institutes and other mechanisms)' 14–15 April 2011, Vienna, <www.osce.org/event/shdm2011_1> accessed 15 February 2021.

Organization for Security and Cooperation in Europe, 'Opinion on the on the Law of the Republic of Lithuania on the Seimas Ombudsmen' (21 September 2011) Opinion-Nr.: NHRI–LTU/187/2011 (AT).

Organization for Security and Cooperation in Europe, *Handbook for National Human Rights Institutions on Women's Rights and Gender Equality* (ODIHR 2012).

Organization for Security and Cooperation in Europe, 'Report of the Second Meeting in the ODIHR Human Rights Discussion Series for Representatives of the Forum for Security Co-operation: The Role of Ombuds Institutions in Protecting Human Rights of Armed Forces Personnel' (Vienna, 14 October 2013).

Office for Democratic Institutions and Human Rights, 'Opinion on the Draft Act on the Independent National Human Rights Institution of Iceland' (6 February 2017) Opinion-Nr.: NHRI-ISL/301/2017 [AlC].

Office for Democratic Institutions and Human Rights, 'Opinion on the Draft Federal Law on the Support to the National Human Rights Institution of Switzerland' (31 October 2017) Opinion-Nr.: NHRI-CHE/312/2017 [AlC].

Office for Democratic Institutions and Human Rights, 'ODIHR Limited Election Observation Mission Final Report: Hungary Parliamentary Elections 8 April 2018' (27 June 2018) <https://www.osce.org/odihr/elections/hungary/385959?download=true> accessed 23 May 2020.

Office for Democratic Institutions and Human Rights, 'Human Dimension Implementation Meeting 22 September to 3 October Warsaw, Poland: Speech by Aydin Safikhanli, Head of the Office of the Commissioner for Human Rights (Ombudsman) of the Republic of Azerbaijan: Activity of the Azerbaijani Ombudsman as a National Preventative Mechanism against torture' Doc No HDIM.DEL/0127/14.

Office for Democratic Institutions and Human Rights and European Network of NHRIs, 'NHRI Academy-Compilation of Pre-Academy Assignments' (June 2014).

Parliamentary Committee of Council of Europe, 'Improving co-operation between National Human Rights Institutions (NHRIs) and parliaments in addressing equality and non-discrimination issues, Committee on Equality and Non-Discrimination, Report by Katherine Zappone (Ireland)' (30 April 2014) PACE Doc 13506.

Pegram T, 'Diffusion Across Political Systems: The Global Spread of National Human Rights Institutions' (2010) 32(3) Human Rights Quarterly 729.

Pegram T, 'National Human Rights Institutions in Latin America: Politics and Institutionalization' in Ryan Goodman and Thomas Pegram (eds), *Human Rights, State Compliance and Social Change: Assessing National Human Rights Institutions* (CUP 2012).

Pegram T, 'Governing Relationships: The New Architecture in Global Human Rights Governance' (2015) 43(2) Millennium—Journal of International Studies 618.

Pegram T, 'Global Human Rights Governance and Orchestration: National Human Rights Institutions as Intermediaries' (2015) 21 European Journal of International Relations 595.

Pegram T and Linos K, *Interrogating Form and Function: Defining Effective National Human Rights Institutions* (The Danish Institute for Human Rights 2015).

Pegram T and Linos K, 'What Works in Human Rights Institutions?' (2017) 111(3) American Journal of International Law 628.

Pohjolainen AE, 'The Evolution of National Human Rights Institutions—The Role of the United Nations' (Danish Institute for Human Rights 2006).

Ramirez FO and Cole WN, 'Conditional Decoupling: Assessing the Impact of National Human Rights Institutions, 1981 to 2004' (2013) 78(4) American Sociological Review 702.

Reif L, 'Building Democratic Institutions: The Role of National Human Rights Institutions in Good Governance and Human Rights Protection' (2000) 13 Harvard Human Rights Journal 1.

Reif L, *The Ombudsman, Good Governance and the International Human Rights System* (Springer 2004).

Reif L, *Human Rights, State Compliance, and Social Change: Assessing National Human Rights Institutions* (CUP 2012).

Roberts K, 'National Human Rights Institutions as Diplomacy Actors' in Michael O'Flaherty and others (eds), *Human Rights Diplomacy: Contemporary Perspectives* (Martinus Nijhoff 2011).

Roberts Lyer K, 'National Human Rights Institutions' in Gerd Oberleitner and Steven Hoadley (eds), *Human Rights Institutions, Tribunals and Courts—Legacy and Promise* (Springer Major Reference Works handbook series 2019).

Roberts Lyer K, 'Parliaments as Human Rights Actors: The Potential for International Principles on Parliamentary Human Rights Committees' (2019) 37(3) Nordic Journal of Human Rights (2019) 195.

Sebihogo G, 'Opening Statement by the Network of National Human Rights Institutions' (56th Ordinary session of the African Commission on Human and Peoples' Rights, Banjul, Gambia, 21 April–7 May 2015) <www.achpr.org/sessions/statements?id=80> accessed 20 January 2021.

Sidoti C, 'National Human Rights Institutions and the International Human Rights System' in Ryan Goodman and Thomas Pegram (eds), *Human Rights, State Compliance and Social Change: Assessing National Human Rights Institutions* (CUP 2012).

Smith A, 'The Unique Position of National Human Rights Institutions: A Mixed Blessing?' (November 2006) 28(4) Human Rights Quarterly 904.

Stein AM and Lord JE, 'Monitoring the Convention on the Rights of Persons with Disabilities: Innovations, Lost Opportunities, and Future Potential' (2010) 32 Human Rights Quarterly 689.

Subcommittee on Prevention of Torture, 'Third annual report of the Subcommittee on Prevention of Torture and Other Cruel, Inhuman or Degrading Treatment or Punishment' UN Doc CAT/C/44/2 (25 March 2010).

Subcommittee on Prevention of Torture, 'Guidelines on national preventative mechanism' (9 December 2010) UN Doc CAT/OP/12/5.

Subcommittee on Prevention of Torture, 'Report on the visit made by the Subcommittee on Prevention of Torture and Other Cruel, Inhuman or Degrading Treatment or Punishment for the purpose of providing advisory assistance to the national preventive mechanism of Honduras' (25 January 2013) UN Doc CAT/OP/HND/3.

Subcommittee on Prevention of Torture, Visit to the former Yugoslav Republic of Macedonia undertaken from 23 to 29 April 2017: observations and recommendations addressed to the national preventive mechanism—Report of the Subcommittee' (26 March 2018) UN Doc CAT/OP/MKD/2.

Subcommittee on Prevention of Torture, 'First Annual Report of the Subcommittee on Prevention of Torture and Other Cruel, Inhuman and Degrading Treatment or Punishment' (14 May 2018) UN Doc CAT/C/40/2.

Sub-Committee on Accreditation (SCA), 'Report and Recommendations of the Sub-Committee on Accreditation' (April 2006).

SCA, 'Report and Recommendations of the Sub-Committee on Accreditation' (October 2006).
SCA, 'Report and Recommendations of the Sub-Committee on Accreditation' (March 2007).
SCA, 'Report and Recommendations of the Sub-Committee on Accreditation' (October 2007).
SCA, 'Report and Recommendations of the Sub-Committee on Accreditation' (April 2008).
SCA, 'ICC Sub-Committee on Accreditation General Observations' (adopted in June 2009).
SCA, 'Report and Recommendations of the Sub-Committee on Accreditation' (November 2008).
SCA, 'Report and Recommendations of the Sub-Committee on Accreditation' (March 2009).
SCA, 'Report and Recommendations of the Sub-Committee on Accreditation' (November 2009).
SCA, 'Report and Recommendations of the Sub-Committee on Accreditation' (March/April 2010).
SCA, 'Report and Recommendations of the Sub-Committee on Accreditation' (October 2010).
SCA, 'Report and Recommendations of the Sub-Committee on Accreditation' (March 2011).
SCA, 'Report and Recommendations of the Sub-Committee on Accreditation' (October 2011).
SCA, 'Report and Recommendations of the Sub-Committee on Accreditation' (March 2012).
SCA, 'Report and Recommendations of the Sub-Committee on Accreditation' (November 2012).
SCA, 'ICC Sub-Committee on Accreditation General Observations' (adopted May 2013).
SCA, 'Report and Recommendations of the Sub-Committee on Accreditation' (May 2013).
SCA, 'Report and Recommendations of the Sub-Committee on Accreditation' (November 2013).
SCA, 'Report and Recommendations of the Sub-Committee on Accreditation' (March 2014).
SCA, 'Report and Recommendations of the Sub-Committee on Accreditation' (October 2014).
SCA, 'Report and Recommendations of the Sub-Committee on Accreditation' (March 2015).
SCA, 'Report and Recommendations of the Sub-Committee on Accreditation' (November 2015).
SCA, 'Report and Recommendations of the Sub-Committee on Accreditation' (May 2016).
SCA, 'Report and Recommendations of the Sub-Committee on Accreditation' (November 2016).
SCA, 'Report and Recommendations of the Sub-Committee on Accreditation' (March 2017).
SCA, 'Report and Recommendations of the Sub-Committee on Accreditation' (November 2017).
SCA, 'General Observations of the Sub-Committee on Accreditation' (adopted 21 February 2018).
SCA, 'Report and Recommendations of the Sub-Committee on Accreditation' (May 2018).
SCA, 'Report and Recommendations of the Sub-Committee on Accreditation' (October 2018).
SCA, 'Report and Recommendations of the Sub-Committee on Accreditation' (March 2019).
SCA, 'Report and Recommendations of the Sub-Committee on Accreditation' (October 2019).
The Arab Network of NHRIs <https://annhri.org/en/2020/11/> accessed 22 February 2021.
The Commonwealth <thecommonwealth.org/about-us> accessed 15 February 2021.

The Hungarian Helsinki Committee, 'Assessment of the Activities and Independence of the Commissioner for Fundamental Rights of Hungary in Light of the Requirements Set for National Human Rights Institutions' (September 2019) 4 <www.helsinki.hu/wp-content/uploads/Assessment_NHRI_Hungary_2014-2019_HHC.pdf> accessed 19 February 2021.

Uggla F, 'The Ombudsman in Latin America' (2004) 36(3) Journal of Latin American Studies 423, 450.

United Nations Assistance Mission in Afghanistan, 'Afghanistan: Protection of Civilians in Armed Conflict 2019' (February 2020) 34–35 <https://unama.unmissions.org/sites/default/files/afghanistan_protection_of_civilians_annual_report_2019.pdf> accessed 18 February 2021.

United Nations Division of Human Rights, 'Seminar on National and Local Institutions for the Promotion and Protection of Human Rights' (18–29 September 1978) UN Doc ST/HR/SER.A/2, 'Guidelines on the Structure and Functioning of National and Local Institutions for the Promotion and Protection of Human Rights'.

United Nations General Assembly, 'National Institutions for the Promotion and Protection of Human Rights, Report of the Secretary-General' (19 November 1984) 39th Session UN Doc A/39/556.

United Nations General Assembly, UN General Assembly, 'National institutions for the promotion and protection of human rights: Note of the Secretary-General' (19 November 1992) UN Doc A/47/701.

United Nations General Assembly, Vienna Declaration and Programme of Action (12 July 1993) UN Doc A/CONF.157/23.

United Nations General Assembly, 'Report of the Secretary-General on the Process Currently Utilized by the International Coordinating Committee of National Institutions for the Promotion and Protection of Human Rights to Accredit National Institutions in Compliance with the Paris Principles' (18 January 2010) UN Doc A/HRC/13/45.

United Nations Secretary-General, 'National institutions for the promotion and protection of human rights: Report of the Secretary-General' (3 August 2017) UN Doc A/72/277.

United States Department of State, '2008 Country Reports on Human Rights Practices—Afghanistan, 2007' (25 February 2009) <https://www.refworld.org/docid/49a8f1b0c.html> accessed 27 September 2020.

United States Department of State, '2014 Country Reports on Human Rights Practices—Afghanistan' (25 June 2015) <https://www.refworld.org/docid/559bd58728.html> accessed 24 February 2021.

United States Department of State, 'Country Reports on Human Rights Practices for 2011: Thailand' <https://2009-2017.state.gov/j/drl/rls/hrrpt/2011humanrightsreport/index.htm?dlid=186310#> accessed 6 September 2020.

United States Department of State, 'Human Rights country reports: Poland 2019' <https://www.state.gov/wp-content/uploads/2020/02/POLAND-2019-HUMAN-RIGHTS-REPORT.pdf> accessed 3 August 2020.

Venice Commission, 'Opinion on the Draft Law on the Public Attorney of "the former Yugoslav Republic of Macedonia"' (Venice 14–15 March 2003) CDL-AD(2003)007.

Venice Commission, 'Opinion on the draft amendments to the law on the Protector of Human Rights and Freedoms of Montenegro' (Venice 9–10 October 2009) CDL-AD(2009)043.

Venice Commission, 'Opinion on the Draft Amendments to the Law on the Protector of Human Rights and Freedoms of Montenegro' (13 October 2009) Opinion No 540/2009.

Venice Commission, 'Compilation on the Ombudsman Institution' (1 December 2011) CDL(2011)079.

Venice Commission, 'Preliminary Opinion on Act XXV of 4 April 2017 On the Amendment of ACT CCIV of 2011 on National Tertiary Education' (11 August 2017) CDL-PI(2017)005-e <https://www.venice.coe.int/webforms/documents/default.aspx?pdffile=CDL-PI(2017)005-e> accessed 23 May 2020.

Venice Commission, 'Republic of Moldova—Draft Opinion on Proposed New Article 37 of the Law on the People's Advocate Finance Provision' (5 December 2017) Opinion No 906/2017.

Venice Commission, 'Opinion on the draft law on prevention and protection against discrimination' (19 March 2018) CDL-AD(2018)001 <https://www.venice.coe.int/webforms/documents/default.aspx?pdffile=CDL-AD(2018)001-e> accessed 25 February 2021.

Venice Commission and Organisation for Security and Cooperation in Europe/Office for Democratic Institutions and Human Rights, 'Joint Opinion on the Provisions of the so-called "Stop Soros" draft legislative package which directly affects NGOs' (25 June 2018) CDL-AD(2018)013-e <https://www.venice.coe.int/webforms/documents/default.aspx?pdffile=CDL-AD(2018)013-e> accessed 23 May 2020.

Varieties of Democracy Institute (V-Dem), 'Autocratization Surges—Resistance Grows' (March 2020) 16–17 <https://www.v-dem.net/media/filer_public/de/39/de39af54-0bc5-4421-89ae-fb20dcc53dba/democracy_report.pdf> accessed 23 May 2020.

Wouters J, Meuwissen K, and Sofia de Barros A, 'The European Union and National Human Rights Institutions' in Jan Wouters and Katrien Meuwissen (eds), *National Human Rights Institutions in Europe: Comparative, European and International Perspectives* (Intersentia Publishing 2013).

Zambara W, 'Africa's National Human Rights Institutions and the Responsibility to Protect' (2010) 2 Global Responsibility to Protect 458.

Index

For the benefit of digital users, indexed terms that span two pages (e.g., 52–53) may, on occasion, appear on only one of those pages.

Tables are indicated by *t* following the page number